SIMON INGRAM was born in Liverpool. An ou
over ten years, he is the editor of *Trail*, the UK's bestselling ......
magazine. He lives in Stamford, Lincolnshire.

Praise for Simon Ingram:

'This is the work of a polymath mountain-lover with a backpack-sized curiosity and the stamina to take notes when most of us would be gasping for
breath. It's not just painstakingly researched, it's also well written ... an
intrepid, original book'   *The Times*

'A welcome and refreshing addition to the increasingly crowded field of New
Nature Writing. Warm, poetic and humane yet shivery with the vertiginous
thrill and allure that mountains cast over some of us.'   STUART MACONIE

'Almost Tolkienian in delivery ... *Between the Sunset and the Sea* turns mountain
climbs into a form of poetry.'   *BBC Countryfile*

'Rich, thought-provoking and lyrical.'   *Scotland Outdoors*

'Accessible and refreshing ... written in an engaging style that quickly takes
the reader into its confidence. The endearing confession of an authentic
mountain addict.'   *Country Walking*

'Makes for an engrossing read ... a book of considerable depth, full of fascinating and well-researched detail.'   *Walk Magazine*

To Mum and Dad, for letting me wander;
and to Rachel and Evelyn, for bringing me back.

William Collins
An imprint of HarperCollins*Publishers*
1 London Bridge Street
London SE1 9GF
WilliamCollinsBooks.com

This William Collins paperback edition published in 2016

21 20 19 18 17 16
10 9 8 7 6 5 4 3 2 1

First published in Great Britain by William Collins in 2015

A catalogue record for this book
is available from the British Library.

ISBN 978-0-00-754790-6

Printed and bound in Great Britain by
Clays Ltd, St Ives plc.

MIX
Paper from
responsible sources
FSC
www.fsc.org   **FSC® C007454**

FSC is a non-profit international organisation established to promote
the responsible management of the world's forests. Products carrying the
FSC label are independently certified to assure customers that they come
from forests that are managed to meet the social, economic and
ecological needs of present and future generations,
and other controlled sources.

Find out more about HarperCollins and the environment at
www.harpercollins.co.uk/green

BETWEEN THE SUNSET AND THE SEA

A View of 16 British Mountains

SIMON INGRAM

WILLIAM COLLINS

There are more reasons for hills
Than being steep,
And reaching only high.

Norman MacCaig
'High up on Suilven'

CONTENTS

1 HEIGHT

Seven miles north of the village of Tyndrum in the Southern Highlands of Scotland the A82 flinches hard to the left and begins to climb. The pitch of your car's engine drops. You slow. Heathery embankments recede around the tarmac and the sky begins to widen as you approach the top of a rise. The road makes a long arc like a tensioned longbow until it finds north-west then, abruptly, it snaps taut. The horizon flees around you. And ahead, beyond the sharp vanishing point of the road and softened by distance, are mountains.

These are not the elegant meringue-and-meadow peaks of the Alps, nor the shrill slants of geology you might find in density in the Himalaya or the Andes. The mountains that lie ahead of you as you drive this road are old and crouched, and etched with lines of incredible age.

The place wasn't always like this. It's the ghost of a once much mightier landscape. They say the ancient mountains of Scotland once stood five or six times higher – as high as the young peaks of the Himalaya stand today. Some of the oldest surface rocks in the world cover their faces and line their gullies and cracks, exposed by the millennia like dead bone to the wind. The mountains here are the ruins of a giant, explosive volcano – violent and vital. Layers of spat, hot rock layered new skin onto already ancient foundations. A million lifetimes later glaciers hung from the gaps between the peaks, carving brittle arêtes and spitting the shavings of worked land at their feet. Again and again ice and time returned to this landscape, shaping it and re-shaping it like a tinkering sculptor. He's on a break now. Give him a few dozen millennia, he'll no doubt be back.

This first sight as you inch into the mouth of Glen Coe never underwhelms. It's astonishing. Even if you've seen it a dozen times, its magnitude is unexpected somehow. We're constantly reminded how tiny Britain is, so it's a surprise to find something so boundlessly big-feeling – especially to people who live in flat places where mountains don't cut the horizon or fill the sky.

But if you're a certain type of person, this sight carries something else, too: a kind of queer charisma. It invades the emotions and tickles something primal, enshrining mountains onto a sensory level far more stately than merely as a pretty backdrop to everything else. And if you don't know what I'm on about, there's an easy way you can find out: come here, drive this road, and see what happens.

You might feel nothing, of course. Maybe looking up at these mountains produces little more than a mental shrug before your mind wanders back to something more interesting inside the car. If so, best you get back to it. Where we're going probably isn't for you. But feel a flutter around your stomach when you enter Glen Coe – a frisson of adrenaline, an indefinable but unmistakable quickening of the pulse – and sense your eyes being tugged upwards, it's got you. That's it for you now. If you didn't know it already, you've woken something up, and it's never going away.

If that part of you is there, everyone's got their own moment when they felt their mountain heartbeat spring to life. It could be something so subtle – passing through this glen or somewhere like it, watching the way evening light climbs across the buttresses of a far-off peak, the sight of windblown cloud snared and tearing from the point of a summit, the yawn of steep height against the sky. For some it remains something that stays at sea level. For others, the compulsion gets too strong, and little by little, the closer they creep.

The A82 continues into Glen Coe. The wastes of Rannoch Moor fall back from the roadside, and the mountains gather around you. Just after you pass that white cottage – the one they always put on the shortbread tins – they begin to leer over you and details emerge. The powerful gable of Buachaille Etive Mòr fills your windscreen, a side-slouched pyramid of wrinkled rock punching skyward. Grey water discharges from summits choked by cloud. All of a sudden the mountains of Glen Coe cease to resemble a distant frieze, the stumps of a range long cut down by time; they become physical and textured things, personalities almost. As your eyes trace the arêtes and buttresses, you feel deep emotions being nudged: awe, intimidation, even something implacable not dissimilar to dread.

It's a strange thing, but it makes sense. Mountains are not the place for humanity to feel at home. They're hostile, barren, bereft of comfort – we're programmed as a species to avoid them. It's a feeling as old as we are, nature's chemical way of telling us that no, we can't live there. It can't sustain us. It's cold. Hard. Find somewhere else to go. A field. A forest. A riverbank. This place isn't for people. Mountains repel us. Fight us. Yet still, you're being pulled closer. What would it be like, you wonder, to be up there?

The act of climbing a mountain – any mountain, anywhere – is to enter an environment that is challenging simply to be in. Up there, a vertical kilometre above you in that high ground, life is dangerously simple. Things wilt down to the basics: get up, move, keep warm, stay alive, get back. Trivialities at sea level, such as shelter and water, become coveted luxuries. All of a sudden we're back in the state of primal essentiality that as a species humankind has been developing away from for thousands of years. It's not like walking through the woods, or a trip to the park. Here you're beyond the darkness at the edge of town. You're walking back in time. It's like anthropological nostalgia.

The things you see here in the high places become a visual drug. Once seen and felt, you'll drive hundreds of miles just to be in this hard ancient landscape, and recapture those emotions. Spend sizeable amounts of money. Make personal sacrifices. Struggle through all weathers and dangers. And you probably won't be able to explain why.

Some have tried, of course. There are many 'justifications' for climbing a mountain, some of them notoriously impenetrable, some of them shamelessly contradictory. You climb it because it's there. You go up, to come down. None of them make much sense. Because in the pursuit of the profound, many of them compromise simple honesty: being on a mountain, a witness to its ways, just *feels* incredible. To hear the silence of a high stream frozen tight; to feel an ice-laden wind sizzle your skin; to stand on the prow of a mountaintop and look down on an ocean of lilac-lit clouds, whilst civilisation below slumbers beneath their shroud – and to live in a country where you can do all of this in the slender gap between Friday night and Monday morning. For anyone with even a vague appreciation of nature, climbing a mountain is a rare blessing: the closest you can get to a full-on sensory epiphany.

But mountains – particularly ours – are so much more than simply things to climb. Mountains aren't things at all; things are just *there*. Mountains are *places*. And places are worth getting to know. Visiting. Inhabiting. Investigating. In places, things happen.

But first, something's got to find that part of you, if it's there. Find it, check its pulse, then really wake it up.

It was late October, and a filthy sky hung above the mountains of Glen Coe as I followed the road snaking its way between them, then continued north. Where I live in England's east the horizon is empty of mountains; it is in fact a place particularly notable for its flatness. But this morning the skies above Lincolnshire had been full of the hard contrasts of dawn, and a solid grey weather front approaching the county from the west gave the convincing and novel impression that there was a tall, plateau-topped mountain range where there was in fact none. I allowed myself to imagine for a few minutes this wasn't an illusion, and immediately the landscape's entire mood shifted. Where before there had been just boundless sky, suddenly here was a presence in the landscape far more noticeable than anything else. Something to look at and, indeed, something looking back. This is the slightest dab of the feeling that fortifies the mood of the places overlooked by mountains for real. Of these, the valley of Glen Coe is perhaps the most overlooked of all – although my destination on this particular afternoon must surely run a close second.

I was driving through Scotland to Torridon, a nest of mountains in the remote North-west Highlands, to climb a peak by the name of Beinn Dearg. The summit of this otherwise anonymous hill isn't on a lot of people's lists of lifetime ambitions. Most people – even seasoned hillwalkers – will never climb it, particularly considering the visually throatier mountains nearby. And yet here I was, returning to climb it a second time, because ten years ago it had been Beinn Dearg that had checked my own mountain pulse.

That day the weather had been flawless. The September air was velvet warm, and blue sky and sun left the sharp mountains of Torridon entirely innocent of the malignant cloud or sudden wind so notorious in the Highlands. My companion Tom and I had sat in the breakfast area of the Torridon Inn that morning over a map of closely bunched contours when a man we correctly identified as both a local and a walker – in that he had a strong Scottish accent, shocked hair and wore a pink jacket that looked like it might once have been red – enquired as to our day's objective.

'Fine wee hill,' he'd said when I pointed it out on the map.

I'd been preoccupied with the contour lines on the mountain's western flank since the previous evening. Contours that were close together meant a steep slope; these ones were touching each other.

'Is it difficult? It looks steep.'

'Steep, aye. Hands-in-pockets job once you're up, though.'

'Hands in pockets?'

'Aye, a bimble. Have a good day, lads.'

He winked and, with the beanpole stoop of an ageing hillwalker, was gone.

'What does he mean?' I hissed across the table at Tom as the door clapped shut behind him and my eyes again fell upon the closely bunched orange lines covering the map. 'Hands in pockets? Bimble?'

Tom – who I should say was rather more experienced in such matters – was busy scrutinising the map for a parking place.

'He means if the first bit doesn't kill us we'll be fine.'

Vernacular is likely to be one of your first obstacles to overcome before you feel at home in a conversation with those who climb mountains for fun. Like most niche pursuits, you'll find yourself absorbing it as you go via a kind of linguistic osmosis. You *bag* summits, you don't climb them. Tricky parts of a mountain route don't yield: they *go*. You're not off to have a walk, you're going *on the hill*. Feel scared on the hill and you're probably doing something a bit *necky*. The thing that's scaring you is probably *exposure*. In plain English you might be reaching the summit but to a mountaineer you're *topping out*. A walk is a *bimble*, a hard walk a *yomp*, something that needs hands and a strong stomach is a *scramble*. If it's *blowing a hoolie* you don't really want to be up there. And all of this isn't really a walk; it's a *route*. Gear is *kit*, sustenance *hill food*, anoraks *shells* and – just in case you get conversationally caught out – underpants are *shreddies*, though it's probably best not to ask why. In addition, a certain amount of understatement is required if you want to capture the severity of the task in hand in a suitably humble manner: hence frequent use of, for example, 'a bit rough', 'a lively wind' and 'a couple of interesting bits' to describe something that most people would describe as twelve hours spent on a terrifying cliff in a hurricane. There's more, but don't worry. You'll pick it up.

* * *

Of the ascent that took place that day in 2004, I remember three things as if tattooed with them. The first was the endless view, which carried our eyes not only over the scenically incandescent peaks of Torridon – I didn't know their names at that point – and beyond to the Isle of Skye, where cartoonishly sharp, island-isolated peaks straddled the horizon like an open bear-trap. The second was the golden eagle we saw hunched against a crag near the mountain's summit not twenty metres from where we were walking: a sight that stopped and silenced Tom and me in unison. We just stared at it, watching it blink, seeing the edges of its feathers quiver in the wind. Then, this beautiful, Labrador-sized thing unfurled its wings – a metre each – and nonchalantly plunged from its crag into the drop beneath it. If it moved because of our presence, it certainly didn't make it obvious.

The third I can remember as if it happened yesterday – and was largely the reason that I was coming back to Torridon.

It had come as Tom and I approached the top of Beinn Dearg's pathless western flank. This was the bit I'd been worried about; the bit where the contours touched. It was indeed steep, aye; not steep enough to turn walking into climbing, but steep enough to make a slip unthinkable. As we approached the point where the flank crested and tipped into a broad summit ridge – the point at which we could put our hands in our pockets and have a bimble, apparently – the mountain began to sharpen. Suddenly the ridge wasn't something distant and removed: we were astride it. Beinn Dearg's grassy rump gave way to ribs of naked rock, and we began to appreciate just where we were. We were no longer climbing a hill; we were nearing the top of a mountain.

From this ridge, I looked south. Ahead, beneath the level of the high balcony on which we were standing, the edge of the mountain terminated in a vertical buttress with a void beyond. It was the same feeling of compressed perspective you might get if you looked out the window of a tall building, to its edge and beyond into the far distance, something both alarming and exhilarating; a feeling of being incongruously, deeply high – out of place, out of comfort, clinging to something that is hovering amidst nothing. You'd think that being on a mountain and feeling so delicately exposed was odd, since a mountain is by its very nature a fairly solid and sizeable thing upon which to cling. But it was less what was beyond that snared that attention; it was what was beneath.

Far below a smelt of silver was catching the afternoon sun: the river. Looking at it from this height, maybe 2,000 feet above its surface, seemed so odd, so *other*. This was something seen from an aeroplane, or an image pulled from Google Earth. Only it wasn't. It was the view from my own feet. Just a couple of hours ago they had carried me across a substantial bridge on that very river and then up to a perspective from which I could view this same river not as a violent cataract of spray but as a mere vein, its motion rendered still by distance. The bridge was there, too, no longer robust and impressive but a mere staple joining the banks.

It was as if I were not looking at a living scene, but a painting in which the landscape was already interpreted by the artist. Yet here, as well, were the processes of the earth, given context and meaning by height. From this elevated perch, the way the landscape interlocked and related seemed so clear.

There was the river, the valley it cut, the sea it fed, the mountains that fed it, the sky that fed them. And the mountains, falling to earth through shades of rust-red sandstone to the grey of their quartzite flanks, to the green of the lowland scored with the deep black creases of gully and ravine.

This view changed everything for me. I'd thought I had a pretty good beat on this little country, but right then I knew that nobody had really seen Britain unless they'd seen it from a mountain. How many people missed this view? Who never got to a position where they could see this kind of sight under their own steam? What percentage of the population moved through the landscape and gazed up at the mountains, without ever realising the thrill of gazing back down upon it from them? There was, of course, the question of effort and time. Of distance and difficulty. Of danger, to a degree. But to me, at that moment, this had ceased to matter. All I felt was deep and electrifying awe.

Today I now realise that day in Torridon was an almost ridiculously fortuitous introduction to the mountains. People wait all their lives for such conditions in a place like that; I felt like I'd received a concentrated dose of beginner's luck, like buying a toy fishing rod and landing Moby Dick on the first cast. My fascination with mountains would grow and change shape over the years for me in both a passive and fumblingly active way, but I'd never shake it. That day in 2004, a part of me woke up, and one mountain journey began.

* * *

The only other thing you need to know about me is that I'm probably just like you – that is, if you're the sort of person who finds themselves gazing at mountains with a bit of a happily confused look on their face. Like many touched by this strange infatuation, mountains had become a big part of my life, even becoming my job in a meaningful way, as since that day in Torridon my days had been spent working for an outdoors magazine – something that put me thoroughly in touch with the physical process of climbing Britain's mountains. I'd seen a lot, and I'd certainly learned a lot, but I'd come to realise more and more that walking to the tops of mountains was only the first step towards really getting under their skin.

And the thing is, I still wasn't very good it. No matter how much I tried to be one of those people who could negotiate the pratfalls of equipment, navigation, physical prowess and danger with Buddha-like calm, I just wasn't someone to whom mountain climbing came as an easy, natural fit. It took constant effort to appear even remotely competent. I forgot things. I still got lost, having a knack for losing even well-trodden paths from beneath my feet – a trait that over the years has left companions initially amused, then bewildered, then genuinely concerned there was something medical at play. And despite ten years of exposure to it, a neuro-linguistic programming course to help me overcome it, and more moments of pause than I care to recall, I was host to a concentrated – and worsening – fear of heights.

But I loved it. I absolutely loved it, in that kind of unconditional, permanent way you know you'll be stuck with until you croak. I'd felt it slowly maturing behind the scenes over the years. It wasn't an *obsession* – obsessions with mountains rarely have happy endings – and it wasn't anything to do with ambition. I genuinely just wanted to linger in, loiter on and explore the mountains – and experience just *being* in these uniquely atmospheric places.

And now I was going back to where it began for me, to take the tentative first steps on another quite different mountain journey.

Over time the idea that you could gather together a small clutch of the most singularly extraordinary of the British mountains had become increasingly distracting to me. This would be a journey in search of one simple thing: what *makes* them extraordinary. For some of these mountains, the most amazing thing about them might be the violent voyage through time they've taken to get here. For others, the tales of science, endeavour and art that have played out on their slopes. The mythology they're drenched in. The history they've seen. The genius they've inspired. The danger that draws people to them. The life that clusters around them, human or otherwise. The extreme weather they conjure. The adventure they fuel. The way that some raise the hairs on the back of your neck and trigger powerful, strange emotions. And moreover, what they're like to be amidst, under, on – just what that indefinable quality *is* that the British mountains wield that takes possession of you so powerfully, and never goes away. Were you to find one mountain that best exemplifies a particular one of these conditions – a kind of natural temple to each – in a way, they would collectively comprise a kind of ultimate summit bagger's list. Something achievable but definitive: a collective interpretation of the British mountains.

All mountains are different, of course. If you were to seek an example of every unique quality they possess the list would easily run to a thousand. But what my list would provide was a kind of experiential mountain hit list for people who don't have the time or will to climb a thousand of them. A list that, were someone to ask you which British mountains they should climb – and you could only pick a dozen, say – would make a pretty impressive answer. This wasn't just a ten highest, a twenty prettiest or a thirty most likely to make you shriek; it was something much more subtle and infinitely more interesting. Although I didn't really yet know it, it would be a journey that would take over a year, and take me high into the rafters of Britain's most forbidding, unflinching and unchanging wild places through all seasons – from the first blush of spring to the deepest, darkest bite of the mountain winter. A journey that, as it turned out, would have sixteen separate destinations. And Beinn Dearg, towards which I was driving in the slanted light of this autumnal afternoon, was the first.

The harmonic buzz of a deer grid beneath car tyres and a rinse of static over the radio accompanied my arrival into the long, broad scoop of Glen Torridon. To the right, stands of skeletal trees, their bark dead and grey, lined the lower slopes of Beinn Eighe – a monster of quartzite mountainside dominating the northern side of the glen for several miles. Its back is turned from this angle; you can't see the drops, the falling arêtes, the dark gullies, the hidden valleys. As the beautiful sea loch that gives the glen its name approached, I began to feel myself moving from one realm to another as the radio weakened further, mobile phone reception died, and above me, the mountains of Torridon sharpened.

Cheerily weather-beaten, the houses of Torridon village cling to a single street between the water of the loch and the bottom of another mountain, Liathach. Liathach is long and tall, but tilted away from the road, like a mainsail in a crosswind. Like Beinn Eighe, all you see from the road is a languid slope, cut by rivulets of meltwater; hidden is the 800-metre fall of the north face, which the map assures us is there but which the eye cannot see from this vantage point. Like Glen Coe, there's only a certain appreciation you can have from a car. The rest you have to earn by foot.

Beyond the village, I found the small car park amongst the woods of Inveralligin, where I'd parked with Tom in 2004. From here a twiggy path led along a series of waterfalls, turns and climbs, then broke out of the trees, following the river earnestly towards the mountains that fed it. Ahead, the outline of Beinn Dearg began to crisp into focus, from this perspective angular, almost trapezoidal. It looked interesting. It also looked weirdly unfamiliar, and it was only as the mountain's broad base approached that I realised just how much I'd forgotten about the ascent. Last time, I was just being introduced by someone else to this place. I was a tourist. Now, alone, I was in charge.

I'd chosen Beinn Dearg as the first mountain in this little quest for several reasons. The first was that it was a mountain that exhibited the feeling of exposure – of raw *height* – to a spectacular degree. There are taller and steeper mountains, not just in Britain but in this immediate area, that could easily compete; but Beinn Dearg to me was the finest example, not least because it delivers in such an unexpectedly dramatic fashion.

How a mountain cuts its dash is, of course, down to its geology. The Torridon mountains, with the exception of Beinn Eighe – which, thanks to the convoluted mangling of British upland rock eschews the typical Torridonian sandstone top for a cap of crumbling white quartzite – have a particularly unsubtle way of climbing to their considerable elevations. Laddered with horizontal terraces of crags, glaciation and weathering have sculpted the flanks of these peaks into a distinctively consistent form: as they climb, they rise first steeply, then vertically, then steeply, then vertically. From high on the mountain, the experience of looking down this sloping-step structure is devastating: beyond tipped, slippery slopes of grass and loose rock, drops open. And these are big, convex drops, whose extent is hidden. It makes you feel like you're sailing towards the edge of a waterfall.

The result is a stepped wall of mountain through which passage has to be found before you can stand on the top. In England, Wales and the higher, more travelled mountains of Scotland, many of these ways have been engineered, or walked so many times they are worn unambiguously into the mountainside. On Beinn Dearg, there are no such ways. Every side of the mountain is steep and outwardly impenetrable, and the way up is not obvious.

I was aiming to climb the mountain the same way as before as I was fairly sure it was the only realistic way up. But whilst I'd in effect be repeating my earlier ascent, I wouldn't be repeating the weather – and that made a difference. Even a subtle shift in conditions can completely change a mountain's character, and today's mizzle was far from a subtle shift.

Down to the left of the path the river was surging. I could hear the hard 'clock' of boulders being spun and punched along its bed. Crossing it would be impossible on foot. Luckily, the last human augmentation to the landscape before the Bealach a' Chòmhla – the high gap or *bealach* between Beinn Dearg and its tall, sheer neighbour, Beinn Alligin – is a bridge. Beyond, as the path's thin ribbon began to climb, it started to rain. I looked up towards Beinn Dearg's south-west face. Though the detail of its buttresses was softening in the drizzle, I could still see clearly what lay ahead. It looked so high, and steep: impossibly steep. I'd been up it before, and had no recollection of it being *that* difficult. Maybe distance would decode it; perspective in the mountains was tricksy, after all. Perhaps at the foot of the slope it would cease to resemble a wall and take on a kinder angle. As eyelash-hung raindrops began to quiver the mountain in my vision, I stooped my head and continued on, the soft gnaw of apprehension in my stomach.

As I got closer, the tiny grains of scree that hung around the lower slopes of the mountain like a valance grew into boulders, some the size of marrows, others the size of cars, the odd one the size of a house. A flicker of memory: had I climbed through this before? I scanned above, tracing a potential line of travel through the boulders onto the grassy shoulders and up, up onto the sharp skyline of the north-west ridge. Possibly. Possibly that would go.

The boulders were chaotically tall and grey, the grey of the cindered ruins of a bombed-out town. The sandstone was sharp and cold, the hard fabric of my trousers and jacket making a scratching sound as I brushed by. All of this must have fallen off the mountain at some point; what a terror it would be to see one of these boulders racing down this face. For the first time on this mountain, my hands touched rock. Using your whole body to move through terrain is less tiring than just using your legs, as well as being more engaging to the brain. Of course, it's usually steeper, too – which has the benefit of gathering height beneath you briskly, although it quite literally has a down side. I found myself enjoying the crossing of the boulder field so much that I forgot to keep an eye on the drop opening quickly behind me. It was only when the ground underfoot pitched enough to give me a thoughtful moment that I noticed the features I'd passed were taking on the altered perspective that only comes from being several hundred feet above them. Streams and stodgy bogs were suddenly sinuous rivulets and sky-mirrored pools interlocking with a messy elegance. I refocused upwards. Looking along the edge of the mountain, I could see that I was approaching a band of crags – the first of several that ran laterally across the mountain like taut waist-belts. After the ease of the boulder field, the way ahead was all of a sudden daunting. This was where things got interesting. This was where the mountain began.

What constitutes the 'special quality' of the British mountains is a big question, but it's one worth asking. To engender such wide-ranging respect and affection – and they do, as we shall see – whatever it is, they must have it in spades. And it certainly isn't height; not height in the numerical sense, anyway.

First, though, there's the matter of exactly what qualifies as a *mountain*. People argue all the time about this. They kick numbers around, use terms like 'prominence' and 'relative height', quibble over a metre here, a foot there, and get sniffy about certain hills because they don't hit a certain all-important benchmark. But in my book – and this *is* my book – it's all a bit unnecessary. Mountains were never meant to be specific; they're chaotic, and all about feeling and aesthetics. If it looks like a mountain and it feels like a mountain, then it *is* a mountain.

This is a convenient viewpoint to take, as a proper definition doesn't actually exist – neither between a mountain and level ground, nor between a hill and a mountain. The *Collins English Dictionary* (and I should probably underline here that it's no worse than any other dictionary in this regard) defines a mountain as 'higher and steeper than a hill and often having a rocky summit', and a hill as being 'a natural elevation of the earth's surface, less high or craggy than a mountain'. The only thing that seems to be agreed is essentially a loose compositional contrast – mountains are rockier and higher than hills, hills are rounded and lower than mountains – but no specifics as to what extent or with what steepness something has to project from the earth's surface in order to be classified as one or the other.

If this were an accepted grey area things would be fine, but it isn't; many still think mountains and hills differ from each other simply because of their height. In September 2008, three amateur surveyors re-measured a mountain in North Wales – Mynydd Graig Goch, in Snowdonia – and found its height to be 2,000 feet, rather than 1,998 feet. The celebratory headlines that followed certainly suggested this constituted the crossing of a significant watermark; the BBC report of 19 September – in a similar vein to many others of the same day – was a simply triumphant 'Survey turns hill into mountain'. So there is clearly a school of thought sufficiently established to make national news that the appropriate point at which a hill ends and a mountain begins is 2,000 feet – or 609.6 metres. In a pernickity sidenote, many of these reports drew parallels to the 1995 film *The Englishman Who Went up a Hill But Came Down a Mountain*, whilst quietly ignoring the fact that in this instance (based on a true story and a real eminence – The Garth, near Cardiff) the point where a hill became a mountain was only 1,000 feet.

Either way, and however wonderful both stories were, they get us no closer to a definition. There are many sharp, craggy elevations below 2,000 feet – or even 1,000 feet – that certainly resemble and evoke the idea of a mountain, just as there are plenty over 2,000 feet and 3,000 feet that struggle to resemble the definition of a hill, let alone a mountain. This merely serves to highlight that all these places are different and defy any kind of numerical ring-fencing: a mountain is simply what is made in the eye of the beholder. The pioneer Scottish mountaineer J. H. B. Bell put it rather nicely when he wrote, 'Whether we are dealing with the little 1,000-foot hill near our homes ... or a 20,000-foot giant of the Himalaya ... in certain kinds of weather and atmospheric lighting, one can look almost as impressive as the other.'

What we do have instead are classifications – lists, basically – which are less definitions and more ways of grouping the natural shambles of mountains together under something approaching order.

It's testimony to the fascination of Britain's high places how many of these lists there are – especially since the presence of mountains does not necessarily an overwhelmingly mountainous country make. Most of Britain's high places are isolated in ranges in North or South Wales, the Lake District and Pennines of England, and the Uplands, Highlands and Islands of Scotland. Yet despite this fairly lean coverage, Britain is far from short of mountain classifications – many of which, whilst inevitably overlapping to a degree, comprise hundreds of mountains. Amongst others we have the Deweys, Tumps, Hardys, Nuttalls, Donalds, Grahams, Murdos, Corbetts, Wainwrights – and, most venerable of all, the Munros.

If this all seems a bit tedious, don't worry. We'll revisit one or two of these lists, but most of them we won't. And either way, it doesn't *really* matter.

Another thing that doesn't seem to matter is absolute elevation. On paper, the mountains of Britain are – relatively, at least – embarrassingly slight. Not a single one gets remotely close to cracking the 2,000-metre mark, which, as I understand it, is the minimum height a mountain has to be before a French mountaineer can justify the energy required to look up at it. There are car dealerships in Italy higher than the 1,344-metre (4,409-foot) summit of Ben Nevis. The million people who inhabit Guatemala City live, sleep and work higher than our highest point and probably don't have to do it in a Gore-Tex coat and walking boots. In fact most countries in the world have enough justification to – in the most literal sense – look down on the height of Britain's modest mountains. Amongst the many, many countries that boast far higher peaks than ours within their borders are the less-than-notably mountaineering nations of Cuba, Guinea, Sri Lanka and Madagascar – with Fiji, Tonga and the Seychelles uncomfortably close to joining that list.

But despite their diminutiveness, people come from all over the world to get our mountains beneath their feet. Many are world famous, and – whilst perhaps not as ballistic or notorious as, say, the Matterhorn or the Eiger – the shadows they throw are far longer than their physical statistics would seem to merit. Perhaps it's the convenient conservativeness of their height; they're robust enough to *feel* big and tall enough to include several distinct ecosystems, but none of them requires more than a day to get up, or hits any altitudes that require acclimatisation. This makes our mountains extraordinarily inclusive, which is further helped by the fact that few require the assistance of a rope to achieve the summit. Given even a basic skill set and fitness, and the willingness to use your hands, outside of winter most people can get to the top of most British peaks under their own steam. Indeed, most host routes to suit all abilities to such a canny degree it's as if this were a conscious consideration in their design.

Not that they always *look* straightforward, of course. An amusing story, which time has sadly rendered apocryphal, concerns a visitor from Switzerland who had come to walk up Snowdon. Upon rounding a corner of the Pyg Track, at a point that offers a spectacular view of the mountain's east face, he froze, before imploring his party to turn back as there was insufficient daylight to make a summit attempt. Snowdon had tricked him; in good conditions the summit from that point is little more than two hours away. This is heartening, because, if you've ever seen the Swiss Alps, you'll know that the mountains there are ridiculous. They're like daggers, and there are millions of them. The fact that someone who comes from a country with mountains like that would want to come and climb one of ours – let alone be overawed by one – tells us something. It tells us 'less is more'. It also tells us that whatever it is our mountains have, it isn't cheapened by abundance or the anonymity of youth. They are dignified. Distinguished. They have something, which, were they alive, you might call a personality.

The names help. Oh, the names. Mountains across the world are usually given evocative names; it's what comes of being the landscape's most dramatic natural feature. But the toponymy – a little-deployed word to do with the etymology of place names – of the British mountains has a curiously unique vintage that is both cherishable and maddening, depending on the dexterity of your pronunciation muscles. Thanks to the interbreeding of Middle English, Gaelic, Goidelic Celtic, Old Norse, Anglo-Norman and the odd humorous landlord with a hill's identity at his disposal, we have within our shores mountains that sound like flaking skin conditions (Slioch); someone choking on a Polo whilst trying to give directions in a Glasgow suburb (Stùc a' Choire Dhuibh Bhig); unpleasant bodily reflexes (Barf); embarrassing bodily parts (Fan y Bîg); a kind of rice-based snack (Canisp); and the fortress of some medieval villain (Bidean nam Bian). We also have a couple of Cockups (one big, one not so big), a Sergeant, several Old Mans and literally hundreds of Bens. And though I jest, the meanings of some of the more colourful mountain names are as fascinating as they are eclectic. To illustrate this point, I'll offer just one particularly good example: a hill in North Wales called Pen Llithrig y Wrach. It means 'Hill of the Slippery Witch'. How can you not love that?

Not all hill names are unique, alas. There are several Beinn Deargs, for instance. It means 'Red Hill', and it's a lazy name, about as plain as you can get for a Scottish mountain. *Beinn* is a typical Scottish Gaelic word for a peak, or hill. The 'red' is probably a reference to the way it looks in a certain light at a certain time of day at a certain time of year, although even by these rules the name is a flimsy fit. But no matter; interesting names aren't always given to interesting mountains, and the reverse is often true. And I knew that this was certainly the case with Beinn Dearg.

I began to feel like there was something amiss with the route I was taking up Beinn Dearg about halfway up the north-west flank. The route through the boulder field had felt familiar, in the manner of a decade-old hunch. But by the time I reached the first crag band at the top of the boulder field, this hunch had gone. I could see a way through this new obstacle: a steepening grassy slope above the drop of the crag, which led diagonally up to a nick in the skyline ahead. What lay beyond it I didn't know – and to get to it would involve traversing out over steep ground leaning towards an awful, convex drop. If this route didn't go, I'd have to cross above the drop twice. I didn't like that idea.

When walking alone, you don't have anyone to help with uncertainty or share in the decision-making; it's one of the reasons they tell you not to do it. All the confidence I had was my own, and today I didn't have much. Shakily, I began to walk towards the nick in the crag ahead. I felt the ground steepen underfoot, and tilt; I swayed my weight accordingly, and kept my eyes fixed forward. I could feel air opening to my right as I moved slowly across the slope. It was only when I reached the rock beyond and took hold of its solidity with a queasy exhale that I realised I'd been holding my breath. Looking through the gap in the crags that had been my goal, I saw more steep ground and a possible zigzag I could take to gain the next band of crags above, which looked like it skirted just to the edge of the drop. It seemed this alarming void was to be my steadily intensifying, inescapable companion for the whole ascent. My eyes searched the ground for comforting signs of human passage: a boot print, piled stones, anything suggesting others had gone this way. Nothing. But perhaps that was how it was all over the mountain. Perhaps this was all part of its challenge.

Satisfied that the route could be reversed if necessary, I continued my upward traverse of the steep ground, cutting back on myself after a dozen steps or so at a higher angle in a zigzag climb, up a skinny vertical corridor ascending the mountain's side. I didn't know if I was right. Britain might have great maps, short distances and relatively small mountains, but this was still exploration of the most vital kind – basic, exciting, nerve-wracking exploration with a simple composition: move. Climb. Don't slip. A fragile, self-balanced pivot between the thrilling and the frightening. Proper adventure, with all the high stakes and uncertainty that this brought: any second I could hit something unpassable. And then, eventually, I did.

On the last section before I met the second band of crags, I came across an overhanging shelf of sandstone. From a distance it looked passable; up close, I could see it wasn't. It would hang me over the drop I'd delicately been trying to keep at arm's length all the way up. As I shuffled in indecision, my foot nudged loose a rock the size of a beer coaster. Transfixed, I watched it gather momentum as it bounced down the mountainside in lengthening arcs, before sailing cleanly off the precipice I now stared down. It was the final kick to my resolve. This route was going nowhere. The map was no use; I was in the nitty-gritty muddle of the face, a place the cartographer had detailed with missing contour lines and stippled crag decals – fair warning of steep and difficult terrain I should probably have heeded.

As frustrating as all this was, this had been the second reason that Beinn Dearg had appealed to me. One of my memories of climbing it a decade ago was hearing it described by someone as a 'proper mountain' – that is to say, not roaded with deep paths punctuated by lines of people, or representative of any kind of soft touch to the hillwalker. To get to the top of it, you needed to earn it. You needed to use your navigation head, be a little bit brave, push on past bits of difficult terrain, and have the resolve to ascend something unrelentingly steep for what seems like hours, as the ground falls mercilessly around you. Beinn Dearg might be a 'bimble' to some. To most, however, it's a test.

I stood for a long moment, looking down the steep fall beneath my feet. There was really no choice. I had to go back. Find another way. Crouched on the slope, I took a few deep breaths and began to descend the way I'd come. I gingerly reversed the zig-zags, re-reached the nick in the rock, then re-crossed the exposed terrace to a grassy platform, where I could rest and reassess.

One other option looked realistic – a shelf of rock that ascended the mountain for a hundred metres or so, with a stony gully beneath it. Midway across the traverse to it, my eyes caught something on the ground. Something faint, but unmistakable: a partial footprint. Someone else had come this way. Whoever this boot print belonged to could have been as indecisive as me, but it was still a comfort to think that I wasn't *completely* misguided. As I reached the shelf I took hold of it and climbed it, using the rock as a kind of human-height banister. It was comforting to be closed-in, instead of exposed. It smelled of moss and echoed my breath. I could hear faint trickles of water.

I followed this slowly as it travelled high above another steeply angled slope, then came up against the spine of broken rock of the north-west ridge. The ridge ascended unbroken, right to the top. This was evidently the way the few who climbed Beinn Dearg typically went. After my own failed attempt at route-finding up the face, I decided to join them. Soon the sky opened ahead, and I reached Stùc Loch na Cabhaig, the lower of Beinn Dearg's two summits.

From here, the mountain becomes a podium. Views open, and the eastern distance hits you with a vision of astonishing depth. There was Beinn Eighe, curled like the rim of an old caldera, brittle quartzite dusting its flanks like fine flour; Baosbheinn and Beinn an Eòin to the north, watchful twins overlooking torpedo-shaped Loch na h-Oidhche between them. And beyond, the watery hinterland of the Flowerdale Forest, a broad place of loch, mountain, bog and bug stretching to the long natural divide of Loch Maree, seven miles to the north. Detail was hazy, but the mountains' outlines were clear, black shapes in the murk.

My companion in the view all the way up Beinn Dearg to the west was perhaps Torridon's most distinguished mountain, Beinn Alligin – which, as

I'd climbed, had gradually sharpened and shifted from being a huge mass of terraced rock to becoming a shapely, flat-topped cone fluted with dark gullies. With its neat architecture and straight edges it looked as if it had been folded like a steepled napkin. So unique. So charismatic.

The winner in the spectacle stakes, however, didn't show itself until I made the final walk to Beinn Dearg's summit. The last stretch to reach it is a bowed whaleback of a ridge, slung like a rickety bridge between the two high points. The most logical line takes you within handshaking distance of the massive drop into Beinn Dearg's secretive inner valley – the floor of which is drowned by the black waters of Loch a' Choire Mhòir.

Happily, the only difficulty here was just one move, little more than a long step. There was a drop – but so long as I didn't dwell on it, only a head appearing from a hole at my feet could startle me into getting it wrong. Soon I was on the other side of the crags. Breathing hard but happy, I began to walk up the final easy slope to the broad summit of Beinn Dearg, beyond which, rising steadily into view, lay one of the great mountain sights of Britain.

From Beinn Dearg's little-trodden high point, the view of Liathach (the 'Grey One', probably in reference to its quartzite scree) is spectacularly vivid: a long battlement of peaks resembling the cardiograph of a racing heart. From the main road in Glen Torridon it's just a lump. You have to walk miles to see this, and to view it at its best you need to climb. It's the reward you get for being intrepid: a great sight, and once seen, your perspective of scale within Britain's humble little archipelago may well shift for good. Amongst mountain walkers, Liathach is famous, and much coveted as a prize. But the view I was getting from Beinn Dearg was much rarer – an unbeatable vantage point that, as I'd found, was no easy win itself. But I'd made it. Here I was, for the second time, on the summit of Beinn Dearg: the culmination – and exact halfway point – of a 1,000-mile round trip.

There was the summit marker cairn: a modest, human-piled heap of native rocks, one the shape of an incisor tooth poking out of the top to the height of my shoulder. Within that cairn – somewhere around the height of my hip – was the 3,000-foot contour line.

And herewith lies the great irony of Beinn Dearg, and the third reason I'd chosen to climb this mountain above all others hereabouts. Beinn Dearg is considered the least noteworthy of Torridon's central quartet of mountains, not for lacking challenge, nor spectacle, nor location: it has all of these in plenty. Despite being the nucleus of the area that contains Liathach, Beinn Eighe and Beinn Alligin, the mountain is ignored by the bulk of human traffic because it's 30 inches too short. Thirty inches: that's the distance between the sole of my boot and the middle of my thigh. You cannot imagine how spectacularly, how *ridiculously* insignificant that is in mountain terms. A 3,000-foot mountain is 36,000 inches high; 30 inches represents 0.08 per cent of its total height. On a 6-foot person, that's the equivalent of cutting just under two *millimetres* of hair from the very top of their head, then dismissing them for being inconsequentially small. The reason for this is that 3,000 feet is quite an important measurement for a mountain in Scotland; it's the height at which a mountain becomes a Munro.

There are, at the time of writing, 282 Munros in Scotland. I say 'at the time of writing' – new mountains don't appear or disappear at a rate necessary to be monitored by hillwalkers, after all – because nobody can really decide what actually *constitutes* a Munro. The original list was compiled by a London-born, Scottish-raised baronet, Sir Hugh Munro, as a way of categorising the hills of his familial homeland into some sort of quantifiable system. It was published in 1891, and surprised most by its sheer length; most people thought Scotland harboured a mere handful of mountains over 3,000 feet, so the whole thing was a splendid surprise.

But despite being thorough, Munro wasn't particularly specific. His *Tables* reflected what he considered 'separate mountains above 3,000 feet', but he neglected to define what constituted 'separate,' and this is of course unsatisfactory for today's levels of numerical scrutiny. Alas, much quarrelling continues about which peaks should and shouldn't be on the list, and it all gets terribly complicated. The debates on the matter are filled with terms such as 'overall drop', 'relative height' and 'subsidiary tops', which all broadly circle around the fact that nowhere did Munro give a specific figure for how tall a summit had to be in relation to the one next to it to qualify it as a separate mountain – and therefore a true Munro.

The reason this all matters is that 'bagging' the Munros, as well as subsequent (and generally rather more specific) mountain lists such as the Corbetts, Grahams, Hewitts and Marilyns – not forgetting the Lake District hills chronicled by celebrated guidebook scribe Alfred Wainwright – has become a way of quantifying experience and achievement, a means of systematising and categorising something which, by its nature, is the antithesis of order and reason: walking into the wilderness, and climbing up something for no other motive other than you can. And – of course! – because it's there.* Frustrating, annoyingly pedantic and wonderfully idiosyncratic. In short, splendidly British.

As of May 2013, some 5,000 people have completed all of the Munros, some of them having done so twice, a few without stopping. That's an awesome achievement. Superhuman, even.

Yet how many of those people looked up at Beinn Dearg, saw it, and thought: 'Wow! But not on *my* list,' before shuffling on?

It's all a lot of fun and certainly makes a pleasingly functional answer to the perennial question 'Why climb a mountain' (Answer: 'I've got them written down on this piece of paper, so I have to'). And whatever legacy Hugh Munro left when he died of influenza in 1919 – presumably without someone sitting anxiously at his bedside imploring him to write a number, *any* number, down on this piece of paper before you go, old chap, because one day this could be important – you have to admire his style. Other than that 3,000-foot criterion, Munro went on instinct rather than anything more mathematical; it was simply a question of how grand a summit *felt*. And at its core this all brings us back to the argument of what is and what isn't a mountain. It really doesn't matter. If it feels like a mountain, then it *is* one.

I didn't have time to do the Munros, even if I wanted to. I certainly couldn't do all the Corbetts, or even the Wainwrights. I admired and envied the experiences of all those who did, but I couldn't invest the precious time I had to spend in the mountains to one geographical area, and certainly not to the same narrow band of the vertical scale.

Stand on Beinn Dearg's summit, make a little indentation in your thigh, and take a moment to consider your context – there's the Atlantic, there's the

---

* Which was of course said by ill-fated climber George Mallory at a lecture in 1923 when asked, 'Why climb Everest?' Nobody really knows what he meant, or even if he said exactly this; it could have been something profound, or it might simply have been irritation at the question. Either way, it has passed into history as the most famous three-word justification of the ostensibly pointless.

river, wriggling along far below, and here you are, alone amongst it – and you'll realise how little numbers matter when it comes to climbing mountains. Beinn Dearg is a *mountain*: each and every one of its 35,970 inches builds towards a top of such elevated spectacle, you'd be mad to discount it on any basis, let alone it not making the coveted slate of a man whose life occupied but a flash of its own existence.

I looked at my watch. Six p.m. It had taken far more time than I'd thought to reach the summit and darkness would soon start falling. Cloud was beginning to mither the higher tops, and was creeping up the gullies and valleys around me. Walking out would take hours. Time I got down.

Taking a last look around, I walked south from the summit cairn, intending to follow Beinn Dearg's skyline as it curved around to the east, then find a comely slope to descend into the valley once the mountain had surrendered most of its height.

Ahead of me, the edge of the summit appeared as a hard line against the sky, like the side of a flat roof or the end of a diving board. I wasn't alarmed: the convex slopes that built these mountains meant that easy terrain beyond – a broad series of rock steps, or a thin path negotiating a steep slope – would emerge as I got closer.

Only it didn't. I reached the edge of the summit plateau and froze. For the first time I saw the descent route, and it was a shock. Ahead of me and below was a thin sail of brown, bitten rock. Curved slightly, its outside edge was completely vertical in its fall to the valley floor, whilst the right side – now filling with rising cloud – had a steeply tilting grassy ledge across which a thin path beetled. Beneath that, a crag, then a drop of similar horror. From the top of the mountain down to the first bit of buttress-cut slope was probably in the order of 500 metres. That was the only way the mountain went. I'd two choices: climb the crest on good rock but over big exposure, or traverse the grassy ledge and pray it wasn't slippery. My company on both of these options would be open intimacy with a drop as high and as vertical as the Empire State Building. I didn't remember this! And this wasn't even the most pressing problem.

At my feet – far from an easy toddle down a few amenably angled rocks – was a vertical step of about three metres. Its bottom was a little platform of rock, on either side of which the mountain fell away with fatal steepness. To get to it required a down-climb as if on a very steeply raked ladder, only with tilted footholds of wet rock instead of rungs, with no guarantees of integrity and no margin for error at the bottom. Piece of cake.

I pulled out the map and looked at it helplessly. I'd no phone reception, and no rope – ropes are not necessary to reach the top of all but a few major mountain summits in Britain,* and next to useless unless you have someone with you. This was the way off; the only other option was to go back the way I came, and I didn't fancy that either. With increasing alarm, I looked around at the clouds and tried to rationalise. The down-climb in front of me looked delicate, but achievable. I must have done it before, though probably under direction and encouragement – and with even a helping hand – from Tom. But I *had* done it. And confidence was two-thirds of the battle. As long as I didn't lose my cool I could do it. Just a few feet of down-climbing and a bit of exposure, and I could be on my way to a meal and a bed. Either that, or I'd just have to learn to live up here.

Descents like this are what fatal-accident statistics are made of. Coming down mountains claims more people than going up by a ratio of about 3 to 1. What was worse, I really hadn't expected this. By ploughing up the hill, waving my previous experience of the mountain as a tool which, as we've seen, turned out to be less than reliable, I'd neglected to do enough research. A failure. But a lesson, too – and one I could learn from provided I could safely find a way out of this jam.

Mustering confidence, I fixed my mind on something random. I'd read somewhere that reciting your telephone number backwards during times of fear engaged a part of the brain that antagonistically quelled your fright cells; as I turned to face the rock and placed my foot on the first ledge a few feet down the crack, I shakily began to do it. Three points of contact at all times; look after your hands, and your feet will look after themselves. I could smell the murk of the rock as I pushed my face close to it, trying hard to make my

---

* Most famously, Sgùrr Dearg's notorious 'Inaccessible Pinnacle' on the Isle of Skye. There are other summits in Britain – indeed, more on Skye – that require the use of a rope, and ability is of course subjective, but there are ways up most of our principal mountains without additional aid, certainly in summer.

entire world the crack before me and the narrow tube of rock at my feet I had to get down. No mountain, no drop – just this little ladder. Nothing else.

Concentrating on moving my hands to where my feet were, striking the rocks with the edge of my fist to check their stability, and mumbling my reverse phone number aloud with my exhales, I steadily made progress down the crack. I dropped down the last foot, landing squarely on the little platform. My heart audible in my ears, I took a deep breath and continued on down the ridge, not wanting to lose momentum until these dangers were passed.

I rejected the crest of the precarious rocky sail in favour of the lower grassy terrace, moving to the right of the ridge's frightening-looking apex. Trying to move as smoothly as I could, I traced the skinny path with my eyes then followed it with my feet, taking care – great care – not to trip. Writhing cloud had now clogged the void to the right, momentarily taking away the psychological impact of the drop. It parted as I approached the end, and I caught the glint of the river far below and the edge of Beinn Dearg's mighty south-west buttress. There it was: that memory, that feeling of height – the kind of feeling that hits you like a nine-iron to the back of the legs. It was exactly what I didn't need at that precise moment, but I stayed focused for the last few feet of the traverse. Then suddenly it was over. I scrabbled over a few rocks onto a little ledge, and when I saw that the mountain was considerably tamer from here on and that there were no more surprises in store, I let out an audible groan of relief, crumpling against the rock, my legs buzzing, arms shaking, breathing rapidly. *That* had been unexpectedly hairy.

Although I wasn't off yet and the descent was still going to be difficult, I now knew that I was going to get down. After that, dinner was going to taste particularly good. I might even have an extra beer to celebrate being able to have an extra beer.

But this was only the first. As it would go, fifteen more mountains lay ahead – each with its own challenge, its own particular conditions, feel and story to tell. Beinn Dearg wasn't the hardest. It also wasn't the highest. But for me this was the mountain I'd always associate with this feeling of *height*; of that elevated perspective you can only get from a mountain, and of the exhilaration and the fear that grips you by the stomach – the basic elements that make these places so special. In 1911 the Scottish-American naturalist John Muir wrote that 'Nature, as a poet ... becomes more and more visible the farther and higher we go; for the mountains are fountains: beginning places, however related to sources beyond mortal ken.'

I rose, and as I did so I pushed my wet hair out of my face and felt a substantial deposit of sharp sandstone grit upon my forehead. Confused for a moment, I realised my hands had picked it up off the rock and I'd wiped it onto my brow every time I'd mopped it. I was literally sweating grit.

My eyes followed the rock at my feet up towards the ridge I'd just climbed. The stuff I was carrying down the mountain on my forehead, these mountains are made of it. That brown, course-grained sandstone is even named after the area best exhibiting it: Torridonian sandstone, they call it. The whole range has rocks made of this grit as their bedrock. It's why Beinn Dearg is called Beinn Dearg: for the way the sun lights the brown sandstone and deepens it to red in the westerly glow of sunset. It's famous for this.

But nobody ever tells you about the lichen. Brilliant white whorls of it, augmenting almost every rock. Unless you were on the hill you wouldn't see it or know it was here. But up on the ridge it's everywhere. It looks as if the mountain is pinned with white rosettes; silly little patches of prettiness adorning its hard skin.

PART I

SPRING

2 SPACE

It was May, and southern Britain was drowning. Winter had been hard, and spring hesitant to commit in its wake. The last six weeks had seen new lambs arrive along with the first, anaemic, blush of colour to the landscape; both were soon buried in snowdrifts. For mountain climbing, this didn't bode well. Whilst such seasonal false starts were happening so dramatically in the valleys, the weather on the tops would be even more alarmingly fickle.

Six months after I returned from Torridon the thaw finally came – and with it rain, on a seemingly biblical scale. It was in between two of these May downpours that I went out to the garage to resume packing the bag I intended to take on the journey of sorts that, with the albeit damp foundations of spring firmly bedded, could now begin.

One of the most important aspects of this journey was my desire to see the mountains at their most wild, and experience their most extreme and dynamic moods. Happily, these conditions occurred every 24 hours without fail, and twice: sunrise and sunset. To really know a mountain you need to see it in all shades of the day and, preferably, at night – and in the high places of Britain contrasts are magnified far more than at sea level. A mountain feels intense and quite different in the dark. My plan, therefore, was to climb as many as I could at the frayed ends of the day, the time when the mountains lose the little civility they tolerate during the daylight and return to the wild. Where I could I'd sleep on them, drink from their streams, seek shelter amongst them and walk in all weathers. And whilst I'm not saying that I *didn't* want to do the living-off-the-land thing and wander in with a stick, a cloak and a big knife (well, maybe I am), I was going in to enjoy the mountains, not survive them. But that still meant that a certain amount of kit was necessary.

It started out as a small bag; just the ascetic essentials for safety and warmth, crammed into a small rucksack that was light enough not to be an onerous burden, but fortified with enough to see me through any blip in the notoriously shifty mountain weather. I wanted it to be there, ready and packed – something I could stash in the car boot for deployment at any opportunity. As time passed, however, and I watched all manner of winter weather scrape by the window, additions inevitably began to creep in: another jacket, an extra pair of gloves, a second hat, my spare compass, the emergency map. There was, when walking at the extreme ends of the day, always the possibility of becoming cold or lost: and, as wild camping was on the cards, a tent – or bivvy bag, if I was feeling intrepid – a sleeping bag and a roll-mat needed to go in there, too. Now there was far too much for a little rucksack and so a larger rucksack was needed. And so on.

It's easy to get excited about outdoor kit. The shops that sell it are little pieces of the mountains dropped into urbania; boutiques filled with shiny, purposefully robust equipment destined to become muddy and tarnished. It's no problem at all to disappear into these places for ages. Inside, you can appraisingly touch the latest waterproof fabrics, assess the tents packed into tight nylon sausages for weight, gaze at the newest boots, and wonder what it might be like to have it all at your disposal. You'll recoil at the price tag, but over the coming weeks you'll come to realise that you not only *want* this piece of equipment but categorically *need* it. Every hobby has its own infectiously fetishistic side, and climbing mountains is no different. There's something slightly gladiatorial about it; layering up with stiff, rugged fabrics and packing everything on your back that you need to self-sustain in a wild environment is a pleasing feeling. But aside from the pomp, drastic financial outlays and painful colour clashes, dressing properly is also absolutely necessary. You need to not only be warm and dry, but comfortable under considerable physical strain. It gets pretty tough out there.

I was fairly sure I was in possession of everything I needed for whatever I was about to face; the problem with our seesawing climate was knowing exactly what that was likely to be. Eventually I gave up on trying to pack the perfect bag and instead lugged the now considerable pile of clothing and kit in various states of garage-induced mustiness to the car boot. Most of it would remain there for almost a year and less than half of it would get used.

But as I packed the last pieces in, it was empowering to think that I'd be comprehensively covered should I be seized at any moment by the notion to turn north in search of mountains. You can choose your cliché. To get away from it all. Escape the rat race. To get some headspace. For many who habitually head for the high, wild places, this idea of space, of solitude, is a key part of the appeal. For many, it's the whole point.

Of the many things you get used to hearing when you live in Britain – the moans about the weather, the speed at which the government of the day is sending the country to hell on a skillet and the fact that petrol isn't as cheap as it used to be – one gripe that's particularly difficult to escape is how hopelessly, intolerably crowded the country is. It would be easy for an outsider to visualise Britain as a kind of unstable skiff of disgruntled, over-jostled passengers that at any moment will crack loudly and spectacularly discharge its contents into the North Atlantic. But in practice this preconception is really complete nonsense.

The next time you find yourself travelling long distance across the country, allow yourself for a moment to be struck by just how physically empty much of Britain is. We're not talking boundless, unmolested wilderness exactly; just *space*. Leave London by car in most directions and minutes after you're outside the M25, the number of buildings falls away and you're amidst the most bewitching countryside. Even in the industrial north – where, if maps were to be believed, cities seem to spill into each other in an arc that starts at Liverpool and doesn't really stop until Leeds – there are huge expanses of not an awful lot. There doesn't seem to be anything sizeable at all between Lancaster and Whitby (the span of the entire country) except high, savage moorland; ditto between Carlisle and Berwick, and Newcastle and Penrith. Of course this is difficult to appreciate from King's Cross or central Birmingham. And on the face of it, the numbers do disagree.

According to the 2011 census, 56,075,912 people live in England and Wales. This equates to just under 371 souls packed into every one of a combined 151,174 square kilometres. That's a lot. But that's also presuming they're spread uniformly, which of course they're not. The 70 most populous towns and cities in England and Wales cover a total of 7,781 square kilometres – around 5 per cent of the two countries' total area. Into that a staggering 60 per cent of the population is shoehorned. A total of 33,899,733 people live in one of these built-up areas, which means the average population density of the remaining 95 per cent of the country exhales to a rather more spacious 154 people per square kilometre. This is a third of England and Wales' 'official' population-density figure, but again in practice this is a rather misleading measure as the remaining population is also by no means evenly spread, being instead compartmentalised even more by the many thousand smaller clumps of population: big towns, small towns, villages and so on.

Scotland belongs in a different class altogether. Covering 78,387 square kilometres and home to 5,313,600 people, its average population density of 67 people per square kilometre drops to a decidedly thin 37 when the ten largest settlements — which cover just 769 square kilometres, or a fraction under 0.9 per cent of Scotland's total area — are disregarded. So really, when you think about it, Britain consists of a small amount of space in which a huge amount of people live, and quite a lot of space where relatively few people live.

Mountains are the unconquerables. They are, in every sense, the last frontier of Britain — and its emptiest places. By their very nature, they will be the last bulwarks to be overcome by the rising flood of population and development that the gloom-mongers tell us is relentlessly on its way. Inhospitable and extreme, they'll become refuges for those seeking escape; pointy little islands of silence and space, too awkward to be developed, too inconvenient to be home.

Of course, for those who crave calm, said solitude and escape from the very real crowding of cities, the mountains are refuges already. They're the greatest empty spaces in a country of otherwise relatively lean dimensions. Consequently, I was keen to find a mountain that might demonstrate exactly this, a wilderness close to something, but bare of anything; a kind of accessible antithesis to claustrophobia.

I spent some time trying to find it. It needed to be a place where you could feel like the only person in existence, where the landscape around you is so limitless and free of human meddling it has the potential to redefine perspective and blow any sense of claustrophobia or overcrowding out of the system. The trouble was — and this was a happy dilemma — there seemed to be too many places to choose from.

Arthur's Seat, standing above the spired city of Edinburgh like a spook over a child's bed, stood at one extreme, given its striking juxtaposition of the brimming and the barren. Such is the intimacy with which the city and the peak nuzzle up against each other you could honk a horn or even open a tub of particularly delicious soup in the city and someone up on Arthur's Seat would notice. Not just that, the visual contrast was particularly unsubtle. The roots of a long-dead volcano hewn and squashed into its present form by glaciation during the Carboniferous period some 300 million years ago, its bold profile grinning with crags made for a strikingly bare companion to the twinkly steeples and townhouses of Edinburgh. But at 251 metres it's tiny even by British standards, and didn't so much offer an escape from civilisation as stand proud as a podium amidst it – somewhere to gaze from a pleasing point of observation down upon the city, but never to feel truly removed from it.

Dartmoor, in the south-west of England, seemed to offer almost limitless desolation with a pleasingly eerie footnote, thick as it is with folk legend and weird, gaunt tors. Much of it sits at around 500 metres above sea level, making it surprisingly elevated for a moor; look north from its highest point at 621 metres and the next comparably lofty ground in England doesn't crop up until Derbyshire. But a quarter of the national park – and around half of the area you would call the 'high' moor – is used by the Ministry of Defence, who, for a few hours most days bounce around on it in jeeps and shoot at each other with rocket launchers and other noisy things entirely unfavourable to tranquillity. To give them their due, the military look after the moor rather well in the moments they aren't using it as a kind of Devonshire Ypres. But to me, the process of having to check access times on a website to avoid the slim possibility of being shot – or inadvertently stepping on something that might cause me to be returned home in a carrier bag – sort of defeated the object.

My search area was beginning to spiral northwards again when a news story caught my eye. Suddenly the answer was obvious, and a decision was quickly made. And fortuitously enough, the solution to this quest for space *came* in the form of space – albeit space of a quite different kind.

Whilst the most obvious menace with the potential to collectively rob us of quality elbow room and the balm of tranquillity is hustle and bustle, cars, noise and overcrowding, it appears there's another, more insidious, space thief at work in Britain. Disruptions of migrating birds, erratic breeding patterns of animals, falling populations of insects and even serious health conditions in humans are being blamed on it. I learned all of this one morning in February during a discussion on the news centred on an area of South Wales that had just become the fifth area in the world to be selected as an International Dark Sky Reserve. What this meant was that the quality of the night sky above this particular area was of such superior clarity, free of the sickly orange bleed of large population centres and their streetlights, that it not only warranted recognition, but also protection. The area was the National Park of the Brecon Beacons. The Brecon Beacons are mountains.

It made perfect sense. Where there are people there's light, and therefore where there's light, you can never truly be away from people or their influences. But there's also light where there are only people some of the time: roads, warehouses, industry, infrastructure. Subtle though it is, understanding this relationship between human-manufactured light and the night sky will lead you to the emptiest parts of Britain.

During idle moments over the next few weeks I learned some interesting things about light pollution. I learned that light that falls away from the area where it's needed or wanted is called 'stray light' and an unwanted invasion of this – be it a washed-out night sky with stars lost to the amber haze of a nearby town or the clumsily angled floodlight on your neighbours' wall that lights up your bedroom like an atomic flash every time a cat walks under it – is given the apt term 'light trespass'. Lighting used to throw dramatic illumination on a building or object is called 'accent lighting', and I also learned that all of these are in general bad news to lovers of dark skies and given the neat collective term 'night blight'. One of the worst-afflicted places on the planet is Tsim Sha Tsui in Hong Kong, where the level of light has over 1,200 times the value defined as the international standard for a dark sky.* The facility where this is measured is, with unfortunate irony, the Space Museum. I also

---

* If you're interested (and who wouldn't be!), the lowest quality for what is considered a dark sky – according to the International Dark Sky Association – is that 'at a minimum the Milky Way should be visible and sky conditions should approximately correspond to limiting magnitude 5.0 (or Bortle Class 6).' The Bortle Scale was created by John Bortle to aid astronomers, and runs from 1 (where shadows are cast on the ground from the sheer brilliance of the stars overhead) to inner-city skies of 8 and 9 (the sickly glow by which Bortle helpfully notes one can 'easily read').

learned – thanks to a charming organisation called the International Dark Sky Association – that an unspoiled sky is visually packed with stars right down to the horizon and the starlight is strong enough to cast noticeable shadows on land. In such conditions, picking out individual constellations is almost impossible to the untrained eye given their sheer abundance above.

I also learned that, perhaps surprisingly, Britain has some of the largest areas of dark sky in Europe. This was illustrated by a natty map of the United Kingdom as if seen from space, with clumps of heat-signature colour spread over the country like an outbreak of digital pox. The largest population centres – London, Liverpool and Manchester, Birmingham and Glasgow – were coloured an angry red, surrounded by a scab of yellow, gradually fading into pale blue. The areas of least pollution were deep navy, tonally seamless with the sea. On land, the places where these were darkest and most extensive were the mountains. Scotland blended with the sea just north of Stirling. The Pennines, the Southern Uplands of Scotland, the moors of the south-west, and the Lake District were all dark – as were blanket swathes of Wales.

The population-density maps had been one thing, but I hadn't seen anything quite so starkly illustrative of this idea of mountain ranges as islands – or voids – amidst British civilisation. This map cut through the intricate camouflage of daylight, highlighting human intrusion like phosphorescence in a murky lake: a true map of British space. And a week into May, with my eye on the weather I picked the best of a bad bunch of moonless days and headed for South Wales, to spend the night on top of the mountain – all being well – that lay beneath some of the darkest, most spacious skies on the continent.

The mountains of the Brecon Beacons – like most British mountains – are totally unique. The name rather evocatively comes from the signal fires once lit on their summits to warn of approaching English raiders. But whilst many other mountains wear the suffix of 'Beacon' across the land, none is quite like the Beacons of Brecon. None is even a bit like them.

Such is the ancient, much-brutalised geology of the British Isles, that every bit of land sticking its neck up has been battered by a particular some-thing, in a particular manner, at a particular point on its long journey, marking it as different to mountains not that distant from it. That's why British moun-tains have long been of interest to geologists: they are some of the most scrawled-on and kicked-about creations nature has ever sculpted, and they wear these signatures like scars.

The Beacons are a perfect case in point. From a distance, as you approach from the direction of south-west England, their character is clearly seen. They look like they've been finely carved from wood by a carpenter with an eye for nautical lines; all elegant scoops, gorgeously concave faces and wedged prows, a natural symmetry that seems somehow *too* symmetrical to be natural. These ingredients rise, gently but inexorably steepening towards the 900-metre contour line, whereupon they are abruptly sliced flat, as if by plane and spirit level. Their characteristic form is best demonstrated by the highest massif – the 'Brecon Beacons' themselves, the central trio of Pen y Fan, Cribyn and Corn Du – but all of these startling mountains display the same touch. The other visible hallmark is their cladding: these are not cragged and hard-skinned like the mountains of Glen Coe or Torridon, or even Snowdonia. All have coats of horizontally ridged green corduroy, the edges of which catch the first winter snows and hold the last, striping the mountains white. Where paths have worn through, the mountains beneath bleed sandstone a vivid, Martian red. The flat 'billiard' tops exhibited by the most distinctive of these mountains are the remnants of 'plateau beds' – a much grittier, harder sedimentary layer that has been chewed into the air by weathering, then resisted further attack. If the mountains look as if they've been cut flat it's because, in a manner of speaking, they have.

These central mountains are the most frequently climbed of the Brecon Beacons, and are rewarding and accessible to all. The drops are huge, the views immense, the sense of achievement fulfilling and the aesthetic tremendous. But it wasn't Pen y Fan I was here to climb. At each of the park's extremes lie two ranges that confusingly share the promising (promising if you're in search of a lovely dark night sky, anyway) name of Black Mountain. Well, they almost share it: the Welsh names for each reveal the subtlety lost in their English translation. One lies close to the English border in the east, and is a high but inauspicious collection of moorland summits bearing the collective name the Black Mountains (Y Mynyddoedd Duon). The other, on the park's spacious western fringes, bears the singular denotation the Black Mountain (Mynydd Du), and this one most definitely earns its chops in the spectacle stakes. Burly and remote, its summits are in fact the hoisted edges of an enormous, wedge-shaped escarpment, tilted into the ocean of moorland like a sinking liner.

The more specific names associated with this mountain and its features are rather bewildering, and you may have to bear with me here. Mountain toponymy – as we will continue to see anon – is not an exact science, and is often inconsistent across a relatively short distance. A summit in South Wales (Fan, Ban, Bannau, Pen) isn't necessarily a summit in North Wales (Carnedd, Moel), although in both places a *llyn* does tend to be a lake, *cwm* a valley, *craig* a crag, *bwlch* a pass, and *fach* and *fawr* little and large, respectively. The Black Mountain as a massif is Mynydd Du; the long escarpment of the eastern flank is given the name Fan Hir, *fan* meaning crest. But *fan* can also mean peak – and there are two of these on the Black Mountain, three if you count Bannau Sir Gaer, which uses the term *bannau*, which is probably derived from *ban*, which is in turn the plural of *fan*. Bannau Sir Gaer means the 'Carmarthenshire Beacon', and this is often still known by its mixed translation Carmarthen Van, *van* being yet another variant of *fan*. Fan Foel is one summit, probably meaning 'bald peak'; Fan Brycheiniog is the other, named after the small kingdom to which the mountain belonged in the Middle Ages. Like I said, bewildering. But if you take anything from this, make it simply the following: mountain names can be complicated. And it was remote Fan Brycheiniog – at 802 metres the highest point of the Black Mountain – that was to be my mountain of space.

The weather was, it has to be said, not good at all. The rain held off long enough for me to enjoy the sinuous roads over the border and the tentatively awakening villages and pubs as I approached Brecon. It even stayed clear enough to appreciate the tall, distinctively clipped top of Pen y Fan as I passed Brecon and headed for the empty western part of the national park. A few miles outside a little place called Trecastle, a left turn led into a long valley of arched hillsides and naked, wintered trees. The road dwindled to such a degree that I began to suspect it led nowhere, and indeed it proved more or less to do just this. It first climbed, then dropped into a scraped landscape of wide-open moorland. This was one of the barest landscapes south of Scotland. And to the west, far away across it, there it was.

The Black Mountain filled the horizon like a wall. Though it was smudged by cloud, I could just about see the top reaches, for the moment at least. I certainly wasn't going to be reclining under an umbrella of stars tonight, that was for sure; although I'd brought a tent, my optimism of a clear night out atop the mountain had faded with every squeak of the windscreen wiper. More concerning was the wind; I could feel it whumping into the car as I sat gazing out at the grey landscape, and by the rate the weather was moving across it, things would only get rougher higher up. Trouble was, whilst camping probably wasn't an option, it would inevitably be night in a few hours. Whether I liked it or not – and regardless of whether the weather improved – I'd definitely be coming down in the dark.

The eastern approach to the Black Mountain involves crossing over a mile of rough, stream-ridden heathland, more moor than mountain. The map says there's a path here, and there might well be, somewhere – but it's so indistinct amongst the soggy brown, lumpy grassland that following it would require constant concentration. It certainly didn't register beneath my boots as I set off into the wind towards the dark cliff ahead.

The place to ascend from this direction is a gentle chink – the Bwlch Giedd – which from this direction dips the escarpment into a shallow 'M' shape. This passage is not easy to miss: at its bottom lies the large lake of Llyn y Fan Fawr – 'Lake of the Big Peak' – so named for its position directly beneath the highest point of the massif.

Walking into a strong wind filled with rain has little to recommend it other than giving a renewed appreciation for how desperately insignificant and fragile you are versus the elements. Within half an hour of staggering into the southwesterly, the left side of my body was beginning to feel the tendrils of cold moisture pushing through my clothing. The volatile time of year meant the usually insubstantial streams that required crossing on the journey west towards the mountain were thick and fast. The only ways across were by balancing on moss-slicked rocks over which water raced with unbalancing strength. One mis-step, and a lively second or so of spasmic body penduluming almost resulted in a dunking – after which I made a mental note to ensure to pack both a pole and a dry set of clothes were I to do anything this foolish again.

After an hour I very nearly gave up. The wind had grown stronger as I climbed above the sheltering hummocks, and it wasn't long before it was pretty intolerable. Just walking was becoming hard, and more and more I took to stopping, mouth gaping, with my back against the wind for respite. Cloud was tearing across the vanishing mountainside ahead like billowing smoke, and with the gloom, thickening cloud and my rapidly chilling legs – plus the fact I hadn't actually set foot on the mountain yet – the outing this was unfolding into bore little resemblance to the evocative plan I'd left home with. Just as I was considering abandoning it for another day and squelching back to the car the mist briefly moved, and I saw the shore and grey water of Llyn y Fan Fawr close by. I was practically at the base of the escarpment; it would be rude not to go and have a look at it. As I climbed towards the grey bulk of the mountain, a frayed path joined from the left. This was the Beacons Way, which climbed the escarpment of Fan Hir at precisely the point I was aiming for. Soon the red soil of the path was joined by a more established, slabby path, and as I followed it into the curl of the cliff, the wind – blocked by the fold into which the path was beginning to climb – fell away.

Suddenly it was quiet. I could hear my own whistly breathing, and my clothing – having spent the last hour energetically flapping – settled heavily against my skin. I was *soaked*.

The escarpment of Fan Hir isn't a huge climb. In fact, given the relative tallness of the Black Mountain's highest point, Fan Brycheiniog – at 802 metres the fourth-highest point in Britain south of Snowdonia – it isn't much of a climb at all; from the shore of the lake to the top of Bwlch Giedd requires less than 150 metres of vertical ascent – vertical ascent being the typical measure hillwalkers use to anticipate the likely exhaustion of an objective. I'd parked the car at close to 400 metres above sea level; most of the rest had been gathered gently on the blustery walk in.

I stopped for a few minutes in the lee of the cliff, enjoying the calm and considering my options. Cloud was coming down and the darkness was deepening, robbing the distance of detail. From the top of the escarpment, the route to the highest point of the Black Mountain – the trig point of Fan Brycheiniog – was less than 500 metres away. I was wet as hell. Stupidly I'd neglected to pack waterproof trousers; although the ones I wore were supposedly robustly resistant, seven years of more or less constant use had evidently depleted their ability to withstand torrential rain and wind, and everything from my hips to my ankles on my left side was numb. I'd spare warm layers in my rucksack, but they were for emergencies. What's more, I knew that once out of this sheltered fold in the escarpment, I'd be exposed to the full temper of the bludgeoning wind – wind that, quite possibly, would have the muscle to blow me clean off the top of the mountain.

I should really have called it quits, but I decided to push on to the top of the escarpment – or until my natural shelter ran out, whichever came first. If I stuck my head above the top and it was too blustery, I could turn round and climb back down without being mugged of dignity. Whether it's Mount Everest or a Brecon Beacon, the basic physiology of a mountain can't be argued with: the summit is only halfway home, and overstretching yourself before you've even made it there is usually a bad idea.

This wasn't Everest, but it was certainly feeling extreme enough for what was originally supposed to have been a leisurely wander under the stars. I continued on up the path, and swiftly – much more swiftly than expected – I was high above the lake and approaching the top of Bwlch Giedd. Good paths make short work of ascent, and bad visibility – whilst a swine for views – can psychologically aid you, as you simply can't see how much further you have to go.

As I reached the top of the escarpment I could feel the wind beginning to gather once more. It seemed bearable, so I tentatively carried on towards the summit. At first, the pushing gale from the south-west was robust, but not extreme; I could walk without too much trouble, albeit with a jaunty tilt of twenty or so degrees into the jet of wet air blasting the left side of me. I was now on the plateau'd top of the Black Mountain – the 'billiard table' – and whilst my eyes were fixed ahead for any indication of the top, I couldn't ignore the huge drop that was now on my right. It seemed perverse that the direction of the wind was inclined perfectly to push me towards it.

In an effort to keep track of progress and stay focused, I kept pace in my head. From practice I knew that, on reasonable ground, every 64th time my left foot hit the ground I'd covered roughly 100 metres. This double-pacing technique was a staple of basic navigation, and for all my hopelessness with remembering my waterproof trousers, I knew that whenever I used this technique it was usually pretty accurate – as well as being a handy mental focus whenever things got stressful. My count was approaching 400 metres when ahead a squat rectangular shape began to solidify from out of the mist. The map didn't indicate the presence of such, but that had to be a summit shelter. I reached it, and it was; a low, roofless horseshoe of slate, perhaps two foot high, but with its back to the wind and substantial enough to hunker inside and take stock.

The second I was beneath and away from the gale, I realised just how silly my decision to push on had been. My clothing was now so saturated my trousers were falling down with the weight of the water they had sponged up, and my sleeves hung limp around my arms. This little shelter would, most likely, have been my place of repose had I been lucky enough to catch a clear, calm night from which to appreciate the dark skies of the Brecon Beacons. But to me, right now, the thought of spending the night up here, in this weather, was chilling. I felt cold, soaked, and – however disappointed I was at not being able to reap the starry benefits of being this far from other people – truly, comprehensively alone. This was certainly an antithesis to comfort and civility, but it was starting to feel a little out of control. Were I to give up and stay here, hunkered down in this little windbreak in these conditions and the saturated state I was in, it wouldn't be long before hypothermia began to gnaw. I can't say the thought occurred to me at that exact moment – huddled and cold, being blasted by storm-force gales high on a mountain, miles from anywhere, with night solidifying around me – but my, what a strange way to spend a Saturday night this was. Or, put a slightly different way, what a privilege.

The safeguarding of Britain's – and the world's – dark skies revolves around a change in people's thinking when it comes to their own use of light. By this reckoning, all that Britain's wild places seemed to need in order to attain what the residents of the Brecon Beacons National Park were now obliged to do was a collective effort to reduce the amount of light pollution projected into the sky.

Something as simple as ensuring an outside light is angled downwards instead of obliquely, using a different type of lightbulb and – heavens – actually turning the things off when not being used to read the paper or shoot a burglar seemed, if embraced en masse, to be all that was needed to make a difference. In January 2012, the Somerset village of Dulverton – which lay within the other of Britain's Dark Sky Reserves* – staged a mass switch-off of

* This is Exmoor, granted International Dark Sky Reserve Status in 2011. As of 2014, the other six reserves are in Namibia, New Zealand, Canada, France, Germany and Ireland. Honourable mention must go here to Galloway in southern Scotland, which in 2009 became a Dark Sky Park and has been decreed as naturally possessing the highest quality of dark sky. The difference between a park and a reserve is that the latter requires the cooperation of neighbouring communities to restore and maintain the quality of the night sky.

the village lights for a live TV event to highlight the difference even a modest settlement could make. As it happened it was pouring with rain, and instead of the jolly amassed crowd cooing in wonder beneath a newly unveiled ceiling of stars, they were spooked by the opaque blackness of a night not dissimilar to the one increasing around me on the summit of the Black Mountain. The last time our cities experienced the same sort of consciously collective darkness – besides the odd power cut, during which people were presumably more preoccupied with reclaiming light than appreciating dark – was during the Blitz.

However modest, the Brecon Beacons' new status was enough to illustrate that, as the anthropologist Margaret Mead once said, we should 'never doubt that a small group of thoughtful, committed citizens can change the world; indeed, it's the only thing that ever has.' And when it comes to the search for space and freedom in the British mountains, it's not just in matters of 'light trespass' where the actions of a few can trigger a reaction that will be influential down the generations in their enjoyment of wild places. In fact, were it not for the actions of one group in particular, weather would be the least of my barriers to experiencing the starlit skies of the Brecon Beacons; in all likelihood, I wouldn't be there at all. Actions which, funnily enough, also involved a trespass.

Today, like all of us in Britain, I enjoy constitutional access to wild places under a law called the Right to Roam. And this is something we should be very, very proud of, on two fronts: one, that we have a country enlightened enough to have introduced such a law. And two, that it did so based on the acts of what our new friend Maggie Mead might call 'thoughtful, committed citizens': namely a bunch of working-class Manchester socialists who, on one otherwise unremarkable morning between the world wars, decided to go for a walk.

In 1932 Britain was a grim place if you were poor. The bite of the Great Depression was being painfully felt: industrial output fell by a third, and that summer saw unemployment hit a record high of 3.5 million – most of them casualties of the downturn in northern industries such as mining and steel. Seeking focus and amusement for little or no cost, many of the unemployed began to walk for pleasure. The problem was, this pastime – 'rambling' – was a play without a theatre. In 1932 there were no national parks, no long-distance footpaths. Land was owned, and enforced as such. Areas that weren't practical for agriculture – that is to say, mountain and moorland – were ring-fenced and populated with grouse, which landowners would make available, sometimes for as little as two weeks a year, to be noisily and gleefully dispatched by those who could afford cars, guns and time to fritter.

The 'ramblers' were almost comical in contrast. Unable to afford specialised gear, they would improvise: army clothing, work shoes, ragged clothing they didn't mind being ruined. In addition, many walked under the auspices of groups such as the British Workers' Sports Federation (BWSF), which were often suffused with broader moralistic leanings – in this case, communism – and which in many people's eyes gave the activity a disagreeable air of rascal politics.

It's difficult today to envision the kind of restrictions early ramblers were subject to. By restrictions we aren't talking about barred access to a few manicured grounds or fenced fields: in the early 20th century an estimated four million acres of mountain and moorland in England and Wales were owned by a few inattentive individuals who didn't – and couldn't possibly – make anywhere near full use of it. Paths existed for ramblers to use, but such was the uprise in popularity in the pursuit amongst the working classes (it's estimated that in 1932 some 15,000 ramblers took leave of Manchester on a Sunday to go walking) that these were often becoming as crowded as the suburbs, and potentially problematic frustrations were starting to mount. Worse, so-called 'respectable' walking organisations such as the Manchester and Stockport wings of the Holiday Fellowship – via deep-running relationships with dukes, earls and other influential citizens – were enjoying the freedom to wander on land forbidden to unemployed working-class ramblers. Enjoying the country-side – whether in the form of shooting, hunting or rock climbing – was, inexorably, a perk of the privileged.

By default, the wilder places of Britain became the scene of a strange class war. Landowning aristocrats were irritated by unkempt, Catweazle-type characters drifting illegally onto their land, and ramblers were increasingly frustrated at being barred from harmlessly entering what was effectively unused wilderness a bus ride from the inner city – and all over what they saw as little more than historic, ceremonial ownership by a few Hooray Henrys. It was a dangerously unstable stand-off: the ramblers had numbers and spirit, but the landowners and gamekeepers had the written law and cash – as well as employees with guns.

One of these landowners was the Duke of Devonshire. His particular 148,000-acre patch occupied an area of northern England known as the Peak District, which – despite a name that conjures pointy drama – is largely peaty moorland and vast, open plateau, reaching its elevational zenith atop Kinder Scout at 636 metres. It's an agreeable if bleak place to wander, and its proximity to the northern industrial cities of Sheffield, Manchester and Huddersfield made it a natural choice for ramblers seeking to escape the depressing, economically stricken cities. But in April 1932 fewer than 1,200 acres of the Peak District were open for them to enjoy. Based on our estimate that 15,000 Mancunians left the streets and took to the upland paths each Sunday, this gave each person an area of considerably less than one tenth of an acre in which to find space and tranquillity. Something had to give – and on Sunday 24 April 1932, it did.

In the weeks prior to this a scrawled leaflet found its way into the hands of interested parties on both sides of the fence. One handed out in Eccles read:

B.W.S.F. RAMBLERS RALLY

This rally will take place on Sunday 24th April at 8 o'clock. At Hayfield Recreation Ground. From the rec, we proceed on a *MASS TRESPASS* onto Kinder Scout. This is being organized by the British Workers' Sports Federation, who fight:

Against the finest stretches of moorland being closed to us.
For cheap fares, for cheap catering facilities.
Against any war preparations in rambling organisations.
Against petty restrictions, such as singing etc.

Now: young workers of [Eccles] to all, whether you've been rambling before or not, we extend a hearty welcome. If you've not been rambling before, start now; you don't know what you've missed. Roll up on Sunday morning and once with us, for the best day out you've ever had.

Scenes photographed in Bowden Quarry near Hayfield – the hastily re-arranged meeting place in an attempt to shake off gathering police attention – on the day of what history would remember as the Kinder Mass Trespass are extraordinarily vivid, despite their age. One shows a crowd numbering in their hundreds gathering amidst an amphitheatre of fractured rock looking up towards a figure standing on a gritstone plinth and purposefully addressing the crowd. Were he holding a medieval sword aloft it would resemble a scene from an Arthurian saga. According to contemporary accounts, the man on the rock launched into a passionate sermon against trespass laws and access restrictions, and after warning the crowd against using violence against whatever they encountered, presumably signed off with something stirring like, 'Right lads, let's go for a bloody walk.' And off they went.

Five hundred people left Hayfield that morning, aiming for William Clough, a comely valley that ascends onto the Kinder plateau – the moorland for which the Mass Trespass was destined. It was here that the group met their opponents, a group of gamekeepers who had been specially drafted in for the day by the Duke of Devonshire, who had caught wind of the ramblers' plans. Violence ensued. We're not talking wanton bloodshed and rambling-crazed savagery (the most serious injury reported by the *Manchester Guardian* that afternoon was a keeper named 'Mr E. Beaver, who was knocked unconscious and damaged his ankle'), but by the time the ramblers reached the plateau – there greeted enthusiastically by another group who had set off from the south – and retraced their steps back to Hayfield, the authorities had decided the landowners' strife warranted some official fuss.

Assisted by several gamekeepers, the police arrested six ramblers, all aged between 19 and 23: John Anderson, Jud Clyne, Tona Gillett, Harry Mendel, David Nussbaum and the man on the quarry plinth – a 20-year-old, five-foot Manchester communist named Bernard Rothman.

'Benny' Rothman was actually not intended to be the rallying speaker at Hayfield Quarry – the original nominee grew meek when the crowd swelled beyond 200 – but the articulate sermon he delivered castigating official rambling organisations for their malaise stirred the crowd into a strident buzz, and Rothman soon became a figurehead for the respect (and the flak) the Trespass would later attract.

Something of a part-time political agitator, the event had been Rothman's idea. He was a regular visitor to the Clarion Café on Manchester's Market Street – a kind of informal parliament for the working class and frequently the scene of stylised political debates between socialists, Trotskyists, communists and supporters of other ideologies. Rothman became a member of the BWSF and took part in many of the weekend camps the group organised in Derbyshire, which would invariably draw unemployed young men, many wearing old First World War surplus kit. Following a scuffle with some game-keepers on the nearby hill of Bleaklow some weeks earlier, Rothman observed that whilst it was not unusual for small groups of ramblers to be beaten 'very, very badly' by the gamekeepers with no rebuke, if there were 40 or 50 ramblers the balance would be tipped. Discussing what they viewed as the historical 'theft' of the moorland, the plan was hatched for the Trespass.

The main headline on the following morning's *Daily Dispatch* read 'Mass Trespass Arrests on Kinder Scout: Free Fight with Gamekeepers on Mountain'.

Rothman and his five companions were brought to trial at Derby Assizes on the charge of riotous assembly, assault and incitement. Tellingly, as regards the motives of the prosecutors, 'trespass' – seemingly the most obvious offence – was absent from the charge sheet, as it was a civil matter. By most accounts the trial was a farce; gamekeepers, members of the police and repre-sentatives of the Stockport Corporation Water Works, which owned and leased some of the Kinder Plateau for shooting, delivered overwrought testi-monies to a jury comprised largely of the rural Establishment. Whiffs of politi-cal perversion in the communist leanings of many of the key figures,* as well as a bit of tokenistic anti-Semitism (the judge made the useful closing obser-vation that several of the defendants were 'obviously Jewish'), seemed to pervade the proceedings.

Rothman delivered another impassioned speech. 'We ramblers, after a hard week's work, and life in smoky towns and cities, go out rambling on weekends for relaxation, for a breath of fresh air, and for a little sunshine. And

---

* It was reported with some degree of disgust that one of the songs the trespassers sang was the left-wing protest song 'The Red Flag', although several renditions of '(It's a long way to) Tipperary' were also given, as well as a modified version of Harry Lauder's 'The Road to the Isles', with key locations in the song replaced with local landmarks for the occasion.

we find when we go out that the finest rambling country is closed to us,' he said, before emphasising that 'our request, or demand, for access to all peaks and uncultivated moorland is nothing unreasonable.' The six men all pleaded not guilty; all but one were found guilty, and sent to prison for between two and four months, with the harshest sentence – predictably – given to Rothman himself.

It was a huge misjudgement. Far from putting down such actions, the convictions dished out to the Kinder trespassers further ignited the cause. The public response had repercussions still felt today; in many respects, the treatment of Rothman and his cohorts was really the best thing that could have happened to wild places. A rally in Castleton a few weeks after the trial was attended by 10,000 people. In 1935 the Ramblers Association was founded, and a year later the Standing Committee for National Parks was formed, publishing a paper titled *The Case for National Parks in Great Britain* in 1938.

A setback came in 1939 when the progressively intended Access to Mountains Act was passed by Parliament in such an aggressively edited form it actually sided with the landowners, and made some forms of trespassing a criminal as opposed to a civil offence. But opposition to draconian access restrictions continued, and in 1945 – just as soldiers were returning home from the war to a country undergoing profound social changes – architect and secretary of the Standing Committee on National Parks John Dower produced a report containing the definition of what a national park in England and Wales might be like. Given what went before – and what would follow – it's worth quoting at length.

An extensive area of beautiful and relatively wild country in which ... (a) the characteristic landscape beauty is strictly preserved, (b) access and facilities for public open-air enjoyment are amply provided, (c) wild-life and buildings and places of architectural and historical interest are suitably protected, whilst (d) established farming use is effectively maintained.

In 1947, Sir Arthur Hobhouse was appointed chair of the newly enshrined National Parks Committee, and proposed twelve areas of the UK that would be suitable locations for a national park. 'The essential requirements of a

National Park are that it should have great natural beauty, a high value for open-air recreation and substantial continuous extent,' he decreed in his report of that year. 'Further, the distribution of selected areas should as far as practicable be such that at least one of them is quickly accessible from each of the main centres of population in England and Wales.'

In 1949 the National Parks and Access to the Countryside Act was passed, and on 17 April 1951 – with an irony not lost on many of the Trespass participants – the Peak District, including Kinder Scout, became the first national park in Britain.

The Lake District, home to the highest mountains in England, followed on 9 May; Snowdonia, thick with legend and shattered geological grandeur, on 18 October; the Brecon Beacons National Park – where I was now being battered – was opened on 17 April 1957, six years to the day since the first, and itself the tenth national park to be opened in England and Wales. Somewhat slower on the uptake, Scotland opened its first national park in 2002 (Loch Lomond and the Trossachs), with the Cairngorms National Park following suit the next year.

For the first time, access to our high and wild places was gilded by law. By 1957, with the opening of the Brecon Beacons National Park, 13,746 square kilometres of the most arrestingly beautiful countryside was officially enshrined as national park – just under 9 per cent of the total area of England and Wales.

The golden ticket in the eyes of access campaigners, however, was not stamped until the turn of the 21st century. The national parks were a giant leap forward, but much of what truly lay open to free access was only the very highest land, where agriculture was poor. Other than areas owned by bodies such as the National Trust, access agreements still had to be reached with landowners concerning the often restrictive rights of way through their land. But in 2000 the Countryside and Rights of Way Act (CRoW) was passed, coming into effect five years later, providing 'a new right of public access on foot to areas of open land comprising mountain, moor, heath, down, and registered common land'. In other words, the balance had finally swung to the benefit of walkers, who could now roam freely in open country – the inverse to the Enclosure Acts of the 1800s that ramblers had fought so hard to repeal. In a stroke, the area of land upon which a walker could freely roam had expanded by a third.

Benny Rothman lived to see the CRoW Act passed. After a lifetime of lending his voice to access causes, the passing of the act was a vindication that came just two years shy of the 70th anniversary of the Kinder Scout Trespass. This he did not live to see; he died aged 90 just a few months before it, in January 2002.

Had he been at the anniversary celebrations he would have witnessed a fitting endstop, when the current Duke of Devonshire – grandson of the man who unleashed his gamekeepers on the trespassers of 1932, and evidently something of a good sport – took the podium. Presumably with a quiver in his voice, he addressed the crowd thus:

> I am aware that I represent the villain of the piece this afternoon. But over the last 70 years times have changed and it gives me enormous pleasure to welcome walkers to my estate today. The trespass was a great shaming event on my family and the sentences handed down were appalling. But out of great evil can come great good. The trespass was the first event in the whole movement of access to the countryside – and the creation of our national parks.

Whether or not the national parks would exist today without the Trespass – and whether I'd be able to appreciate the feeling of gradually being ripped from my feet on the top of the Black Mountain in the chilly spring air – we cannot know. But what is clear is that access to the British countryside took a great leap forward that day in 1932, and the degree of freedom we can all now enjoy wasn't easily won.

However grumpy I was feeling in the summit shelter atop the Black Mountain, I was glad to have made it. Now all I had to do was make it back to the car. Emerging from the shelter, I caught sight of the trig point – a slim concrete pillar found on many British summits, for reasons detailed later – twenty metres or so away. Staggering over and touching the top, I snapped an awful summit photograph and, with no small degree of haste, turned in the direction from which I'd come.

It was now almost totally dark, the descent seemingly destined to be desperate. While my eyes had become accustomed to the gloom, night was biting, and soon I'd barely be able to see where I was placing my feet. I had a head torch somewhere in my bag but I didn't want to use it unless I had to. Any bright light would destroy my night vision in a flash, and besides, I didn't want to stop – not even to rummage in my rucksack.

It turned out that walking back towards Bwlch Giedd was a hell of a lot harder than walking from it. The wind was now punching me directly in the face, chilling my skin and making the simple matter of looking up almost impossible. I could barely see where I was going and the wind was doing its best to exploit this. Every time I took an uncertain step I felt the gusts attempting to pick me up, or snare my backpack sideways and try to pull me from my feet. I focused on my pacing and tried not to panic. All I had to do was get down before I became too cold to walk. That was all.

My instinct had been to get as far from the cliff edge as possible, but walking on the grass wasn't so good; the grip between my boots and the ground wasn't as positive as on the stone of the path. Trying not to lose balance or composure, I pushed on along the stones, distracting myself by trying to figure out how strong the wind was. A steady 50 mph was my guess, possibly gusting to 70 mph. This might not sound much when you're sitting at home listening to it rattle the windows, but on a mountain trying to walk, anything over 40 mph and you're struggling.

I reached Bwlch Giedd with considerable relief, and stepped into the shelter of the path that descended the escarpment down towards the lake. The sudden silence caused by the drop in the wind made me realise my ears were ringing. The path was rocky and trip-prone, but I managed to stay upright all the way down to the shore. Pulling out my compass and wrestling with the flapping, shiny cased map, I struck a straight bearing from the edge of the lake to the point where I'd parked the car. It would be a cold, damp walk out – but at least I was down. Now I had to get back across the rolling grass and several streams, and I'd be out of this wind, and out of this rain.

It took a while, but I managed it. Along the way I discovered the batteries in my head torch were almost flat, so the stream crossings were done in a darkness that was rather too profound for comfort. My compass bearing had been spot on, though, despite it being the headlight streak of a distant car that finally guided me back to my remote parking space. My final steps were beckoned by the little red blinking LED of my car alarm indicator. Even in mountain places – and dark-sky reserves, at that – it seemed electric light had its minor uses. I was intensely glad to be back at the car and, however foolish the decision had been, equally glad I'd pressed on, albeit at the cost of comfort. My trousers were so sodden I drove the 200 miles back home in my boxer shorts. Things *had* to get easier.

3 LEGEND

Somewhere between the Brecon Beacons and the country's north coast, the mountains of Wales sharpen and slough off their grassy skins. Southern Snowdonia marks the changing point, and here there's a belt of mountains evidently conflicted about which camp they belong in. The shapes of these ranges waver between the cutting ruggedness of the peaks in the northern part of Snowdonia and the queer emerald forms of their counterparts in South Wales. The names of the big groups of hills here tickle recognition for some, but only just: the Arans, the Tarrens, the Dovey Forest, the Rhinogs. Journey from the south into this region and steep diagonals, or the jag of a peak on the skyline ahead might symbolise your steady transition to the wild, hard north. But conversely, enter from the north and you might describe the landscape around you as softening, easing towards the sprawling south. It's a fascinating, disjointed menagerie. Then you see Cadair Idris, and suddenly you're not looking at anything else.

A month after being nearly drowned on the Black Mountain, I found myself in southern Snowdonia during a spring that had finally sprung. Colour had returned to the landscape. New life was exploding. Bluebells bobbed on embankments beside roads sweeping through richly-carpeted passes and tired-looking villages. Sunlight diffused through new leaves, lighting the world through miniature shades of green and giving the afternoon a feeling of intense optimism.

I'd spent an uncertain twenty minutes dividing my attention between the road and the skyline – punctuated occasionally with visits to the rumble strip – trying to establish whether my objective was sliding into view ahead in some distance-skewed fashion. When it finally did appear, it seemed preposterous to think I could miss it.

There's evidence that the Elizabethans considered Cadair Idris to be the highest peak in the British Isles, and it's an easy mistake to forgive. Approach it from the north and it smacks you in the face from a distance of ten miles. It's massive: a wide, wrinkled battlement of brown, crag-hung rock sprawled across the southern horizon with intimidating abruptness. Showell Styles – author of *The Mountains of North Wales*, of which more later – described the vision of Cadair from the north as a 'hunched eagle with a tremendous wing-span', and it's wonderfully apt. Cadair isn't the highest peak in this part of Snowdonia – not quite – but its visual presence is enough to make it seem as if it is. Perhaps this apparent brawniness is because the mountain's base is at sea level, thereby earning every millimetre of its 893-metre height over a rela-tively short distance. The town of Dolgellau, just to the north, sits on the zero contour and so completes the contrast on a human scale. But the reflex assess-ment upon sighting Dolgellau isn't that it nestles up against Cadair Idris; it's more like the town cowers beneath it.

I chose the climb from Talyllyn, a way known as the Minffordd Path. Some say the path from the north – the Fox's Path, which climbs the cliffier aspect of the mountain directly – is the best. From the north Cadair appears as a massif of three summits, split into upturned prows in several places by aggressive staircases of ridge. It appears impossibly impregnable, and impres-sively immense. The Fox's Path offers superb views of the Irish Sea, Dolgellau below, and the bristly Cyfrwy Arête, probably the most blisteringly dramatic ridge climb south of Scotland. But this route doesn't take you into the moun-tain's inner keep; it climbs this northern wall and, once atop, walks the ramparts to the highest point, missing one of the main arenas of the moun-tain. Plus, instead of one hard ascent, the climb from Minffordd is a languid, gentle rise, followed by one mercifully swift but screeching pull. To me, it seemed to be the best choice to appreciate the many levels on which Cadair engages the senses. Plus, with memories still raw from the Black Mountain, it clearly seemed the preferable option – especially since, having not learned my lesson in the Brecon Beacons, I had a summit sleepover planned.

Rounding the corner at the Gwesty Minffordd Hotel, I swung immediately right into the smooth, wooded car park. I was late. Dinner in the seductive surroundings of a fast-food restaurant – and many stops along the road to admire the views amidst the day's deepening shadows – meant that my plan for getting to the summit by sunset was now on a perilously tight schedule. In my pocket was a mobile phone newly loaded with GPS mapping software, which

I'd decided to bring as a backup to my map following the collapse of my planning on the Black Mountain. It was not only prudent, but genuinely useful; although keen to find my way by my nose as much as possible, with traditional navigation as a failsafe, I had no qualms about using reliable gadgetry to ease my way. If anything, it would help me keep my eyes on the landscape rather than buried in a map. Pulling my overnight rucksack from the boot, I hastily chucked in a few provisions already bagged up in waterproof bags – some of which I'd labelled with helpful words like 'food', some of which I hadn't – doubled-back to check the car was locked and set off into the mild evening air in something of a fluster, giving a quick look around the car park as I went. It was deserted but for one other car. With a plunging feeling I realised its owner might have similar designs on inhabiting the summit for a night, but just as I approached the gate onto the path I saw two walkers emerging into the car park, looking pink and happy. One, a greying man with a map case around his neck, smiled as he held the gate for me. 'All yours,' he said. And with that, I had one of Britain's most atmospheric and intricately legendary mountains all to myself.

The mythology associated with mountains is prolific, and pervades cultures regardless of time or place. The reason for this isn't really a mystery: they are the land's most obvious, most dramatic physical feature. But those early peoples who settled beside mountains didn't see them as objectives, or assets; they feared them.

Since the earliest ages of civilisation the mountains have been the homes of gods and demons. Like the sea – that other great unconquerable – the mountains' physical size and fickle moods meant that they were seen as both forbidding and forbidden. Although many people saw them as dark places of evil and the meddling of spirits, some optimistic cultures viewed them as protectors, even mothers. But neither saw them as places for people to tread.

Understandably, it's the most striking, massive or isolated peaks that demand the most attention and stir the most potent awe, and it's hardly surprising that such mountains across the world have become sacred.

Kailash, an enormous, free-standing peak in Tibet, is perhaps the most famous of these, amongst both mountaineers and students of religious philosophy alike. Unfeasibly dramatic, 6,638-metre Kailash rises sheer, a topographical exclamation mark ascending so drastically from the mud-brown of the Tibetan plateau the vision of it is surreal from all sides. Located near the source of several rivers, including the Indus and Brahmaputra – which collectively irrigate land supporting over a billion people – the mountain is sacrosanct to several religions. In Hinduism, Kailash is said to be the home of Shiva, destroyer of ignorance and illusion. Buddhists believe the mountain is the place where the Buddha Demchok sits on the summit in eternal meditation. Many believe the summit is the final step to heaven; yet all consider that stepping onto its slopes leads to death, damnation or the opening of Shiva's third eye – a highly undesirable event said to trigger the end of the universe.

Pilgrims to Kailash brave altitude and often brutal sun to be in the mountain's presence. A common form of worship is to circumnavigate it, some 33 miles of rough path and sharp rock. Many feel suitably moved to make this journey in penance, prostrating themselves at full length on the ground, indenting the dust with their fingers, resting their heads on the rock and saying a prayer, repeating this for the entire length of the walk. This can take several weeks, after which the successful pilgrims return home, often with enormous welts on their fingers, feet and foreheads, and one hopes enlightenment in their souls.

No mortal has climbed Kailash; to do so would insult those to whom the mountain is sacred. As for immortals, it's written in legend that 1,000 years ago, the Tantric Buddhist Milarepa challenged Naro Bön-Chung of the Tibetan Bön religion to a contest decided by a race to the mountain's summit, although their method of ascent cannot be strictly considered 'mountaineering' by today's standards.* Several Western mountaineers have come close, but either declined their permits or found themselves pressured into doing so by others in the mountaineering community. One of these – the Italian mountaineer Reinhold Messner – stated of Kailash: 'If we conquer this mountain, then we conquer something in people's souls.'

In the Indian Himalaya above Sikkim, Kangchenjunga – the third-highest mountain in the world – is another such sacred summit. Again, the mountain's

---

* Milarepa rode the rays of the sun, while Bön-Chung sat cross-legged on a magic drum that ascended the mountain while he meditated. Milarepa won, but as he arrived at the summit he threw a handful of snow onto a nearby peak in honour of Bön-Chung. I once interviewed Reinhold Messner – a mountaineer deeply respectful of Tibetan beliefs but deeply pragmatic about his own climbing – about Kailash. When I commented it had never been climbed, he vehemently corrected me to the effect of the above, before deadpanning: 'Though, this sun-ray climbing technique – I don't know how it functions.'

physical presence is striking, and directly linked to the reverence it's accorded by those of the Kirant faith. Its name means 'Five Treasures of the Sacred Snows', referring to the mountain's five summits and the holy repositories they are said to harbour: gold, silver, gems, grain and holy books. As with Kailash, to step on its very summit is considered a desecration, and in 1955 – in a most admirable demonstration of self-restraint – the British climbers Joe Brown and George Band, having just made the first ascent of the mountain, stopped several feet short of the pristine snow cone on the very top in deference to this belief. This tradition continued on every ascent until 1980, when members of a large Japanese expedition reputedly trampled all over it.

Closer to home, mountains have been accorded similar – if somewhat more niche – respect. Above the southern Lake District, the Old Man of Coniston is a stately 803-metre mountain that draws many walkers to it for pleasurable day walks. Most don't know it's also considered the fifth most sacred mountain in the world by a religious sect called the Aetherius Society. To them, the mountain is a store of spiritual energy that, when unlocked by prayer vigils, is said to radiate out to those in need across the globe. The focus of this is said to be a table-shaped rock located just north of the summit, near which the group often congregates to pray. Basing their beliefs on the existence of extra-terrestrial intelligence – or 'gods from space' – Aetherians see mother earth as a deity who sacrificed herself to provide a home for a flawed, brutal humankind. The religion was founded by Dr George King, who in 1958 was visited whilst climbing Holdstone Down in North Devon by a 'great being of love', who sent streams of energy through him deep into the mountain, making it forever a holy repository. King was then instructed to travel to eighteen other mountains and 'charge' them with spiritual potency. Nine of these lie in the British Isles, the others being iconic (or obscure) peaks abroad.* Aetherius pilgrimages are organised to these mountains to this day.

* The mountains in Britain are Ben Hope and Creag an Leth-Choin in Scotland, Carnedd Llewelyn in Snowdonia, Pen y Fan in the Brecon Beacons, Kinder Scout in Derbyshire, the Old Man of Coniston, Brown Willy on Bodmin Moor, Holdstone Down on Exmoor and Yes Tor on Dartmoor. Notable mountains abroad include Kilimanjaro in Tanzania, Mount Kosciuszko in Australia, Mount Adams in the eastern United States and Madrigerfluh in Switzerland. These kept King busy – 'charging' the mountains took him three years in a journey he dubbed 'Operation Starlight'.

And so to Cadair Idris, which is perhaps the most concentrated meeting of myth and mountain, certainly in Britain. For that, we can thank the rich seam of Welsh legend that perfectly complements the mood of the landscape and its reflective, storytelling people. This is the land of the *Mabinogion*, the collection of eleven medieval folk tales that coalesces thousands of years of fable into one delicious mix. The *Mabinogion* takes the form of a book; if it took the form of a mountain, it would be *this* mountain.

The legends that haunt this place are strange and old. Many have become exaggerated over time; most were fantastic to begin with, although some have their roots in history and in truth. The name *Cadair* is the mountain's correct spelling, despite frequently being given as *Cader*. There's no deeper reason for this than the pronunciation of the longer word in the local dialect. The translation of this prefix is both 'hill-fort' and 'chair'. The suffix, however, is a name.

Your first steps onto Cadair on the Minffordd Path take you through a forest of sessile oak, where the path ascends slopes veined with stepped waterfalls. It was mild enough to set off wearing a T-shirt, and soon I was beginning to sweat. The sun had long dropped below the point where it could pierce the canopy and light the ground, and the forest was darkening and thickening with clouds of biting midges, which made stopping unwise. My pack felt heavy – heavier than it should, somehow – and my breathing soon became laboured, and progress unsteadily erratic.

Climbing alone didn't seem to be something I was yet particularly good at. Of all the mountains I'd walked up over the previous years, I pretty much always had someone with me – and that someone was usually in front, setting the pace, taking the worry out of route-finding and being, physically and psychologically, something to follow. Climbing a mountain is a very measurable commitment. You either get to the top, or you don't. And like every commitment, whilst sharing it gives it much more retrospective cachet, on the hill the act often turns into a who-blinks-first matter of pride.

This gentle competitiveness helps you get through the physically hard moments. It pushes you on for just a few more metres of ascent when you feel like all you want to do is curl up, leak sweat and carbon dioxide for a few minutes, and then maybe die. Looking at a mountain on a map at home is easy. It's just a squiggle, rarely bigger than the base of a wine glass and usually small enough to eclipse with your thumb. This – more so if the wine glass happens to have had something in it – has the effect of inflating your ambitions. But out in the real world the second you hit a steeply raked slope with a rucksack on your back, your pace slows, your breathing gets stiff and you're staring up at something impossibly high above you. It's at this point that those ambitions have the habit of playing dumb and mutinously slinking away – and you remember just how much harder climbing a gradient is to walking on level ground.

If you're alone nobody will judge you for it. You can go as slowly as you like, and no one will see. I could babble to myself, have a wee without saying 'I'm just having a wee' to anyone, or sit down for ten minutes every five metres. On the occasions you pass another walker, of course, you puff your chest out, close your mouth so as not to appear out of breath, quicken your pace and do your best to look like a strident mountain person before deflating and re-reddening as soon as they're out of sight. But by and large, when alone you're your own motivation – and there's nobody to silently scold you for being slow or unfit but yourself. You can turn round if you want. Go home. Nobody's stopping you. And that takes some getting used to.

Tonight, at least, I had the sunset to race – though after twenty minutes this wasn't going so well. It was approaching 9 p.m. when I entered Cwm Cau to see the last blush of sunlight colouring the very tops of its crags. Half an hour later, and it would be sinking into the Irish Sea. If I wanted to get to the top to see it do so, I didn't have long.

A *cwm* is the Welsh word for a valley, usually a glacial cirque, and Cwm Cau is perhaps the most perfect glacial cirque in Snowdonia. A sculpture fashioned by massive glacial forces, the beautiful black-blue lake at its centre has inspired much of the mountain's legend, and some of the more questionable deductions of scientists who have studied it. The lake is almost fifty metres deep in places. Resembling the broken neck of a glass bottle, the dramatic ring of peaks surrounding it once led many to think Cadair Idris a long-dead volcano – and the image still appeals. But it's wrong. The rock is volcanic, like that of much of Snowdonia. But this rock erupted onto the floor of a great sea, was thrust upwards in a period of mountain building, then worn down and defined in form by aggressive glaciers over hundreds of millions – possibly billions – of years. Smothered by the Pleistocene glaciation, the ice lay so steeply against the mountainside that it slid in hard rotation, grinding against the dolerite rock and slowly scooping out the basin we see today. The headwall against which the glacier terminated – the pyramid of Craig Cau – was frost-split, clawed at and dragged against by the glacier, leaving the mountain's impressively scored appearance as a legacy and adding to the raw allure of the *cwm*. Why anyone would want to miss this part of the mountain is a mystery all of its own.

The crags rise vertically several hundred metres from the lake to a big-dipper skyline, which, seen from the entrance to the *cwm*, climbs from the left to the dominating peak of Craig Cau – often, due to its pyramidal shape, mistaken for the massif's topmost summit – before dropping to a nick in the ridge then climbing again to the right, up to the highest point of the mountain itself, known as Penygadair.

Away from the shifting of the leaves of the lower path, the *cwm* was noise-less. In the same way your eyes become tuned to the dark, so your ears respond to silence. As I entered the huge basin and began to edge around the lake, my senses were numbed. I stopped to take a breather, and slowly sonic details began to peep through. The delicate sound of water tickling the shore, the hard 'chack' of a wheatear ground-nesting nearby somewhere; faint, audible traces of nature emerging from a landscape so quiet you had to listen hard to hear it. As I moved I noticed white crampon scratches like tapeworms doodled up the rocks at the water's edge. Walkers had been here when all of this was white. In winter the lake would be frozen, perhaps snow-covered. You wouldn't know where the edge was.

My route lay in the north-west crook of the basin, and looked steep. It climbed the slope via a shallow, rocky groove to the 'v' in the ridgeline between the pyramid of Craig Cau and the summit, still invisible above and to the right. In the gloom I could see a patch of white that looked about mid-way up – probably a quartz vein – which I made a mental note to look out for. Gauging the progress of your ascent from a slope can be tricky; everything above you looks closer than it is, and everything below further away.

I looked up, and then down at my watch. Darkness was chasing the light east to west across the sky. Invisible, beyond the bulk of the mountain over the sea, the sun would be setting. Night was coming.

* * *

Cadair's 'Idris' was most probably Idris Gawr, a king of Meirionnydd – a region of medieval Wales. Today most of Meirionnydd is part of the county of Gwynedd. But at the time of Idris, around AD 600, it was a kingdom of mountains and coast occupying the area of southern Snowdonia in which Cadair Idris sits.

It's at this early juncture that things get a little muddled. The direct translation of Cadair Idris is literally 'chair' or 'stronghold of Idris'. Some versions of the legend state that Idris was a giant so large he could sit using the entire mountain as a throne from which to survey his kingdom. Other versions state that the mountain received its association because Idris the king would climb to the summit and stargaze. Yet more state that the king retired to a hermitage – or fort – on the mountain in his later years. Further ambiguous threads of the tale indicate that the 'chair' referred to was an actual rock-hewn object on the summit, natural or otherwise, upon which Idris would sit and do whatever it was that he did.

However delicious all of this is, whoever Idris was, it would seem that in this region, at some point he *did* exist – and for whatever reason he became inexorably associated with the mountain.

It was written as far back as around 1600 by Siôn Dafydd Rhys in *The Giants of Wales and Their Dwellings* that 'in this high mountain formerly lived a big giant, and he was called Idris Gawr.' He goes on to describe some other myths about the mountain, including one that seems to suggest an early version of subterranean Poohsticks: 'If a stick or other piece of wood be thrown into any you may choose of those waters, you will get that wood in the other lake on the opposite side of this mountain.' There are many references to Cadair's numerous lakes being bottomless, or home to the *afanc* – a kind of water serpent that had been cast into Llyn Cau by King Arthur, no less.* Gwyn ap Nudd, the Celtic Lord of the Underworld, was also said to dwell here, and his scarlet-eared *cwn annwn* – loosely, hounds of hell – are said to glide across the summit, seeking souls to steal and no doubt ghostly walls to pee against. It's said in mythology that the howling of these dogs (loudest further away, and quietest close to you) was a premonition of death to anyone who heard

---

* Snowdonia is thick with Arthurian connotations, although these are mostly concentrated on Snowdon itself.

them. Many associated the bark-like honking of migrating geese by night with the legend. But the story that really stuck – the one most enigmatically associated with the mountain – is also contained within *The Giants of Wales and Their Dwellings*. 'On the highest crown of this mountain is a bed-shaped form, great in length and width, built of slabs or stones fixed around it,' it states. 'And it is said that whoever lies and sleeps on that bed, one of two things will happen to him: either he will be a poet of the best kind, or go entirely demented.'

Long before the 17th century, Celtic lore speaks of pilgrims who journeyed to Cadair Idris with the express intention of climbing to the top at sunset and spending the night there. The experience, if successful, was said to lift the traveller to a higher spiritual plane, becoming a *filidh* – which means both 'seer' and 'poet'. The *filidhean* filled a void that druidism was rapidly vacating, and were seen as conduits between the spirit world and humankind who could see beyond the world of convention and impart *imbas* – the knowledge of enlightenment – to the people. It was said the process of becoming a *filidh* required the traveller to shed all identity and return to the world with a new narrative – hence 'poetry' – for life. This process could, of course, go wrong. If unsuccessful, the result would be too much for the pilgrim to bear, and he would descend into madness or die on the spot.

It's a common motif. Mount Zion, Mount Horeb and Mount Sinai in the Old Testament, and Mount Olympus in Greek mythology, are summits dense with religious symbolism or host places where dramatic enlightenment has taken place. But it's striking that this comparatively modest mountain in North Wales appears with such potency in so many legends. And, because spending the night on the mountain seemed such a recurring feature of these legends – whether to gaze at the stars from a giant chair, look over an ancient kingdom, be eaten by a ghost dog, dragged to hell by the god of the underworld, ascend to a higher plane of wisdom, become a poet, go insane or simply die – well, it seemed like the thing to do.

Cwm Cau was deep in shadow, and chilling quickly. Finding the outlet to the stream that fell from somewhere near the top of the mountain, I filled my water bottle from the place where it flowed the fastest. This would be the last of the water I'd find now, and the safest to drink, relatively speaking. I unclipped my bag and filled the clear bottle I carried. Normally I'd hold it up to the light to see if I'd caught anything interesting in there, but there was no light. Of course, if there was anything *really* sinister in there I wouldn't see it; viruses, protozoa, the gunge from the mulching body of a dead sheep unseen upslope. High, mossy streams like this are pretty good at breaking down contaminants, given a clear run of flow, but wild water is always a gamble. A measured gamble, but a gamble all the same.

Nearby, a rough footway began to ascend. I took it, feeling the cold of the rock bristling against my bare arms as it steepened, closer to my body than before. Next to me, the crags of Craig Cau ceased to be a wall of cracked rock, more a side of broken ribs descending from above, separated by gullies scraped into the mountain.

It was hard going. Breathless, I began to set targets. A stop at the sheep. A drink of water at the white rock, whenever it appeared. To get me there, a few sweets. Finally, I reached the white rock I'd spotted from the Cwm. It was quartz – a massive cataract of it, bent and fractured where it broke the surface. I stopped, looking down at the darkening water below, and back up at the slope stretching above me. Maybe a hundred metres left.

The next section was tougher, both in terms of the terrain and my dimming evening energy to tackle it. The path was starting to lose its mud-and-stones constitution, and more and more stretches of bare rock had to be crossed and climbed. Soon I was amongst sharply raked cracks of stone that required both hands; several times as I hoisted myself into these I caught sight of the increasing drop through my legs below. As I began to draw level with the skyline, a sniff of breeze began to drift downwards from above, suddenly becoming a gust as the sky grew wider. There was the white nape of the coast and its necklace of amber lights. The horizon was gone, smudged by gloomy mist. And to my right, a mercifully gentle-angled path began to lead upwards through jumbled boulders to the summit of Penygadair – the top of Cadair Idris.

After a few moments' rest I slowly but robustly began a slumping gait upwards along the path. It was getting cold, but I'd soon be on the top, and soon able to layer up and get warm. The world was now deepening blue tones, with no trace of the colour of sunset left except for a messy smear of orange across the western sky.

My ears were becoming nervy. A sheep's cough sounds disturbingly like a human choke – at least it does when you're high and alone on a mountain in increasing darkness, and the silence seemed to have bulk, a kind of sonic hiss like distant traffic, as I continued along the ridge. The views on each side began to widen and I started to feel like I was reaching the top of something. At last, barely perceptible, the white Ordnance Survey trig pillar – perched atop a tall pile of rocks evidently comprising the summit – appeared ahead. I clambered up, pausing for the briefest moment to enjoy being at the apex of that massive ridge I'd seen earlier from the road, then quickly began a visual search for Cadair's second most distinctive summit feature. Glancing around from the trig point, beneath me to the right I spotted a uniform row of stones, and then a patch of corrugated tin they edged. In the blurred contrast of the gloaming, so well does it mimic the native stone of the summit you could easily mistake it for a weathered sheet of metal lying on the ground, perhaps covering some sort of hazard. But it isn't. It's a roof.

The hut was built in the 1830s by a guide named Robert Pugh. He had a vested interest in constructing a building in this rather auspicious place – if not for a financial gain then certainly a practical one, as Cadair Idris was big business for local guides in the late 18th and 19th centuries. Its status as one of the most southerly big chunks of proper mountain in Britain, and its dramatic qualities – which mirrored many of those of Snowdon, twenty miles to the north – drew visitors from afar. The guides they hired were often colourful local characters typically acquired at inns in Talyllyn and Dolgellau who could make their sole living escorting artistic travellers and science buffs – to whom Pugh applied the neat collective 'curiosity men' – to the summit of the mountain.

Geology was a major preoccupation for these early travellers. Before glaciation and erosion reduced its height by thousands of feet and carved it into its present form, the Ordovician volcanic rocks and Precambrian sedimentaries that form the bedrock of the mountain once extended northwards in a huge arch of layered rock beds. This arch reached its apex high above the central region between Cadair Idris and Snowdon, and is known as the Harlech Dome. This is an ancient sea floor, folded like a rucked carpet and considered one of the oldest geological formations in Britain. It's also the reason fossilised seashells have been found on Snowdon's summit. The rocks in the face of

Craig Cau can be seen to tilt southwards, showing the slope of this arch, like the abutments of some collapsed Roman fortification. We know all of this now, but in the 19th century it was all still a fascinating puzzle waiting to be solved. Cadair's botany, too, was and is of particular interest; today the mountain's status as a nature reserve comes from the delicate and unusual alpine plants that can be found at their most southern extent on its slopes, including purple saxifrage, the prehistoric-looking green spleenwort and pretty little white-flowered spignel.* The summit ridge is a bouldery grassland, where can be found the evocatively named hare's tail cotton, and wavy hair grass.

A telling early description in literature of Cadair comes from Daniel Defoe, who visited the area in the 1720s. He was not a man to delight in wilderness; he describes the area as being home to mountains 'impassable ... which even the people themselves call them so; we looked at them with astonishment, for their rugged tops and the immense heights of them.' He goes on to mention the 'famous Cader-Idricks, which some are of the opinion is the highest mountain in Britain'. Alfred Lord Tennyson was another visitor to the mountain – in a storm in 1856 – and was sufficiently moved by it to say he had 'never seen anything more awful than the great veil of rain drawn straight over Cader Idris'. The diarist Francis Kilvert was escorted to the summit by Pugh's son in 1871, and his account was similarly bleak: 'This is the dreariest, stoniest, most desolate mountain I have ever been on.'

Pugh's shelter was constructed so that travellers could take rest and enjoy refreshments until such time that the clouds parted. It was, as he put it, 'to be had for those wishing to see the rising sun, or in case of a shower or likewise.' The original shelter was probably built of wood, and during summer months housed a lady of maturing years who climbed the mountain at dawn and dispensed tea. Later on it was fortified, and now stands of squat native stone.

---

* Plantlife, a charity for wild flora in Britain, pulls no technical punches in its description of Cadair's botanical interest: '[Cadair Idris] is noted for vascular, habitat and bryophyte interest. Euphrasia hotspot. Calcareous rocky slopes with chasmophytic vegetation; Oligotrophic to mesotrophic standing waters with vegetation of the Littorelletea uniflorae and/or of the Isoëto-Nanojuncetea; Siliceous rocky slopes with chasmophytic vegetation; Siliceous scree of the montane to snow levels (*Androsacetalia alpinae* and *Galeopsietalia ladani*).' I couldn't have put it better.

However welcome it may be in a winter blizzard or summer rainstorm, it isn't inviting in the dark. It's amazing how open to suggestion your senses become out of your normal surroundings, especially when combined with the crepuscular aesthetic of the old stone and the myths that circle Cadair like a stubborn smell.

Happily, though lacking a door, the hut has a kind of porch with a bench where one can sit and look out of the open entrance into the northern view without venturing into the main room. Slinging down my pack, that's what I did now, glancing briefly into the wall of darkness to my right as I did so. It might as well have been a black curtain; I couldn't see a thing in there. I'd my head torch with me, but I wanted to avoid switching it on if I could, partly to protect my now-established night vision from bright light, but also because of a silly youthful fear I still harboured of shining a beam of light into a dark room and coming nose to nose with something unpleasant.

Entering the hut's little porch, the wind died as if a switch had been flicked. The chill I was beginning to feel on my sweaty back subsided. Stone buildings like this usually cool the air, but this one didn't. It was almost warm. Heated by the afternoon sun? The roof was metal, after all. This relief at the change of conditions wouldn't last; I needed to get a warm jacket and my bivouac equipment out of my backpack. Once I was warm and the sweat had dried off my back, I could move around the summit and explore a little, snatching some sleep in between. I found my bivvy bag, some food, my sleeping bag and mat, and pulled out the bag containing two snug jackets and a waterproof.

Only it didn't contain two snug jackets, or a waterproof. I'd brought up the bag with my tent in – and nothing warm at all. Well, this was annoying. I slumped down on the bench and looked out into the darkness, and down at my thin, sweat-soaked woollen T-shirt – the only thing I had to keep me warm overnight on top of an 893-metre mountain in spring. I'd never previously forgotten anything really major on a trip like this. My eyes slid to the Thornton's chocolate cakes I'd brought up with me. These were my little treats for later; now seemed like the time to have one. A bit of sugar, bit of pep. All fine.

The truth is, I *was* fine – but had this been a cold or rainy night, or a period of unstable weather, I could have been in quite a bit of trouble. The weather was good and set to continue as such, and the walk down off the mountain in the morning should, if the forecast held, be warmed by the sun. I was sweaty, but not irredeemably soaked. The problem was the wind – nothing chills you down more quickly, and if you're wet, water will sponge the heat from your body with alarming speed. I'd a light summer sleeping bag with me rated to around 5°C, but seeing as it was the single warm thing I had, this I'd have to look after. Sleeping bags stuffed with down feathers don't go well together with moisture. And I'd made enough rush-triggered mistakes for one day; my priority now was staying warm and dry. I looked again into the blackness to my left, into the hut. Then, resigned, I reached for my head torch. 'Thank God I remembered *you*.'

Enclosed spaces on mountains have a distinctive atmosphere to them, man-made ones particularly so. Perhaps it's the discrepancy between them and their surroundings that concentrates this. For instance, all journeys to the summit of Cadair Idris end here, and if shelter is what you seek, you and whatever emotion you bring with you will find it under this one, isolated roof. Whilst any spot on a mountain can hold a story, the mountain is still a mountain, full of spacious distractions – and you share the atmosphere of that spot with the view, the wind, the birds and the sky. But the curious intimacy of an enclosed space on a mountain – which by definition is a limitless, wide-open thing – is entirely different, and very potent. In that place, centuries of meetings, fears and moments of exhausted relief have gathered within the same few square feet, under the same roof. It's a piece of our world. A comfort. A sink of concentrated humanity in a wild place.

But Cadair's summit shelter didn't comfort me. Certainly not at first, anyway. I turned on my head torch and – holding my breath – shone it into the black hole of the shelter, quickly bouncing the beam into every corner to ensure there were no nasty surprises lurking there. It was, to my relief, totally empty and surprisingly clean, mercifully free from litter or screwed-up reeds of toilet paper used for their intended purpose, but not in the intended place. The room beyond the porch was about the size of a suburban living room, with a bench running round the edge and a square, coffee-table-sized brick platform in the centre. On it sat the burnt-out remains of a candle on a saucer of melted wax. I could hear the erratic wind funnelling through gaps in the corrugated roof like tin whistles. Two small windows – just big enough to frame a face – hung lightless in the gloom.

I began to worry about the batteries in my torch. I didn't like the thought of them running flat and there being no relief from the dark. It was thick and unyielding, and I found it unsettling. Some people can be as the animals and embrace nature in all its pragmatic barbarism without hesitation, but I'm not one of them. Don't get me wrong; I love the atmosphere of places that carry the fears of childhood – the dark corridors of a forest, the brush of fog against an ancient window, the bleakness of a Hebridean moor. Like most I seek them out because they stimulate an immersive sensory reaction – invigoration to one degree, fear to a significant other. The emotional mechanics are very much like climbing a mountain. But it still spooked me.

Given the circumstances, I could tolerate a night alone in a 150-year-old hut on the summit of a lore-thick mountain, but I was damned if I was going to do it without a light. Turning the beam down to its lowest setting, I set the torch on the central platform and went about making up a bed, set back away from the draught of the doorway. This done, I had another chocolate cake, pulled a hat onto my head and my spare socks onto my hands and wandered out of the hut onto the summit plateau, leaving my torch shining dimly within.

The wind was cold. Frost was beginning to shimmer like a fine fur on the summit rocks. Above, stars were piercing through a sky grading to mauve in the west. This would be an unwise dwelling for a sleepwalker: in front of the hut, the rocky ground gave way to a thin wig of grass atop a convex slope that bulged forward then plunged nearly 900 metres down the northern scarp of the mountain. Far below, the valley held the mythically bottomless lake of Llyn y Gadair. Beyond that, the mist-muted lights of Dolgellau. Stretching north like embers in a smouldering carpet, patches of amber light – villages, towns, isolated homesteads. How this lightscape must have changed since the first villages arrived here and looked up to the mountain in awe and trepidation. And how little – aside from a few paths and a hut – the mountaintop upon which I was standing had evolved. The people and their perceptions of the mountain had changed a lot; the mountain itself, hardly at all.

I walked a little way along the ridge, enjoying the solitude before I began to chill down, my hairs bristling where the wind touched them. Beginning to shake, I turned back towards the hut's boxy silhouette. As its front came into view, I noticed the yellow light of my torch shining dimly but warmly through the window. It almost looked cosy.

It's reasonable to assume that those who would gather in mountain shelters like this would automatically have more in common with each other than people meeting in most buildings at sea level. Therefore, conversations in this ramshackle little building over the last couple of centuries would have had much more of a synergy, and the meetings in general potentially more fortuitous simply because of the incongruity of the meeting place.

In his book *Visions of Snowdonia* writer Jim Perrin describes arriving at Cadair's summit shelter late one winter's evening in the mid 1970s in cruel weather. He had to slide in through the door past snow that almost blocked it. Soon after he arrived, another man entered and perched himself on the benches at the far end of the shelter. Perrin noted: 'He was quite short, a little arthritic in his movements, and his face was deeply lined with deep-set, intense eyes that dwelt on you in unnerving, long consideration.' The man lit a pipe, and Perrin offered him coffee, which he accepted with the grumble both that quality coffee was impossible to obtain in civilised Britain these days, and that in the little shelter on top of Cadair, 'of all places, he might have expected to enjoy a solitary pipe on a day like this'. The two traded good-natured swipes together awhile, principally about the human race – a man in his twenties finding common ground with another in his seventies, both in an ice-encased shelter at 893 metres above North Wales for ostensibly the same reason: solitude, escape, adventure, space.

Perrin knew more or less immediately who the older man was. He was famous: the explorer and mountaineer H. W. 'Bill' Tilman, one of the 20th century's most prolifically adventurous figures. As a teenager he'd fought at the Somme and between the wars had climbed Nanda Devi in the Indian Himalaya, at 7,816 metres then the highest peak summited to date. Parachuted into the Balkans during the Second World War to incite resistance to the Nazis, between the conflicts he had met Eric Shipton whilst picking coffee in Africa, with whom he made some of mountaineering's most important ascents, as well as significant attempts on Mount Everest during the 1930s. In later life he would shift his focus somewhat to the ocean, adopting and restoring old craft and casting off for bleak corners of the world such as Patagonia,

Greenland, Baffin Island and Spitzbergen, where he would anchor up and close in on mountains inaccessible by land, exploring their shores and often climbing them.

Tilman and Perrin became acquaintances for a very brief period, the inquisitive younger man visiting the old explorer at his home in the Mawddach Estuary, where he was to be presented with 'a parable of [Tilman's] relationship with the world'. Perrin would become one of mountaineering's leading authors and thinkers; in 1977, Tilman – aged 79, and just weeks after his meeting with Perrin on the summit of Cadair Idris – put his dogs into kennels and joined as a crew member a boat that left Rio de Janeiro bound for the Antarctic. The boat was lost in one of the many storms lacerating the South Atlantic and no trace of it was ever found. There went a man who loved solitude, and travelled to the far corners of the planet to tackle its most austere and extreme places; it would appear Tilman met his end without ever breaking his intrepid swagger.

It's quite possible that Cadair Idris was the last mountain Tilman climbed. His last moments atop a summit were spent with Perrin, here, within sight of his own house. Perrin described his meeting with Tilman as 'completely remarkable ... one of the most singular gifts to me'. And that gift was kindled just feet away in the strange, entirely out-of-the-ordinary little room in which I was now lying on the summit of Cadair Idris.

The hopes I'd had earlier in the evening of being alone on the top of this mountain had switched to a desire for company. I could hear scimperings on the tin roof above. Mice, maybe. The fidgets of wind, perhaps. Turned down to its lowest setting, the trade-off for saving my batteries was the particularly eerie, candle-yellow light my torch produced. Every time I moved, a wild curl of shadow was thrown across the wall. Out on the mountain, the silence would have been a natural part of its sonic 'scape. But the shelter muddled the dynamic, and in here silence wasn't welcome. I thought about using my phone to play some music, an audiobook, anything, but I resisted, and eventually turned off the torch and tried to sleep.

I managed a few hours, waking briefly in the night coughing violently and feeling an obstruction in my throat. I thought for a grim moment something cobwebby and ancient had dislodged itself from the ceiling and plummeted into my gaping mouth, or a curious insect had wandered in. A few slugs of water and whatever it was became nutrition. Now wide awake, I leaned forward and peered towards the door, seeing beyond it a scrape of orange brightening on the horizon opposite where I'd watched it fade just a few hours earlier. It was 5.15 a.m., and already brighter than it had been when I arrived the previous night.

Struggling up, I unzipped the sleeping bag to its base, then put the foot-box on my head and wrapped the rest of it around me like a blanket. Pushing my feet into unlaced boots I wandered out onto the summit, the grass crunching under a soft frost, found a rock and sat for a while.

The mountain was awakening in total silence. No birds, no sheep, no distant static of road or airplane. As I watched, red exploded from the horizon, bleeding through the thin ribbon of cloud and lighting the crisp grass of Cadair Idris's summit ridge, upon one of many boulders, where I sat. The grass started to shimmer, then glisten and bead as the frost upon it began to melt. It seemed ridiculous that such an awesome event as a sunrise could unfold without an accompanying sound; a sizzle, a hiss, a roar, operatic music. Nothing, alas, but pure quiet, as nature began to light the mountain. I sat and watched, as many had here for hundreds and hundreds of years – possibly expecting rather more to happen than a sunrise. Enlightenment, the ascent to a higher spiritual realm. And, of course, insanity or death.

A specific reference to Cadair's most emblematic legend came in the form of an 1822 poem by English writer Felicia Hemans, titled 'The Rock of Cader Idris'. A poet of the late Romantic period, Hemans was born in Liverpool in 1793. Romantics had a profound affinity with mountains – as we shall see – and Hemans was no exception.* 'The Rock of Cader Idris' is rather dark; Hemans describes waiting alone on the bed-shaped boulder on the summit of Cadair, 'that rock where the storms have their dwelling,/The birthplace of phantoms', viewing the 'dread beings' that hover around the mountain:

---

* Hemans also has the distinction of coining the term 'stately home' in the first line of her 1827 poem 'The Homes of England'. The first line reads: 'The stately Homes of England,/ How beautiful they stand!'

I saw them – the mighty of ages departed –
The dead were around me that night on the hill:
From their eyes, as they pass'd, a cold radiance they darted,
There was light on my soul, but my heart's blood was chill.

Needless to say, the poem's protagonist lives through the horrors of the night, and – upon watching the sunrise on Cadair, as I was now – feels suitably illuminated.

I saw what man looks on, and dies – but my spirit
Was strong, and triumphantly lived through that hour;
And, as from the grave, I awoke to inherit
A flame all immortal, a voice, and a power!

Showell Styles, aforementioned author of *The Mountains of North Wales*, thought the whole legend a displaced mistake, and that Hemans had transferred the legend of a rock on the slopes of Snowdon – the Maen du'r Arddu, or 'black stone' – to Cadair, adding to a long list of folkloric confusions that exist between the two mountains through written history, probably due to their both being high, craggy peaks overlooking small, deep lakes. Styles, incidentally, was something of a poet himself – penning the bouncy 'Ballad of Idwal Slabs', named after a well-known climbers' crag in the Ogwen valley, 25 miles north of Cadair.

English-born and a prolific fiction writer, his non-fiction (and many of his stories) centred around the mountains. Humorous poems and novels aside, too few know Styles for his mountain writing. It's a travesty that most of his books are now out of print, as in this he ranks as one of the very best – particularly in Snowdonia, his adopted home, where he died in 2005. *The Mountains of North Wales* was his masterpiece.

Styles was great because the mountains clearly got to him. His interpretations are suffused with intermittent outpourings of emotion and feeling that came from his being amongst them. Far from being screeds of dry practicality, his descriptions of routes up the peaks of Snowdonia were imaginative, curious and peerlessly articulated, fortified by the mythology of the region and its mountains. After describing being chased off Cadair by a storm in 1971, Styles remarks that 'the only country you can feel nostalgic for whilst you are still in it is mountain country, and only the Welsh have a word for that feeling – *hiraeth*.' Of the highest peak he says this: 'Snowdon has everything ... from any angle, distantly or close at hand, Snowdon is the noblest and most shapely peak in sight, and obviously the queen of the lot ... five main ridges converge at the summit, each with its own special characteristics.' And it was one of Snowdon's ridges' 'special characteristics' I'd be exploring next.

I sat outside in the infant warmth of the sun until it sat four fingers' height above the horizon, then shambled back to the hut and began to gather up my possessions. Eating another chocolate cake and slugging back some of my remaining water, I stayed wrapped in my sleeping bag and gently dozing, giving the air long enough to warm a little, until outside the door the sky had turned from deep blue to bright white. Pulling down the broom lodged in the rafters, I gave the floor a quick sweep, picked up a dead candle to dispose of later and gave a last glance around the hut. With daylight streaming in through the window, it was a quite different place.

I walked out into a veil of white cloud. The morning sun was warming the grass and steam was rising like bushfire smoke into the air. It was beautiful. Following the shape of the ridge, which I could just see, I walked the brief distance to Mynydd Moel, the furthest east of Cadair's triple summits. To the north, the heads of northern Snowdonia's mountains rose from the morning mists, hard and bare; of rock, not grass. Where I was now standing was a sort of bridge – the link between the verdant south and the austere, brutal north. Reminiscent of both, but resembling neither entirely.

At the rock buttresses of the northern flank, I took a look over the edge before turning south. The slope began to tilt downwards, and at my feet hoverflies dozily awoke and rose where I stepped.

4 DANGER

At around 3 p.m. on Saturday 2 April 1960, three sixteen-year-old army cadets vanished on the slopes of Snowdon. They were part of a group of five who had left Pen-y-Pass earlier that afternoon for the summit of Wales' highest peak during their much-anticipated ten-day adventure-training holiday.

The weather was a mix of rain and low cloud – reasonably gruesome by sea-level standards, but nothing odd for this part of North Wales. Snowdon's high elevation and proximity to the coast meant waiting for perfect conditions hereabouts was hardly the done thing, and certainly wasn't character building – at the time a prerequisite for most forms of youthful outdoor endeavour. Besides, these boys had been assured that the route they were taking up the 1,085-metre peak wasn't anything worth fretting over; according to their instructor, the ridge that would be the outing's highlight 'had been walked by women in high heels'.

Initially, the headlines that began to creep into the national press were coyly optimistic. The *Daily Mail* began its story of Monday 4 April with the comforting image that the three boys had 'settled down to spend their second night in mist and drizzle', clearly confident that nothing more malign than a twisted ankle or disorientation could be preventing the boys from reappearing, weary but chipper, when the mist finally cleared.

But at 8.30 a.m. on Monday 4th, hope was abandoned. Two members of a rescue team came across three bodies with severe head injuries lying amongst rocks at the base of a 100-metre drop, in an area known as Square Gully. The boys – John Brenchley, John Itches and Tony Evans – were roped together. The rescuers' report delicately implied that their injuries were such that death would have been instantaneous. It had taken a team of 100 nearly two days to find them.

Piecing together what had happened wasn't difficult. The three boys, separated from their instructor in rain and sudden Snowdonia mist, had taken a wrong turn on the ridge. Becoming lost in a catacomb of tall rocks and terrain that coaxed them towards dangerous ground, amidst tiredness and fear one had stumbled and fallen; the others, tied together, had been pulled down with him. According to one seasoned rescuer, what befell the boys that day was 'sheer bad luck'.

Even in 1960 it wasn't uncommon for people to lose their lives climbing British mountains. But the story of the three teenaged boys lost on Snowdon touched something sensitive in the national consciousness – and with the final, tragic outcome, something snapped.

Over the next few days, the stern faces of Search and Rescue personnel, teachers, police officers and mountaineers filled the pages of the national press, all proposing competing theories as to how this tragedy could possibly have occurred – not just on a mountain, but on a mountain damningly described as 'safe'. The papers had a thorough chew of the case, announcing the tragedy with predictably hysterical headlines such as 'The Ridge of Death Row' (*Daily Mail*) and 'Peril on a Peak' (*Daily Mirror*). Both stories featured grim photographs from the mountainside – grubby and speckled in the way only 1960s news pictures can be – of rescuers manhandling stretchers down sharp rock, and each came loaded with blame cross-haired in various directions: chiefly towards mist, bad luck and, inevitably, the boys' instructor, an experienced and 'highly competent' 28-year-old mountaineer named Peter Sutcliffe.

Many of Sutcliffe's critics claimed that the young instructor's charge of five boys was far too much for him alone to herd safely to Snowdon's summit, and that the deteriorating weather should have prompted him to turn the group back. Others focused on details, highlighting the inherent flaws in the 'roping-together' technique the boys were using – an arrangement common in the Alps that relies on the principle that if one person takes a tumble, the others are required to quickly and deftly fling the slack over a handy spike of rock to arrest the fall (the problem here being, of course, that if no spike immediately presents itself the rest of the party is yanked towards whatever doom awaits). But most extraordinary in all of this was the disagreement amongst practically everybody as to exactly how serious the route the group took up Snowdon – that 'Ridge of Death Row' so subtly christened by the *Daily Mail* – really was.

Surely this was straightforward: it was either a route from which you could easily fall to your death or it wasn't. Even in the tragedy's aftermath, Sutcliffe stuck to his assertion that the ridge was 'not a climb, but a walk', along with his aforementioned reference to untroubled women in high heels. Reportedly, the reason the boys were using a rope was for training purposes, not for any concerns over safety.

An inquest was held in a tiny stone chapel in Llanberis, during which Arthur Bell, the guardian of John Brenchley, repeatedly pilloried Sutcliffe on this seemingly very complicated point. One exchange began with Bell levelling: 'Am I right that in places this ridge is just a narrow pathway with a drop on either side?' Sutcliffe responded that yes, this was correct. Bell then countered: 'Yet you say you don't think this is dangerous?' Sutcliffe simply replied that no, he didn't. Then a senior member of mountain rescue gave Sutcliffe's defence some much-needed solidity. When asked if he considered the route dangerous for inexperienced people, he responded with: 'No, sir – I've seen young children up there.'

A verdict of 'misadventure' followed, with coroner E. Lloyd-Jones citing mist as the principal cause. But Bell remained adamant that the route itself – and the decision to tackle it – was to blame. In a statement he said: 'I have been told that the ledge from which they fell is only two foot wide. I think this walk was dangerous, and I don't think the boys should have faced such risks.'

Lloyd-Jones delivered a statement in acknowledgement, worth noting for a simplicity that verges on the profound: 'Of course there is danger. It is one of the objects of the course.'

Over 50 years later, people continue to argue over the severity of the route that those boys took on Snowdon. In fact, people argue about Snowdon as a whole all the time. The muscular, four-peaked mountain that dominates North Wales' arrestingly contoured uplands is a superstar, drawing upwards of half a million visitors each year. It's not only Britain's most-climbed mountain; it's probably the most-climbed mountain in the world. Some come looking for a pleasant walk, some for a challenge, some for thrills – and few are disappointed. But there's danger here, too, and nowhere are arguments about mountain safety found in sharper relief.

What isn't in dispute is this: at a rate of about two a year, people still die on the ridge that claimed those three lives in 1960. This upsetting tally has steadily made the ragged arête – bitten into Snowdon's east flank 600 metres above the Pass of Llanberis – the most notorious mountain route in Britain. Its name is Crib Goch.

Empty, foam-streaked glasses and the living remains of a funeral party were spread around the lounge of the Douglas Hotel in Bethesda when I arrived just after 6 p.m. and took a seat in the corner to wait for Mal Creasey.

Mal is a mountain guide and a veteran of the Llanberis Mountain Rescue Team – volunteers whose self-imposed duty is to locate those who find themselves in trouble high on the Snowdon massif. It's one of the busiest teams in Britain, having the dubious honour of working a patch that's the very definition of a black spot. It's been known for the team and its neighbouring units to attend call-outs from people in distress on the slopes of Snowdon 170 times in a single year. For one Welsh mountain, that's pretty exceptional.

Ten minutes after I arrived the door opened and I heard the clip of crutches from the lobby. Seconds later Mal swung into the lounge, looking out of breath. He nodded a hangdog hello, before scowling at his crutches. 'Arthroscopy. Both knees.'

I gave him a blank look.

'Where they go into the joint and scrape off all the crap.' He shrugged. 'Hey – live a sedentary life and you could die of a heart attack at 50. Or live a long life outdoors and expect a few squeaks.'

There's no longer really any debate about whether Crib Goch is a walk or a rock climb. Today it's considered neither, occupying a grey area between the two that's actually more dangerous than both: scrambling. Any route above a potentially damaging drop that demands the use of your hands to negotiate it is considered a scramble. It would seem the activity is addictive, too: given the proximity to vertical danger and the monkey-business it demands, devotees will tell you that it's the most thrilling thing you can do in the mountains. Routes are given grades, going from 1 to 3 in ascending order of difficulty.*

---

* Few people use ropes on the lower scrambling grades, which is what makes them so dangerous. Rock climbs, whilst technically more difficult, are usually protected by ropes and so are generally safer, although there are the lunatic few who tackle the toughest rock climbs in the world unroped – a pursuit known as free soloing.

These grades were originally established by guidebook writers as a general indication of a route's toughness when combined with how far you could fall if you screwed up, but the system has proliferated into a more-or-less universally adopted yardstick of overall difficulty.

At Grade 1, Crib Goch is considered amongst the easiest of scrambles from a difficulty point of view. But there's a catch. What Showell Styles called a 'special quality' was also noted by Irvine Butterfield in *The High Mountains of Britain and Ireland*: 'The ridge is magnificently precarious for about 400 feet and whilst technically easy, commands respect – with a sensationally sharp summit ridge above a steep precipice.' These evidently awesome drops mean that exactly how anyone will fare on Crib Goch is still fiercely and unpredictably subjective. Some inexperienced walkers can skip across with nary a care, yet there are bedded-in mountaineers who blanch at the thought of going anywhere near it. In mountains this seems to be the thing; you can describe how difficult *you* found it and why, but how anyone else will get on is down to them.

Perhaps because of this, your Crib Goch status – more than any other mountain route in Britain, it seems – says something about you. After its many years of notoriety, today the ridge inevitably presents something of a rite of passage; a mountain-shaped question mark that only a firm constitution, a certain element of skill and a generous endowment of sheer balls can answer. Nail it, and you can proudly attest to hitting the top of the thrill curve for what a gutsy mountain walker could be reasonably expected to achieve. Miss it out, and you're missing out. You're below the watermark. You're a wimp. Right?

'Dangerous way to think,' said Mal, as we sat down at a corner table away from the increasingly horizontal mourners. 'With that kind of attitude, all that happens after you've beaten it – if you beat it – is you end up sizing up something even scarier. Some climbers feel that way if they haven't climbed the Matterhorn. Everest, even. Can you believe that?' He considered this for a moment, before chuckling. 'Anyway. Crib Goch.'

There are harder, more overtly threatening mountains in Britain – in this book, even – but in terms of a personification of all that is deviously hazardous about the British hills, no shadows fall on the staircase of Crib Goch and the pile of sharp contradictions that is Snowdon itself. The slightest glance at incident reports reveals that the mountain is a high-volume cautionary anthem for what can and does go wrong in the British hills.

All this aside, on a more personal level I knew exactly why *I* was scared of Crib Goch. An enthusiasm for mountains and the ability to be at ease with horrible drops are not necessarily easy bedfellows – heights hate me, and I hate them back. Some people can keep their head and enjoy the thrill of tight-roping along ridgelines; me, I stay back from cliff edges, avoid tall buildings and take the aisle seat on an aeroplane. Inability to focus on objective difficulties when faced with 'exposure' – the mountain name for a drop that will pretty much definitely kill you – meant I struggled with any terrain that wasn't wide enough for me to sprawl messily over it should the need arise.

From reading up I knew that the crest of Crib Goch certainly did not possess much width. Five hundred metres of bony, severely angled rock over drops many times the height of Big Ben, this thing was sheer, sharp, long – and didn't have much patience for the acrophobic.* As many claimed after the tragic accident in 1960, from a point of view of actual physical difficulty the ridge isn't really that hard at all; like climbing a stepladder, or boulder-hopping on a beach. But raise these little exercises to a platform the thick end of 300 metres above spiky ground, and – whilst from a coldly technical point of view it shouldn't make a difference – psychologically the consequences of a slip suddenly become harder to ignore.

I needed to talk to someone who knew the ridge in forensic detail. Someone who could tell me, with nothing in the way of macho marinade, exactly how much trouble I would be in. That's why I'd called Mal. You can use a map to traverse the rump of any mountain, but on something as hefty as Snowdon you needed someone like Mal to really get you under its skin. A sturdy 60-something with an air of permanent bemusement, I knew him to be straight-talking, likeably mischievous and peerlessly experienced. If anyone could reassure me – or at least give me a couple of pointers – it was Mal.

'Well, I don't want to worry you,' Mal began, 'but if you got rid of Crib Goch … I'd say rescue call-outs would drop by 80 per cent.' He sipped his pint. 'Give or take.'

'Falls?'

---

* Acrophobia is the fear of heights – not, as is often claimed, vertigo. Vertigo is a physical condition related to dizziness, balance and equilibrium. Obviously for this reason, heights and vertigo still aren't the best combination.

'Yeah, some. A few get lost. But most people just get cragfast.'

This is a term you come across regularly in association with Crib Goch, and steep mountains in general. 'Cragfast' means, quite simply, stuck – stuck in a trap of your own making, when you've climbed up something you can't climb down, and then freeze, barnacle-like, to whatever you're clinging to. This could be because of physical difficulty; more often it's because every way looks precarious and you're too scared to move.

'So where on the ridge does it happen?'

'The Pinnacles, usually,' Mal said, taking another sip. 'And the beginning, the first big rock step. And sometimes descending into that first steepening.' He frowned. 'Oh, and don't go left or right off the crest – all that does is take you onto a load of loose rock. Hit everything straight on,' he said, blading a hand in my direction for emphasis. 'It's steep and exposed and it looks horrible, but the rock's solid. And it's better than the alternatives.' I saw the look on his face and I didn't like it: a kind of bouncy-eyebrowed I've-got-a-story-you-don't-want-to-hear look. Mal probably had a lot of stories I didn't want to hear – as well as a whole bunch he probably didn't want to tell.

Loosely, mountain rescue teams are the emergency services for the British mountains – only they aren't, certainly not in the conventional sense. Nobody gets paid; few teams are even funded beyond the odd bit of clothing or radio gear, and they scratch sustenance from donations and tax breaks to keep volunteers equipped and trained. Beyond a doubt they're heroes – but the cost can be steep. A mountain fall is not a pleasant way to go; it's violent, tearing, shocking. Those dispatched to accidents where they sometimes literally have to pick up the pieces often suffer lasting psychological trauma. Some volunteers harden to encountering death in the mountains. Many, somewhat understandably, can't.

If the fact that our mountain rescue personnel are local volunteers like Mal rather than paid-up professionals who ride around in helicopters all day is a surprise to many, the idea that Britain's mountains are dangerous enough to need rescue personnel at all might come as another. In terms of their physical attributes, our mountains are laughable in comparison with those found in many other mountainous countries in the world. We've no glaciers filled with bottomless crevasses; no oxygen-drained high-altitude death zones in which pulmonary or cerebral oedema can stealthily kill you; no bears or mountain lions to keep an ear awake for in a quiet mountainside camp. But what we do have are hundreds – thousands – of steep, storied and striking mountains, and a lot of people interested in climbing them for amusement or thrill. The urge to climb mountains has complex, but largely pointless, sources – and often the feeling of danger is cited as justification in itself. The swaggery adage of 'feeling more alive the closer you are to death' often crops up at this point. But sometimes, for reasons often beyond control, close gets too close.

Before you even insert humans into the equation, mountains are in any case pretty hairy places. Avalanches and rockfalls are difficult to predict, and impossible to control. Freak weather gets freakier and more frequent the higher you go, and even the most benign gland of a hill can rapidly turn malignant given inclement conditions. Pieces of mountains fall down from time to time. Temperatures fall by around 6°C per 1,000 metres, a phenomenon known as the lapse rate – which, on a British mountain in spring, can mean the difference between dewy grass at sea level and solid ice at the summit, with damaging consequences for the unprepared. Lightning can strike without warning and with impunity, sometimes out of a clear blue sky, and wind can blow you off an exposed mountaintop in an unexpected gust. In the UK alone, all of these account for victims in double digits each year.

Sometimes when it comes to death or injury the mountains are merely aggravating bystanders. Heart attacks, strokes and the occasional suicide (including some extraordinarily odd cases in the Highlands of Scotland*) aren't at all uncommon.

But most accidents in the mountains occur as the result of the smallest human error. Misjudgement, poor timing, inadequate clothing, distraction, panic, inexperience, over-ambition, under-preparedness, over-reliance – then the most simple and common of all: a split second of physical failing. A slip in

---

* The oddest of these is without doubt that of Emmanuel Caillet, the Frenchman whose body was found at a lonely spot near the summit of Ben Alder in 1996, having lain there for months. All the labels were missing from his clothing, he wore slip-on shoes and carried no identification. He had apparently shot himself in the heart with an antique replica Remington revolver, which lay nearby.

a dangerous place. A trip. A tired stumble. Even something as innocuous as a broken shoelace or a dropped compass can be the spark that ignites a crisis. Head for a dangerous mountain and you need your head screwed on – a second can be all it takes.

Between 2002 and 2011 mountain-rescue teams in England, Wales and Scotland responded to 11,558 incidents in the hills. Of these, 6,862 yielded injuries, of which 564 were fatalities – almost exactly 10 per cent. The pattern of these statistics is unnervingly consistent but makes perfect sense when you think about it. 'Slip, trip or stumble' is the number one rescue-triggering mishap, year on year. 'Falls or tumbles' come a close second, with 'lost' as the number three cause of reported distress in the mountains. What's interesting about these otherwise unsurprising figures is the nature of the wounding activity when broken down by region. In terms of objective dangers, Scotland has by far the most severe ground and weather, but their hills feel comparatively fewer feet – and the ones they do tend to be more experienced. Thus, Scotland has a much lower overall rate of incident when total area and potential high places in which to come unstuck are taken into account.* The Lake District has by far the most incidents for hillwalking, largely injuries to the lower legs befitting an ugly slip or a fracturing step. But Snowdonia's principal cause of damage is rock scrambling – almost to the point of exclusivity. If you're going to fall off a ridge, chances are you'll do it in Snowdonia. And with one or two exceptions, you'll very likely do it on Crib Goch. Which is why I wanted to talk to Mal.

'So,' he said after a while. 'What's your plan?'

I explained that later tonight – preferably after a splendid and unhealthy pub meal – I intended to drive up to Pen-y-Pass, wander into a secluded valley beneath Crib Goch and wild camp for the night. Then, come the dawn, I'd hit the ridge. Mal pulled a face.

'Bad idea?'

'Have you seen the forecast?'

I confessed that I had, but only the general forecast. Everything had seemed so meteorologically settled I hadn't gotten round to it yet.

---

* In 2011, Scotland saw 415 incidents and 21 fatalities; England and Wales, 1,078 incidents and 33 fatalities.

'Well, the *proper** forecast shows a front arriving early tomorrow morning. Gales, rain ... Can't say I'd want to be up there.'

'Oh.' Balls. This I should have checked.

'May I suggest a compromise?' said Mal. 'Do the first section – the, ah, exciting section – tonight. Then you can slip down into the little valley beneath the gap in the middle of the ridge, camp, relax – and do the rest in the morning. You've got the nasty bits over with whilst it's dry, then.'

'Nasty bits?'

He bobbed his eyebrows again. '*Exciting* bits.'

I looked at my watch. 'It's gone seven.'

'Well then,' Mal drained the rest of his drink, 'best get your skates on.'

*   *   *

The fast road to Snowdon from Bethesda takes you first through the broad half-pipe of the Ogwen valley. Here, ancient mountains spill slate to the roadside, lining the grand valley like a colonnade of towering, crumbling gargoyles. You pass Tryfan, a freestanding 918-metre arrowhead crowned with two tiny pinnacles: Adam and Eve. It's a popular picture on the postcard racks; positioned just far enough apart to allow an uncomfortably nervy leap from one to the other, performing this summiteer's tradition is said to gain you the 'freedom' of the peak.

Then the road bends and you brush the village of Capel Curig, before entering quaggy open ground, scudding along the shore of Llynnau Mymbyr towards the dark mass of Snowdon. From here, the triangular sweep of Crib Goch guards its parent peak in a protective curl, like a drawn cloak. The building overgrown with vegetation that appears to the right is the Pen-y-Gwryd Hotel, marking the corner turn into the Pass of Llanberis – the road that wiggles up to the foot of Snowdon like a dropped cable.

Crags tower either side as you ascend, including some of the most storied in Britain. Find similar outcrops in Spain or Switzerland and, chances are, they're

---

* General sea level forecasts don't really cut it in the hills. Ironically, given the might of the Met Office, the bespoke upland forecasts 99 per cent of mountaineers rely on are the MWIS reports produced seven days a week by an extremely clever man called Geoff from his house in Scotland's Southern Uplands. SportScotland give him some money for it; but the forecasts he provides for England and Wales are, at the time of going to press, unfunded.

just crags – unremarkable, unexplored and unexploited. But in Britain, being the confined menagerie of interested parties and interesting terrain it is, almost every significant cut of rock in Snowdonia will have been looked at with a devious eye and quickening pulse at some point. The crags on the Pass in particular have made history, home to climbing routes teased from the dark North Wales rock and given bleak, strikingly alliterate titles: Cenotaph Corner, Cemetery Gates, Cobweb Crack. Snowdonia has a certain darkness to it: the rain-streaked remnants of dead industry and hard, Welsh nomenclature lend the region something of a sinister air, which – combined with the region's abrasive mountains and frequently tough weather – makes for an atmosphere so thick you could punch it.

Architecturally, the mountains hereabouts are sharp and broken. The clichéd postcards of this place consist of high summits studded with flakes of rock in silhouette, bristling at angles, like the radial spikes of a medieval torture machine. Occasionally these contain a climber, gazing out to a bruised sky, or swinging off a frozen seesaw of rock. Snowdon itself is extremely ancient, composed of some of the oldest exposed rock in Britain – a mixture of pressure-hoisted sea-floor sedimentaries and volcanics brutalised by pressure and glaciation into a sharp, arrestingly fractured massif. It's an angrier landscape than the Lake District, and more claustrophobic than the Scottish Highlands, one of geological menace and home to a more chilling breed of outdoor adventure than the Lake District's cuddly persona. It seems to say that if you want to find small animals wearing floral dresses and drinking tea, go to the Lakes. If you want dark, cold rock that hates you, go to Snowdonia.

I reached the corner turn on to the Pass of Llanberis a little before 8 p.m. A quick supply run in Bethesda had yielded a few comforts for a night out on the hill – sugary snacks, crisps, noodles, hot chocolate and some whisky to liven it up. It seemed a little unreal and adventurous that I was going to be approaching this dreaded ridge in little over an hour. It was the sensible choice, given the forecast – but tackling the ridge with darkness coming seemed even more intimidating than doing it in bad weather. Even in rain, there might possibly be someone else crazy enough to be up there with me – probably wearing shorts – who would be able to pat me on the back and gee me up. But at this hour, I'd almost certainly be very alone up there.

Slowing the car, I rounded the corner onto the Pass and entered the cloud, brightening to a dappled gold as I climbed. A building sharpened to the right as the

Pass levelled, a few vehicles and a hut to the left. This was it: Pen-y-Pass, the place from which to wave a handkerchief in the direction of most who head for Snowdon. For those three boys in 1960, this was their last glimpse of civilisation.

The car park was practically empty when I pulled in, turned off my engine and sat, listening to the gentle whumps of the wind against the car and the ticks of its cooling engine. Cloud was clawing the Pass frantically, one moment allowing glimpses of lofty context down its rain-glistened length, the next snatching it away. I left the car and laced up my boots, wondering what I should leave behind.

I imagined the worst happening, and somebody coming across the car days from now. They'd find discarded Twix wrappers on the back seat, filthy loafers in the passenger footwell, a warm jacket in the boot, batteries – trivial comforts awaiting someone never coming back, and now the object of post-mortem scrutiny. Could that spare jacket have prevented the hypothermia that killed him? Could that Twix have saved his life? Spare batteries – surely they could have done something?

Ridiculous, yes. But this particular hill was giving me dreadful feelings. Part of me thought it couldn't possibly be *that* bad. I'd seen the shrugs and heard the 'No big deal' bravado from people who had done Crib Goch, but I also had a suspicion that, no matter how convincing the patter, most of them had felt a little shake on the ridge at some point. Now, with the act of leaving the car having been laboured over and over in my head, I was analysing every act for *that* critical choice: the moment when I'd make a decision from which I couldn't come back.

Locking the car and taking a last look – wondering, ever so briefly, if the next person to acknowledge it would be from a search and rescue team – I set off onto the path known as the Pyg Track, which leaves the corner of the car park at a forgivingly gentle incline. Constructed from huge boulders, it has the effect of appearing to have been made for a giant, ascending grandly but gently to a narrow pass called the Bwlch y Moch. Continue over the pass and you enter the basin of the smashed cauldron of peaks comprising what is known as the Snowdon horseshoe,* invisible from this angle. Or, on arrival at the

* The Snowdon horseshoe takes in the four peaks of Snowdon in a circular route from Pen-y-Pass. The peaks – Crib Goch, Garnedd Ugain, Yr Wyddfa (Snowdon summit) and Y Lliwedd – are colloquially referred to as the 'nails' in the horseshoe.

pass, you bear right and take the much steeper route onto the cauldron's broken rim, and eventually onto Crib Goch. Here, the scenery inhales grandly. Muscular hills, glistening water, and everywhere the dark, lichened Snowdonian rock, cracked and fractured in fragile-looking blades, like ancient, natural porcelain.

The air was warm, becoming slightly chilly only when enlivened by the wind. It was the sort of temperature that suggested a thunderstorm, but the atmosphere was thin and the cloud – whilst prolific – looked weightless, certainly for the time being. I passed two walkers on their way down, a couple who looked knackered enough to have been to the summit. I lifted my head and smiled with the kind of eye-roll, aren't-we-mad, this-weather-eh? kind of look walkers often give each other, hoping that they might engage for a moment. I wanted to ask whether or not they knew of anybody else still on the mountain, but they didn't look like they wanted to chat – they were on their last stretch, and obviously weren't in the mood. All I got was a murmur of acknowledgement and the sound of their stiff breathing as they passed. Alone, I continued, the path steepening until after about half an hour I reached the pass, out of breath. Ahead the Pyg Track descended into a steep, broad depression before arcing right over a stile and barrelling into a huge basin beneath a ring of mountains that peered down upon it like a circle of faces. From here the distant summit of Snowdon nudged out from behind creased cliffs to my right. It looked far above, and far away.

Part of the reason so many people get to the summit of Snowdon is because there's a train running up it, a café on the top and paths from every direction that resemble small roads for most of their length. Unsurprisingly, these do little for the mountain's credibility as an objective for adventurers. After hours of walking, arriving at the top to stand in the same place as a festival of day-trippers clad in the meagre clothing of sea level who haven't shuffled more than 100 metres – not to mention a natty building and a puffer train – must be a disquieting experience, and one I was curious to have the following day after my night camping alone on the uncivilised mountainside. The railway is an enormously popular draw, and doubtless a wonderful day out for people who can't, or won't, walk up Snowdon. But the walking routes see their fair share of bizarre traffic, too – cursed with the status of 'highest', the mountain attracts all sorts of feats that lay claim to an ascent with a particular, quirky caveat. Over the years a number of extraordinary sights have lumbered out of the mist on Snowdon's slopes – from groups clad in pyjamas, dressed as gorillas or, on one memorable occasion, driving a car.*

That this perception has caused Wales' highest hill to be viewed as something of a sacrificial lamb to tourism is a shame, because as a mountain Snowdon is absolutely bloody stupendous.

The four peaks that form the massif aren't arranged in a neat, linear manner like a child's drawing; from above, the range looks like a slender starfish with its limbs mid-flail. Those limbs are sharp ridges that themselves rise to summits – including Crib Goch, and its more genteel mirror across the *cwm*, Y Lliwedd – and the gaps between them are chasms, floored with lakes and walled with bitten cliffs. Snowdon itself, seen from within the embrace of its eastern arms, is a black, fantastically sheer pyramid that, when not wearing its hat of cloud, rises to a pleasingly sharp point. It's a drastic spectacle, and entirely unexpected by those imagining something blousy and accommodating. Unsurprisingly, this dichotomy between the mountain's public persona as something of a tame kick-about and its very real qualities as a 'proper' mountain has caused big problems. The briefest scan over incident records unquestionably reveals that Snowdon's popularity has prompted a serious lack of respect.

In 2008 two walkers came across some rubbish poking out of the snow heaped in the doorway of the summit café at around 7.45 a.m. Closer inspection revealed it wasn't rubbish, it was a man – an unconscious 40-year-old who had climbed the mountain in trainers and a shirt, with not much else besides. Pinned to the mountain by bad weather, he had been forced to spend the night on the summit at −5°C and in 60 mph winds – which in combination reduced the effective temperature to a brass-monkey-killing −18°C. The walkers briskly placed him in all of their spare clothes and a survival bag, then scrambled the Llanberis Mountain Rescue Team. The man was taken down the

---

* This one occasion was actually two. A Vauxhall Frontera was discovered near the summit of Snowdon in September 2011. The driver had followed the railway line in the car and abandoned it near the top. Arrested and bailed after the car's recovery, he promptly drove it to the summit again.

mountain by the train, then to hospital by helicopter, where he was found to
be suffering with hypothermia and severe frostbite to his feet. Without doubt
the swift action of his rescuers saved his life. It was October.*

The Principality's highest peak certainly hasn't always been viewed as such
a soft touch. Before the railway made its debut in 1896, Snowdon was considered a rather scary mountain. In *Wild Wales*, George Borrow's dandyish 1862
meditation on the country, he quotes an old Welsh proverb: "'It's easy to say
yonder is Snowdon; but not so easy to ascend it." Therefore I'd advise you to
brace up your nerves and sinews for the attempt.'

And if Snowdon's conditions are difficult to predict year-round, in winter
they become hell for the unprepared, occasionally and unpredictably reaching
near-Himalayan severity between November and February. Yet for some, even
this has its perks. In the winter of 1952 the strange spectacle of a party of tall,
rangy climbers could frequently be observed setting off up the slopes of
Snowdon and the nearby Glyders whenever a poor forecast was issued,
adorned with severe-looking equipment and long lengths of rope. Months
later, in May 1953, members of the same team would make the historic first
ascent of Mount Everest. For these men – which included John Hunt, Edmund
Hillary and George Band – Snowdon galvanised preparations for the world's
highest peak, worthily testing their storm-gear and ice-climbing skills during
some of the mountain's shriller moments. It was a good choice: in winter snow
and wind, Snowdon's angles and ridges weren't so far removed from the slopes
of Everest as you might expect in terms of physicality, although obviously
lacking the freezing, asphyxiating altitude. So attached were the team to the
region, and so instrumental were the small but fierce peaks of Snowdonia in
cementing the convivial bond of teamwork gained through shared hardship,
that their annual reunion was held at the team's old haunt, the Pen-y-Gwryd
Hotel – less than a mile from where I now stood on the Bwlch y Moch. By
2003, however, the group's numbers had dwindled to such a point that there
was nobody in robust enough health to attend.

---

* The same man was rescued five months later after a 15-metre slip lower down on the same
mountain. Though he remained unnamed in the ever-respectful protocol of such things, a
spokesperson for Llanberis Mountain Rescue drily confirmed the twice-unlucky – or, indeed,
twice-lucky – man had been identified as 'a previous client'.

But even amidst such freezing peril, people think of the café and the train, and set off under-prepared up Snowdon's slopes right into the bones of winter. Expecting good cheer, a cup of tea and an easy way off at the top, the unwary expend all their energy on the ascent and fail to realise that the summit is only half the effort. For your mind, the top is the finish line – the apex towards which all your concentration is directed. But for your body, it's merely the half-way point. The physical and emotional crash of summiting, coupled with the underestimation of what a descent demands as your wits slowly unravel, are the reason why – on all mountains, everywhere, and by a considerable margin – most accidents occur on descent.

The light was softening, and cloud was quietly filling the valleys around me by the time I reached the path split beyond Bwlch y Moch. Onward: the Pyg Track, marked by a smart stile emblazoned with the path's name in English and Welsh on sympathetic blue plastic. Right: a rough, steep path that ascended towards a tall, knobbly bulk. Immediately my pace dropped as the ground tilted and I felt the first pulls of grassy steepness beneath my boots. Within minutes, my choice of route had begun to assert its personality, the path zigzagging up the prow of increasingly defined mountainside. The next stile bore the words 'Crib Goch'. This sign was signal red.

Around twenty minutes later, the ground started to steepen again. Then came the first naked rock on the ridge. It was aggressive-looking – many small flakes, angled skyward, like the spines of a balled hedgehog. I took hold of it. It was abrasive and eel-slick. Where the rock had weathered and crumbled to grout the spines it was a weak pink, a clue to the source of the translation of Crib Goch: literally 'red ridge'. The path – such as it was – slinked vaguely amongst the outcrops, their ledges and flakes offering grab handles for balance where the path was too steep. Modest drops began to open to the left and right, until – about ten minutes from the stile – I could go no further.

In front of me was a large rock buttress, 40 or 50 metres wide. To carry straight on looked woundingly steep, but there were signs of a path on both sides of the obstacle – a thin, pink ribbon of scree draped over the rock. I took the one on the right, which vanished after a few metres at a series of mean-looking slabs. Traversing back beneath the buttress onto the left path, it began to wind beneath large, increasingly precarious overhangs that swiftly became awkward – like trying to limbo-dance under an eave. A potential way through lay up a narrow gully, but as I took hold of the rock and pulled, it became clear this was a move I wasn't going to be able to reverse should it turn out to be a dead end. My right leg, jammed into a crack for purchase, began to shake.

This was ridiculous. Barely onto the ridge, I was already in trouble. Maybe it was my nerves making me indecisive. Maybe I'd taken a wrong turn and was on a path to nowhere. Maybe I shouldn't be doing this at all.

Mal had told me to take the ridge on the nose at the first rock step; I hoped this wasn't what he was talking about. I pulled out my phone and called up the map, zooming right in and peering at the little blue arrow that represented me, frantically changing direction, mirroring my movements. According to this the path climbed Crib Goch just to the right of the ridge's crest – a few metres from where I was now standing. I'd tried that, and it hadn't felt right. Clicking the map off, I looked around my little ledge. On a ridge like this, it was pointless trying to follow the map with microscopic faith. I needed to feel my way up.

Gingerly, I began to descend the way I'd come. Reaching a broad, grassy bower below the buttress, I took a step back and studied the rock face. Head on, it certainly appeared possible. Big holds, large cracks to wedge parts of my body into – there were plenty of things to grab onto and hang off, but I still didn't like it. From the looks of things, that was pretty much how this ridge was going to go: physically doable, but requiring a certain mental commitment. I leaned against the cold, briny-smelling rock. Standing there, running through the consequences of a mishandled traverse in my head, thinking of home and headlines, family messily sobbing unanswerable 'why' questions … this wasn't doing anything. What the hell was stopping me here: the intimidation of the route itself, or my own horror-story-driven fear?

Using a flake of rock, I pulled myself off my feet as if peeping over a wall. The rock ahead ascended steeply, but it was broken, full of holds. I *could* climb that. Could *probably* climb down it, too. All it took was a decision.

A breath, then I pulled myself onto the step. A surge of adrenaline hit my legs as I lumbered up the first six feet of the rock. Don't fall. Stay confident. This was it: I was on Crib Goch. Up or bust.

It felt good to have made a decision. Right or wrong, it didn't matter now. As I climbed, my hands and feet finding holds easily, a tentative confidence grew – a kind of pragmatic resignation to the simple job in hand, which now simply had to be done. I could sense a drop opening to the right; I ignored it, keeping my movements as smooth as possible. I kept waiting to get stopped for long enough for my senses to realise the trouble I was getting myself into, but it never came. It wasn't easy – I wouldn't tackle it in high heels, that's for damn sure – but after the initial rock step my uncertainty began to subside. For the time being I could breathe.

Ahead was a long and tapering ramp of stubby rock. It was broad in comparison with the claustrophobic cracks of just a few moments earlier, high enough to be exhilarating, yet secure-feeling. The surroundings were beginning to take on the jaunty perspective of great height, but I was still very much on the mountain's flanks.

It didn't last. A finger of rock tilting out over a drop marked the beginning of the stretch known as the Pinnacles, collectively comprising the knife-edged part of the ridge that Crib Goch was famous for. This rocky frill was the second of Mal's 'exciting' bits. Again, two choices: the technically easier climb over the top, no doubt accompanied by the sort of airy, hit-the-deck-and-hold-on panic of great height on both sides; or an awkward, slip-friendly traverse beneath it to the left over one long drop to the right. I could see that the extent of the exposure was going to be hidden until I'd made my choice, so any ideas about just 'having a look' before committing to a move wouldn't work.

Another moment of pause. The light was fading rapidly, and here I was at another uncertain commitment. Scraping a solid foothold from the loose scree beneath my feet, I took a breath to steady my knees, then – taking option one – hauled myself untidily onto the top. And there it was: the crest of Crib Goch, flat and straight, an upturned comb of rock spines as wide as a park bench. At its centre, the ridge was cut by a monstrous vein of white quartz, from a distance resembling a tangled parachute draped over the bristles – minus a dangling, panicking sky diver. Beyond, a thickening and jumbling of the rock suggested the end of the Pinnacles and a descent into the Bwlch Coch, the grassy notch at which I'd be over the worst of the bad ground, and in search of my camp for the night. All I had to do was get there. It looked a long way off.

The first pinnacle was tall and comfortingly huggable. Inching round to the left of it, I stepped out onto the crest in a low stoop, arms spread in a wide triangle in front of me, as if trying to ward off jumping terriers. A draught of air came from below as voids opened to both sides and I inched beyond grab-distance of the pinnacle. A few steps along the crest and I'd reach a small cluster of pointy rocks I could crouch against. All it took was four or five steps, and the means to link them together. One step, two, don't look down, three, four … there. I spotted a gearstick-sized needle of rock; I lunged and grabbed it. It moved. I froze.

Heights, as far as your body is concerned, are the enemy. Look over a drop and you trigger a sequence of chemical events between your brain and your limbs – a kind of biological Mexican wave – that begins with a massive dump of epinephrine (otherwise known as adrenaline) from your adrenal glands. This hormone quickens your pulse rate, increases respiration, re-routes energy from your digestive system to more pressing physical applications, and releases nutrients and sugar flow to the limbs for a bit of short-term muscular zing. Hang out over a huge drop and you might describe such feelings as a hollow belly, a fluttery heart and a feeling of jittery, almost narcotic energy in your extremities that you could mistake for the irrational urge to 'jump over the edge'. You don't want to jump over the edge, of course. What you're experiencing is a primal biological reaction from your body that you're somewhere you shouldn't be. A reaction that says, hey – if you feel like escaping whatever peril into which you've gone and landed yourself, here's an evolution-crafted helping hand designed to channel all your available energy into doing just that.

This response is commonly referred to as 'fight-or-flight', though a more contemporary – and apt – term is 'fight-or-flight-or-freeze'. It's probably what has led to all those cases of people becoming cragfast on Crib Goch: a realisation of sudden, frightening vulnerability followed by a mutinous physiological rush, which, in delicate situations demanding calm and considered movements, might actually add to your problems. Not moving is therefore a fairly logical, if temporary, tactic – especially when you're in an environment where gravity is against you and simply 'letting go' will be the end of you.

My knees were shaking. I was hoping I'd be bolder than this and not succumb to fear this early, but I'd seen the drop – and now couldn't ignore it. The moving shard of rock had something rather more solid adjacent to it; I now clung to this and considered my next move. Ahead, the ridge was taking on an eerie quality in the thickening dusk. The light had softened, and the landscape was beginning to lose its contrasts. Fighting to keep confidence – and therefore decisiveness – under my control, I stepped up onto the crest again, and focused on my feet. Just like walking along a pavement. A very tall pavement.

The crest itself is fairly linear, maybe a foot wide, made of crenellated, fractured rock that's broken up into halved-brick-sized blocks – small enough to step over, but the perfect size to trip the boots of the cocky or complacent. It's given a certain potency by the ever-present drop to the right. The bedding planes of the rock are tilted in such a way that the north face is cut at a severe angle, meaning that the ground is shallower to the left – a long, loose slope at an angle of about 70 degrees. If you took a slip this way you still wouldn't stop, but psychologically the drop was easier to deal with, and as I continued to inch along the chewed crest I could see the polished rock where thousands of feet had found passage a few feet down on this slope using the very apex as a handrail. This wasn't hard to understand, because a fall to the right would be comprehensively fatal – hundreds of feet of air, terminating far below with a deep ramp of pink scree. The sense of dread isn't relentless, however, as several grassy platforms and accommodatingly flat slabs of rock punctuate the ridge's narrow first stretch – good spots to stop, breathe, have a chocolate bar and a little cry if you want, before reviewing your progress and looking further along the ridge to what's coming.

A level block the size of a car bonnet appears a few feet beyond the big quartz vein – up close, it no longer resembles a stranded parachute but a rock sprayed with whitewash – and I chose this as a place to take a moment's rest. From here, the architecture of the ridge is awesome, and your position – dare I say – incredibly exhilarating. Snowdon itself squares up to you now; a massive pyramid, slightly offset, its face acres of grey, deep-wrinkled rock punching skyward from its glacial valley, where the black waters of Glaslyn stare blankly upwards like a dead eye. It's beautiful, and brutally so.

Beyond this point Crib Goch begins to undulate like a sine wave, rearing up into impressive rock turrets then dropping down again into slacks of narrow crest. It also begins to slink, snake-like, from side to side, creating tall, semicircular buttresses that bulge from the cliff and accentuate the long drops.

From this promontory I caught a glimpse of the way ahead. It was a sight to raise blisters.

The ridge rose into two blade-like towers of shocked-looking rock, one after the other. I followed the line of travel with my eyes over the first, and felt sick; its crest tilted over the biggest chasm on the ridge, an overhang. It looked horrible – the prospect of climbing it like shimmying up an angled flagpole on the roof of a skyscraper.

Reaching the first of these towers, the rock underfoot became grander – shed-sized pieces of cracked rock replacing the fidgety, crenellated crest. Looking for polished rock that would suggest a line of travel, I began to ascend, the rock closing in around me for the first time in a while. This was not an unwelcome feeling, but, as I climbed, an uncomfortable thought began to creep in to my head amidst the echoing scratches of my steps. I couldn't see the drop any more. Where was it? Was I over it? Was I suddenly going to pop my head above the skyline and be confronted with it?

Feeling suddenly vulnerable – perhaps because the end was in sight – I steered clumsily around the block on the very top and I found a truncated staircase of boulders that led down into the slack between the two towers with a deep gully opening in between. The next tower pushed me off the left – a labyrinth of cracks and slabs above Crib Goch's steep southern slopes. Traversing around led me to a few scrubby descents and a messy scramble over abrasive rock, but then a gap appeared round the rocks to my left, broad and tufty. Two more moves, then a fizz of relief that shivered through my body.

Crib Goch was done and I allowed myself a little whoop of elation. The platform I was on felt huge, luxuriously so. If I so wished, I could even fall over and not die. I felt like doing it just because I could. And the rest was within reach: an easy descent to my right led into Mal's valley, and somewhere to put up my tent.

Enjoying the silence, the feeling, and the surge of my heartbeat in my ears, it began to dawn on me where I was standing. Ahead was the Clogwyn y Person arête; the place where, in 1960, John Brenchley, John Itches and Tony Evans became lost in the mist, and fell to their deaths. Right there.

I traced a plumb line from a point on the arête to the valley floor, then another. Any fall from there looked a chilling prospect; even in the comely weather of the evening it was easy to see there wasn't a thing the boys could have done to save themselves.

After rewarding myself with a biscuit, I pulled my phone out to send a text message to Mal before beginning my descent into the valley for the night.

I had an unread message that I must have missed whilst high on Crib Goch: 'Forecast poor tomorrow, but rain isn't due until 3 to 4 a.m. Might be worth heading for the summit tonight. Mal.'

Oh, hell. Really? It was now 10.30 p.m. The legacy of a diffused sunset still faintly lit the sky, but it was weakening. I read the message again, my heart heavy. I could ignore it. I was tired and looking forward to my sleeping bag; and now here was the prospect of another couple of hours' walk to a much more exposed, rockier place. An ascent into the gathering darkness with a forecast of bad weather wasn't in my plan – but Mal was right. The last thing I needed was to be clobbered by bad weather in the night, then be faced with either a wild climb to the summit in the rain or a dejected descent back to Pen-y-Pass. I looked down from the col into Cwm Glas, my intended campsite. Immediately I could see two or three accommodating spots a few hundred metres down the valley; one by a stream, another by a small lake. Cups of whisky-spiked cocoa, good, natural shelter, a reprieve from strength-sapped nerves … splendid. I could be there, tent up, in twenty minutes. A hard image to resist.

I looked over to the south-west and balked. A bank of cloud had spilled over Y Lliwedd on the opposite side of the horseshoe – the first wave of an advancing charge of bad weather. Visibility would be the first to go, and much sooner than dawn. If Mal's forecast was right, rain wouldn't be far behind. I had no real urge to experience the weather rife within Snowdon's accident statistics, nor did I have any real urge to become one. One thing was inescap-able: the narrow window of stable weather that had remained open for me on Crib Goch was now rapidly closing. If I wanted to get to the top with any degree of decorum I'd have to summit tonight, and quickly.

Pulling out my drink bottle, I peered into it. Half a litre left, at most. Snowdon's top was a bare cap of rock; no streams, no little lakes with outflows from which to scoop water. I had 300 metres of ascent to go and my throat was already dry as a stick. Rationing my water would be miserable, but possi-ble. After a longing look down the valley towards the campsite that wasn't to be, I started up the other side of the ridge – the Crib y Ddysgl – this time in haste. The ground was easier, less steep, but still complex. I might even have enjoyed it had I not been eager to beat the weather to the summit.

I can't tell you when it happened, but at some point I lost the path.

Although the ground beneath my feet no longer had any definition, I could still see. Without the sensory bludgeon of artificial light, darkness quietly creeps up on you. You'll walk and walk, and then eventually you'll stop to adjust your clothing or have a wee and realise that at some point, whilst your back was turned, it's gone and gotten properly dark on you.

I'd been avoiding getting out my head torch, partly to enjoy the primal oddness of climbing a mountain in the cool, grey-blue tones of dusk, and partly because my night vision – slowly matured over the last hour of failing light – would be instantly buggered the second I looked at something bright. My phone map was bright, so I didn't give it due attention, and before long I was groping up a black slope following my nose. I could see the angled skyline of the mountain above me against the sky – but any sense of scale had long disappeared, along with the detail of the ground. *Surely* I was almost up by now.

A noise caught me as I stepped over a small gully. It was the giggle of running water. With a cry of happiness, I downed what I had left in the bottle, then found a fast-flowing part of the burrowed-in stream and refilled. Now at least I had something I could cook with.

I continued to freelance along the slope, which was covered in dinner plates of loose scree. Perhaps the darkness was a blessing, as I now had no idea of the consequences of a slip. If it descended smoothly to the valley floor – unlikely, given the considerable height I'd quickly gained – little more than bruises and scuffs. Or perhaps I was on a scree fan draped atop a vertical cliff – in which case, a mis-step, an untidy fall, a roll and a swift acceleration down the loose ground towards an edge …

I shuddered, and focused on my feet and balance. Some of the most dangerous spots on this mountain weren't knife-edges; they were slopes like this, which didn't present the same kind of instant, shake-you-by-the-lapels danger that makes your movements delicate, like on Crib Goch. Up there, the peril you're in is hardly subtle and you can react – if not exactly in a way that will expedite your escape – in a manner that will at least make you pause for considerable thought and a re-check of your movements. But on a slope like this – darkness notwithstanding – it's quite possible to swagger onto danger-ous terrain with your hands practically in your pockets, ignorant of just how lethally steep the ground you're on is until a slip sends you tumbling down it. This sort of scenario appeared to account for many accidents on Snowdon, particularly in the winter, when snow hid the subtle shifts of the ground. I'd heard a story of a rescue team who were dispatched to find a casualty below a notorious steepening next to the Snowdon railway, which – in winter – becomes a hardened ice slope above the lip of a cliff. The team found a man dead at the base of the cliff, but it was only when descriptions of clothing and timings were compared that the team realised that these didn't quite match – this person was another victim, as yet unreported. The man they'd been called to assist was found later, also dead.

Amber lights appeared below like the view from an aircraft when I pulled myself over the lip of the ridge and stood up on the broad shoulder that arced towards the peak of Yr Wyddfa* – Snowdon's summit. The views from here in daylight are said to be some of Britain's most expansive; in optimum clarity four countries – England, Wales, Scotland, Northern Ireland – can be seen, as well as the Isle of Man. Although almost hypnotised by the odd sense of seeing this view at night and in only a gentle breeze, I spotted the path and joined it, grateful for the opportunity to relax and enjoy the feeling of approaching the highest point in England and Wales in exhilarating darkness.

Ahead, a splinter of angled rock known as the Finger Post marked the top of the Pyg Track, the beginning of which I'd left earlier before turning on to Crib Goch. All around, the smouldering carpet of light was punctuated by huge holes of darkness; it took a moment for me to realise that these were the mountains. It's an odd reversal; in daylight the mountains take the stage, with humankind very much in the wings – hidden even. But with darkness nothing

---

* Meaning, literally, 'the grave'. It's thought this title relates to Arthurian legend – King Arthur is reputed to have died on the mountain, having tossed his sword Excalibur into Llyn Llydaw. Nearby Bwlch y Saethau means 'Pass of the Arrows', where Arthur's knights did battle. After Arthur's death it's said they crawled into the cracks of Y Lliwedd to await his return. This is one bizarre sight that hasn't as yet been seen on Snowdon.

natural is lit, and the sinuous extent of man's touch on this landscape is revealed.

Continuing towards the summit on the breezy walkway, my peripheral vision was snagged by something unnaturally linear slinking up to me from the right: the railway. That was it. As much as anyone could – or would want to – on this mountain, I was able to relax. Even if the worst happened, if meteorological hell broke loose tonight and I had to beat a hasty retreat – this was my handrail. It was an odd anticlimax. Normally, such comforting civility is encountered lower down when your expedition is unwinding, not just as you reach the top. This summit was hardly going to be a wilderness experience; but after the emotional test of Crib Goch, maybe I'd earned a bit of security.

A summit camp hadn't actually been in my plan, but it might be a fun feeling and would certainly fit the *modus operandi* of being on the mountain at its quietest, most changeable time: of all the 56 million people in England and Wales tonight, I'd be the highest. And more importantly, I had the grand podium of Snowdon entirely to myself, with the warm feeling of having done Crib Goch. Normally this place would be heaving with all manner of traffic, even in ropey weather. And yet here was I, feet from the summit, all alone – the mountain equivalent to finding the keys to the Louvre and sneaking in after closing time. Maybe this wasn't such a bad idea after all.

I reached the summit shortly after midnight, the low hum of a generator and the strange, mysterious-from-a-distance glow of a vending machine inside the crouched café a surreal greeting, and reminders of this mountain-top's queer civility. Keeping the long, grey building and the railway behind me, I climbed the steps to the concrete pillar that marked the very top, trying hard to imagine the summit without them, as indeed has everyone seeking wild-ness here since the first building went up here in the 1820s.

It was colder up here. The wind was kicking up too, and very quickly. From Snowdon's brass summit plate, I stared out into an opaque, squally blackness. The dark shapes of the horseshoe's limbs were gone. In fact, there was nothing – no lights in the distance, no twinkles in the sky – just depthless gunmetal. It took a moment to realise why: I was looking into a wall of cloud, barrelling onto the mountain from the south-west and pouring into the deep valley beneath the summit like floodwater breaking a levee. Pretty soon the expanse of lights that had held my attention on the last stretch to the summit would be gone, too. Good timing, in that the bad weather had held off for the tricky stuff; bad timing in that it had arrived just as I reached the highest, most exposed point of the country. Nothing to do now but hunker down, batten up and hold on.

Crouching in the stony lee of the café's wall, I threw down my pack and started to pull out the rudiments of a camp – less a place to sleep and relax, more somewhere to keep out of the weather for a few hours. Pulling out my little tent, I quickly bowed the poles into position. The summit ground was solid rock; tossing a few helmet-sized boulders into the tent to weigh it down, I wrangled the flysheet over the frame, the wind doing its best to mischief any attempts to secure it. Within a few minutes – after some guy-rope fiddling and a lot of swearing – the tent approached some sort of solidity and I was able to dive inside.

The night was uncomfortable. After some inflatable noodles and hot chocolate, I attempted to sleep as the weather continued to break against the summit. The wind went from unnervingly persistent to worryingly determined, gusting severely enough on occasion to prompt a moon-eyed, sit-up-and-brace-the-walls position, all the whilst accompanied by the sound of heavy rain hitting the nylon in sharp, radio-static crackles. Constructed to complement the mountain's natural lines, the café offered little shelter and if anything seemed to give the wind a more aerodynamic trajectory towards my camp.

I spent the rest of the dark hours in a state of twitchy half-doze. A streak of torchlight went across the tent at 3.30 a.m., accompanied by men's voices. In a soundscape you so want to be comfortingly silent, voices on a mountain are an alarming addition – like lying in your bed at night and hearing a creak you can't place. Concerned as to who could possibly be up on this summit in these conditions in the deep hours and not be inside a tent, I almost investigated – but the wild weather and the darkness of the situation convinced me otherwise, and whoever they were departed as quickly as they came.

At 5 a.m. the flysheet pulled free and began flapping wildly, allowing daybreak's watery light to leak into the tent. Packing up my sleeping bag, mat, stove and sweet wrappers, I waited for a lull in the wind and left the tent into the dawn. The gale didn't seem so bad out of the tent. The landscape, soft in the half-light, was covered in a burst duvet of cloud enlivened by the still-robust wind, and a steadying rain had established itself on the mountain. Occasional peaks on the horseshoe popped out of the fluff now and then as I watched – Y Lliwedd, the summit of Crib Goch – but the cloud was thickening in the warming air and soon visibility would be lost in grey sludge. Brewing up some coffee in the shuttered doorway of the café – the very spot where that unfortunate frostbite victim had lain unconscious in a snowdrift whilst his digits slowly hardened – I tried to shift the fuzzy, detached feeling of being up in a chilly dawn after a night of little sleep.

Amongst its summit buildings and straight-cut concrete, it was hard not to view Snowdon as vexed, torn between its status as an elemental, dangerous environment and the crowd-pleasing persona it had been forced to adopt. You can't knock its primal qualities: this thing is a crocodile. But with its station and concrete and shuttered, platitude-engraved summit building, it's a crocodile forced to wear a party hat.

But whatever has become of Snowdon's very top in its recent history, crossing Crib Goch hadn't disappointed. Exhilarating and worthy, besides the thrilling experience the route had given me something else – confidence. This was good, as higher, wilder peaks were coming.

Cooling the stove in a puddle, I waited for the hiss of steam to subside. Then, securing my rucksack and zipping up my jacket, I walked out of the sheltered doorway and set off down the Pyg Track, into the rain.

5 PLUNDER

From a ceiling beam in the bar of the Pen-y-Gwryd Hotel a row of walking boots hang by their laces like dangling feet from a line of gallows. Some are very old: the hobnail type, collapsed and discoloured, their soles stiff with age.

This place is part hotel, part museum, part tomb. The walls are panelled with dark wood, and many are hung heavy with mountaineering memorabilia. Facing you as you sit sipping a pint of dark beer in the lounge is a cabinet filled with yellow tanks the size of marrows, each emblazoned with a Union flag. To the first men who climbed Kangchenjunga – third-highest mountain in the world – in 1955, these prevented them succumbing to sickness in the thin air, filled with life-bearing oxygen to top up the deficit burgled by altitude. Behind you hangs a photograph of Mount Everest's first ascenders Edmund Hillary and his friend Tenzing Norgay. Tenzing's skin is crisped and blackened by sun and dirt, and both of them sit drinking lemonade from tin mugs. One of those mugs is displayed in a cabinet in the next room, alongside the white rope that tied the pair together on their ascent of the mountain and fragments of rock carried from the highest place on earth. Also present are the many signatures of mountaineers old and new who have made a solemn stop at the isolated hotel – crouched on the corner of the Pass of Llanberis in Snowdon's northeast shadow – to be in the presence of the ghosts who made that remarkable journey to the highest point on the world.

Legend has it that when news of the successful ascent of 29 May finally reached the hotel at 1 a.m. on 2 June 1953, the owner announced that any guest not in the bar with a glass of champagne in their hand in ten minutes would be thrown out the following morning. It describes itself as a 'mountaineers' hotel ... which is a haven from the relentless grind of modernity'. You can well believe it.

A line of pictures runs along the northern wall of the 'smoke room'; a group, pictured in the same place year after year – outside the door, just there. A sudden lurch into colour in the mid-sixties is followed by increasingly modern clothes, shrinking hair and steadily diminishing numbers. They were all here, that first summit team; they trained on the mountains nearby for the expedition that would carve itself into mountaineering history like no other. And year after year, back they came. The tall, wild-looking one with the big grin; his name would be the one people would remember most, although it was the summit photograph of his partner – diminutive, smiling – that people would see, axe aloft, flags straightened by the jet stream, the harsh tones of snow and space, and him, bridging them with his iconic pose. It was a long way for Tenzing to come back to Snowdonia from Darjeeling. But he still came back when he could.

They're all gone now, this climbing team. The last one, George Lowe, died in 2013. It's over 60 years since those vital young mountaineers first gathered here at the Pen-y-Gwryd Hotel, warming themselves from the savage air of the Snowdonian winter, to eat and be merry before tramping off to the frigid climbing huts where they slept.

Some would say the mountain they climbed has gone, too – or at the very least plundered beyond recognition. In 1953 Mount Everest was the Third Pole, the realm of elite, trusted, specially selected adventurers. Today it can be had for money. Base Camp is now a small town, people step over the dead and the dying as they climb for the summit on fixed ropes, children have climbed it, and all have witnessed its troubling mix of horror and glory. It's perhaps understandable the Pen-y-Gwryd Hotel does its best to cling to the atmosphere of a seemingly more honourable time when such things remained an inconceivable dystopia. Then mountaineering was truly steps upwards into the unknown, and all you had or needed were those you were with, and the collective will to try.

After a disgracefully lavish breakfast in Llanberis, I'd had a snooze to allow my body to recharge. Then, with the sun over the yardarm, I treated myself to a drink at the Pen-y-Gwryd. I'd never been there before, and it seemed a fitting place to reflect on the excitement of my own slightly more modest achievement, amidst mountaineering's greatest ghosts. These aren't the only ghosts you can find in Snowdonia. They certainly are not the only ones who inhabit the long shadows of these mountains, and not all of them had climbing on their mind when they entered into their cold pall. Perhaps one place above all others could offer the perfect podium to appreciate this: a place carved by both of Snowdonia's distinctive, dichotomous mountain conditions, and a place of great aesthetic beauty long revered by climbers. From where I was now sitting in the Pen-y-Gwryd Hotel amongst the spoils of Mount Everest, this mountain stood five and a half miles south, amidst a landscape littered with the legacy of a very different kind of human plunder.

In his 1952 book *Three Bear Witness*, the novelist Patrick O'Brian – later of the successful nautical books featuring 'Master and Commander' Jack Aubrey – describes arriving in a Welsh valley to find a fictitious mountain, one he calls the Saeth. 'I had expected hills, little more, yet here was a mountain. Its height in figures meant nothing: there was the majesty, the serene isolation, that you expect only from ten thousand feet or more. It was a mountain as a child draws a mountain, a sharp, stabbing triangle.'

An Englishman by birth, O'Brian lived in London during the Second World War. During this time it's claimed he worked in Intelligence, before moving to an isolated, Welsh-speaking valley in Snowdonia named Cwm Croesor.

Anyone who knows Cwm Croesor even vaguely will realise that the Saeth is no fictional peak; it's a faithful rendering of a real mountain, renamed. Whilst living in the valley, O'Brian befriended a young shepherd named Edgar Williams, and the two often discussed the mountain that stood grandly above the valley. It was said the mountain resembled the shape of a jousting helmet, and that its Welsh name was a modified version of the English word *knight*. But Williams didn't think so, and it was he who suggested the name *Saeth* – meaning 'arrow' – when O'Brian asked the shepherd what he'd have called it. This became its name in fiction. Its name in fact is Cnicht. And as I approached the valley of Croesor in the slanted afternoon sunshine, it was this striking mountain I could see, peering through a quivering aperture of backlit spring leaves.

Cnicht isn't a particularly big mountain, but then it doesn't have to be. See it from the road separating Beddgelert and Aberglaslyn and it snares your eye like a fishhook, as it emerges from behind a wall of anonymous, knobbly crags – instantly the most enticing thing in the view.

As O'Brian described the Saeth, Cnicht is indeed a classic, cartoonish rendering of a difficult mountain: a triangle with crenellated sides rising to a sharp summit, the kind you'd plant a flag on. Surely to climb this you'd need axes and clanking implements. You'd have to ascend its near-vertical slope with a rope, step after step, like Batman and Robin ascending a skyscraper. The view from the top would be the best anyone had ever seen. Then you would return from the summit for salted pork, vast fires and brandy, ideally without too many casualties. But as is often the case with mountains, appearances can be deceptive.

An ascent of Cnicht isn't merely a climb, either; it's a cultural experience. Croesor is isolated, but the reward is a place quite extraordinary. In summer, when the trees are brimful with leaves, it's hard to gather the extent of this little place of handsome, solid buildings with cheerful blue window frames. Our old writer friend Showell Styles lived here, raising his family, working as a guide and running the local post office. Styles knew Cnicht rather better than most; on his return from the peak in 1994 – aged 86 – he announced the ascent was his last. It was his 879th.

What is obvious immediately is that the residents of Croesor regard the mountain almost as a deity. The first thing you see as you cross the river from the car park is a small circle of fractured slate plaques like broken headstones. Upon them local children have carved tributes to the mountain. It's unique and touching that a community would form such a symbolic dialogue with the peak overlooking them. It certainly gives the place an atmosphere.

It's perhaps not that mysterious, though. Whilst today Croesor's connection with the mountain leans more towards the artistic, its story began firmly with industry. Everywhere its legacy is in the walls, is laid in the fences and keeps the rain out of every building. And whilst its sharp, fractured evidence is today seamlessly absorbed into the village's character as it is in its structure, in the mountains above it stands starkly in ruin, destitute and austere. Built with swift vulgarity, the scars this industry left are yet to be reclaimed by the slow, healing touch of nature.

Before they were used as training grounds for climbers tackling the roof of the world, the mountains of Snowdonia once literally roofed the world itself. The explosion of the Industrial Revolution during the 19th century pushed the demand for quality slate through the roof – and most of this was provided by Snowdonia. The ghost of what was a monstrous slate industry looms large over the region, sometimes literally so. In their Victorian heyday, the towering works at Dinorwig above Llanberis and Penrhyn near Bethesda were the biggest slate quarries in the world, with Blaenau Ffestiniog – a crouched town surrounded by massive, scarred cliffs and waste heaps just a few miles over the hills from Croesor – the biggest mine. This plunder was rightly prized: beautifully smooth, deeply coloured and perfect of split, Welsh slate was – and still is – considered the best in the world.

In 1865, around the same time that the working class and the mountains of North Wales were being brutalised in the quarries of Snowdonia, Edward Whymper was making the first ascent of the Matterhorn on the border of Switzerland and Italy. He was a product of another class, and a champion of another plunder: the conquering of continental peaks in what has come to be known as mountaineering's 'Golden Age'. Climbing was a game for the rich in the 19th century. Whilst the Industrial Revolution was flourishing in North Wales and northern England, young men and women of privilege with money and time to fritter on sporting achievements in far-flung places were making many of the most significant ascents in the Alps. It was a time of peculiar contrast. Quarrymen braved the cold and dirt, squalid accommodations and predictably horrific industrial accidents in an attempt to make a meagre wage whilst appalling weather, dangerous ascents and inevitable incidents were braved in the name of recreation by the rich in the Alps. The first ascent of the Matterhorn in 1865 was accompanied by appalling tragedy; four men were killed when a rope snapped near the summit. It seems that were you fortunate enough not to have adversity as a necessity, for some it was a necessity to seek a suitable replacement.

If Cnicht were to truly deserve its nickname – the 'Welsh Matterhorn' – this might be the case. But, happily, it's nothing like the Matterhorn, and it certainly doesn't need such a cheap comparison to make it extraordinary in its own right. Spend enough time spidering through guidebooks and you'll notice this 'Matterhorn' moniker is applied to quite a number of vaguely sharp and triangular mountains; several upland places in the UK have one, for instance, with varying degrees of tenuousness. It isn't a canny comparison, principally because the Matterhorn is terrifying and huge, whereas Cnicht is 689 metres high and can be climbed in an afternoon. But it does *look* daunting, and getting to that pencil-nib of a summit provides just the right amount of thrill.

The path from Croesor towards Cnicht is friendly and doesn't really start to ascend steeply until you're on the mountain itself. Instead it crosses the toes of the mountain's long south-west ridge, and toddles alongside it awhile as it gains its direction. Then it sharply traverses onto the mountain just beneath the spot where Cnicht bursts out of the ridge like a thorn through tweed.

I'd taken the track leading out of Croesor, which led through gladed farmland. After a few minutes of climbing, the trees peeled back and the landscape emerged.

Ahead I could see another walker, perhaps twenty minutes ahead of me, moving in and out of sight behind outcrops and the steepening skylines. At first I thought he was going more slowly than me and that I'd catch him; but every time I lost sight he would then reappear the same distance ahead of me, further up the mountain. As he approached the final pyramid of the peak I watched what he did. From where I was standing it looked almost impassable. To his eyes, up close and beneath, it would look much more amenable. From my vantage point, by way of my unsuspecting participant, I could indulge one of Cnicht's great allures: the illusion of extreme adversity.

Ahead, the mountain looked less daunting than it did earlier, more ant hill than arrowhead, but still an exciting and severely angled prospect. Mountains often do this: distance sharpens them, makes them look insurmountable. The mind sees them as objects of human scale, and imagines these faraway, javelin-sharp summits as barely wide enough to place both feet on. Then you get close, and they broaden, soften, become more accommodating. But their challenge becomes bigger, too. Suddenly the raggedy little rock point you saw from a mile away becomes a long, curving ridge line of considerable extent, weathering to bare rock steps and bristles that must be surmounted before the summit can be yours. Look at photographs of Mount Everest as seen from a distance and it's mind-lacerating: steep and frightening, impassable, impossible. You imagine a person would cling to it as if shimmying up a church steeple. But a steeple is an object on a human scale; a mountain is not. At close quarters Mount Everest is huge. Its slopes look more surmountable, its summit spacious enough for a dozen people to wander around in a stumbly wooze, their bodies in a confused fight between exultation and the desire to sit down and die.

This illusion has its advantages. See Cnicht from a mile away and you can impress people when you tell them you've climbed it. 'It looks so sharp!' they'll say with awe. 'It's not so bad up close,' you'll say back. (Actually you'll just fold your arms and concur with a contented 'Well, yeah,' a smug nod and misty eyes, aware that only you and the mountain know the truth.)

But get the opportunity to observe somebody on the mountain from a distance and illusion and reality combine, and you can witness human being in context with mountain. I watched him as he arrived at the base of the rock pyramid and, barely breaking stride, began to climb. He looked tiny against it, a little fleck of blue wending his way in and out of the rocks, with an occasional flash of pinky-white as he raised his arms to pull himself up. He stopped for a while, then crawled on, moving out of sight a few times before eventually, just as I was about to give up my vigil, I spotted a movement on the apex of the pyramid, a tiny silhouette rising briefly against the sky, then vanishing out of view, presumably onto the very top, tilted away from my low vantage point. And again, I was alone.

I'd climbed Cnicht twice before, and both times was struck by how perfect it was as a podium upon which to view the rest of Snowdonia from an unfamiliar angle. Cnicht has, throughout its entire western sweep from south to north, a view of intensely beautiful, rugged country. Catch it at this time of the late afternoon and the small lakes – *llyns* – that punctuate the angled outcrops of rock and mossy grasslands catch the setting sun and turn brilliant white. And in the distance, mountains layer deeply to a horizon of bulky shadows, arched and steep, the wall before the sea. The long, rollercoaster line of the Nantlle ridge, the messy silhouette of Moel Hebog – and further north, the unmistakable plunge of Snowdon's dramatic east face diving towards its lake-drowned cwm, from here lost to shadow. The sea is close: Porthmadog, its beach reclaimed from the estuary by the slate industry, and the languid snake of the Afon Glaslyn, fed in its infancy by Snowdon's lakes, winding thickly for the coast. But to the east, things look different. Something wounds the view.

The path climbed right to the crest of the ridge. Crossing a stile, for the first time I caught sight of Cwm Croesor, a long, deep trench running south-west to north-east parallel to the ridge as it climbs Cnicht. The drop is unexpectedly cavernous. I looked down into the valley, then up left towards Cnicht, and felt a familiar twitch in my stomach as my eyes travelled along the ridge to the summit, then traced the plunge-line down again to the valley floor. Illusion or not, it suddenly looked far more daunting than I remembered. Above it stood Cnicht's less dramatic but much higher mirror across the valley, Moelwyn Mawr. Then, like details emerging from one of those magic-eye paintings, my eyes began to catch things in the landscape. Irregularities. Or, rather, the opposite.

Being landscapes of slant, twist and knobble, anything linear in a mountainscape sticks out. Fences and walls, the ancient dry-stone divisions of farmland; these tend to – but don't always – peter out at an elevation of around 500 metres. Paths, with the notable exception of those on Snowdon (which, of course, also has the railway), tend to follow natural creases in the land. Often they're ugly, but most at least make some effort to blend in. But industrial scars – tramways, levels, hard-surfaced paths – are always orderly vulgarities amidst nature's beautiful chaos. They make no attempt to hide themselves, and even after the industry has long gone they lie straight and tight across the skin of the hills like drawn wires.

Other details. Opposite me, on the flanks of Moelwyn Mawr, a patch of grey rubble, the colour of pencil lead. It was a platform cut into the hillside, and on it stood what looked like the chars of a fire – blackened buildings, half decayed, completely abandoned, high on the mountain. The remains of the Croesor quarries. Though small, look hard and their extent begins to bleed, subtly but prolifically, into the rest of the view as you trace the long-quiet paths of industry through them.

I continued to climb. The grass was beginning to give way to rock, and as I arrived at the last buttress separating me from the summit of Cnicht the mountain's green skirt was pulled away. Angled steeply in front of me was the final ridge to the top, the right-hand skyline of that shocking triangle seen from a distance to the west.

The rock rises easily, a passage weaving steeply in and out of sharp outcrops but not so steeply for your hands to be needed: not at first. The lines of travel of hundreds of years of footfall following the most logical line through the rock, made the first section untroubling. Then the path began to disappear as the rock became steeper and the way less defined. From here, you could make it difficult if you wanted. Beds of slate, angled as if blown by the wind then frozen to its prevailing direction, rise out of the mountain at a steep rake. You can climb between the slate, grappling sheets of it above your head for balance like the overhead handrail of a tube train, and feeling on its edges the polished smoothing where others have done the same.

Cwm Croesor deepened even further to my right. The frayed edge of the mountain was more apparent now, its slope uninterrupted until the valley floor. Describing the Saeth, Patrick O'Brian called these 'great runs of shale, beds of it tilted up in ferocious slopes, and the lines of its fall'. Sure enough, from my vantage point on Cnicht these long chutes of pale fragments would take you all the way to the bottom were you silly enough to slip, gathering momentum as you went. Falling was not allowed.

Thankfully, it didn't seem likely. There was something comforting about the mountain, something oddly unthreatening. Of course, I might have felt differently were the rain and the wind and the cloud kicking the side of it, but the weather was still holding, the sky beginning to whiten where the sun had dropped, grading to deep blue on the eastern horizon. It was perfect weather for being out on the hill.

I tried to keep as close to the line of the sun as I could, but most of the route I was taking lay in shadow. Moss and grass grouted the rocks I climbed on, and it was colder and more enclosed, the sound of my boot scuffs and laboured breaths as I pulled myself up step after step close and scratchy.

The scramble didn't last long. I wanted it to, but before the novelty had the chance to wear thin, the skyline began to drop ahead of me and suddenly I was there, making the final few moves onto the summit.

It's a fantastic place. It feels like a mountaintop should, in polar contrast to arriving on top of Snowdon to find a Coke machine, a station, and rocks smoothed of their geological stories by a million feet. Compact, unadorned with a trig point or cairn, Cnicht is a summit as nature formed it. Weathered claws of volcanic rock browned and pitted by age angle out of the mountain's scalp; you have to walk across them to say you've stood on the very summit. Even someone short like me stands far proud of the highest rocks; reach the summit and you are without doubt the most prominent thing on it, and you feel it in the sensation of space and air. And it's small – not the precipitous point you see from a distance, but certainly a compact knub. That you're scrambling and using your hands until popping out on the very top again corresponds to this feeling of a mountain adventure conceived in a child's imagination, an ascent requiring your whole body right up until the final, grunting seconds when you stand up on the summit, the skyward extreme of that triangle.

I looked back from the summit down the ridge. Seen from a height lends it elegance, distance smoothes it of its imperfections, and it sweeps from the summit in an arc that's at once steep, then eases to a long, graceful trajectory back into the glades of Croesor. It's novel to think of that long sweep as being the same ridge that seems so dramatic from below. Viewing a mountain from the ground is all too familiar, but looking down from its top isn't and is worth enjoying for its unfamiliarity.

Taking a moment to appreciate just that – the inverse of the view from the road a couple of hours earlier – I did a little thing I like to do. You can do it too, if you're daft like me: stand at the roadside, close one eye and, arm outstretched, block out with your thumb the summit you're about to climb, as if trying to stem a leak from it. See how much of it you can cover. Then climb the mountain and find the roadside where you were standing a few hours earlier and do the same, noting how much of the ground your thumb covers. It's pointless, but an oddly addictive way of visualising your journey from one to the other.* Plus, get it just right and it also looks like you're doing something technical and important to anyone who happens to be watching. (Get it wrong and to the same observers it looks like you're giving a wonky thumbs up to somebody who couldn't possibly see you, which makes onlookers think you're either a bit mad or a bit drunk – neither of which is welcome on the summit of a mountain.)

Admittedly, it has a tough act to follow, but Cnicht's north-east ridge is something of an anticlimax. From the top it descends gently over a second,

---

* Primitive distance-measuring techniques were often practised by sailors and wilderness travellers, who would use their hands (or fingers) to measure the distance between the sun and the horizon, therefore the time left until sunset. The depth of four fingers, bladed and held horizontally outstretched (as if trying to compare a note on your palm to the text on a distant billboard) is around an hour – or 15 minutes a finger. On a much more profound scale, Apollo astronaut Jim Lovell would do a similar thumb-eclipse with the moon and the earth. He was once quoted as saying that, whilst blocking the earth out with his thumb from the cockpit of his stricken spacecraft Apollo 13, 'It dawned on me how completely insignificant we are. Everything I had ever known – my family, my country, my world – was behind my thumb.' Similar feelings are unlikely on Cnicht.

minor, top then gradually merges into a grassy whaleback. It's pleasant, but as a route it isn't spectacular in the doing, however spectacular the seeing; there's no intrepid descent from the pinnacle in a similar style to the ascent on the other side, as you would expect from such a triangular peak. But it's when crossing the mountain from south to north that you realise a certain amount of perspective is in play, and that this part of the mountain's backside is hidden from the road. Its sheer appearance is actually down to the steep ground on the north-west face, whereas the north-east ridge eases into a skywalk. I wandered along this whilst the mountain returned from bare rock to soft, hummocky grass.

All the while my eyes were fixed across the valley, where the mountain had been exposed. Something was emerging from the crook of the hill opposite: a black scratch, scabbed and charred, like a burst sore.

*   *   *

Y chwarel nid yw mwy – mae'n adfail prudd.
Heb swn peiriannau yn y llethol hedd,
A llu o'r gweithwyr heini yn y bed.

This is a passage from 'The Old Boys of Rhosydd', a poem written in Welsh by a slate quarryman named Richard Owen in 1930, the year the Rhosydd Quarry closed. Translated in Jean Napier's photobook *Rhosydd: A Personal View*, in English the lines read thus:

The quarry is no more, it is a sad ruin.
No sound of machines, the stillness overwhelms,
The wind whistles between the loose stones
And a host of lively workmen are in their grave.

Rhosydd is today much more of a ruin than it was in Owen's day. Whilst the most dramatic mountains of spoil and sliced mountainsides above Llanberis and Blaenau Ffestiniog are now tourist attractions, Rhosydd is too remote, too hidden, to be developed in this way. Today it stands bereft, its buildings a strange and erratic hyphenation on the landscape, and very slowly returning to the mountain.

Industrially cut slate is an extraordinary substance. Dry, it's a purple-grey matte, but its cut edges are things of brutal, parallel texture that brilliantly catch low sunlight when angled in walls and arches. It's quite beautiful. Wet, though, it goes black. Buildings built from it transform from stolidly handsome to brooding, and radiate a grim pall. They frown. And this place is the bleakest frown of all.

As I entered the quarry ruins through the gate at the head of the valley I smeared some water from a puddle onto the unblemished face of a table-sized fragment and watched it mirror, the evening sun catching its subtle relief. Then the moisture broke up, spread out and dissipated.

Walking on, a gigantic sprawl of hubcap-sized slate fragments – millions and millions of them – covered an area as big as a football pitch to my left. I walked on them, their clink beneath my feet like breaking china. On the other side of the path the buildings began. There was a row of rough-cut, hip-tall slabs of slate arranged in parallel lines facing each other, like the opposing pawns on an unplayed chessboard. They reminded me of the inscribed slates I'd seen in Croesor. For a moment, because of their order and appearance, I thought they were graves, or some sort of memorial, in keeping with the atmosphere of the place. But the stones were blank.

Work started near Rhosydd in the 1830s when slate was discovered by two men from Croesor. Its height and the site's remote location – then reached by packhorse – made transporting the quarried slate difficult and slow, and the early days were lean. But by 1886, despite considerable ups and downs in its fortunes and finances, the changing of ownership from entrepreneurs to a co-operative of local workers, and thanks to the addition of tramways in 1864, Rhosydd Quarry was one of the largest underground operations in North Wales outside of Blaenau Ffestiniog. Rhosydd slate was even used to roof London's Royal Mint.

During that period some 200 quarrymen were based here. Walking the miles up the mountain to the remote quarry before a day's work, then returning home at the end of the day – often in dreadful Welsh mountain weather – wasn't a viable option for most workers. Instead, they stayed on site.

What remains today of the barracks where the men of Rhosydd lived is a striking, lethal ruin, like a bombed-out Blitz site abandoned for nature to reclaim. Wandering between the tall, stern buildings, roofless and decaying, it struck me that the place was probably little more welcoming when in use.

The barracks resembled two rows of modest houses around fifty metres in length, facing each other across a muddy, grass-haired track where a street would have been were this a row of real homes. Instead, a tramway ran here for the disposal of rubbish. There would not have been much refinement in these dwellings, their inner walls resembling their outer walls, and their outer walls built from the very thing the men were digging from the mountain.

Although they appear almost identical on account of the uniformity of their construction material, the buildings to the south were built around 1860, those to the north in 1890. Some of the ruins still had recognisable features within; where they remained, the chimneys had their little fireplaces (bigger below, smaller up above where the second floor would have been), but many of these chimneys had collapsed into the houses, sometimes taking entire walls with them. As you'd expect – and confirmed by their advanced state of decay – the buildings were clearly constructed with convenience in mind; but it was a convenience that their hard-working residents would have had to live with up to six days a week, far from home, high above civilisation.

Alongside Richard Owen's poem, in her book of Rhosydd Jean Napier quotes a Mines Inspectorate report from the late 19th century that described the conditions within the barracks. It was, to say the least, damning. 'The men were nearly all sleeping two in a bed ... the rooms were dark, with a bad floor and an indifferent roof ... The inside walls were unplastered ... the whole arrangement showed a great disregard for comfort.' With no sanitation other than the nearby stream and often improvised protection against the weather – mud and turf were sometimes used to hold roof slates down against high winds – conditions here were thought to be amongst the worst, if not *the* worst, in the industry.

For some it was too much. They'd rather brave the elements than the squalor of the barracks (which, of course, the men had to pay for) and they walked to and from the quarry each day. Those who stayed seemed to rely on comradeship for comfort, and there are many accounts of Rhosydd quarrymen being a highly cultured bunch. As well as religious debate and education, which ranged from scripture to science, the Rhosydd Quarry Choir – whose recitals would often reverberate through the mountains (what that must have been to hear in this place!) – became revered, despite being allegedly reliant on a conveniently pitched shackle coupling for a tuning fork.

The conditions in the tunnels themselves were desperate. After the open-cast quarrying was exhausted, the quarry had to become a mine. Tunnels were dug at an incline where the slate met the next rock layer – typically these beds dipped north at around 25 degrees – from which the miners would cut horizontal floors into the slate at various levels, which would form the beginnings of chambers. At its peak there were 170 chambers, with over 5,000 tonnes of slate extracted per year. Work was undertaken with hand tools and by candle-light, only a few major tunnels being serviced with electricity. It was noisy, difficult and dirty work, which, like mountaineering, required strong physical endurance, tenacity and the ability to negotiate dangerous stretches of rock with confidence.

Today there are plenty of places in the old mine tunnels where you can get yourself into considerable trouble. An event known as the 'Great Fall' occurred in 1900, when a large section of the underground network collapsed, but even though many of the tunnels are today still explored by experienced potholers, I'm at pains to stress this is desperately dangerous for anyone who doesn't know what they're getting themselves into.

I had the briefest glimpse of this many years ago when, after an assignment for *Trail* magazine, two colleagues and I entered the tunnel known as the No. 9 Adit, following a tip-off from a caver who'd told us it was possible to access another part of the mountain via the tunnel. It was an appalling day; we'd seen nothing of the Rhosydd ruins bar some dark shapes set back in the mist as we delicately navigated towards the grid reference we'd been given. No. 9 wasn't hard to miss: a toothed hole the size of a garage door, draped with water threads at the end of a tapering cut set back from the buildings.

Bolstered by the courage that company inspires – never wise – and eager to get out of the rain that was leaking through our clothes, we went in, the water shin-deep in the tunnel. Head torches at full beam, we walked – and walked, and walked – first confidently, then hesitantly, as the white light of the tunnel door shrank to a pinprick behind us. Strange things were illuminated by our torches: old wagon tracks, assorted wreckage and peculiar white leach-ings from the walls. The water gradually shallowed our feet. The tunnel went on to such a distance that rendered the entrance an ineffectual pinprick of light. Turning off our torches briefly to experience it, the blackness was unbearable when we remembered where we were and, coupled with the acrid air, almost possessed actual physicality as if it were a solid thing, pressing in around us.

We continued for a few more minutes, until our torches alighted on something written ahead. One scrawled word: 'Rockfall'. Suddenly our resolve cracked, and a briskly unanimous decision was reached: flee.

Twenty minutes later, standing in the rain again and breathing in the fresh air, the three of us agreed we'd just done something pretty dumb. But my research back home – conducted largely with hubcap eyes and a gaping mouth – revealed that our experience had been relatively tame. There was a whole network of caves beneath Rhosydd that experienced considerable human traffic, albeit much more expert human traffic than us. There were zip-wires over chasms, fixed ropes, abseils, bridges, even an inflatable dinghy anchored for underground lake crossings over water the kind of blue you see in the tropics, but all enclosed in chambers of black slate amidst rust-reddened, century-old industrial wreckage. Some of these underground places had names – the Bridge of Death and the Chamber of Horrors being two particularly inviting examples – and all of them squirrelled through terrain that was constantly collapsing and flaking, using equipment whose reliability couldn't be assured. It was mind-boggling to think that beneath the armour of the mountain ran an underland of industrial, claustrophobic and Tolkienesque labyrinths, and even more mind-boggling to think that people went down there; a kind of mountain climbing in reverse, using the same arena in a very different manner. It was, obviously, exceedingly dangerous. But like most dangerous things, those who operated in these places clearly did so near the sharpest end of adventure's thrill.

Caving in general is a relatively youthful sport, and not – with the exception of old mines like Rhosydd – one whose challenge can be quantified by visual inspection, like in mountaineering. The fact is, nobody really knows how much there is to explore down there. One of the most important recent discoveries was made beneath the limestone cave systems of the Pennines, when a link was found between two extensive networks. The breakthrough – called 'Bruno Kranski' – meant that one caver could descend in Yorkshire, another in Lancashire and a third in Cumbria, and they could all sit and enjoy a game of cards and a sherry – or whatever it is cavers do down there – in the middle.* This was what many called the Holy Grail of British caving: a contiguous 55-mile – *55-mile* – system of grottoes, shafts, squeezes, tunnels and cathedral-sized caverns explored, mapped and described by the intrepid few who make this strange, dark, nightmare world their arena. The caves were linked in November 2011, making the mythical 'Three Counties' system a physical reality and creating the deepest caves (253 metres) in England and the longest in the UK, relegating the 41-mile South Wales system of Ogof Draenen into second place. This latter was discovered in 1994, and is continually being revised. Both prove that frontiers of exploration – true frontiers – continue to be pushed beneath the British hills. What once were places of work have become places of play – notwithstanding a few interesting historical digressions en route. The 'back door' that linked Rhosydd and Croesor quarries was only rediscovered in the late 20th century by a caving club from Hereford. Its finding was greeted with no small amount of alarm; both by the explorers who found their supposedly 'unknown' chamber packed to the rafters with high explosives, and by the well-known industrial chemical company who had locked them in there. It was, as this company presumably briskly learned that day, pointless bolting the front door when there was a back door standing open. Famously, the quarries of Manod near Blaenau Ffestiniog were used to store paintings from the National Gallery during the Second World War, and it's said many other forgotten bunkers lie beneath the mountains to this day.

Back in Rhosydd, I found the entrance to No.9 Adit once again. I knew what was in there beyond the empty black wall of the entrance, although, of course, any number of rockfalls might have occurred in the eight years since I'd been in. Just for ceremony I walked into the shaft, just under the lip of the entrance. Immediately I was hit by a deep chill that instantly raised hairs. It was as if

* In all seriousness, whilst a certain amount of insensitivity is obviously required for anything life-threatening conducted for fun, triviality probably isn't on the cavers' list of prime attributes. This particular system is considered deeply unpleasant, and only the hardest cavers can cope with it. Put less delicately, on a caving forum that broke news of the Three Counties breakthrough, the poster described it as 'a desperately horrible and dangerous choke'.

the mountain were exhaling through this ragged mouth from a core bereft of heat and of comfort. I quickly retreated into the comparatively balmy air of the hill: no doubt this was a feeling experienced by the many miners who went down there not out of choice or fun, but out of necessity, for work.

Before coming here, I'd mentioned to Mal Creasey that I'd be visiting the ruins at Rhosydd. He told me of other places in Snowdonia – places above Bethesda where parallel lines of slate are driven into the ground across the mountainside like roofless corridors to guide the men across the treacherous ground to the quarry in thick mist, and on the flanks of Snowdon, where great holes gape in the side of the mountain like bomb craters.

'Trouble is,' he said, 'Snowdonia slate lasts a hundred years. If it only lasted twenty, the mines would still be open. It's too good. That was the problem.'

He then added a destination to my list I hadn't considered. 'You've been to the Quarry Hospital, haven't you?'

I said that I hadn't.

'Well, if you're interested in what it was like to work up there – and what happened when things went wrong – you must go.'

The next day, I made my way across to Llanberis, and there, above the shores of Llyn Padarn in a glade on the grounds of the handsome National Slate Museum, I found the Quarry Hospital. Lovingly restored – right down to the slight whiff of chemicals – inside its bright, high rooms is a collection of the tools used by Victorian doctors to make the best fist of fixing everything from crushed limbs to popped eyes.

Unlike the mountaineering that took the privileged classes out to the Alps during the second half of the 19th century, mining was resolutely the realm of the poor. Health was diabolical amongst the miners, many living only on bread and butter throughout their working week, and they were subject to rheumatism exacerbated by the damp and lung disease caused by slate dust. This was called 'miners' phthisis', similar to the notorious 'black lung' of the coal industry, and is now known as silicosis.

The local average life expectancy in 1875 for men in the Blaenau Ffestiniog area was 67; for a quarry worker it was 38. Half of Rhosydd's quarry deaths were a result of respiratory maladies, an extraordinary proportion considering the physical risk involved in a job that in the late 19th century ranked as one of the most dangerous in the world. Were slate mining practised as widely today it would probably still be dangerous, even with modern equipment. As I wandered the corridors of the hospital in morbid fascination, I found a particularly eloquent description – boy, they knew how to write back then! – written by an inspector and concerning the Welsh quarrymen of the time:

> God turns them out a very even lot as babies; look at them above sixty as they pour out of a large quarry, and pray that the Almighty might give them the sense and the knowledge to understand what produced the awful change. How terribly numerous are the tubercular class of affliction ... and how frequently they die when a well-fed man would recover.

You'd be right to imagine that mining accidents have to rank amongst the most unpleasant that could befall a manual worker of the era. Falls from the lethally slick slate, limbs becoming trapped and injuries caused by splinters of rock were commonplace, particularly in winter when the frightful cold would put the men into careless stupors in dangerous places. Limbs were often amputated on site, in the rain, on the rock face in order to free their owners. Slate splinters frequently led to blood poisoning, against which there was no effective treatment, and death would eventually follow. Fatalities were often mercifully swift: blasting accidents, crushings, catastrophic blood loss, shock, wagon collisions and falls due to inadequately prepared ropes were all causes of fatal accidents at nearby Dinorwig Quarry between 1878 and 1886.

In addition to – or perhaps because of – this, the quarries seemed to be run with a culture in which blame was held at arm's length by quarry bosses. On a wall of incident reports, I caught one concerning a fractured thigh from 1924, which ended with: 'The accident occurred whilst the man ... was riding a tramroad incline ... which is contrary to the rules of the quarry therefore compensation is not payable.' The person involved in the accident was, as here, often blamed for it, possibly with a view to future prevention, but then possibly not. It was remarkable in this list of horrific fatal accidents how many ended with somewhat castigatory lines such as 'Failed to hold on to his own rope'; 'If the lad had stood five yards further back, he would been safe'; 'Rope not properly secured'; and 'Wilful disobedience to blasting rules'.

Said rules included the banning of meetings or of leaving the quarry on weekdays between 7 a.m. and 5.30 p.m. except for meals, the insistence that any damaged equipment be paid for, and – with strikingly frosty language – in the event of accidents, the edict that men must return to their work after 'disposing of the injured, provided they reach the hospital prior to one hour and a half of last whistle'.

There are suggestions in the documents pinned to the walls of the hospital that the quarry bosses tried to rubbish claims that workers were being struck down by silicosis by suggesting slate dust was not only harmless, but actually beneficial to health – fortified by iron and sulphur it was, they said – and that it was rarely inhaled.

I wandered through the rooms of clinically dressed, austerely framed beds, Tiny Tim crutches and revolutionary stretchers shaped for the human body. But it was the cabinets that held the most brutal fascination; here were the tools of the Victorian trauma surgeon's trade, and frankly he can keep them. Teeth extractors like old pliers, eyelid retractors that looked like something you'd rip up a carpet with, amputation knives, skull saws, a finger saw (is that in relation to its size or intended use? I think the former but I'm still not completely sure) and something horrific called a urethral speculum, which I dared not type into a search engine.* I'm sure without the lesson taught by the tools of this time modern medicine simply could not be as advanced as it is today. But wander round the quarry hospital in Llanberis and two emotions will haunt you: one of immense sorrow for the poor people wheeled into what must have felt like an industrial field hospital, and another of deep gratitude that things have moved on considerably in the intervening years.

Leaving the last room, my eyes alighted on a set of pictures of the quarry gangs at work or posing for group shots. Although all pictures of a certain age have similar qualities, it struck me again how alike these images of quarrymen, poised with their hammers and chisels – expressions characterless but

---

* I did, in the end – something I wouldn't advise – and it is, I'm afraid, as you imagine it. Though how the object I saw could be used to do that is beyond imagining; let's just say it would be like trying to look up a drainpipe with a lighthouse.

earnest, eyes looking fixedly to one side of the camera lens – were to photographs of mountaineers of the same period. Images of ladies with umbrellas and frilly mountaineering dresses alongside bearded, axe-wielding men with a backdrop of dripping Swiss mountains placed beside images of the Rhosydd quarrymen, the grey shoulders of the Snowdonia peaks at their backs, would be oddly complementary were it not for the evident contrast in the wealth and social class of those pictured. These aside, Edward Whymper in his 1860s Alpine heyday, photographed before his Matterhorn ascent, ice axe in hand, could so easily be holding a slate hammer, risking his life and learning his mountain skills in the bowels of the Welsh peaks.

The First World War would bring the classes into physical proximity in the trenches, then they would go their separate ways once more – the climbers to chip away at the seemingly impregnable Himalaya, whilst the miners went back to the quarries to do the same in Snowdonia. Rhosydd closed in 1930; other slate quarries in North Wales limped on until 1960, with a few mechanised mines continuing to this day.

I walked out of the quarry hospital into the late sunshine glistening on Llyn Padarn. For all its harsh undertones, there's no denying it's a beautiful spot. Off the back of the lake, the Pass of Llanberis and the high peaks stood, a dramatic backdrop that bore its visible scars well. The wind-wobbled toot of the Snowdon Mountain Railway rose from somewhere in Llanberis, on its way to the summit of the country with its payload of passengers. And with that, it was time to say goodbye to Wales.

6 WEATHER

Considering we're a nation genuinely obsessed with elemental conditions, hunting out truly distinctive features of the British climate isn't actually that easy at sea level. For the really good stuff, you have to go up.

For most of us for a lot of the time our weather seesaws between the pleasant and slightly less pleasant, although we do of course bitch heartily about both. Every now and again the M5 will be covered in two inches of snow, and the news will be filled with helicopter tracking shots of abandoned cars caterpillared along carriageways, news correspondents in puffy coats and much talk about the country never getting a summer. Then a week later the sun will come out, the snow will vanish, the papers will carry photographs of Brighton beach beneath headlines like 'Wow! It's hotter than Malta', and for a brief moment everything will be wonderful. By the following week the news will be full of brown pictures of cobweb-cracked river beds, repeated use of the phrase 'since records began' and concerned-looking scientists intoning that if it stays this warm, we're all in deep trouble.

However mercurial all this seems, leave it behind, head for the mountains and things become even more volatile. The uplands of Britain are genuinely extreme. Winters in the Scottish mountains can be more fearfully unpredictable than those in the Antarctic, on account of their propensity to mix the 'very wet' with the 'very cold' over the course of a very short time. This is not actually a particularly common combination, although it's one that can have disastrous consequences for anyone feeling their combined effects in an exposed and committed place. The merging of even moderate cold with wind, wet and being unprepared means that death by exposure in the British mountains is a real threat. Whilst it's a famously British conversational icebreaker in the lowlands, in the hills the propensity to exchange opening comments about the weather is practically a survival tactic. Things change very, very quickly here.

Whilst rain crackles around everything like background static, you could say that each area of mountains in Britain has its own particular bouquet of elements amongst which generally one smells stronger than the rest. Snowdonia is famous for hill cloud. Scotland's landlocked Cairngorms are generally the best place to find snow. Drizzle plagues the Lake District. And in the Pennines it's wind. Actually, in the Pennines it's everything, as the highest parts of this 180-mile range of battered, limestone-and-grit hills suffer by far the most extreme conditions south of Scotland. Long shaven of trees and beaten smooth by the climate, here the winds blow hardest, the temperature drops lowest and the snow lies deepest. One particular quote sums up rather nicely the two-faced nature of British meteorological conditions in general: 'By some, it has been described as the best in the world. For others, the astonishing variety of small-scale effects that it can and does repeatedly provide induces resigned tolerance, irritation or downright dislike – accompanied by declarations that the British Isles have no *climate*, but merely *weather*.'

The author of this was a geographer named Gordon Manley, and it's him we have to thank for bringing to wide attention an authentic freak of the British mountains, and a true phenomenon of our weather. Between 1937 and 1939 Manley was often to be found crouched in a small observatory on an anonymous moorland summit in northern England preoccupied with an extraordinary quirk of weather peculiar to this region. It was, essentially, a wind – but no normal wind. A thing of violence, with ominous, visible hallmarks, this wind had claimed lives and terrified locals for hundreds of years, and was described evocatively by John Ruskin as 'one of the plague winds of the world'. The world has many such regional winds – amongst them the European Mistral and Bora, and the American Diablo and Chinook – but Britain has one alone. And it's to be found only in the highest reaches of the Pennines, on the western slopes of a mountain named Cross Fell. It's also the only British wind to have its own name: the Helm Wind. And purely by its reputation alone, it had to be worth a look.

* * *

Cross Fell is easy to spot when you know where to look, but easy to miss if you're not sure what you're supposed to be looking for. I'd driven by it for years without realising. It's deceptively high by English standards; at 893 metres, were it not for a few summits in the Lake District it would be the highest ground in the country. As it stands, it's the highest point of the Pennines, the long thread of upland that stretches from the Peak District in the south to the Cheviots in the north. This is no serrated wall of peaks, instead a high moorland range of startling bareness, scraped of features and worn to a knub by stiff winds and endless years. In such a place you tend to notice anything at all out of the ordinary. And it's the golf-ball radar station atop Great Dunn Fell that you tend to notice the most when driving west on the A66, as I did on this particular spring morning. Only this time I'd learned that the plateaued, snow-dappled ridgeline to the left of this was Cross Fell – home of the Helm Wind.

The fact I could see the summit at all from this distance didn't bode well. After a week of rain and gales, I'd picked this moment to scramble for the north as being the most likely to yield an occurrence of the Helm Wind – in that it was spring and generally dreadful weather. But as it happened, I parked the car in the pretty hamlet of Milburn and set off down a farm track towards the open fell into the best weather this part of Cumbria had seen for months: a flawless blue sky, a breeze that barely tickled the skin and 20°C. The landscape was full of birdsong, the lowing of cattle and delicate new life. It was beautiful. I was crushed.

'You're off the path, you know.'

A small lady with about six dogs of various sizes emerged ahead.

'Pardon?'

'I said, you're off the path,' she repeated, as the dogs engulfed me.

'Oh.' How embarrassing. Five minutes from the car in weather like this and already I'd gone wrong. 'Sorry.'

'All you need to do is head through t'gate. Come *by*,' she admonished a terrier as it wiggled through my legs. Anyone with this many dogs was clearly a local, and probably a farmer. I suspected she was probably from the farm that worked much of the land I'd be walking through towards the fell.

'Do you know about the Helm Wind?' I asked, hoping she might be able to point me in a profitable direction.

'Difficult not to, in these parts. Quite a thing.' She threw a dismissive look at the sky, then back at me. 'Don't think it'll trouble you today, though. You're lucky.'

'I was kind of hoping for it, to be honest. What's it like?'

'Quite a thing,' she said again, before adding darkly, 'It roars, you know. If it was on, you'd look to see what was behind you.'

I looked around at the crisp conditions and felt a pang of longing for something – just *something* – of the wild weather of the Pennines to show itself.

'When was the last time it happened?'

'Well, it was a semi-Helm yesterday. We could hear it from the house. But I wouldn't worry about it today. Come *by*.'

Typical. A day earlier and I could be getting blown off my feet and battered with severe gales around now. Instead I was in danger of getting a tan. Rotten luck.

The locals around Cross Fell and Great Dun Fell have had an understandably fractious relationship with the Helm Wind. Stories as to the origin of Cross Fell's name are colourfully varied; an amusing argument is that it means 'angry' fell (as in, 'She was *cross* with him for the mess he left in the sink'), and certainly wherever you look you'll find reference to the mountain being viewed with suspicion and fear. Like Cadair Idris, there was just something about Cross Fell that stood the hairs on the back of people's necks on end. Another explanation for its name lies in a tale of a bishop – St Austin – who erected a cross on the summit in an evidently unsuccessful attempt to exorcise the mountain 'from evil Spirits',* as said Revd Robinson, vicar of Ousby, in 1709. Cross Fell was definitely known as Fiend's Fell in the Middle Ages, perhaps in reference to the captivating visual and auditory qualities that make the Helm Wind – and Cross Fell itself – so elementally distinctive.

The 'roar' my new friend described is perhaps the wind's most famous attribute, described as resembling everything from the deep screech of an

---

* '... who continued their Haunts and Nocturnal Vagaries upon it, until St Austin, as is said, erected a Cross and built an Altar upon it, whereon he offered the Holy Eucharist, by which he countercharm'd those Hellish Fiends, and broke their Haunts.'

express train and the sound of distant thunder to the bellow of a charging wild animal. Gordon Manley, in his much-lauded *Climate and the British Scene*, offered various insights into this mysterious wind, which was clearly a key reason why he chose this particular spot as the site of his observatory. Its ferocity is notorious: as far back as 1831 there was a report in the *Westmorland Gazette* of a Helm Wind being 'so heavy it carried up the peats high into the air on its whirling eddies and scattering them', and even spooking a horse so much that it ran 'headlong off a precipitous crag and was killed dead on the spot'. Other sources report farm machinery being lifted off the ground, sheep being blown around like discarded pieces of fluff, haystacks overturning, riders being blasted out of their saddle, and – colourfully – Brussels sprouts being stripped from their stalks and propelled towards one (presumably highly alarmed) onlooker like bullets. There's even a story that the wind flattened a Norman army during the invasion of 1066, blowing the invading soldiers off their horses.*

The second – and perhaps even more ominous – hallmark of the wind is the Helm cloud, which when in bloom must have resembled to onlookers of a more superstitious age a true hell above the Eden valley. It's most likely that this cloud gave the wind its name, being shaped like a helmet and worn like one by the mountain. Occurring when the Helm Wind blows, 'This helm or cloud exhibits an awful and solemn appearance, tinged with white by the sun's rays that strike the upper parts, and spreading like a gloom below, over the inferior parts of the mountain, like the shadows of night', as Hutchinson's *History of Cumberland* has it. A second cloud – the Helm Bar – forms in front of the mountain, above the river. The local lore is that the Helm Wind never crosses the Eden valley.

The nature of the wind has long seemed linked inexorably with the specific architecture and situation of the fell. This part of the Pennines comprises one of the largest stretches of high ground in England, and certainly the barest. Great and Little Dun Fells and Cross Fell form a ramp that gathers height

---

* Some accounts link this event to Grasmere in the central Lake District (where, incidentally, there's a Helm Crag), and the Helm Wind is often referred to in this area although what is being talked about is just a locally strong wind. The true Helm Wind only occurs on Cross Fell and the narrow band of land above the Eden valley.

slowly from the east, terminates in a long string of summits, then – squeezed between this and a 'glass ceiling' of warmer air above – falls dramatically to lower levels in a smooth drop free of much interrupting vegetation. Many learned observers over the years have suggested that the Helm Wind is a *Föhn*-type wind – one composed of dry air that gathers height then accelerates when it meets the lee slope of a mountain. In the case of Cross Fell, north-easterlies blow from the North Sea coast, rise and cool, then meet the rock step that drops from high on this line of mountains into the Eden valley, which is filled deep with warmer air. Meeting this gradient, the cool air rushes unchallenged into the valley with considerable urgency – a waterfall of air – with dire consequences for anyone or anything in its way. Manley would describe an encounter with the Helm Wind in a radio broadcast in 1939: 'To walk up the fellside against it is an unforgettable experience, and whilst I don't object to wind, I don't recommend going up in a Helm for pleasure,' he said. 'One stoops against it with everything buttoned up as tight as can be, and slogs wearily up the hill with this steady roaring torrent of air pressing against one at sometimes fifty or sixty miles per hour.'

If anything Manley got away lightly that day. Recent Helm Winds have been less forgiving, with the highest wind recorded in England clocked at 134 mph on the slopes of Great Dun Fell in January 1968. That's the speed of a Category 4 hurricane. Instances of the wind during the first decade of the 21st century have also been damaging, with one particularly violent gale obliterating a stone barn with metre-thick walls.

It was peculiar to be at large in an environment subjected to such legendary torment on a day so conspicuously free from it. As I began to climb gently through the intake fields, sheep and new lambs watched, stiffening then skittering as I came close. It was so still that when I paused, birdsong from distant clumps of trees gradually emerged, like stars slowly greeting light-grilled eyes in a night sky. Every now and again I'd spot evidence of an obvious climatic villain: stripped trees, vegetation combed towards the west – but the day was peaceful, and as the view began to emerge and the slope steepened, I started to enjoy myself. Occurrences of this kind of weather in the Pennines were undoubtedly rare in themselves; perhaps I was just experiencing a different kind of extreme.

Before the mountain began, a dip. A slick streak of black caught my eye within it, accelerating out of the valley away from me up the steep grass of the fellside: a sheepdog. Not wanting to interfere with the dog's task, I watched for a moment the sheep above me coalesce, then move as a clump over a grassy spur towards lower ground. The angry-sounding whistle-bellow of a shepherd and the putter of a two-stroke engine soon followed, and a few minutes later I received an acknowledging head-twitch and a wink as he bounced by on his quad bike, flat cap on head, smiling dog perched on the rear pannier.

Ahead, the radar golf ball atop the summit of Great Dunn Fell was leaning back and dropping out of sight as the slopes of the valley began to rise around me. Cross Fell, the long escarpment of its summit plateau finely frosted with late-lying snow, lay to the left beyond a nick in the skyline. The river slinking from the valley I was now in presumably had its source somewhere near this. Looking quickly at the map I saw the river split into three main tributaries, like a fallen branch. Wanting to follow as natural a line as possible – particularly on reasonably unthreatening terrain like this – I decided to follow the left-most of these, then cross when it became delicate enough. I made for the river and began to slowly track it backwards up the valley. A small deer burst out of the undergrowth six metres ahead and pogoed away, its rump resplendent with brilliant white. As I climbed against the descending river, the landscape around me began to empty and harden, as the valley ended and the mountain began.

Gordon Manley perhaps had a greater threshold for hardship than most. Born in the north-west of England 'amongst cloudy hills', he held the theory that keen minds in the earth sciences tended to come from similarly tempestuous roots, as if a proclivity – bordering on a preference – for bad weather were somehow part of their make-up. It also helped that he was a disciple of Frank Debenham, a geologist and veteran of Robert Falcon Scott's fatal *Terra Nova* expedition to the Antarctic,* who was later instrumental in establishing the Scott Polar Research Institute in Cambridge. After several years

---

* Debenham only escaped Scott's final journey to the South Pole as a result of a knee injury sustained after a slip whilst playing football in the snow. Instead, he and fellow expedition members mapped the western mountains of Victoria Land.

making observations from a weather station he'd set up at Moor House – 'probably the highest inhabited house in England' – Manley decided to tackle the Helm Wind head on, so to speak. He built a small observation hut on Great Dun Fell, measuring a mere eight feet by six, in a little hollow more or less directly in the path of the north-easterlies breaking over the crest of the ridge.

During the period between 1937 and 1939, the Durham-based geographer made over 100 trips across the Pennines to the hut – at the time a considerable distance by car, followed by a hard walk – in order to conduct his experiments, frequently spending the night in the hut, either by choice or otherwise. Equipped with camping equipment and snow-clearing tools, the hut was frozen solid on several occasions by a case of ice whilst the geographer attempted to get in – or out. It must have been utterly desperate, but by all accounts he enjoyed himself, writing that 'Occasional misadventures in the darkness, mist and snow of a December night were offset by so many pleasures.'

Halfway up the river valley I was having exactly the opposite experience. The sun was beginning to burn the right side of my neck and my right ear. I didn't have sunscreen, and remembered clearly the moment when, the previous night, in front of a radiant heater and under my rain-tapped garage roof I'd slung it aside dismissively in an effort to save weight. Pulling a bandana from my bag, I wrapped it around my neck and pulled it up, bandit-like, over my mouth, nose and ears. Ridiculous or not, this would have to do. Deer tracks littered the path I was following, although the ground was steepening sharply on both sides. I was walking into the creases of the mountain now; soon I'd have to leave the path and start climbing more steeply. I looked up at the slopes around me and decided the one to my left looked like the keenest ascent. Crossing the chattering water, I started the steep pull up the grassy slope, falling to my hands and knees immediately and clutching bushes of grass as handholds. It was *just* too steep for comfort: slip, and you'd probably roly-poly all the way down, unless your fall was interrupted by a rock or two. There was little to grab other than tufts of grass (not the most reliable thing to trust your balance to) or the rusted remains of a fence to my right (ditto). Eventually I made my way up to a point where the level eased a little, and I could see ahead the slope ascending into rockier ground, where the mountain's skeleton – brown, fractured limestone – poked through its skin. It looked broken and ancient.

Manley's endeavour, heroic as it was for one man to accomplish, must sadly take second place in the elite field of making gruelling weather measurements at altitude – having been beaten to the top of the pile by another absurdly tenacious individual. This man, from whom Manley no doubt drew inspiration, is now sadly mostly forgotten, despite his extraordinary tale and his awesome legacy: quite simply, modern weather forecasting. The story begins on the slopes of Britain's highest mountain in the late 19th century.

Were you in the vicinity of the meandering Red Burn on Ben Nevis at around 6.30 a.m. between June and October of 1881, you might have had the interesting experience of encountering a cadaverous, slightly desperate-looking man in a perpetual hurry named Clement Wragge.

Wragge was by all accounts an astonishing human being. With a 'mop of flaming red hair, an explosive temper to match and the adjectival luxuriance of a bullocky',* he was born in Worcestershire and represented a fine contradiction to Gordon Manley's theory – that those from England's blasted north had the greatest affinity for ferocious weather – given his own near-constant dance with it. After rejecting a career in law in favour of seafaring, Wragge relocated to the Antipodes, joining the South Australian surveyor-general's department in 1876, where he cultivated a passion for meteorology. But between 1 June and 14 October 1881, then again in the following summer of 1882, Wragge – often accompanied by his long-suffering Newfoundland dog Renzo – could be found in Scotland, climbing Ben Nevis every day on a strict, self-imposed observation schedule.† The reason: plans by the Scottish Meteorological Society to set up a weather observatory on the highest point

* 'Bullocky' is an Australian term for a driver of bullocks – that is to say, someone of a rather blunt turn of phrase. Descriptions of Wragge alienating almost everybody he met are legion.

† The schedule was this: sea level, 4.40 a.m.; Lochan Meall an t-Suidhe, 6.30 a.m.; shoulder spring at 1,029m, 8.15 a.m.; summit, 9 a.m., 9.30 a.m. and 10 a.m.; spring, 10.50 a.m.; Lochan, 1 p.m.; sea level, 3.30 p.m. At each of these times the long-suffering Mrs Wragge (who bore the opulent name Leonora Eulalie Edith Florence d'Eresby, and would bear the couple an incredible eight children) made observations in Fort William at sea level.

in Great Britain. Wragge had been enticed by Alexander Buchan, the Society's secretary, to undertake a series of daily observations over nearly five months to establish results interesting enough to justify a permanent year-round observatory on the summit plateau of the mountain. The object would be a greater understanding of the weather systems operating in Britain, with the subsequent aim of improving forecasting.* The summit of Ben Nevis – on account of its position almost a vertical mile above sea level, its location on the climatically tumultuous west coast and its enormous mass – was and remains the wildest, most elementally extreme place in Britain, although at that time it was merely conjectured to be such. Quite simply, there was no knowledge as to what the weather was like on its summit from one day to the next over a long period of time. All the Society needed was someone tough enough to make the daily journey to the summit in whatever conditions presented themselves to provide readings for wind, barometric pressure, rainfall and temperature. In Clement Wragge – who would later garner the unkind but inevitable nickname 'The Inclement Rag' – Buchan found that someone.

Wragge's findings would depict an environment much more extreme than previously thought. His journals, today held in the archives of the Edinburgh Meteorological Office, make for harrowing reading, yet – written as they are in the matter-of-fact manner of a dogged and somewhat eccentric Victorian with an arduous job to do – aren't without amusement. Ben Nevis's vast top, as we shall later see, can be a very dangerous and frightening place; such is the way the mountain is put together – a benign flank on one side, vertical cliffs on the other and a summit plateau approached via the former but ringed by the latter – that the thousands who climb it each year occupy a thin corridor of benevolence and consequently many remain gloriously ignorant of the mountain's more dangerous facets as they scoot up and down the well-engi-

* Experiments with regard to altitudinal variations in temperature had thus far been fraught. In December 1881 – the winter after Wragge's first series of Ben Nevis ascents – three observers attempted to ascertain the vertical distribution of temperature using a balloon loaned by the War Office in Somerset. Near Bridport, the balloon made unexpected groundfall, jettisoning two occupants, who escaped with broken bones. The unfortunate third was about to alight when the balloon suddenly rose again. The last time he and his craft were seen they were over the English Channel, and stridently ascending.

neered mountain track. But even then, standing as it does in the path of Atlantic storms, the elemental assault that can open up on the summit with little warning can be absolutely furious – something in which Wragge (and presumably Renzo) would enjoy a thorough apprenticeship in the months and the many, many miles that followed.

Wragge stuck to his daily schedule as if bolted to it. On occasion he was unable to operate the key that unlocked the small cage on the summit housing his measuring instruments until he had lit a fire to warm his numb fingers. In the margin of his entry for 19 July 1882 he wrote: 'Hands so swollen owing to the wet that I couldn't reset [the barometer] ... I had indeed the greatest difficulty turning the vernier screw this morning, having to sometimes use both hands, right hand being almost useless. Such is the effect of wet and cold upon the flesh.' And this was midsummer! Wragge had a small stone shelter erected on the summit to house the barometer; it provided him with some rude respite from the summit conditions, and contained a stove on which to make a drink. In October 1881 this shelter fell foul of Ben Nevis's weather, with Wragge reporting in a letter to *The Scotsman* that 'The canvas roof of my hut, having been carried away during the late storm, I have no shelter, and the winter has set in with extreme severity ... I much regret that the observations must now be discontinued.'

The following year he acquired two assistants, one of whom was a man named Angus Rankin, who would replace the now presumably deeply weary Wragge on his daily observations for at least a couple of journeys each week. Rankin described reaching the summit plateau, which had now garnered the ominous nickname 'the plateau of storms', one day shortly after midsummer in June 1883 to find a wind so ferocious he had to 'three times lie down and take hold of stones 'til the squall was past ... [It was] lifting old snow in large pieces from edge of precipice and carrying it across.' Rankin reported a Force 10 gale. Another entry described the snow being so horrific he was 'unable to untie my coat to make a note, look at my watch ... sit, nor walk easily, as my clothes were one solid mass.'

The efforts of Wragge and his assistants, and the value of the results they captured, were enough to convince the Scottish Meteorological Society that a permanent observatory was both desirable from a scientific point of view and practically necessary; the conditions the observers had experienced on their treks up and down the mountain had stretched them to their physical limit, despite lying entirely outside of the winter months. In 1883 there was no equipment that could be relied upon to withstand the kind of conditions likely to befall Britain's highest place under even more extreme conditions, and no observer physically qualified to make the dangerous trek daily to Wragge's already well-established schedule. Thanks to a *Times* reporter who'd accompanied Wragge on a particularly diabolical ascent during which they crossed the summit plateau in a Force 11 gale on all fours – and the horrified but awestruck three-column article that followed – the scheme received a much-needed boost. Soon the weight of the British scientific community, buoyed by considerable public interest, was behind the observatory project. A public appeal was launched, and by summer had reached the necessary sum of £4,000, which, amongst other things, would cover the £1,237 for the observatory plus £793 for the path. The first donation – of £50 – was made by Queen Victoria.

First things came first. In order to transport the necessary supplies for the observatory – both for its construction and daily subsistence – a path of sufficient quality needed to be built. With the assistance of a local geography teacher, its course was determined up the gentlest slope of the mountain, rising from Glen Nevis and performing a series of sharp zigzags near where it met the summit plateau.* With it went an armoured telegraph cable to link the summit to Fort William.

Based on a series of plans made by lighthouse designer Thomas Stevenson nearly a decade earlier, architect Sydney Mitchell then created drawings for a building with double-skin, felt-filled walls, 3.5 metres thick at their base, made from the native granite of the mountain. The building was a cosy affair, although it would grow considerably during its lifetime. The Ben Nevis observatory was officially opened on 17 October 1883 on a day of blinding cloud and hailstorms. Wragge – for reasons still debated, but most likely because he was presumed disagreeable when snowbound in a small space for long periods – did not win the role of first superintendent of the observatory. This went to a

---

* This 'pony track', so named because most of the supplies for building were transported on horseback, remains the normal route up the mountain as it is the clearest, gentlest route to the top of Britain.

man named Robert Traill Omond, who along with assistants Robert Mossman and Wragge's old colleague Angus Rankin took their place in the observatory and waited for winter.

What followed was the most extraordinary human witness to the extremity of British mountain weather – a meticulous record, uninterrupted for twenty years, of a range of diverse phenomena documented at the nation's 1,344m highpoint.

After the first winter two things became apparent: first, the observatory was far too small to accommodate three observers and their equipment in comfort. Second, once considerable snowfall began to accumulate around the building, it was impossible to get out without first digging a snow tunnel that could be anything up to ten metres long and climbing four metres to the surface* – a considerable inconvenience if fleeing a fire, say. That first winter was particularly hard; the observers needed to be roped together to take their readings, and the snowfall – constantly windblown into the exit passage – frequently made observations impossible. Nine months' worth of stores were kept, on the off chance that the weather would become so bad that the ponies and road-men tasked to resupply the observatory couldn't make it. As a result, the larder was full of tinned food such as tomatoes, tongue, beef, peas, peaches and prunes.

The observatory also hosted an array of the latest and strangest measuring equipment; hours of sunshine were quantified on a Campbell–Stokes recorder, which used a glass orb to focus the sun's rays on a curved strip of wood or thermo-sensitive paper. In summer, wind speed was measured using a Robinson anemometer, but when this iced up in winter a system was employed that – and this is true – determined relative velocity by the angle at which an observer could lean into the wind without falling over. The ferocity of the gales experienced led to the adoption of a new scale of measurement in place of the Beaufort scale, which was deemed inadequate. Force Ten on the Beaufort scale was a wind of 64 knots; the equivalent on the Ben Nevis scale was 84 knots. The unofficial top reading of this is rumoured to have the disappearance of the observatory from the mountain as its measure. Mercifully, that was never reached.

---

* This was the length of the tunnel as recorded on 1 March 1884.

An expansion in the summer of 1884 saw the addition of several more bedrooms, a tourist's room and a nine-metre tower, within which some of the more critical observation instruments were kept. The thermometer was kept in here, and raised step by step up the ladder as the snow deepened. The tower also offered a conning-hatch exit, which would maintain access into and out of the observatory in even the worst snowfall, and allow round-the-clock observations in all conditions other than intolerable wind. Rankin discovered the latter on 21 February 1885, when 'at 16h the observation logbook was torn in two and blown away. At 18, 19 and 20h [the observer] went out on a long rope at the tower door and had to be hauled back.' He added drily: 'After that, the observer didn't go out.'

A place of lantern- and candlelight, little heat and very long nights (lest we forget, this was the 1880s; the Wright brothers were still scratching their heads in their garage, and in London Jack the Ripper was preparing to terrorise the streets), the observatory in winter was an austere place. Despite the stove burning constantly, it became intensely cold and must have felt isolated to a degree more extreme than any other place in Britain. Perhaps the most vivid description of winter nights in the observatory comes courtesy of W. T. Kilgour, a copywriter from Fort William who spent several weeks at the observatory and would later make it the subject of his book *Twenty Years on Ben Nevis*: 'In the day-time there was always the same blank whiteness ... and at night an awful pitch darkness that might be felt. There was the terrible boom of the gale on the sides of the hill ... the constant vibration of the tower and the ever-present feeling that the rest of the universe was tearing past at double the speed of an express train.'

However traumatic the storms, they were usually considered a lively respite from the tedium. The observers – who in general numbered three, plus a cook and, between 1895 and 1904, a cat – would warmly welcome weary winter climbers caught out by the short days and hard routes, and a knock at the door in the dead of night was a fairly common occurrence. Tourists would also visit during the summer months, often making use of the telegraph machine to send amusing messages – 'Missed the view but viewed the mist!' – to their sea-level recipients. Tourist outings became so popular on the mountain that in 1894 a small hotel was built on the summit adjacent to the observatory, and ten shillings would entitle you to one of the four highest rooms in Britain.

On 19 June 1895 a deafening bang and a flash filled the observatory. Smoke began pouring from the telegraph apparatus and a fire began in the kitchen where the cook lay sprawled, having been knocked unconscious. The fire was soon under control, and the observers were able to take stock of what was probably the closest the building came to destruction – somewhat fittingly, by lightning strike. It was all too much for the cook, who left the following day, although a high turnover of cooks was apparently (and perhaps understandably) normal.

In 1892 the aurora borealis was seen on 38 nights. In November 1898 a violent storm blew a tonne of spindrift into the hotel lobby, and that year also saw the greatest annual rainfall on the summit, with over 240 inches recorded. St Elmo's fire, a peculiar electrical phenomenon, was also witnessed at the observatory, causing jets of electricity up to three inches long to bristle on the edges of all protruding objects, accompanied by a kind of hissing sound.

The tower is the most striking feature in the exceptionally vivid photographs from the observatory's short life. These images, particularly those taken in winter, have a quality of the ethereally extreme uncannily similar to Herbert Ponting's famous pictures of Captain Scott's fateful *Terra Nova* expedition to the Antarctic. In snow, the tower projected from a sea of white like a submarine breaking the surface. In many pictures the tubular structure is encased in a thick ruff of two-metre-long ice crystals collectively clawing outwards into the wind on an identical bearing; the figures of the observers in the snow are blackened by underexposure to faceless, coal-coloured silhouettes in a world of sepia-tinted blankness; and in one, a lone observer takes notes in a cluttered, wood-panelled room with a gaunt iron stove at its centre. These were days when there was no mountain rescue, no high-tech clothing, a Victorian knowledge of a human being's ability to withstand cold and little clue as to the likely conditions they'd face in the extremities of winter on the summit of Ben Nevis – that was, after all, the point. Yet some of these observers undertook dogged ten-month stints in the observatory, dropping to three-month rotations only when a sea-level observatory was opened in Fort William in 1890. Tobogganing (one picture shows a participant with a pipe defiantly jammed in his lips), curling on the frozen lochans and the surreal spectacle of a table-tennis match conducted on a table fashioned from a sheet of timber on a base of snow were lighter moments of what in winter must surely have been a gruelling commission.

By 1904 it was decided that the £950 a year to run the observatory was over-indulgent, and after 21 years of continuous log-taking, the closing entry was made on 1 October 1904. A week later the door of the observatory was shut and bolted for the last time amidst a gentle snowfall. The fire, which had burned continuously since the opening, was finally snuffed out and the observers made their last journey down the mountain. 'It is ... a matter of profound disappointment that in this wealthy country it should have been found impossible to obtain the relatively small sum to carry on a work of profound scientific value and interest,' was the statement made by the directors.

The observatory became first vacant, then ruinous – the latter exacerbated in 1950 when a group of climbers removed the lead from the roof of the main building, allegedly to finance a mountaineering trip to the Rockies. Today, elements of the structure remain in ruin; the steel frame of the shelter cage in which Wragge used to house his instruments (and himself); 'Wragge's Well', a wooden trough that allegedly had its origins in the Sudan and that tapped a spring on the edge of the plateau; the stone slab where the observatory stove used to sit; a few walls, and the base of the tower, which now holds a metal emergency shelter.

What's perhaps most remarkable is the observatory's legacy. Robert Louis Stevenson, son of the man who drafted the first plans for the observatory and who designed the Stevenson thermometer screen that stood on the summit of Ben Nevis (a device now ubiquitous in weather stations worldwide), would write *Treasure Island*. Charles Thomas Wilson, who spent a fortnight on the summit of Ben Nevis in 1894, would invent the cloud chamber in order to replicate, scientifically define and understand what he called the 'beautiful optical phenomena ... seen on the mountain top'. He was awarded the Nobel Prize in 1927.

As for 'Inclement' Wragge, he didn't disappoint. Having been rewarded with the Gold Medal by the Scottish Meteorological Society for his tenacious daily observations, he left Great Britain before the opening of the observatory (perhaps angrily, we're not sure) and arrived back in Australia in 1883 after a voyage in which his Newfoundland hound Renzo – Wragge's 'hero of a hundred gales' – and his Persian cat caused considerable chaos.* In the three weeks following his arrival, an unprecedented nineteen inches of rain fell in Brisbane, an event that was possibly the source of his latterly infamous nickname. Wragge had received a considerable windfall from an aunt, and built a fine house with it. Founding the Meteorological Society of Australasia in 1886, he became involved in the prediction of tropical storms and, remarkably, can be credited with the systematic naming of cyclones and hurricanes after people. Tropical systems he named after South Sea Islanders he admired; fierce Southern Ocean storms after politicians he didn't. After antagonising just about everyone in the Australian meteorological community, he retired to New Zealand in 1906 with an Anglo-Indian named Louisa Emmeline Horne, with whom he practised the esoteric spiritualism of theosophy and established the Wragge Institute and Museum – later destroyed by fire. In his twilight years he nurtured a fascination with the occult and took up yoga, before succumbing to a stroke at the age of 70. Photographed in his latter period in his jungle-like garden, Wragge cuts a striking figure. Whippet-thin, he stands defensively, hands on hips, pipe jutting from his cadaverous cheeks and a mystic's turban round his head: an extraordinary and, unlikely destiny for Britain's original mountain weatherman.

Two hundred miles south-east of Ben Nevis on the slopes of Cross Fell, I was beginning to win my battle with the ascent. The sun was now reaching its zenith, and just as I was beginning to wish for a moment of respite for my sizzling forehead I found one high on the slope above me. A cave with an aperture about two-thirds the height of a front door gaped out of the steep boulder slope like a dark window in the mountain. I was well off-path; the cave was as surprising as it was welcome, and as I reached its entrance I set down my pack, pulled out my head torch and peered into the mouth of the cave. Steam was rising gently from inside, curling out of the darkness into the sun's path; there must be moisture in there that the sun was just beginning to hit.

---

* Renzo escaped his kennel on several occasions, with his preferred hiding place being 'under a settee in a brand new saloon to the steward's horror, whilst puss soon distinguished herself … by demolishing seven canaries, and was consigned to the hold, there to live on rats for the remainder of the voyage.'

A new feature of my car-boot kit arsenal was the brightest head torch I'd ever seen. I'd made people fall out of their chair with it, but as I fired it up and shone it further into the cave the darkness swallowed the beam as if it didn't exist. Confused, I looked at the bulb to check it was on and shone it back in the cave once more. Nothing, save for a limp illumination of the first two feet or so. It was as if I were shining the torch onto a painted black wall.

Curious, I reached for my camera and switched the flash on. This is the sort of thing you see in horror films; someone points a camera into a dark room and the flash fires for a millisecond, capturing some horrifying image from the darkness. But as I reviewed the picture on the screen I was surprised to see it didn't reveal a small cave, but a long, engineered tunnel. It was arched like a catacomb, with walls hung with green weeds and algae, floored with a few inches of water and ploughing straight into the hillside, disappearing once more into thick darkness at the limit of the flash beam. It was clearly a mine of some sort: nothing was marked on the map, so I could only assume it was a 'hushing' channel – an old technique that used fast-flowing water to expose minerals – or some kind of drainage ditch. It seemed very well built.

Sitting in the mouth of the tunnel, enjoying the feel of the emollient, water-cooled breath of the mountain on my back, I looked out down the valley. Cross Fell was a much more impressive-feeling mountain looking down from it than looking up. Down the infant course of Crowdundle Beck – the stream I'd been following up the mountain – into the valley it had carved presented a view of startling spectacle that felt high-hoisted and spacious. To the east, beyond the head of the valley I was working my way up, I imagined the uplands would roll out in a fairly consistent fashion to the horizon across the wastes of the Pennines. But to the west, Cross Fell falls both suddenly and steeply. Here, looking down at the 'step' of the Pennines – the drop exhibited in many places and going by many names to the north and south, although this was the biggest example of all – I could see what Gordon Manley was getting at when he compared the Helm Wind to a 'fast stream passing over a weir'.

I was almost up. Above the mouth of the tunnel the gradient lessened, and soon I was on the bouldered crest of the mountain. A path joined me from the left as I climbed through the peculiarly spacious, almost Martian landscape of the mountain. The gradient seemed to lessen the closer I climbed towards its top, which formed a vast plateau: the flat roof of the Pennines.

Today, where Manley's hut once stood on Great Dun Fell, is another structure dedicated to observation. If you're flying into the north of England, the chances are you make use of it without even knowing: the radar station, or 'golf ball', that assists much of the air traffic in the upper half of the country. Some sort of structure has been on top of this unlikely fell since Manley himself had a hut up here; curious when you consider Cross Fell's proximity and superior height. Alfred Wainwright – the meticulous and somewhat misanthropic writer of quaintly detailed guidebooks to Lakeland and the Pennines – would describe the fell in typically measured fashion in 1967: 'Happily there is no other [summit] so defaced, so debased. A monstrous miscellany of paraphernalia, most conspicuous being four tall masts, disgraces it. Additionally there are wind and sunshine recorders, other grotesque contraptions and several squat buildings of no charm whatsoever. Quite the ugliest of all summits.'

Back then the summit observatory was evidently cluttered. If anything, the golf ball – properly called a 'radome', which was added in the 1980s – neatened it up by hiding some of the more sensitive equipment from view. In a way it has assumed the mantle of what the Ben Nevis observatory started and Manley continued. It still hosts a weather station, recording wind speed, direction and temperature, as well as a complement of researchers from the University of Manchester's Centre for Atmospheric Science. Today they use the station to study the behaviour of clouds. As I continued along the increasingly defined path towards the summit of Cross Fell I wondered what Wragge would have made of it. Pausing on the way up, I used my thumb to block out the golf ball in a feeble attempt to imagine the landscape without it. Ugly or not, it certainly provided a focal point for an otherwise leanly featured mountain; without it the place would be truly empty.

Just off the path was a cluster of cairns – frail pyramids of rock, like peculiar Stone Age graves. I've always wondered how these structures, often used to denote the indistinct course of a pathway, remain erect up to their most precarious top tier in areas prone to high winds. As the gradient eased and the ground underfoot tipped forward, I felt the soundscape around me change;

gone was the gentle 'whoosh' of the wind from a distance, replaced by the hard clink of rock underfoot and a peculiar calmness. But something else was there, too – something I only caught on the odd tickle of wind. Something strange.

It wasn't an obvious noise, and it certainly wasn't the Helm Wind – I daresay that such was my disappointment on missing the latter that if I'd listened even harder I would probably have heard the sound of straws being clutched at – but it was certainly *something*. It was a strange sound; a sort of fluting, such as when you hear a draught coming under the door or the thrust of a jet on a runway queered by distance into an odd, fragile whistle. There were neither poorly fitted doors nor airports hereabouts, and the oddly mobile direction of the sound suggested it wasn't coming from a single source. I looked around me for possible explanations, on one or two occasions dismissing it as my imagination and moving on, only to be stopped in my tracks by it again.

It could have been anything, but it did seem associated with the wind's ebbs and flows. I considered the options as I continued along the path, concluding it must be the wind being piped through hidden mine entrances or gaps in the boulders. I remembered reading that the Helm Wind was often accompanied by a 'shrieking' noise, and I wondered what would happen to the noise I was hearing had it been propelled by a more robust gale. Then, as I was preparing to give up once more and made a mental note to check up on weird noises on Cross Fell when I arrived home (and possible names for my discovery if it turned out that I'd found a *second* strange wind), high above me the sun glinted off a pair of gliders lazily wheeling in the warm thermals rising from the slopes of the mountain. I didn't know what sort of noises gliders made – if any – but it certainly seemed a possible fit. I was almost disappointed. But it seemed neat in a way that this noise was a result of the same strange mountain air patterns that produced the Helm – and also the thermals these gliders relied upon for their lift. Without it, they probably wouldn't be here.

I reached the gap between Cross Fell and Little Dun Fell at around 2 p.m. To my left the rocky plateau of Cross Fell's 893-metre summit was within reach. All of a sudden I wasn't alone; people appeared at varying distances to my right. Despite the weather, I got the feeling that this was less to do with the mountain than with the row of paving flags that suddenly appeared in a line ahead of me. It was a path – but not just any path. This was the Pennine Way, the 268-mile footpath that goes from Edale in the Peak District to Kirk Yetholm in the Scottish Borders. The oldest of 15 'official' national trails in Britain, it was conceived by writer Tom Stephenson in 1935 when he bemoaned in a newspaper article the lack of a 'long, green walk' to rival American routes such as the Appalachian Trail. It took another 30 years for the route to become reality, and today it's estimated that some 10,000 walkers complete all – or a significant chunk – of the route each year. Anyone who completes it is thought to open 287 gates, cross 432 stiles and 204 bridges, pass through three national parks, and walk past the door of Britain's highest inn and arguably its most famous waterfall before crossing the border into Scotland.*

Most people take just over two weeks to walk it; I was due to be on and off it in about half an hour, but in that time I'd reach the highest point of the walk and arguably its best view, which sounded like a good deal to me. I'd never set foot on the 'Way' before; even though it was the biggest path to snake through a lot of the Pennine's key areas, I'd managed to avoid it, so it was with slight ceremonial hesitation – I'm not sure what I was expecting to happen – that I stepped onto the flags and turned left towards Cross Fell's summit.

The summit is vast. As I approached it I noticed the clutch of people I'd seen wandering by on the Pennine Way before I'd joined it simply carried on. Typically on a summit, people stop – certainly on one as important as Cross Fell, crowned with such an impressive feature: a huge cairn like a pointed finger, built from artfully constructed rocks of a grandness certainly befitting a summit. But in fact this doesn't crown the very top at all, despite giving every impression of doing so until you're standing beside it. As I reached it, the true top, with its broken wind-shelter and what looked like a standard Ordnance Survey trig point, rose into view a few hundred metres beyond. I lingered momentarily next to the cairn, which stood as tall as a bungalow above me. A lycra-clad mountain-biker joined me after a few moments, and I watched the same expression of surprise ripple the parts of his face not covered by helmet and acid-yellow sunglasses. 'Bloody mountain. Just goes on!' he near-shouted, before wheezily moving off. If I were looking for a place of reflective

---

* Respectively, the Peak District, Yorkshire Dales and Northumberland national parks; the pub is the Tan Hill Inn, at 538 metres above sea level; and the waterfall is High Force, near Dufton.

tranquillity, this probably wasn't it, and after a few more moments I followed him.

The summit shelter was shaped like a laid cross. I wondered briefly if this could be St Austin's 'cross' – but popular summits often have cross-shaped shelters, open-topped but robustly walled and designed to give protection from the wind whichever way it happened to be blowing. A few walkers and my cyclist friend had stopped and were in the process of devouring food from their rucksacks. Everyone had their own little ritual. One serious-looking chap was necking energy gels from wrappers with short, bright words like 'Zap!' written on them and sucking on a plastic hydration tube as if it were oxygen and he was on Mount Everest; an older couple had sandwiches in tin-foil and Scotty flasks; the cyclist a sports bottle and a muesli bar.

After trading nods and comments about destination, origin and, of course, the weather (it *is* amazing how reliable this is as an opening comment, as if it's the only thing we have in common; why not footwear or choice of snack?), everyone returned to their rucksacks and I slinked over to the shadowy north-west side of the summit shelter to eat my own embarrassingly juvenile rations (Monster Munch, a Sherbert Dip and a Mars bar). This side of the shelter was heaped with snow; a bit of a shock, even though it's not uncommon to find high mountains holding snow deep into summer. The summit shelter and its system of shadows had created its own little microclimate of suntrap and shade in this extreme place, meaning the difference between snow and no snow, so it's perhaps not difficult to appreciate how a mountain like Cross Fell could give rise to a local wind like the Helm. My only regret – and it seemed odd to be feeling it in such rare and splendid weather – was that it wasn't blowing today.

I finished my lunch and wandered out to the trig point, with the frenzy of ground-nesting birds and the gentle chatter from the shelter the only audible sounds. From the top of Cross Fell it feels as if you can see the entire country. The emptiness around you is colossal: beyond the barren brown boulders of the summit the mountain tapers away to shoulders overlooking cardinal points that carry one's gaze to very different destinies. South lay the Howgills, those steep, blunt moorland mountains with skins like old felt, untroubled by paths and crowds. East, the intimidating blankness of awesome, gently descending nothingness towards the Yorkshire Moors, peppered by occasional and unexpected pockets of water, hidden in amongst inaccessibility. West, the Lake District in its rumpled entirety. A great history of mountains, peoples, communities and adventures in one half of one head-turn. I scanned the horizon for recognisable hills. The bulks of Skiddaw and Blencathra, the latter like a collapsed roof-pitch to the extreme right; the Old Man of Coniston, High Street, probably the most bulky things to the far left; Helvellyn, the hunched shoulders in the middle. Someone climbs Helvellyn every day in winter to check the conditions on the summit; they call this modern equivalent of Wragge and Manley a fell-top assessor. Then to the north, Scotland stood moodily beyond the Solway Firth, the hills of the Southern Uplands compressed into a flat horizon. Beyond them lay mountains that dwarfed in number everything in England and Wales combined. In a month or so I'd be crossing the border and heading hundreds of miles beyond this view for the strange, remote mountains of the far north; as far north as I could get. The chances of finding a summit with a shelter up there were slim. The chances of finding a summit with other people on it slimmer still.

As I looked north, the elderly man from the shelter, flask-lid of tea in hand, wandered idly over to the trig point, breathing heavily through a happy grimace.

'Lovely weather!'

I debated abruptly shifting the tack of the conversation to see what would happen. But standing there on the summit of a mountain famous for wild conditions with a rucksack full of waterproofs, a view that seemed endless and ripening sunburn on my neck, I couldn't help but smile and agree. What a country.

And on that note, for the time being, it's time to leave it.

PART II

SUMMER

7 SCIENCE

My head torch lit, and with it the world snapped from murky grey to vivid and quailing red and yellow. The tent was still up, at least – but it was definitely protesting. A strong gust of wind had probably woken me, and by the anchor-less flapping at the far end of the tent, this one might have been powerful enough to require some damage control.

It was late July, and a hell of a night to be up high in Scotland. I was pinned at just over 650 metres to the northern slope of a mountain whose name I'd somewhere read translated as 'constant storm'; in hindsight, this was a warning sign perhaps worth heeding. My watch read 3.33 a.m and it wouldn't get light for another two hours. Come dawn I was supposed to be climbing to the summit, but this wind was striking the tent like a cannon loaded with buckshot. If things stayed like this it really didn't look good. The rattling nylon above me had prevented anything other than a camper's doze for hours. Perhaps I should have bailed whilst this was merely a breeze. Around me in the tent was the usual paraphernalia of a wild camp: sleeping bag, water, food, a much-annotated map, mobile phone, various bags for stuffing things in. Also lying around were a number of text-dense papers, one of which featured several graphs and diagrams – reminders that all of this had to do with something remarkable that happened 250 years ago, right here on this slope, on this very mountain. Something that would have seismic repercussions in the worlds of physical science, our understanding of the world as we know it today and the way we draw our maps. Something, rather more specifically, to do with a gentleman called Nevil.

* * *

It's probably best if we back right up and start at the beginning. A couple of props may be of assistance here: a bar of Toblerone – if you don't have supplies in, please learn from this mistake – and any British Ordnance Survey map.

British maps are the best in the world. There really isn't much point arguing about it; they cover, to a degree of useful accuracy regardless of the uselessness of the terrain, every one of the 88,744 square miles of Great Britain (that is, not including Northern Ireland), every kink of the 11,072 miles of coastline and each of the 6,289 islands crumbling from it. Not only that, they do so to a detail that inspires an unconditional trust in the user. This is something to be proud of, as making accurate maps is unbelievably, ridiculously difficult.

Now imagine it's 1784 and there are no such things as cars, computers, airplanes, calculators, cameras, a United Kingdom, roads, telephones, efficient means of cutting one's fingernails or even a pen that doesn't require a supplementary bottle of ink to operate. Your name's General William Roy, and you've just been given the job of accurately measuring and mapping the entire nation. Not only that, you know exactly how you're going to do it.

There are other extraordinary tales of science in the mountains, which we'll get to in a bit. But the story of the mapping of Great Britain is a story of one of the great endeavours of any age. To become acquainted with the basics is incumbent upon everyone who has used an Ordnance Survey map, if only to have the vaguest notion what an astounding scientific adventure the whole thing was. And as most adventures start with a map, we're starting with one too. And this is also why you need the Toblerone.

Break off three pieces and arrange them on the table in front of you. Chances are you'll end up with a triangle of some sort. Now imagine that they aren't pieces of Toblerone, they're mountains and, instead of lying a few inches apart, they're several miles from each other. Suppose you want to measure the distance between them, horizontal and vertical. You can't use a ruler. You can't use a tape measure, or one of those clicky-wheel things. Nor do you need to, provided you have three things: the length of one of this triangle's sides, and two of its angles. Find those, and you can measure every dimension within the triangle without leaving your seat.

The really clever bit – the bit, if you're a non-mathematician, you might want to fall off your chair clutching your head when you hear it – is that providing you have these three known values, you can measure the distances within *any* triangle in this way. The triangle made between your chair, the window and your car keys. Between your car keys, your car and where you work. Between where you work, Milton Keynes and Jupiter.

This is, of course, trigonometry – and reasonably basic trigonometry at that. These days we're spared the more maddening aspects of it by three purposeful-looking buttons on a scientific calculator, namely *Sin*, *Cos* and *Tan*, and triangles with unknown dimensions are more likely to haunt the dreams of schoolchildren than those of military officials. But in 1784 William Roy proposed, entirely without the use of shaped confectionery, that as long as you begin with one extremely precisely measured triangle with its points fixed on three immovable and ideally prominent points – a steeple, a head-land and the top of a mountain, say – you can systematically propagate this technique *ad infinitum* across the entire country. If done with sustained preci-sion, the result will be a highly accurate skeleton map – the perfect frame-work from which to hang detail. The 'muscles' of this skeleton – the more artistic detail of rivers, coastline and relief – can then be filled in by cartog-raphers. The result will be a national map of great integrity. And in 1784, that was quite a novel thing.

The method, however, wasn't quite so novel. Trigonometry had been used to measure distance and height – triangulation – since Classical times. In the 6th century BC, the Greek philosopher Thales is said to have attempted to measure the height of the Great Pyramid by comparing the length of its shadow with his own, a method now known as 'intercept theorem'. On the subject of theorems, Pythagoras is supposed to have come up with his epony-mous formula – that the squared length of the long edge of a right-angled triangle equals the squared lengths of the other two sides combined – at around the same time.* And diagrams dating from 2nd-century BC China clearly show trigonometry being used in a seemingly accomplished manner to determine the height of sea cliffs above a beach. The triangulation of distant

* There's no evidence that Pythagoras ever put his theorem to practical use. Indeed, the man was so secretive and accounts of his work have been so mangled by time, that many doubt whether he came up with it at all, instead attributing the theorem's discovery to an eager student who named it in his honour.

objects specifically for mapping purposes had been proposed in 1533 by the Flemish cartographer Gemma Frisius in an influential paper that was read and used by cartographers and astronomers across Europe, although local British maps of the time were shocking enough to suggest that the paper might not have made it across the Channel. Most maps at this point were piecemeal documents produced by a number of different makers, and were highly eclectic in terms of style and level of precision. Even the fine mapmakers of France and Scandinavia had not produced anything approaching an accurate map on a national scale using systemised triangulation. But what finally convinced the Board of Ordnance – based in 1784 in the Tower of London – that a truthful map of one's own country was required wasn't the idea that civilisation or cartographical science should be advanced. It was war.

William Roy – about whom not a huge amount is known, other than that he was shy, conducted cartographical experiments in his spare time and had a fondness for cataloguing Roman ruins, which I suppose tells us something – was particularly qualified to do this, as we shall see. The critical thing that was required was the side of the first triangle; the foundation upon which the huge, national structure of subsequent triangles would be grafted. Given the long-term implications of incorrectly measuring this first 'base' line – imagine owning up to that! – Roy required unimpeachable precision and a location that would allow its execution with the minimum of interference.

This was the reason why on 26 May 1784 a dozen men of the 12th Regiment of Foot began clearing a long, extremely straight pathway of vegetation and other obstructions between King's Arbour and the edge of Bushy Park – a distance of five miles running south-east across, amongst other things, Hounslow Heath in south-west London. The site was chosen 'because of its vicinity to the capital and the Royal Observatory [at Greenwich], its great extent, and the extraordinary levelness of its surface'.*

To get an idea of the precision of this process – or of Roy, or both – you need only look at the method used to measure this line. You'd think that even

---

* Today such things as level ground, great extent and proximity to large population centres are similarly prized, though for different reasons. Anyone who feels a tug of respect for these early surveyors and decides they would quite like to go and walk Roy's baseline – as I did – will arrive to find their way blocked by a substantial development called Heathrow Airport.

in the 18th century this would be reasonably straightforward, but apparently it wasn't. Far from it.

Roy had put in a request to the great Joseph Banks – then President of the Royal Society – for costs that would cover 'Mathematical instruments of the best Kinds about' (£200), 'a carriage on Springs, Secondhand or otherwise' (£25) and 'Pay of six men for sixty days' (£45). The total cost was estimated at £350; the final bill for measuring the Hounslow Base – simply a long straight line, remember – would swell to over £2,000.

Particularly when considering the intentionally comely location, the measurement proved astonishingly troublesome. Roy initially employed a steel line known as a Gunter's Chain as a suitable rigid length of measurement. This was found to expand and contract with the spring frosts and was therefore of an inconsistent length, however minutely. He then moved on to using rods of New England pine cut from a ship's mast placed end to end. Again, the weather thwarted proceedings, with rain causing the wood to warp and bow to untrustworthy lengths. Finally – and presumably with no small degree of exasperation – came an intricate and delicate-sounding system of glass tubes laid upon wooden trestles, which were lined up in a slow creep across Hounslow Heath. Finally, on 30 August, amidst considerable festivity (certainly compared with other revelries related to the measurement of straight lines), the baseline measurement was complete. The length of the line was computed by Roy as being 27,404.7 feet (5.190 miles).* Roy had one side of his triangle, and the First Trigonometrical Survey of Great Britain could begin.

One of the many, many great things about Scotland is that it couldn't be anywhere else. I crossed the border at Gretna – as most do – at speed and without ceremony, but it only takes a few miles heading north for this scraped part of Britain to visibly inflate. First, the vast Southern Uplands build the

---

* The modern, GPS-facilitated measurement of this line is 27,376.8 feet – around 27 feet shy of Roy's measurement. It's not difficult to lose 27 feet over five miles, and considering the date this measurement was extraordinarily accurate. Nonetheless, given his toils and evidently exacting personality, it's still tempting to imagine that Roy is extremely angrily spinning in his grave.

canvas's scale, comprising soft, muscular hills across which few paths wander. This area is home to some of the roughest terrain in the country; the fantastically dark names of the summits and ranges west of the M74 – like the Dungeon Hills, the Rig of the Jarkness and the Range of the Awful Hand, not forgetting a notorious bogland amidst them known as the Silver Flowe – make up the nucleus of a landscape awesome in scope and sinister of feel.

Whilst the mountains of Scotland's west coast perhaps edge a win when it comes to sliced, storm-battered spectacle, it's those in the centre and the east that provide the awe in terms of desolate scale. The sprawling ranges of the Monadhliath, Atholl, Breadalbane and the great mountains of the Cairngorms fill this region, bulking north towards the Great Glen and west towards the massive wastes of Rannoch Moor. Here, isolated giants such as Ben Alder, Ben Lawers and Creag Meagaidh break the 1,000-metre contour to number amongst the very highest mountains in Britain. And it was one of these lonely-cast peaks that was my destination on this particular windy afternoon. It was a distinctive mountain that held a special kind of mystique, rising above the forested terrain of Perthshire in, it's said, quite unmistakable fashion. I couldn't wait to see it.

The weather was typical of Scotland in that it really didn't know what the hell it was doing. Rain, wind, squally sun: Perthshire seemed to be a symposium of meteorological conditions as I crossed the blustery Firth of Tay and headed for Pitlochry. If this sounds like I'm moaning, I'm not – it was actually electrifying. Everything was so vivid: sunlit hayfields adorned with blood-red barns bordered by wet emerald forests under skies of purple-grey. It was as if the landscape had the saturation turned up. Intending to travel as far as Faskally before leaving the A9, I spotted a sign for Foss and on impulse dived off the main road, immediately entering a beguiling world in which a scrawny, dapple-lit road tunnelled through thick trees. To the right flowed the huge River Tummel, practically level with the road. And ahead of me through the canopy, the hillsides were banked with layered teeth of conifers. Everything was wild and green and thunderous and big. And just like that, I was in the Scottish Highlands.

*   *   *

Long before William Roy began doing exacting things with glass tubes on Hounslow Heath, you could rightly say that the English knew Scotland better than they knew their own country – at least as a complete, consistent unit. The main reason for the sudden clamour to gain an intimate knowledge of Britain's wild northern sway was the Scottish Jacobite rebellion in 1745. Pretender to the throne Charles Edward Stuart – known more romantically to history as 'Bonnie' Prince Charlie – had unsuccessfully attempted to usurp King George II, his uprising bloodily ending at the Battle of Culloden. But even despite their victory in this, the last official big fight on British soil, Scotland continued to be a niggling worry for the government and its army.

To them, Scotland was a place of disparate clans and unhinged terrain – a country positively oozing menace. And whilst they had a geographical knowledge of Scotland that was at best sketchy, the clansmen who had assisted the uprisings of previous years had the ability to truly understand their land. A now apocryphal written quote sums up the English attitude of the time towards their northern cousins, as being themselves a metaphor for the brutal land of mountains in which they dwelled: 'Such "noble" men as these are like Barren Mountains, that bear neither Plants nor Grass for Publick Use. They touch the Skie, but are unprofitable to the Earth.'

Of the many things that caused pain for the British Army during this bloody campaign – rain, bugs, bogs, rain, thickets of forest, rain and 7,000 Jacobites – evidently the thing that made any kind of strategic thinking impossible was the inability to effectively navigate the Scottish terrain. The British felt they were at a fundamental disadvantage, and until the Highlands were comprehensively 'reformed' to prevent future skirmishes, as such they would remain. Following extended periods in the Highlands, those in the military felt that the biggest problem wasn't the Jacobites, or even the weather; it was the maps. Or rather, the lack of them.

That's not to say that maps of Scotland didn't *exist*. Some were even reasonably accomplished. Timothy Pont's fascinating late 16th-century maps of the country certainly gave an idea of its extent and terrain – some even featuring local names for the mountains – and were later published in Joan Blaeu's *Atlas Novus*. But these early maps were somewhat impressionistic and had obvious strategic limitations.

It was a soldier named David Watson who convinced George II to sanc-
tion what was termed a 'Compleat and Accurate Survey of Scotland'. This
would address what Watson – an engineer who had been in charge of the
British Army's provisions during the 1745 uprising and who was a particularly outspoken advocate of ridding the Highlands of 'barbarism' – considered an acute embarrassment. He proposed that what was stopping the army
from subduing the Highlanders – as well as being key to dealing with any
future uprisings briskly and confidently – was an intimate knowledge of the
country. '[The] rebellion and its authors are to be come at in the most inaccessible parts of the Highlands,' he wrote in a letter to his brother-in-law
Robert Dundas in 1746. The Dundas family were wealthy landowners in
Lanarkshire, and managing their land was a family whose twenty-year-old
son had shown extraordinary flair for sketching land features with great accuracy. At some point when visiting his in-laws this son crossed paths with
Watson, whom he evidently impressed to such a degree that he was selected
to execute the first full cartographical survey of Scotland. It would be the first
and by far the toughest challenge he'd face in a career that would follow some
(occasionally very straight) lines already familiar to us. His name: William
Roy.

The challenge the young Scot faced was monstrous. With no formal carto-
graphic training – though he did have a 'sound drilling in Latin and
Mathematics', thank goodness – Roy was expected to set forth and systematically interpret wildly complex and largely unknown terrain with a view to
making it orderly to the eye. Not only that, with the Jacobites still sore after
their defeat at Culloden, the threat of surprise attacks was never far from his
thoughts – especially as it would be difficult to hide the rather official-looking
nature of his work.

The Highlands in 1746 were not as they are today. Modern Scotland is one
of the leanest populated areas of Europe thanks to the notorious Highland
Clearances of later years; but up to that point they were teeming with crofting
settlements, most of them entirely peaceful. However, Jacobites notwithstanding, many locals viewed any kind of land audit as a precursor to bad news –
usually a tax hike or some other form of state interference – and altercations
that stopped perilously shy of murder had been experienced by surveyors
attempting to move through the Highlands piecemeal in previous years.

The most influential of these early surveyors was George Wade, then a field marshal, who had taken a leading role in suppressing Jacobitism in Scotland during and following the uprising of 1715. Wade had built a system of roads – in the most Roman sense of the word – through the Scottish interior intended to aid the passage of troops between important strategic forts such as Fort Augustus, Fort William and Fort George over a total distance of some 240 miles. A gruelling exercise conducted by a band of labourers known rather darkly as 'Highwaymen' – who are alleged to have survived the horrors of the Scottish weather by drinking vast quantities of alcohol – General Wade's Military Roads (as they are still pleasingly titled on Ordnance Survey Maps) were completed in 1738, with Major William Caulfeild continuing to expand the network to over 1,000 miles following Wade's departure.* Roy intended to use these roads as the initial bones of his slowly developing skeleton map.

Roy's progress was, predictably, an agonising creep. His notebooks of the time are lost, but it's thought he spent two years in the Highlands with – it's assumed, and this only because it would have been practically impossible for him to have worked alone – a small band of untrained assistants crossing the Highlands mile by mile across diabolical terrain, using Wade's lean infrastructure where possible. His primary concerns were roads and rivers, the strides and wriggles of which were calculated using a perambulator (a rolling, clicking wheel still often used to measure distance), a Gunter's chain and an early form of basic handheld theodolite known as a circumferentor, with which he would sight the angles of prominent features such as mountains, then sketch their outline by eye. Accuracy – although far better than in any previous surveys – was somewhat loose; where they could not be measured, distances were guessed, but it appears that Roy's guesses were better than most.

In around 1749 he was joined by five junior surveyors and a man named Paul Sandby, whose duty was to look after the matter of physically rendering

---

* Despite Wade's greater fame, it was Caulfeild who shouldered many of the more problematic road projects in Scotland. His network was far more extensive and covered more challenging terrain, including the infamous zigzags of the Devil's Staircase in Glen Coe and the Corrieyairack Pass, both of which were awesome pieces of road building for the time and are today home to some of the most celebrated views in Scotland.

the terrain. Sandby would later become an influential landscape painter and is today known to history as 'the father of English watercolour art', but to Roy he was the rather less romantic 'Chief Draughtsman of the Plan'. Surveying would take place during the summer months, whereupon the mapmakers would retire to Edinburgh to continue working up the composite map, known as 'the original protraction'.

The team cracked on, and by 1752 their survey of most of the Highlands was complete. The presumably weary band then moved south towards the English border into more comely terrain, to finish the job with comparative ease.

The best and most consistent map of Scotland of the time was on a single sheet at a scale of one inch to 13.5 miles, produced by John Elphinstone in 1745. Roy's map sharpened the knowledge of Scottish geography to an impressively focused improvement of one inch to 1,000 yards. He was reluctant to accept the praise that was heaped upon it, perhaps as he was more intimately acquainted with its limitations and conjectures than most. He regarded the map more as a 'magnificent military sketch, than a very accurate map of the country' and implored any user that 'no geometrical exactness is to be expected, the sole object in view being, to shew remarkable things, or such as constitute the great outlines of the Country.'

Roy was possibly being self-effacing, but critics have not always been wholly complimentary towards his map either. In their 1986 academic critique of the military survey Whittington and Gibson described it as 'one of the most intriguing and at the same time infuriating documents available to the researcher into Scotland's past landscapes'. Around the time of the First World War Sir Charles Close – then the director of the Ordnance Survey, no less – referred to the map with curious bitterness as 'little more than a glorified compass sketch'.

Whilst I personally can't profess to be a cartographer – I did once assist in trying to make a map of a small area of Wales; it ended up looking like a ceiling stain – I can say that to my amateur but map-familiar eyes Roy's 'sketch' was a stunning achievement, considering how difficult it must have been to execute. Given the context of the time, to niggle about its accuracy is to be wildly unappreciative of his hardships. You might as well criticise Leonardo da Vinci for not making greater use of a computer.

Speaking of computers, on the National Library of Scotland's website there's a wonderful toy to help you appreciate Roy's efforts. In the maps section, you can view a zoomable digital version of Roy's entire interpretation of Scotland and overlay a modern map that you can fade in and out to see how the two inter-relate. What's immediately clear is that it isn't perfect, but whilst you may notice fairly quickly the things they got wrong – and for reasons of logistics and time all of the islands were excluded, leaving the finished rendering startlingly naked-looking – what's most impressive is how much they got *right*.

Physically, it's beautiful. Rendered in pen and ink colour wash, natural features are displayed with logical, organic faith – green for woodlands, blue-green for water, buff for moorland. Mankind's mark is unsubtle and bold: red for buildings, yellow for farmland, orange for roads. But the map's most striking attribute – by far – is the mountains.

From the neatly delineated valleys and settlements rise wave upon wave of elegantly knuckled, dramatically shaded mountain ranges. Their height, texture, the way they intersect and the violence of their terrain were re-created so skilfully in two-dimensional form that they made the peculiar, oblique-angled viewpoints of earlier maps seem childlike. Nobody had seen anything quite like it before, either mapped or for real; let's not forget that in the mid 18th century nobody had flown over these things, so bird's-eye views were entirely products of imaginative conjecture.

Most historians attribute this artistic showboating to Paul Sandby, who used the map to shunt forward the development of mapping and the depiction of relief using shading (an early example of a technique that became known as 'hachuring'), as well as his own development as an artist. Sandby was just eighteen years old when he joined the survey in 1749, and before setting forth for Scotland received only a brisk mapmaking apprenticeship at the headquarters of the Board of Ordnance – the commissioners of Roy's survey – in the map room of the Tower of London.

Sandby's more conventional illustrations from the military survey are equally illuminating. The young artist would evidently draw to amuse himself, and also to document the survey as it crept ever onward. One – a basic, coloured sketch – shows a man in military dress: a long, red coat with blue lapels and a tri-cornered hat beneath which wisps of hair protrude. Round-faced, the man looks out of the picture with a strong, steady gaze. In his hand he holds a slate upon which he rests a scribe. Most sources conclude that no surviving likeness exists of William Roy, but this portrait – from Sandby's casual sketchbook, dated 1749 and untitled by the artist – could quite sensibly be deduced as one. Some say it could be Sandby himself, or someone the survey encountered, or anybody in it. Perhaps it's nobody at all.*

Another of Sandby's sketches would prove to be somewhat prophetic. In *A View near Loch Rannoch* we get a snapshot of the functioning military survey: two redcoats with a chain, two more tending horses and casually conversing with kilted locals, another holding a flag in the crook of an elbow as if accustomed to doing so, and a distant figure in blue – almost certainly Roy – hunched over a tripod-mounted circumferentor. Many have looked for meaning in the most obvious omission from Sandby's sketch; it has been claimed that the purpose of the image was to show how calm British control was in a region of particularly traumatic Jacobite bloodshed. By making British soldiers the focus of the picture minus any obvious distractions, the scene of the Loch Rannoch lakeside conveys a confident, strident military at ease with their surroundings and those in it. But it's suspected that if Sandby had been faithful, the figures in the survey would not have been the focus. Something else entirely would have captured the attention and the eye, something so dominating as to render them almost comical in its sway. That same something that Sandby consciously chose to omit from his now famous image would in the coming years have great significance to Roy, to mapmaking, to endeavour – and to science as a whole. And it was my destination tonight.

It was nearing dusk when I arrived at the lochside where Sandby made that image. Nobody knows exactly where he was standing when he made *A View near Loch Rannoch*, other than that it was somewhere near Loch Rannoch, with a view looking east. In reality there aren't that many places with a shore along the loch, so these days at least the choice is limited. Perhaps it's the sudden release from the claustrophobia of sinuous, leaf-walled lanes (one of which, I was later delighted to discover, was an old military road of General Wade's),

* Another likeness – a period cartoon – exists of Roy, and is reproduced in Edwin Danson's book *Weighing the World*, although the source of the image is unclear.

but Loch Rannoch feels enormous. I'd found a little pull-in just to the west of Kinloch Rannoch, a merry but adrift little place seemingly composed almost entirely of hotels, many laying claim to be the 'Centre of the Highlands'. Leaving the car and grimacing for a second at my journey-deadened legs, I made my way down to the waterside, where the remains of a firepit amidst the brown rocks of the shore suggested recent occupation by wild campers. The wind this afternoon had chopped the loch into white horses, and it felt more like an inland sea – something exacerbated by the flatness of Rannoch Moor to the west and, beyond this, the shadows of the distant mountains of Glen Coe spray-hazed on the horizon. To the east, conspicuously absent from Sandby's picture, rose the mountain I'd come here for, sweeping from the loch to a height of 1,083 metres and a striking point of near-perfect symmetry.

Way back at the beginning of this chapter I asked you to get two things. Assuming the Toblerone is now long gone, I suggest you turn your attention to the map. Unless you have a sheet covering Romney Marsh or Norfolk in front of you, you'll notice it's covered in faint wiggly orange lines occasionally interrupted by numbers. These are contours, and they're the means your map employs to display the third dimension. That's to say they're the flat language of relief, and a numerical indication of the change in height on the ground. The numbers relate to each particular contour line's height (or depth) relative to sea level, in metres. In trying to visualise how contours work, it's helpful to imagine the protruding earth – a mountain range, say – as cut into horizontal slices stacked on top of each other in ten-metre intervals. If these were stepped, they might resemble a rice terrace. Contour lines are, amongst other things, the mountain walker's tool as they describe the nature of the land. From them you can tell how steep a slope is, how narrow a ridge will be, how uniform the ground is and how difficult it's likely to be to navigate. Such is the behaviour of these lines and their representation of the landscape, if you were to faithfully follow a contour line you'd eventually end up where you started – even if it took you months of walking – and you'd remain at exactly the same altitude the entire way.

What is remarkable is that their inception as far as cartography was concerned was a by-product of something else. A happy accident, nothing more, caused by one of the most scientifically extraordinary – and extraordinarily gruelling – experiments of our age. The place where this happened is the empty space behind those surveyors in Sandby's *View near Loch Rannoch*, the space I was now eyeing over two centuries later and which had unequivo- cally snared my full attention. Sandby neglected to include it, but if he had, rising behind the surveyors to a muscular height would have been a mountain of startling spectacle: near-symmetrical, elegantly scalloped, utterly dominat- ing. This was – and remains – the famous Schiehallion.

In the early summer of 1774 a man named Nevil Maskelyne arrived at the southern flank of Schiehallion to find a small bothy waiting for him. It was here – and in another, similar, site on the north side of the peak – that he would spend sixteen and a half weeks tinkering with a variety of devices, making stellar observations and doing other rather exacting things thor- oughly incongruous to the terrain. His goal was as simple as it was strange: to determine the mass of the earth. Or, put in a slightly more romantically inaccurate way still repeated to this day, Maskelyne wanted to weigh the world.

You may well wonder how one large and admittedly fetching mountain in the Southern Highlands could provide a fitting location for an experiment of such gravitas. But Schiehallion was not only fitting. It was perfect, and had two things that made it so: symmetry and great bulk.

'Perthshire afforded us a remarkable hill,' Maskelyne would later write, 'of sufficient height, tolerably detached from other hills, and considerably larger from east to west than from north to south.'

The idea was this: hang a uniform weight on the end of a line – a pendu- lum on a plumb line, say – and it will hang vertically down towards the earth, with gravity acting upon it evenly on all sides. The line hangs straight because the weight is being pulled downwards by the gravity of the earth; Newton's apple stopped mid-fall, if you like. By 1774 it was known that the planets orbited the sun, and that there existed a relationship between the gravitational pull of an object and its overall mass; basically, the bigger an object the greater its gravity. The biggest object hereabouts is the earth, which is why things tend to fall towards it unless otherwise directed. But what if an object of great bulk, abrupt prominence and similar composition to the earth was located near to wherever you were standing? Something big enough to conceivably have its *own* gravity that might be significant enough to cause a ripple in the earth's own uniform forces? We're not suggesting the effect of such a thing placed adjacent to Newton's apple would be enough to make it fall sideways out of the tree or cause a pendulum to be drawn towards it like a magnetised necklace; just to cause a *twitch* – the tiniest of sways – in the forces acting upon a falling object. If you could measure the magnitude of this twitch, by the behaviour of the object being pulled you could determine by what magnitude the earth's gravitational pull was *greater* than that of the nearby bulk. If that nearby bulk (which at this point let's just call Schiehallion) was known intimately – its composition, dimensions, volume and mass – with a whizzy bit of mathematics you could probably determine, by way of a ratio, the mass of the earth itself.

The question was whether the gravitational effect of a mountain on a dangled plumb-line pendulum – the 'bending' of gravity, or *deflection* – would be sizeable enough to measure. Isaac Newton didn't think so. He had considered a similar experiment in the second volume of his *Principia* in 1713, noting that 'Whole mountains will not be sufficient to produce any sensible effect. A mountain of an hemispherical figure, three miles high, and six broad, will not, by its attraction, draw the pendulum two minutes out of the true perpendicular; and it is only in the great bodies of the planets that these forces are to be perceived.' In addition, an attempt to disprove Newton's dismissal had already been made – and had failed – on Chimborazo in Ecuador by a pair of French scientists. The scientists could scarcely have made life more difficult for themselves, though. Chimborazo is immensely high – 6,268 metres – and the levels where they attempted their deflections was, at 4,680 metres, well into the zone where altitude sickness and frequent drops in temperatures could rightly be expected. In addition, for their experiment to work the scientists would need to know both the general composition and exterior dimensions of the mountain in detail. Chimborazo being as big as it is – and as a volcano, quite possibly full of holes – this was a task that would require perhaps more conjecture than was acceptable, and unsurprisingly the French scientists returned home with little confidence in their results.

Maskelyne himself was no stranger to enthusiastic foreign enterprises in the name of science. Despite being an ordained minister, he was a scientist and a significant Enlightenment figure who, in addition to being a Fellow of the Royal Society, also held the distinguished position of Astronomer Royal. His appointment followed several active years that had seen him dispatched to various exotic parts of the world to make planetary observations – notably to St Helena in 1761 to measure the transit of Venus, and to Barbados in 1764 to establish the longitude of the capital by observing Jupiter. However, in August 1773 Maskelyne's own refusal to accept Newton's conclusions saw him send a surveyor of considerable repute named Charles Mason on horseback into the Scottish Highlands in search of a mountain of very specific quality. It needed to be tall, steep, running roughly east–west, 'with as few scoops & hollows as possible' and standing above a deep valley. Previously considered were Whernside in Yorkshire and Skiddaw in Cumbria, but neither tallied with Maskelyne's strict criteria. But after a week of surveying, Mason delivered in style, finding a mountain which, as Maskelyne would later write, 'was called by the neighbouring inhabitants Schehallien which, I have since been informed, signifies in the language "constant storm"* – a name well adapted to the appearance which it so frequently exhibits.' After St Helena and Barbados, Mason had identified the somewhat less comely venue for the exotically acclimatised Maskelyne's next experiment: a Perthshire hillside.

Schiehallion isn't quite as it appears from Loch Rannoch. In fact, it isn't at all as it appears from Loch Rannoch. From there it looks like a cone of extraordinary elegance, its slopes subtly concave and its summit pointed, a 1,000-metre peak of piped icing. But as you begin to circle the mountain it elongates, first resembling a long, tapering shark fin cutting through the surface of the land in a westerly direction, and then – when you're broadside to it – simply a lump exhibiting a curious but unremarkable smoothness. It was certainly not a complicated, tortuous swirl of ridgelines, and it was easy to see why it was a canny choice for an experiment that required a thing of great and uniform bulk.

I took the military road back out of Kinloch Rannoch and found a small pull-in where I could discreetly leave the car. My rucksack was already packed. Shoving a few extra sheaves of paper into the top pocket and glancing round at the unsettled weather, I threw in a spare jacket, locked the car and crossed the road. A few moments later I set foot on Schiehallion and began to climb.

---

* Although Maskelyne had written of the mountain's name as 'constant storm', it seems this was a mistake – albeit an appealingly apt one – on his part. The mistake endures, though.

Following his identification of the 'remarkable hill' for Maskelyne's experiment, Charles Mason decided to withdraw from proceedings upon being offered the paltry (by scientific standards) sum of a guinea a day;* such a tiny sum seems odd, particularly as it was clear Maskelyne initially had no intention of performing the experiment himself. The Royal Society, however, insisted the ageing astronomer personally execute the complicated and gruelling plan in the wake of Mason's departure (it's tempting to think that this would have amused them, given Maskelyne's penchant for couched living).

Maskelyne took this as a rueful compliment: 'The Royal Society were pleased to do me the honour to think my assistance necessary to ensure the success of such a delicate experiment ... [This was] sufficient motive with me to encounter whatever difficulties and fatigues might attend ... in so inconvenient and inclement a situation.' Despite his outward chipperness, Maskelyne certainly seemed dimly aware this was going to be hell. Spending months in an observatory pinned to the side of a mountain, in a fearful landscape notorious for its weather, trying to conduct measurements of startling delicacy; there seemed little illusion that this would be the scientific equivalent of trying to thread a needle in a tornado. Already on site was a local surveyor by the name of William Menzies and, on secondment from Greenwich, a brilliant mathematician named Reuben Burrow. Both had been tasked with establishing the observatories on either side of the mountain and furnishing them with suitable equipment – no easy task given the weight and delicacy of the instruments, and the steep and decidedly indelicate mountainside.

Burrow was evidently quite a character. A man of undeniable genius but unstable personality, the 27-year-old Yorkshireman was extremely chippy about his lower-class roots. Varied backgrounds were not exactly uncommon in scientific circles at the time, but Burrow's coping strategy evidently was. By all accounts a spectacularly angry and disagreeable man, Burrow would not moderate his lack of tact for anyone, least of all the genteel Maskelyne and his

---

* Mason's final years are a mystery. Returning to America – where he had measured the Mason–Dixon line between Pennsylvania and Maryland – with his wife and eight children, Mason enjoyed a friendship with Benjamin Franklin, with whom he intended to begin a major scientific project. He died in 1786; of his project nothing is known, but a landmark on the moon – the Mason Crater – is named after him.

fellow alumni at the Royal Society. 'Burrow is a good mathematician,' one would later write, 'but eminently scurrilous and slanderous.'* Sadly this infamous reputation bewildered his superiors and probably ruled Burrow out from supervising the experiment himself – and with Maskelyne stoked a breathtakingly bickersome odd-couple relationship over the gruelling months ahead.

But all of this was in the future when, on 30 June 1774, Maskelyne arrived on Schiehallion. It's at this point that our two threads of lengthy digression merge, as travelling with Maskelyne on the journey north was none other than our old pal William Roy.

Roy and Maskelyne were, if not friends, certainly contemporaries. In 1772 Roy had been in the audience when Maskelyne presented the idea of his 'gravity experiment' to the Royal Society. By now a celebrated mapmaker, Roy was invaluable in assisting Maskelyne with locational intelligence and background for his experiment, as well as his expertise in conducting delicate surveys of brusque Highland terrain. Maskelyne and Roy would spend their final night before setting foot on Schiehallion at Castle Menzies, in the same room's Bonnie Prince Charlie had occupied on his way to Culloden.

On Schiehallion, waiting for Maskelyne and Roy, were Burrow, Menzies, a small squad of labourers and two hastily constructed bothies located at over 550 metres on the north and south sides of the mountain. Each of these bothies had a small tower into which was installed a zenith sector – essentially a telescope designed to be pointed straight up – and a plumb line. Due to Schiehallion's symmetry, it was hoped the plumb line would be pulled minute but measurable amounts towards the intervening mountain from opposing sides of it. To add further complication, the plumb line's incline from the vertical would have to be determined from the stars, as the instrument ordinarily used to measure whether something was vertical or not – ironically – was a plumb line.

---

* Evidence of this is too amusing not to quote, given Burrow's particular fondness for insults. Two unfortunate contemporaries who professionally wronged the Yorkshireman received the accolade of being 'Two of the most stupid and dirty of all possible fools, rogues and scoundrels', with one of these singled out as 'Not only the dirtiest scoundrel that God ever made, but the dirtiest scoundrel that he possibly could make. Amen.'

Considering the additional computations to allow for a moving planet, the precise nature of the measurements themselves – plus the headache of having to deal with the Scottish climate, ground that had to be made level before measurements could begin and the fact that Schiehallion was often smothered in cloud* and therefore not the most natural choice for a celestial observatory, let alone two – Maskelyne really did rather well.

Roy helped him for the first two weeks before repairing to survey a nearby group of hills above Strathtay. Maskelyne remained at the southern observatory for six weeks, making 169 observations of 39 stars. A crew of local labourers then relocated operations to the bothy on the north of the mountain where, after a fortnight being thwarted by bad weather, a similar programme of observations began. Maskelyne made 168 observations of 37 stars, finally completing his work on October 24 1774 after sixteen and a half weeks on the mountain and – practically miraculously – successfully acquiring the crucial measurements he came for.

I had no ambitious notions of weighing the world or suspending anything from a line other than a damp jacket or perhaps a head torch. My mission was simpler than Maskelyne's: find the site of his ruined northern observatory, and camp there. I could contrive some deep reason for so doing, but there wasn't one. I simply wanted to be on the spot where it happened, and see and feel what it was like. But first, I had to find it.

You'd think that this would be a fairly simple task. The problem was that the precise site of Maskelyne's observatory isn't particularly well documented. His own writings referred to a 'large level area had been cut away [on the north side of the mountain] with great labour', but he didn't say where. There are a number of photographs of the site, but these are generally vague, generally old, and most of the people who took them generally dead. What I therefore had on my hands was something of historical treasure hunt, and one with precious few clues.

---

* Discounting Maskelyne's erroneous 'contant storm' translation, Schiehallion had various other names. Locals called it Maiden Pap, whilst an over-romantic translation of its name was 'fairy hill of the Caledonians', as some legends link Schiehallion to these mythical creatures. A more believable interpretation comes from the Gaelic *Hill of the Ancestor Spirits of the Caledonians*, which states that it derives from the pronunciation of the word 'Sithean', meaning 'ancestor spirits'.

In the weeks leading up to my trip I'd called various people and left messages. Sent emails. Trawled books and the internet, all to no specific and often contradictory avail. Maskelyne's observatory was evidently anything between 550 and 750 metres on the north slope, the platform upon which it stood was either still visible or no longer visible, and the ruins comprised of anything from absolutely nothing to entire walls. After reading of the latter I'd prowled over aerial imagery of Schiehallion – something which these days anyone can do with the click of a button – to try and spot some kind of unconformity of slope, any peculiar flatness, anything at all to suggest that a building might once have stood there, all to no avail. This I found surprising given the otherwise bare nature of Schiehallion's northern side. The southern slope, contrary to the popular notion that the mountain is wholly symmetrical, is really quite craggy and markedly steeper than the side I was heaving my way up this evening.

Even in the references that noted traces of the observatory as still being visible, the closest thing I could find to an actual specific location – on the eve of leaving for Scotland – was also tantalisingly vague. I found it in a delightful and otherwise detailed 1957 academic paper by a noted Scottish optical physicist named Richard Sillitto. Evidently Sillitto, who died in 2005, had a soft spot for Maskelyne and his experiment, but apparently lacked one for numerical co-ordinates. Instead, what I got was this, and I quote:

> Two streams which cut straight down the hillside form an unmistakable feature of the northern aspect of the hill … at about 2,300 feet, and roughly 150 yards west of these streams, there are two rectangular, level platforms, 5 or 6 yards wide and 10 to 15 yards long. At the ends of one are the remains of the stone end walls of the bothy. On the other platform you can still trace as a different texture of the turf a five-foot diameter circle where the circular wall to house the astronomical quadrant was raised.

Well, how exciting. Not only were there detailed (sort of) directions to find where Maskelyne huddled by night for all those stormy months; you could actually still see *traces* of it, and stand where his zenith sector stood.

The previous night I'd diligently printed out a map and marked the point where this mission would take me. There were the two streams, unmistakable as promised – and a few metric conversions later, I had a location bullseyed on my map where I'd seek this abandoned, scientifically significant ledge.

The north slope of Schiehallion today sees little footfall. The east side of the mountain is partly owned by Scottish wild-land caretakers the John Muir Trust, who have gone to great lengths to safeguard a mountain that – by Highland standards – sees many ascents, doubtless due to that deceptive but striking profile from Kinloch Rannoch. The main path most of these take to the summit is broad and clear, following the length of the slack-backed ridge, whereas mine was bare, pathless and steep. Whilst perhaps not the most aesthetically pleasing way to climb the mountain, it certainly looked direct – and was definitely the direction from which to appreciate the peculiar smoothness of the mountain's flank.

I latched on to the westernmost stream and used it as a natural handrail up the mountainside. Following this was satisfying in itself; crossing and uncrossing the thinning waterway gradually led me beneath an ancient Scots pine, through scrubby heather and onto mountainside clad in a layer of grassy peat. It didn't look like a long climb – Schiehallion's summit in fact looked oddly close. Surely there couldn't be too many places between here and there suitable for an observatory. Several times I came across what looked like a path, and each time I was struck by the idea that maybe this was a track created by the scientists to ferry supplies and building materials up the hill. But their inconsistency and failure to lead anywhere at all meant they were more likely to be old stream rivulets or sheep tracks.

Eventually the stream began to weaken, and I began to pay more attention to the map and the altimeter built into my watch. By the time it read 700 metres above sea level – approximately 2,300 feet – I began traversing west along the steep, frequently mushy mountainside, pacing out the metres as I went. I knew that 64 of my double steps equalled around 100 metres, a touch more in the choppy wind and steep terrain. Sillitto's instructions stated that the first of Maskelyne's observatory ledges lay at this height, 150 yards west of the westernmost stream. This was about 140 metres, or 90 paces. Trying my best to maintain the same height, I started to walk. It's worth noting here that this process of walking level at the same height along a slope is a common technique in hillwalking. It's called contouring. And without Schiehallion, the term probably wouldn't exist.

Once the more delicate aspects of his task were completed, Maskelyne's work still needed the second piece of the puzzle to make any sense – and it would prove diabolically complicated. He may have measured Schiehallion's gravitational pull on his plumb line, but without knowing the precise mass of the mountain he couldn't work out the factor by which its gravity was smaller than that of the earth – and therefore in turn work out how much greater the earth's mass was than Schiehallion's. Essentially, then, he needed to know the physical anatomy of Schiehallion to a degree of precision never applied to a mountain before. Which meant more measurements – and lots of them.

Tasked to do this, inevitably, was Burrow. The mathematician had been kept busy assisting Maskelyne in his observatory, attempting to establish a baseline from which triangulation could be established and (if Burrow's own accounts are to be believed, and the consensus seems to indicate they probably should) wearily fixing mistakes the evidently shambolic Maskelyne was making. One of many such instances recalled by Burrow was how it was he who had set up the instrumentation and put it in order, whereupon Maskelyne then 'put it out of order and did not know how to put it right again'.

However good Burrow was at clearing up after the errant astronomer, there's little denying that the fiery-tempered Yorkshireman's own survey was pretty chaotic. In attempting to measure as much of the mountain as he could from which to triangulate relative height – and therefore volume – he and Menzies set up over 50 bases, from which they used theodolites and wooden poles to survey thousands of individual points on the mountain. From these grew a bewildering network of several hundred trigonometrical triangles in varying orientations.

It's therefore unsurprising that, when the eagerly awaited field notes from Schiehallion didn't materialise, all eyes fell squarely on Burrow. The Royal Society certainly seemed under the impression that he was in possession of them, and in the nervous wait between 1774 and 1775 even speculated he was embezzling them because of some unsoothed grievance. Burrow finally pointed out that Maskelyne had taken them back to London and had evidently been in charge of the 'missing' observations all along. The pair's mutual animosity deepened when it transpired that Maskelyne had been recounting the Schiehallion saga to his influential friends with little if any mention of Burrow, Menzies or even Roy. Burrow retaliated by painting a deeply unflattering picture of the Astronomer Royal, who duly countered with aspersions that Maskelyne had only dragged himself to Scotland as it was deemed that Burrow 'could not be depended upon ... on account of his inferiority of education'. Maskelyne also claimed he had agreed to 'make the direction of the experiment ... not without reluctance [and] not out of any wish to depart from my own observatory to live on a bare mountain'. It was amidst this potato-throwing – and the thickening storm clouds of the American War of Independence – that the results of the survey (on the computations of which rested the fate of the entire experiment) were then quietly passed to Charles Hutton, the self-taught son of a Newcastle coal miner.

To say Hutton's task was enormous would be a titanic understatement. Not only did he have to correct much of the data, he then had to make sense of it, devise a way of putting it to use, then complete the task and actually determine the mass of Schiehallion and – eventually – the earth.

Fortunately, Hutton's capacity for computational mathematics was exceptionally generous. Having made a map over a metre wide, he agonisingly plotted the corrected survey data and – using trigonometry – calculated the heights for the thousands of individual points surveyed on the mountain.

Hutton then hit a problem. He had worked out that the easiest way to calculate the overall mass of the hill was to divide it up into horizontal segments via a series of concentric circles. This would, in theory, make the calculation a matter of simple arithmetic. But he found in practice that the concentric circles he drew on his map seldom coincided with Burrow's scattershot observation points. The result was a mess of different heights within the same segment, requiring a maze of additional calculations. Hutton's solution was to link 'by a faint line all the points that had the same relative altitude'. Hutton's simple act would have consequences that would have far more practical impact than the results of the experiment itself.

To claim that the Schiehallion experiment was the first use of contour lines – or isolines, if you want to sound clever – wouldn't be strictly true. Contours as a concept of diagrammatically linking equivalent values had been applied to various tasks in Europe – initially to convey areas of equal depth, not height – since the early 1700s. In 1701 Edmond Halley (he of the comet, amongst many, many other notable scientific side notes) used similar lines in an 'isogonic map' to link, of all things, areas of magnetic declination across the Atlantic. The result is startlingly like the topographical contour maps of today, the difference being that the lines are much more baggily spaced, cover the whole ocean and link invisible data values rather than being the representation of something physically appreciable.

It's unlikely these early users of contour lines were riffing on each other's idea; given their eclectic end uses and the rampant scientific productivity of the time, it's probable that each method was discovered independently. Whatever the case, Hutton's epiphany would echo through the ages as the canniest application of the contour, not only allowing a reasonably accurate assessment of a hill's volume, but allowing the viewer to make a judgement about the flow and form of the land. This therefore enables the mountain walker to predict the pitch of the terrain he or she will be travelling and tell from a glance at the nature of the lines covering the map just how mountainous an area is.

Back on the side of Schiehallion I was having a frustrating time simply trying to find the site of Maskelyne's old observatory, let alone anything more ambitious. Everywhere were little levellings, a few feet square, covered in grass. It certainly sounded from Sillitto's description as if I'd know this place when I found it, but I just wasn't finding it. I tried ascending and looking back down the hill to see if elevation would reveal anything, but no – just hummocky grass, dark patches of bare peat and boulders.

I searched this small area on the mountain's north slope for over an hour, crossing and re-crossing streams, clambering over boulders, ascending over ledges and traversing across the slope – all with one eye on my altimeter and another on the ground. Darkness was beginning to creep across the sky and the wind was noticeably increasing. These, and the odd squall of fine rain sweeping through the glen, slowly chipped away at my optimism, and – not knowing for sure if there was even anything to find – I began to resign myself to the idea that perhaps the ledge was no longer visible and the mountainside itself would have to suffice. It was then that I spotted something about 50 metres below – a ledge of peat forming an edge about a foot high, in a suspiciously straight line. Straight lines don't occur all that often in the mountains – even on the notably regular Schiehallion – so I began to descend towards it in the gloom.

What I'd found was a lean ledge walled on one side with a small hummock of peat. The straight line I'd spotted was simply where the peat's grassy covering had sloughed off, exposing the dark soil in a long, vertical crack. I paced keenly around the area, looking for more signs of possible occupation, but found none. This might be it; but then again, it might not.

Crestfallen, I pulled out my phone, loaded up its map and dropped a digital map waypoint to mark the spot. As far as sleeping in the remains of an ancient observatory on a Highland mountain went, this was clearly as close as I was going to get tonight.

The tent went up just as a heavier rain began to set in, the silvery Loch Rannoch now a grey smudge on the horizon. Throwing the tent up to form at least a workable shelter, I dived inside to escape, going back outside to fix the guy ropes more stably when the rain eased.

It didn't look like it would hold off for long. In the west the sky was just reddened by the last fire of the sun, but to the east the sky was leaden and I could see the higher wisps of cloud churning upwards as if boiling. Maskelyne, Mason and Burrow variously spent up to seventeen weeks on this mountainside nearly 250 years ago. They drank from the same stream I'd collected water from. Perhaps they'd stood frowning at the weather more or less right where I was, then slept right here on the side of the mountain with the same concerns about being blown off the hill in the night. Although I hadn't found the observatory, this had been the experience I was after. All these minor things we had in common, these elemental experiences and basic worries we shared – the great thing about this mountain, and mountains in general, was their ability to draw people together over the centuries, reducing the differences incidental to their times. As Maskelyne stood here, the American War of Independence was getting under way. The Battle of Trafalgar lay in the distant future. He'd never heard of Darwin or Dickens, seen a train or conceived of a car. There were no antibiotics or antiseptics, no electrical devices, no plastics, no waterproof clothes. But the experience of the mountain and the view from it – give or take a few pylons and the odd ember of electrical light far down the valley

– was exactly the same, an island of inertia amidst an evolving sea of civilisation.

All was finally said and done for the Schiehallion experiment on 21 May 1778, when Charles Hutton handed a very long report to the Fellows of the Royal Society. He noted rather drily as he did so that the delay was because the necessary calculations were 'naturally and unavoidably long and tedious' and the supplied data caused him 'much trouble to reconcile'.

Given Schiehallion's now-known volume, the plumb-line deflection that Maskelyne recorded was not as dramatic as expected. In fact it was less than half of what Hutton computed it should have been were it to be assumed that both Schiehallion and the earth were of comparable overall mass – which had been calculated, from rock analysed from the mountain, as being around 2,500 kg per cubic metre. In order to explain the figures – which suggested the mean density of the earth as being closer to 4,500 kg per cubic metre, or a ratio of 5:9 – the conclusion Hutton drew was simply that material was denser deep in the earth than at the surface. This disparity would explain why the gravitational pull was more pronounced than expected, and suggested a much more compacted material than rock within the bowels of the earth. Not only was the earth clearly not hollow as suggested by many at the time, but something down there was denser – probably to the tune of 65 per cent denser – than rock. Hutton suggested metal. Science still thinks he's right.

Science also still thinks that his figure for the 'weight' of the world – which, as we've established, was actually its mass per cubic metre – is not far off, either. Hutton estimated a mass of 4,500 kg per cubic metre; today's scientists think it's closer to 5,500 kg. And for a surreal eighteenth-century experiment on the side of this very Perthshire hill, that's really not bad going.*

*   *   *

* It was expensive, mind. In 2005 Dr Peter Clive of Glasgow science consultancy Counting Thoughts led a team that re-created Maskelyne's experiment. Pithily summing up the exercise in *The Scotsman*, he said: 'We carried out a similar experiment using the same sort of principles as Maskelyne, but where we did it in a single day at the cost of £100, Maskelyne took 17 weeks and bankrupted the Royal Society.'

I retreated back into my tent and set my stove rolling. As the wind continued to increase outside, accelerating across the smooth slopes of the mountain and slapping straight into the side of the tent, I sat huddled over whisky-nipped hot chocolate, re-reading an account of Maskelyne's experiment by torchlight. As time passed, the darkness deepened and the wind strengthened further, changing from constant and tent-rattling to staccato pits of stillness punctuated by massive, gusting slaps. A couple of times I slipped into an uncomfortable doze, during which I'd slide downhill slightly on my uneven sleeping level – I never seem to get this right – before being woken with a start by a gust that seemed to come from nowhere.

One of these was extremely violent – worryingly so – and came at exactly 3.33 a.m., causing me to fumble for my head torch to check for damage. And this, I believe, is about where we came in at the start of the chapter.

Struggling out of my sleeping bag and unzipping the top of the tent door to create a window into the bluster outside, I peered out into the silver murk. A heavy cloud sat on the mountains to the north-east, backlit by the moon. I could see two of the guy lines were loose, swinging about in the wind. Wearily, I tested the integrity of the tent by grasping a pole and giving it a waggle. Either it felt sturdy enough to do, or I was too tired to care. Either way I zipped closed the door and hunkered down again.

The wind continued for the rest of the night with similar ferocity. After spending much of the night fretting rather than sleeping, at some point during the hours that followed I dropped into a deep slumber only to be woken seemingly moments later by the glow of dawn warming the tent intensely. A few moments of apathy and indecision followed; my body was desperate to rest, but it was clearly a morning for a mountaintop. Schiehallion's summit lay about 400 vertical metres above me, and tired as I was, I wanted so badly to get to the top of this one. It would be swift. Then I could sleep.

In the end I left the tent, stove and heavier pieces of my camping gear where they were in order to give my sleep-starved body the easiest ride possible. I could simply pick them up on the way down – possibly enjoying a light snooze if I was feeling decadent – before heading back down to the car.

The night before I'd remembered thinking the summit looked close enough to touch. This, as it turned out, was a cruel trick. Schiehallion's feature-less slopes, whilst evidently useful for the physicist, are less agreeable to the mountain climber. This is for the simple reason that there is nothing on them with which to scale the task in hand. What looked like small pebbles of scree from below were actually torso-sized boulders up close; insignificant scratches turned out to be meltwater gullies, and so on. This is compounded by the fact that perspective also messes with your sense of scale, foreshortening the upper reaches of a slope so that they look far closer than they truly are. The upshot of this was that the mountain just kept going – the summit bulge above me to the right remaining static and ever-distant as I waddled in shallow zigzags towards it.

It was super, though. The weather was bright, with a crisp sun, the occasional squall of rain and a brisk wind all lending the morning a vital air. What's more, there's something pleasingly basic about just pushing hard up a really steep slope, no paths to funnel you, no myriad route options or ridgelines to skew your line. Just you versus the slope, all the way to the top. This was in addition to the fact that the boulder field that unavoidably crossed my path in ever-increasing slashes amongst the grass was the most unstable I'd ever tried to negotiate. Apart from the rakish angle of repose that asserted itself every time I looked westward to the tilted skyline of the mountainside cutting the horizon at, I'd guess, about 40 degrees (and if that doesn't sound steep, just try standing on it with a straight slope of 1,500 feet underneath you), every now and again the boulders would shift beneath my feet, adding an undesirably precarious frisson to each step. This wasn't just restricted to the small boulders, either. The most memorable move of the whole ascent came when I pulled myself over a sofa-sized piece of quartzite and the whole thing started to shift slowly but inexorably down the slope, as if on invisible rollers, along with a considerable amount of the surrounding rock. Leaping off it with a screech – quicker than I've ever leaped off anything in my life – my thoughts then turned to the very real possibility of an imminent rockslide when, as suddenly as it had started, it stopped. As the smaller rocks settled with delicate tinkles, I crept above it (below didn't seem sensible) and continued up more gingerly than before.

In 1784, long after the Schiehallion experiment and even longer after his heroic mapping of the Highlands, William Roy completed his baseline measurement at Hounslow Heath. From this he created a map of great trigonometrical triangles. These spread along the south-west coast, establishing precise distances between landmarks and producing a skeleton map, which then evolved into a cartographer-enriched image of the area of England most at risk of continental invasion. From this grew plans for a 'General Military Map of England', which would accurately triangulate the entire country upon this single, five-mile standard. But Roy would never see the complete fruition of his work. He died in 1790, and a year later the Board of Ordnance was rechristened the Ordnance Survey (OS), which it remains to this day. In 1792 Roy's team continued what he'd started, extrapolating what the late mapmaker had begun on the south-east coast across the entire nation – an undertaking that became known as the Principal Triangulation of Great Britain. This mammoth task would take over 60 years, and the result would become the envy of the world.

A *re*triangulation of Great Britain was commenced by the Ordnance Survey in 1932, and lasted until 1962. It was during this refining of the work begun by Roy that perhaps the most iconic symbol of the Ordnance Survey came into being: the trig point.* These typically smooth white pillars come replete with theodolite threads and brass levels; evidence they began their lives as scientific tools and are now universally recognised as the distinctive end of uphill for mountain climbers.

The retriangulation of Great Britain, during which they were built, was the last monumental survey of the country before the advent of GPS technology – and was in itself an evocative prospect. By night, surveyors would huddle atop the mountains in all weathers with great lights mounted on the trig points for surveyors on another mountaintop to sight through their theodolites and record the angle. Every mountaintop trig point offers lines of sight to two others, thus creating the spreading triangles that would collectively form the skeleton map. Often the surveyors would be on the mountaintops for days whilst calculations were made, working to tough schedules through the season, often with heavy gear.

It's a mistake to think that trig points denote the tops of mountains, although that's often where they're found. They were in fact originally positioned to occupy the most distantly visible point of a mountain, usually – but

---

* 'Trig' as in trigonometrical, rather than triangulation, as is often mistaken – although these terms in this context essentially mean the same thing.

not always – the very top, which is why so many of them ended up there. Often they were built on site; a diverting footnote* concerns the building of Cadair Idris's summit trig, which was evidently something of a traumatic affair. Trig points are found in the lowlands, too, and – just like Roy's first survey of the south coast – are often sighted to clear landmarks such as churches.

Today they're redundant, but remain, together with the contour lines on your map, enduring symbols of applied science in the mountains.

It's ironic, then, that the summit of Schiehallion – the top of Maskelyne's grand apparatus, and no doubt a usefully distinctive object for Roy when making his 'magnificent military sketch' – is today bereft of a trig point. Personally, I loved the fact that the summit was bare. It was a nice change to find such a popular top suffering from no such intrusion. A single brass nail pierced one of the many white rocks around the summit, possibly a relic of an old trig point that no doubt stood there at some point.† Instead, a small pile of stones lay adjacent to this as a substitute to denote the highest point on the mountain. It's curious that the summits of our hills always seem to need marking with a physical, human-made statement of their topmost elevation, as if the top isn't reward enough. A few names scratched into the summit rocks – graffiti is not a common feature of British mountaintops – bore testament to Schiehallion's popularity.

The wind was incredible on the summit. Not strong enough to blow me over, but certainly pushing hard into my face, and sufficient to dissuade me from walking too close to the steep edge of the southern face lest the wind suddenly ceased and I fell forward over it. From here the mountain felt more wedge-shaped than ever, the roughened tip on which I was standing descending and broadening into a wide ridge curving down towards Foss.

---

* The trig took nine days to erect in August 1936, and the surveyor's diary of the time makes for amusing – if dark – reading as progress was repeatedly thwarted by rain and the mists, which 'on Cader are terrible every day.' Similarly, the entry of 19 August simply reads 'Weather today is terrible, raining all day. Nothing can be done. Fed up with it.' Two days later, the surveyor remarks that he is staying 'on the top of Cader Idris in an old hut for the night.' Yet another occupant of the little stone shelter from Chapter 3.

† There was a trig point here at one point. Many reports attribute its demise to lightning, Schiehallion being the highest peak in the region.

Morning sun was lighting the mountain from the east and all the way along its spine speckles of quartz glinted. Bursts of light rain gusted into my face as the western tip of the mountain met the summit and the view back down towards Loch Rannoch was revealed. This was something to savour: the perfect inverse of that famous aspect seen the previous evening from the loch-side. From there at least, Schiehallion was a formidable, perfect cone; now I was stood atop its very point, looking back down towards the grey slick of the loch. Once again the mountain was deserted – at this early hour I had this famously busy peak, and all its history, to myself. The wind meant staying long probably wasn't wise, and it was obvious that the fragile truce between sun and rain wasn't going to last. Taking in the glorious prospect of bulky, anonymous mountains carpeting off in all directions one more brief time, I turned and began to descend.

Getting down didn't take long. Because of the mountain's unusually smooth northern slopes, it wasn't far from the summit that I spotted the tiny dot of my tent a long way below. From the tent my eyes could follow the stream out to the roadside, and the dot of my car, tinier still. This was a considerable novelty: being able to see every stage of my ascent, overnight stay and prospective descent in one view down one long slope. This was indeed, as Maskelyne had said, a remarkable hill.

Sadly, as much as my eyes searched the mountainside – even from this elevated perspective – I couldn't see any ledges, ruins or suspicious uncon-formities that may have been the place where in late 1774 scientific history was made in the most unexpected way. Today, a plaque at the Forestry Commission car park near Braes of Foss celebrates the event. Maskelyne and Hutton get namechecks. Happily, so does Burrow.

Maskelyne's farewell to Schiehallion carries with it an amusing endstop that – whatever Burrow thought of him, and however much of a self-glorify-ing ingrate he quite possibly may have been – can't help but endear you to the old rascal. On his final night in the northern bothy Maskelyne threw a party. Present were many local shepherds, the surveying team and a young ghillie named 'Red' Duncan Robinson – better known locally as Donnaeha Ruadh – who was a gifted fiddle player. Ever canny to his own comforts, Maskelyne had employed him as a cook with additional entertainment benefits.

This party was evidently quite a success as at some point – whilst Robinson serenaded the increasingly inebriated guests – the bothy swiftly and dramatically caught fire. None of the observation equipment remained inside, so most found the burning scene an amusing and oddly convenient end to the building's short life. Robinson, however, was inconsolable; inside, presumably burning, was his precious violin. Maskelyne, clearly feeling guilty at the young man's loss, assured him he would find him a replacement when he returned to London and send it north. Months later a package was delivered to Robertson, and in it – sure enough – was a violin of particularly pleasing quality. Maskelyne had sent the young ghillie a 1729 Stradivarius, one of the finest instruments ever made. Were the violin still in existence today it would be worth millions.

Postscript

When I arrived home a week later I found a letter waiting for me. It was a reply to an enquiry I'd made to the John Muir Trust, the venerable and admirable wild-land foundation that owns a chunk of Schiehallion – although not the side I'd climbed. Beneath a jauntily written 'Hope this is what you're looking for!' compliment slip, I unfolded the letter, which comprised several typed sheets, a map, some photographs and a diagram. As I slowly realised what it was, my jaw dropped. It had been sent to the John Muir Trust in 2003 by an enterprising individual by the name of Andrew Sinclair, who had titled it: 'Attempt to determine the location of Maskelyne's observatories on Schiehallion'.

Sinclair had triangulated the site of the observatory working backwards using Hutton's complex measurements from various sites on the mountain. Needless to say, he'd found it, and enclosed a picture of the site – two stone walls, still visible, and a large, flat platform. Sinclair's detective work deserves recognition here, and in a way – despite being deeply disappointed to have missed the site – I felt better for seeing it. If this is what it took to find Maskelyne's site then I really never stood a chance, unless I'd literally tripped over it.

I was tempted to write the observatory's grid reference here, but I haven't – partly out of respect for Sinclair's work, and partly because I had such fun trying to track it down that adding a grid reference might prevent anyone ever doing the same and make it a matter of simply walking to it. So what I'll do is simply stir another clue in to the brew. The description I unsuccessfully followed said to search 150 yards west of the westernmost of the two major streams on the north slope of Schiehallion at around 2,300 feet. Following this, I'd say you're over 30 metres too high, and you shouldn't be looking west of the two streams; try looking between them.

8 LIGHT

To the north, then. Relentlessly north – as far north as you can go without getting wet feet. Here, the place where Scotland frays and dramatically terminates is a sequestered region of singular atmosphere where the sky seems to inflate around you, the population thins out and, one by one, the things you rely on back home – phone signal, radio, other people – waver and sputter, then vanish altogether.

This was fine by me. As far as I was concerned it heightened the sense of occasion and the feeling of otherness that any trip to this lonely northernmost part of Britain does and should bring. Because it *is* different here. It really is.

It's so special even the weather can't spoil it, which is just as well because this afternoon the sky was hung like old sheets. After stocking up on camp food at Inverness I crossed the kilometre-long Kessock Bridge over the Beauly Firth, its red lights and skeletal bar-and-cable structure brooding out of a morbid sea mist. This bridge leaps the topmost point of the Great Glen, which all but decapitates Scotland's northern third. Filling it is an arrow-straight series of lochs and rivers, including Loch Lochy and Loch Ness, in a great welt running south-west to north-east. Here in Inverness the glen opens into the North Sea in a broad inlet; and as my wheels rolled over this and onto the land of the Black Isle, I entered the Northern Highlands.

With Schiehallion now a happy memory, ahead of me lay four days – and three more mountains. Beside me on the car seat were three books that I intended to leaf through during the inevitable idle moments spent marooned by rain. One was a newly bought selection of poems by Norman MacCaig; another a colourful book about the ecology of the Scottish Highlands called *Hostile Habitats*; and lastly, a thin volume that I can only describe as a background guide to a notorious Highland enemy.

I'd been well informed before leaving for Scotland that I was about to experience the thing that all British mountain walkers – even the flintiest and most seasoned – dread more than anything. And it wasn't a mountain, an injury or a disease. If accounts were to be believed it was worse. Much worse.

Some weeks earlier I'd been sitting in Scotland's Southern Uplands drinking beer in the garden of Lyle Brotherton, a friend who – amongst many other things – had more experience doing exciting things in wild places than anyone I knew. He'd taken a sip of beer, composed himself, then leaned in with a serious expression, as if about to enquire as to my current bank balance or the health of my prostate.

'You *do* know it's the wrong time of year to go to the north of Scotland, don't you?'

I'd nodded maybe a little too casually and said something like: 'Right. Midges?'

Perhaps something in my tone suggested I was approaching this with something of a cavalier attitude, or I wasn't according the subject its due respect. Either way, Lyle's expression darkened.

'Fucking sparrows with great big fucking teeth, Simon.'

He then proceeded to tell me stories of idyllic canoe trips that suddenly turned into chaotic races for shore through vision fogged with buzzing, biting clouds; of orange tents turned black with a carapace of tiny, twitching wings; and of people returning from the Highlands covered in so many angry red dots there was little unchewed skin left between.

'It's a shame, as this year they thought it was going to be a bad year for midges because of the cold spring,' he continued sadly. 'But the bloody things are thriving.'

In the dozen or so times I'd been to Scotland over the past ten years, somehow I'd managed to dodge the worst of the midge season – which is at its most intense between June and August – so this was all new and improbably extreme to me. I would never for a second want to suggest that people were exaggerating their stories of this two-millimetre scourge of Britain's hardiest country (well, a bit perhaps) but part of me was eager to see just *how* bad it was.

I was heading for the remote region of Sutherland. Sutherland is very huge and very empty. With an area of just over 2,000 square miles it could swallow Snowdonia and the Lake District together and still have room for a decent meal, yet its entire population – around 30,000 souls – is marginally less than that of a small market town like Alnwick. Many of these people are tied up in far-spaced, fiercely remote communities like Dornoch, Durness and Lochinver, leaving an awful lot of space in between and not a lot to fill it besides a skeletal road system and wild, boundless country. There are no traffic lights in Sutherland and no roundabouts. Those used to convenience might feel uncomfortably exposed here; those seeking solitude, space and endless sky might find their promised land. It doesn't take long for the emptiness to assert itself as you drive north. The agricultural land around Inverness soon thins out and you pass distant forests of tightly dark trees, sometimes with a halo of birds. Turn off the A9 and head for Bonar Bridge and the trees creep to the roadside, markings disappear and the wilderness begins to win.

'Sutherland' actually comes from the Norse word for 'south'. Odd as this sounds for an area that comprises the most significant portion of Britain's northernmost territory, it was denoted as such by the Vikings, who landed in Caithness in the 9th century and immediately declared everywhere beneath as *suder land*, literally, 'southern land'. This area makes up a big chunk of the central far north, including the coastline – in every sense Britain's ragged, northern climax. From here Cape Wrath's wild lighthouse gives sailors Britain's final – or indeed first – wink. The island-speckled sea lochs of Laxford and Eriboll, serenely slicing into Scotland where it falls into the sea, create great bays upon which tiny communities huddle against the windstorms of the northern ocean. And it's here that two great mountains stand side by side and look out to sea.

Lairg, a handsome little town at the southern end of unexpectedly mighty Loch Shin, calls itself the crossroads of the north. It could equally call itself the full stop of the south; beyond Lairg, you're pretty much on your own as Britain slowly scuds towards the sea. There's a meat market, a railway crossing, a fine little church and a portion of the lake on which this afternoon canoeists were splashing in the heavy weather. Once that's done with – and it really doesn't take long – the road kicks down to a single lane, its hard edge blurs with vegetation and the view out of the windscreen becomes like the view down the wrong end of a telescope. Everything starts to become very empty indeed. And not just empty, but intimidatingly unshowy in its boundlessness. There are no arterial rivers, no deep glens or viewpoints with picnic tables; huge swathes of densely packed conifers quickly give way to low shrubs of juniper, giving uninterrupted lines of sight for dozens of miles. It's like driving across a thinning scalp.

This extraordinary, ancient landscape is also called the Flow Country, a more evocative-sounding name for blanket bog:* areas of poorly drained ground, where acidic conditions promote the growth of a coat of sphagnum moss. It's a classic circle of symbiotic dependence; the moss grows, then rots, and over the millennia becomes compacted and forms deep deposits of peat, which in turn promotes the growth of more sphagnum moss. It's a slow process: the peat here deepens about a millimetre in a good year, and it's been doing so since the end of the last ice age. Dig down a few metres and you'll be digging into remains of plant life 4,000 years old.

The Flow Country is massive. At roughly 1,500 square miles and straddling Sutherland and Caithness, it's the biggest blanket bog in Europe, and one of the biggest – if not *the* biggest – in the world. Agriculturally useless on account of its acidity and resistance to drainage, the bog can't be farmed, which is why the landscape has remained blessedly unchanged and unpeopled, suspended in a state the ecologist Sir Frank Fraser Darling called the 'wet desert'. *Dubh lochans* – 'black pools' – nestle amidst the peat, giving the area a queer skin of thousands of sky-reflecting speckles when viewed from afar or from height. But up close, most of what you see is moss.

Sphagnum moss is pretty miraculous stuff. You find it all over the uplands of Great Britain, this bristly carpet of green- (or pink-, or red- or orange-) leafed sponge. It's often referred to as the living surface of a bog, and it often feels as such. 'Floating' on waterlogged peat and dead vegetation, thick sphagnum is a strange surface underfoot. Walking on it can feel slappy and hollow, and sometimes you can see it quiver or thump beneath your feet from the vibration of your step, like the patted belly of a sleeping dog. It can hold up to

* That is, it *sounds* evocative, although instead of signifying some slow, elegant motion, it's actually an archaic translation – as is much in this part of Britain – from Old Norse. In this case, the original term was probably *flói*, meaning 'wet'.

eight times its own weight in water, making it incredibly succulent, but nothing eats it. It clumps together into hummocks that can reach the height of your knees as its individual constituents scrabble for light. As the sphagnum keeps the ground waterlogged and acidic, there's little oxygen present in the soil – and the bacteria that typically break down dead matter can't survive. So when sphagnum dies it just sits. Fresh moss grows on top and gradually it compacts into peat, like a kind of soft fossil.

Without sphagnum there would be no bogs. And without bogs, a lot of creatures would be in a lot of trouble: adders, merlins and red-throated divers all breed here. The wet soils provide an ideal environment for insects, which are predated by birds and reptiles, which in turn are eaten by larger creatures. And people need it, too – although on occasion we've been a little over-enthusiastic with it. Bog myrtle was drunk as a liquor by the Vikings; cuts of peat were – and still are – burned as fuel by crofters and used as natural roofing on those picturesque, remote buildings toupee'd with green moss instead of slate. And because of sphagnum's absorbency and antiseptic qualities, it's been used as dressings for wounds since the 16th century. Unlike cotton, which becomes saturated on top of an injury, sphagnum transports the blood, gunge and bacteria away from a wound whilst allowing the moss in contact with it to remain absorbent. The moss also contains a carbohydrate called sphagnan, believed to be responsible for the preservative qualities of peat such as are witnessed to spectacular effect whenever something interesting is found in it, like a 4,000-year-old tree stump or a body,* as well as immobilising the bacteria and pathogens that lead to infection. It was this property that probably saved a huge number of lives and limbs during the Great War, with the wounded receiving dressings of sphagnum shipped down in bulk from the far north of Scotland. Even the humble camper can use sphagnum for cleaning pots and pans after a camp meal. It's abrasive and has iodine in it – a natural purifier. Like I said, miraculous stuff.

---

* Particularly the latter. The most exceptional of these is probably Tollund Man, who was found in the Jutland region of Denmark in 1950. Such was the exceptional preservation of the body – his stubbled face looks like he is sleeping, albeit uncomfortably – he was initially thought to be a modern murder victim. He was later found to be a human sacrifice over 2,500 years old; other than tanning him black, the peat had perfectly preserved his features, organs and even his last meal.

Twelve miles north of Lairg a building appears ahead, a white dot in the brown. This is the Crask Inn. The only hostelry for many miles, it's a place where people can find some shelter, share a song, have a drink or simply be with others, even in the depths of the fierce Highland winter. As I passed it on this grey afternoon I imagined being huddled inside with hill-tired limbs under candlelight, curled around dark beer, home-cooked food, a spitting fire, snow heaped up against the door and somebody noodling on a guitar. It sounds like a cliché, but that's often how it is up here. Life returns to the basics. Food, shelter, warmth, company. I suppose some people might wonder why you'd want to stay in such a barren place; I find the idea seductive. Human things in an austere landscape like this cannot help but be beckoning.

A mile or so beyond the inn I pulled over, got out of the car and walked to the roadside. Stepping onto the scrubby grass, I looked north-west. Ahead, a cloud of dust from an unknown source eddied somewhere close to the horizon. And beyond it the shadows of distant mountains bled through the cloud like faces through a veil.

The peaks here are scattered and disparate. Perhaps it's because they aren't part of bigger ranges, instead rising individually from the rolling Flow landscape, standing alone and spaced against the horizon, they look immense and tantalising, like something remembered from a dream, their isolation giving them dramatic profiles against the sky. Mountains like Ben Hope, Foinaven, Ben Hee and Ben Klibreck – strange shapes bridging land and sky. And most dramatic of all was the mountain I was here to explore: Ben Loyal.

Ben Hope and Ben Loyal are indelibly associated with this part of Sutherland. One is most famous for its status, the other for its shape. Ben Hope is Scotland's northernmost Munro. Seen from the north it looks massive, whilst from the solemn coastal lands it overlooks – its name means 'Hill of the Bay' – it's a proudly colossal sight, and climbed by many summit baggers via a good path from the west.

Ben Loyal, however, makes a far more fascinating proposition – but despite this, it's far quieter. And as happens depressingly often, it's all down to numbers. Like our old friend Beinn Dearg in Torridon, not being a Munro and falling short of Ben Hope's height by 150 metres, Ben Loyal sees a fraction of its footfall. But unlike Beinn Dearg, this is in spite of being visually *more* interesting than its bigger neighbour. Looking like a mountain that's decayed to its bones, and lacking Ben Hope's considerable visual muscle, it is nevertheless a craftily complicated little set of peaks, and incredibly formidable-looking from a distance.

It first caught my eye as a silhouette on the eastern horizon the evening before I'd climbed Ben Hope – as most do when they come here for the first time with mountains in mind – some years ago. Black against a mauve sky, it looked extraordinary: a trap of sharp summits, surreally dramatic between the boundless flats of Sutherland and the sea. I'd looked at the map to find its name and it had since stuck in my head as a place to explore one day.

But trips this far north don't come along often. Ben Loyal isn't on the way to anywhere, unless you have a boat and a fondness for rough seas. And over the years that followed, Ben Loyal began to feel like a kind of unicorn mountain, forever beyond practicality. It was, however, a reason for me to come back. And now, with four days at large in the Northern Highlands to play with, Ben Loyal was the next peak on my list.

Standing by the roadside, I was beginning to get attention. It had taken a few minutes but now they were beginning to arrive in droves – my first introduction to *Culicoides impunctatus*, the Highland midge. Over the silence of the deserted roadside I could hear a shrill whine from their tiny wings, occasionally augmented by a deeper buzz as a horsefly scudded through them, like a bomber through a cloud of fighters. Making a flustered swishing with my hands, I retreated to the car. Moments later they were crowding against the window, already hosting several horseflies that were stuck to it as if gnawing on the glass. I watched with amusement for a moment, then started the engine and continued north.

I arrived in Tongue at an awkward time in the afternoon. The last few miles had been all brewing clouds over bulky, mountain-sized shadows. Occasionally a peak poked into view from the murk, prompting a stamp on the brakes and a squint. These soon gave way to the unmistakable, spacious skies of imminent coast. This was it: I'd reached the tip.

I needed gas for camping, and had cleverly waited until I'd reached one of the most remote places in Great Britain before addressing the matter. In the local shop I was greeted by a friendly chap who informed me that he had run out, but not to worry because he was pretty sure he knew a place in Thurso that would probably have some. Thurso was a 90-mile round trip. I thanked him and left with the feeling that a seemingly insignificant but inescapably vital bit of planning I'd neglected was slowly but surely beginning to bite me. Noting a hand-drawn map in the vestibule showing the location of local services in Tongue, I saw a hotel that looked to be just round the corner. Figuring that as it was creeping towards 4 p.m. a bought dinner wouldn't be the end of the world, I left the shop and quickly found it, disturbing a conversation between the barmaid and several fishermen as I walked in the door.

'Do you do meals, by any chance?'

'Aye, we start at six,' she replied.

'Oh.' Bugger.

'Would you be looking to have something now?' she said brightly. 'If so, the Craggan's the nearest,' she said.

'It's not in Thurso, is it?' I said, perhaps a little too sarcastically.

'It's over the causeway. Just a few miles.'

The Craggan was actually in Melness, the next village along the coast. The causeway the helpful barmaid had mentioned is a concrete bridge crossing the Kyle of Tongue, a tidal inlet that this afternoon was catching a heavy dose of luminous sea mist. I made the turn towards Melness at a little graveyard where stern, spired graves overlooked the bay, and immediately was enveloped in a bright, translucent fog. A mile or so of steadily climbing the edge of the inlet and houses began to appear – weather-battered bungalows perched like barnacles on hills of grass, billowing washing strung on lines outside. I pulled in briefly to let a pick-up pass, and was immediately struck by the ethereal view down the bay out to sea: the sunlight – invisibly diffused from here – was shining on a golden stripe of beach that burned through the fog, a floating coastline. The sand looked like it was glowing. It was quite beautiful, and immediately I felt an ache to be on the other side of the bay and on it.

Instead I carried on into the village and found the Craggan, a friendly place with decent food. I was the restaurant's only customer, apart from a pair of teenage girls on whom I eavesdropped as I ate. Their discussion seemed to revolve around the usual subjects of boys they knew with customised cars, the length of time it took to get to Inverness, the drudgery of work – as well as the slightly more left-field subjects of shooting rabbits and sleeping in beachside bothies. I wanted to ask them what it was like living this far north, but they probably just thought of it as normal, nothing special. They seemed very happy.

I changed into my hill gear in the bathroom and filled my water bottle. Behind my table on the wall was a picture of Ben Loyal, cloud free, looking magnificent. Dinner done and gas no longer needed, the mountain was my next stop. Parking the car at the roadhead near Ribigill, I walked the good track past a fine house now abandoned – to the degree that trees were growing amusingly out of the chimney stacks – then the landscape opened and very slowly I began to climb. The low fog of earlier was beginning to disperse and a watery sunlight seemed just a second away for a long time. Then, rounding the final corner of farm infrastructure, I saw it, properly, up close, for the first time – the last bit of my exhale snagging an obscene word of wonder as I did.

Ben Loyal is called the Queen of the Scottish Hills, although nobody seems to know why it's called that, as its name actually means 'law hill'. One possible theory is its striking shape, which – from the north, as I was approaching it now – is seen as a series of peaks arranged rather elegantly in a line, with deep-scooped corries between them. From this angle it's not unlike a crown, which could have led to its nickname. But what it *is* very reminiscent of is a kind of steepled marine shell, alternated with knotted spires and scoops along its crest and aligned in a diagonal row of four. Either way it's striking – almost pretty – and flaunts itself as such from afar.

Up close, however, it retains its phenomenal drama. This is unlike, it has to be said, Ben Hope – which only ceases to be a huge, seemingly endless lump when you finally reach its summit. Ben Loyal, by contrast, seemed to get more and more dramatic the closer I crept, with the 712-metre Sgòr Chaonasaid – the first of Loyal's knurled spires – poised over me as I walked into its sway.

There wasn't much of a path and what there was I easily lost. I knew that mountains this far north – all barring the most popular peaks – would probably lack obvious lines of travel, and I was looking forward to finding my own logical way up the mountain as best I could – just to see if I was able to. Since my failure to successfully do this back on Beinn Dearg, I'd been paying special attention to the way paths moved up mountainsides on the routes they took, and trying to develop my own sense for following the lines of least resistance on the ground – of drawing a path with my eyes where there was none.

The way, at least, seemed perfectly obvious on the map: pass the abandoned cottage at Cunside, then follow the course of a stream to a startlingly flat area between Loyal and neighbouring Ben Hiel – a place devoid of the pink squiggle of contours named on the map as the Bealach Clais nan Ceap.* From there, I'd cut uphill to strike the saddle between Sgòr Chaonasaid and Sgòr a' Bhatain – steeples one and two of the 'crown'. Then, hopefully with daylight to spare and a confident swagger, make a leisurely ascent to the very top whilst congratulating myself on a crack piece of navigation – 'It was really nothing, old boy' – before enjoying the rare and splendid view of Britain's northern shores and its weird mountain sentinels as a reward.

Although the peak was mostly clear, it was wearing persistent cloud that seemed to be perched atop it like a hat. Occasionally as I walked, this spilled momentarily over, furring the topmost battlements of the mountain. If the cloud persisted, not only would a view be off the cards but navigation would shift into an altogether different realm. This preoccupied me a little as I began the ascent towards the *bealach*, before something happened that changed everything.

You'll have noticed that this chapter is called 'Light'. I'd kept quiet about it until now as it really didn't look like I was going to be able to explain in any meaningful way why I'd selected this place, and this word, as a mountain element important enough to explore. But as I climbed, nature drew the curtain on a spectacular show of *exactly* why.

Earlier I mentioned that it 'feels' different in the far north. You could say there are a few easily definable reasons why this is: that amazing Flow landscape, the isolation and charisma of the mountains, the remoteness between communities that contradicts the image of our overcrowded little country and seems to belong in another place of altogether wilder renown. But something

* I looked this up, hoping for something stirring or mythical relating to its odd flatness. The translation is disappointingly rather literal: 'Pass of the Hilly Gorge'.

that's perhaps the most difficult to define is also the most obviously emotive. It's the light. There's something extraordinary about it.

Anyone standing next to me that day as the sun found an opening in the cloud and set the flanks of Ben Loyal ablaze with spilled afternoon light would understand what I mean by this, but it's not something that lends itself easily to description. Crisp but soft-hued, weedy but warm, it feels like it should crackle as it lights the ground with that peculiar, slanted glow. It's as if the light is coming from somewhere other than the sun.

The strange thing is, there isn't really any reason for it. You hear the term 'northern light' bandied about a lot but nobody can really explain what it *is*. In Britain, a true oceanic coastline that faces an uninterrupted northern aspect is relatively rare. But this one is very extensive. Take a bearing from the top of Ben Loyal and, floating polar ice notwithstanding, you'll hit no solid land whatsoever until you cross the Pole, enter the Eastern Hemisphere and make landfall in a frigid outpost of Siberia a few miles shy of the Bering Strait – at a place called Wrangell Island.* But remarkable as this may be, it doesn't explain that weird, magical light. Of course, the further north you get the more severe the seasons become; particularly at the solstice and equinox. It's here the contrast between summer and winter is at its most extreme, and Scotland's northern regions become a kind of toned-down domestic version of Svalbard, Tromsø or Reykjavik – although in these places the behaviour of natural light asserts itself far more explicitly, with their white nights and crushing winters of darkness. Winter days are short, the sun clings to the horizon and the phantasmal aurora borealis frequently dances across the sky. Then, come summer, everything flips: days stretch out, night never really arrives, and when it does it's anaemic and half-cooked. Scotland offers a more practical, domestic version of this extreme.

I was making my way to the top of Ben Loyal almost a month to the day after the solstice, so I'd feel this to a degree. The sun wouldn't set until 10 p.m., and would be up again before 5 a.m.; I'd have one more hour of light tonight than I'd have back at home in Lincolnshire. Had I been here on 23 June, at sea level the sun wouldn't have set until 10.30 p.m. and would have woken me up

* Of course, by that point your 'north' bearing will have become 'south'. But we shan't get into that.

at 4 a.m. A few thousand feet up and these would nudge even further to their respective extremes. Hardly Arctic, but certainly northern.*

You could of course argue that it's not the light that's different but the landscape itself. Perhaps it's the interplay between the sunlight, coastal weather that rarely settles and the enormous, unstifled sky in which the two can tussle that creates the illusion of this rarefied light. Perhaps its often fleeting nature – the way it cuts through the clouds, bathes something for a moment, then is gone, leaving the landscape breathless – marks it out as unique.

Or however implacable, maybe there *is* such a thing as northern light – queered by latitude, and bent across the earth's curve like a stubborn cane. It seems absurd to think this can happen in the globally slight distance of Britain's length, but it's there nonetheless. At least it's how it always has been for me, in my mind.

It had occurred to me that perhaps my mind was the only place it actually was. Before I'd left I spoke to a couple of photographers I knew, eager to get their thoughts on this peculiar, indefinable thing. Photographers make their living from light, so if they didn't know what I was on about, it probably wasn't worth knowing. One clearly had little idea what I was talking about and just nodded with a kind of sympathetic confusion. The other offered a more enigmatic answer that at least assured me I wasn't completely crackers: 'It is what it is. I don't know what it is, but I know what you mean.' And whatever that is, on the side of Ben Loyal on this particular afternoon, there it was.

I stood and watched awhile, enjoying the way the sun lit the nodding heads of cotton grass around me. I looked west towards Ben Hope, a lozenge of grey on the horizon beneath a massive and lively sky of cloud. After a couple of minutes of peace a malingering cloud of midges was beginning to gather around me; they get you when you stop, it seemed. Moving off with a little

---

* The UK's northernmost town, Skaw – on the northernmost Shetland of Unst – surprisingly doesn't see a much later sunset at the solstice than Ben Loyal, at 10.36 p.m. and 10.29 p.m. respectively. However, dawn comes 30 minutes earlier to Skaw at 3.35 a.m., and a state of 'nautical twilight' – that is to say, the period that ends when navigation at sea using the horizon is no longer possible – meets in the middle between sunrise and sunset, and therefore exists in perpetuity around this time of year.

shake, I carried on up towards the *bealach*, over which a very soft breeze was moving.

The Bealach Clais nan Ceap was at about 320 metres – just under halfway up the mountain. Broad but sheltered between the little cone of Ben Hiel and the jumble of rock peaks that formed Ben Loyal's upper reaches, I was surprised how well drained it was given that it must see a fair amount of storm runoff from the two hills. It was blissfully dry, and as I arrived at the *bealach* and saw the slope that lay ahead up the eastern flank of Ben Loyal, it was immediately clear that here was the sensible choice for tonight's camp. Much as I had done on Schiehallion, I could pitch up, ditch the heavier items of kit in the tent to save me lugging them up the hill, then climb to the top unencumbered.

As I arrived at the *bealach* I took a long slug on the water I'd brought. I could easily have downed the lot as the day was muggy and the stiff climb had made me sweat. I should have carried an extra litre for camp and, leaving about half the bottle, a niggling worry briefly popped into my head that tonight might be a thirsty night. Clinging to the hope that I might find some water higher up, I set about pitching my tent, angling the entrance towards the northern view out to the coast. I could see the white streak of the causeway in Tongue and pictured myself now on the beckoning mountain I saw from there just a couple of hours earlier.

A few moments of stamping about yielded a flat area upon which to throw out the tent, the groundsheet struggling to lie flat atop the thick, natural mattress of grass and moss. Tent up, I hurled my sleeping bag, mat, inflatable pillow, breakfast – biscuits and a bag of crisps – and spare underlayers into the tent and, with most of the load off, began to walk towards the short, steep ascent onto Ben Loyal's higher reaches. Still in my pack was my first aid kit, a down jacket stuffed into a waterproof bag, my half-empty (or half-full) water bottle and a bit of food. As something of an afterthought, when I hit the first gradient I loaded up the digital map on my phone and dropped an electronic waypoint where I stood. This way, no matter what navigational befouling might occur, so long as the battery held I could find my way back to this point, from where it was just a few yards to my tent. I took note of the time as I did so; 8.05 p.m. It soon became clear that this would probably be something I'd be glad of. As I began to climb, the cloud fell.

The air was intensely still. I couldn't remember ever being on a mountain, at this height, and being greeted with such an absence of movement in the atmosphere. There wasn't even a tickle of wind. Maybe it's the heightening of other senses that creates this feeling, but walking into cloud is sometimes like walking into silence. The world becomes muted, as if the cloud really is as it looks – a muffling layer of isolation, beyond which nothing that can make a sound exists.

The way was steep. It was difficult to plough a straight course up the slope, and I found myself travelling mostly up the dry rivulets of minor streams descending the mountain's shoulder like stray hairs. Above me, the peak of the mountain had gone from being a sharply defined horn of rock to a weakening smudge, its detail stolen by the failing light of evening and the murk. Ben Loyal's complexity meant that just finding the top in these conditions was going to be a challenge, and far from a simple matter of climbing until there was no more 'up'. The map revealed that once the highest ground on the mountain was reached, the pinnacles which from afar make the mountain's profile so snaring to the eye spread out around a featureless plateau into high tors, like watchtowers surrounding a keep. This architecture is reflected in the name of the highest of these tors, An Caisteal; literally, 'the Castle'. From where I was now standing, this 764-metre high point lay 1,200 metres south-south west, somewhere up there in the gloom. I looked at the map and tried to translate the frantic contours I was looking at to the terrain I was seeing. Each blue grid square on the map was a square kilometre, 1,000 metres by 1,000 metres. Imagining a straight line between myself and the summit, the contours first bunched, then separated, then bunched again.

That meant the steepness continued for maybe 300 metres, then eased to a plateau, then steepened again to a gap, before turning south for the final pull to the top. The trick would be staying on course over this steep ground. I had my digital map, but whilst it was invaluable for determining position, actually navigating with the damn thing was rather different. Walking with satellite navigation isn't like driving with satellite navigation. In a car ground is covered quickly and your satnav has the predictable certainty of the road network to rely on. Walking speeds, on the other hand, are slow and directions variable, and the little black triangle that represented 'me' on my map didn't seem to know which way it was facing half the time. In practice this meant I'd walk a considerable distance before it became apparent that I was walking in the wrong direction, then I'd have to correct myself and walk in the vague direction I should be walking in – all the while with my head buried in a screen, and zero attention given to basic navigational nous.

When crossing steep mountain terrain in mist using traditional map and compass methods – provided you haven't got something clear to follow, like a ridgeline or a stream – you invariably end up walking in a series of short, straight lines, using a compass to sight a bearing then picking something in that direction like a charismatic tuft of grass or a rock to walk to. You then repeat the process until, gradually, you reach your goal. But for this to work, of course, you need to know exactly where you are to begin with.

It seemed satisfying – as I pulled out my compass and laid it on the digital screen of my map-loaded phone to take a bearing – that the method of navigation I was most comfortable with to get me to the top of the mountain was a mix of old-school navigation and technology. Or, more plausibly, that I was so useless at both that it would take an awkward combination of the two to get me through it.

Whichever, it worked – I had a bearing. And over the next 500 metres I tried my best to stick to it, difficult though it was. The cloud was becoming a soup, and it wasn't long before I could only see a few feet ahead of me as I shimmied on a sideways ascent up the slope, taking bearings off whatever I could to keep me vaguely on track. There was no sound whatsoever. Just a close, crushing silence. It felt odd to be alone this far north, this far away from anyone or anything else, yet at the same time to feel mildly claustrophobic.

I was at about 600 metres when something made me stop. A noise, from somewhere unseen ahead. In a soundscape devoid of anything else you notice everything. I froze, waiting for it to happen again. When it did it brought the hairs up on my arms. It was part choke, part growl, and definitely mammal – an 'oof'. It sounded hollow, guttural, with a resonance that suggested a large pair of lungs; not the sort of sound you could imagine coming from a squirrel, put it that way. I hadn't seen any sheep on the way up here so it had to be something else. I pushed on across the slope, my mind working frantically to identify any possible candidates. Naturally, I considered the least likely and most dangerous first. Escaped, pissed-off farm dog; that wouldn't be good. A bull, ostracised from the lower fields for being just too aggressive; again, not good.

I didn't have to wonder long. As I walked, a shape emerged from the fog and stood, looking at me quite coolly, about twenty metres ahead: a stag. He looked magnificent – stocky, ears alert, resplendent with short but sturdy-looking antlers. I could hear the end of his out-breaths, less frequent than mine. For a moment I was completely still, simply enjoying the feeling of looking at him, this graphic Highland silhouette, just staring straight back at me through the mist. Britain's biggest wild animal, and me – a species merely playing at being wild. After a minute or so I shifted my weight and, briskly but without alarm, he turned away and trotted back into the mist.

Odd how he'd come to have a look instead of just legging it. Stags are noisy come September's rutting season, but this was July, and the noise I'd heard sounded like a warning. He didn't seem afraid. As I moved off I heard it again; like a dog's bark, but not quite. I wondered if there was a herd nearby, perhaps with young, and that the sound I was hearing wasn't the stag I'd seen, but a hind I hadn't, warning her calf of some fellow nearby who didn't look like he knew what he was doing.

It was darkening more rapidly now. Sunset wasn't for another 45 minutes, but as I continued roughly along my bearing the gloom was noticeably thickening. Stopping to have a mouthful of water, I noticed I was soaking. It wasn't raining, and I wasn't sweating that hard. It took a moment for me to realise I was literally covered in cloud.

The ground around me had levelled off, and I found myself on what felt like a broad, grassy saddle. This didn't feel like I expected it to. Looking at a map and thinking about a mountain a lot, from afar you begin to formulate an idea of what it might feel like to be on, and what it will look like when you are. If this isn't replicated by reality it can throw you. The fact I couldn't see a damn thing didn't help, either.

I took a moment to take stock of my position using the map. It felt like I should be in the dip between Sgòr Chaonasaid and Sgòr a' Bhatain, the first two pinnacles of Ben Loyal's crown. I couldn't be sure – there were no landmarks around me against which I could orient myself. So I took a careful guess and pulled out my phone to check. I wasn't *that* wrong, but I was wrong nonetheless: I was actually standing in the dip between Sgòr a' Bhatain and An Caisteal itself – which meant I was closer to the summit than I thought.

Trying not to focus on what I'd have done if I didn't have the ability to check (answer: be more careful in the first place, of course!), I took a bearing due south across the grassy plateau that grouted Ben Loyal's summit tors. No, this wasn't what I expected at all. From sea level Ben Loyal's summit looked like it was going to be all angry rock and drama, not a bowling lawn. As nice as it was to be surprised, it would also have been nice if it was a little bit more, well – mountainous up here. Perhaps it was the low cloud that was robbing me of the finer points of Ben Loyal's spectacle. This damned cloud, which was also preventing me from looking out across the Flow Country, that marvellous, peculiar landscape, from a raised throne. And then I saw it: Ben Loyal's final little surprise.

I only notice it now looking back at pictures of the mountain, but you can see this feature in that classic view of Ben Loyal – the one you see from the causeway over the Kyle of Tongue, and the one that I'd seen in that picture in the Craggan – between the first and second pinnacles. It's a little step of rocks of quite rectangular form. Atop that slab is the summit.

It doesn't look like much from sea level, but get beneath it on a misty evening with a view to getting to the highest point of the mountain and it demands rather more consideration than a momentary glance. It's a magnificent piece of rock, a cap of what looked and sturdily felt like white granite – to all appearances a single piece fissured in many places and spidered with lichen. I'd expected a fairly easy amble, but this looked difficult. So difficult, in fact, I couldn't see a way up.

The fog was now so dense I couldn't see more than a few feet. I daresay I could have found an easier way, but by the time I'd selected a crack that looked wide enough to take a foot and begun to shimmy my way up I was really too focused on the task in hand to consider it. It was like crawling up the side of a wet football – awkward, sweaty and undignified. But it certainly felt like mountain climbing.

The crack was about twenty feet long, and I reached the top to find, with great relief, that the ground levelled off and that in the middle of it all was the trig point marking the summit. Less pleasing was the drop that opened through a gap in the crags to the left, a drop I couldn't see the bottom of. In reality it probably wasn't a long fall, but in the complete absence of any other kind of context it might as well have continued forever and I might have been climbing the final paces to the top of a terrifying, scythe-like ridge. That's one thing fog's good for, at least: self-delusion.

I walked the final few steps to Ben Loyal's summit trig point just after 9 p.m. I stood for a few seconds in the gloaming, just enjoying the stillness and being there on the top of that dramatic, broken-glass mountain that can be seen from so far away, right in the topmost snip of Britain. Taking out my compass, I laid it flat on top of the cold trig point and watched the needle rotate lazily towards north, then settle. Again I was struck with the thought that, looking out in that direction, the next solid land lay some 3,000 miles away in Siberian Russia. Between here and there lay the cold subarctic seas, and a few million square miles of polar ice.

Only slightly less significantly, between me and my chocolate biscuits and sleeping bag lay a misty descent. I went back down the summit slab more or less the same way I came up, clamping the soles of my boots into the granite fissure and trying to muster as much friction from the smooth-surfaced rock as I could. Leaping the last metre, I landed hard and flat, a buzz travelling up from my feet into my back and to my fingertips. Waiting for a second for it to subside, I looked at my phone and – again taking a bearing from the digital map on the screen – found the straightest line of descent back to the little waypoint flag that marked camp. Bearing fixed, I set off.

Descent was a lot quicker. I must have veered pretty sharply off course on the way up, as within 30 minutes I was making good progress down the final slope to my tent. Frequently sliding on wet mud, I realised I was following a rivulet; stones slick with algae, different vegetation and the occasional juvenile frog leaping clear showed that water habitually travelled this way.

The time was 9.45 p.m. when I checked my position. I remember thinking to myself that if it had been clear I'd have been able to see my tent; just then, a wave of cloud moved out of my line of vision, and there it was, as I'd left it. It was still far below, but I was practically down; close enough to make out the reflective guy ropes in the quickening dark. And close enough for something else, about a hundred metres to the north of the tent, to snag my eye. At a glance it looked like a piece of rock; but as I looked harder, I realised it definitely wasn't.

*   *   *

At around 1.30 p.m. on 25 August 1943 a Handley Page Hampden bomber was returning to RAF Wick when it issued a distress call from above Sullum Voe in the Shetlands. Part of the metrology unit assigned to measurement and meteorological analysis, its mission had been to assess the weather patterns moving over Iceland, Norway and the Faroes. Its last communication mentioned engine trouble; ten minutes later the aircraft went down.

That afternoon a second Hampden was dispatched from Wick with a five-man crew under the command of 22-year-old Flt Lt Mick Puplett to look for signs of the lost bomber. After almost eight hours of searching, this second bomber turned south to return to Wick. As it approached the Scottish coast – with almost painful irony – the bomber ran into the huge lightning storm its predecessor was likely to have spotted had it returned. At about midnight the crew of the Hampden, now severely off course, saw a blinding flash, then felt a catastrophically violent blow as the Hampden flew into the eastern flank of Ben Loyal at 150 mph. What happened next on the bleak mountainside I was now descending is probably one of the most miraculous survival stories from the sad litany of British mountain air crashes.

A 23-year-old flying officer named Cecil 'Guy' Faulks was thrown clear of the aircraft and would later awake near its burning wreckage. All around him ammunition was detonating on the hillside. He had a broken leg and left foot, and a torn mouth, yet managed to crawl behind a rock as his aircraft and its contents exploded amidst sheets of rain and terrifying lightning. Faulks managed to climb under a piece of the wreckage, unaware that another survivor lay nearby. He drifted in and out of consciousness over the following hours. The storm continued.

At some point during this long and agonising night the young airman spotted a line of lanterns moving uphill on the distant mountainside below him. Unable to shout, Faulks could do nothing but wait and hope that the line of lights turned towards him. They did, and the injured flyer was soon strapped to a piece of wreckage as a makeshift stretcher. He was administered morphine by the local physician, Dr McHendrick of Tongue, and carried back to the village by the doctor and a local shepherd named Campbell. The other survivor died during those desperate early hours. The journey to the main road was made by horse and cart, from where Faulks was transferred by ambulance to Golspie, the nearest hospital, some 50 miles from the foot of the mountain.

Both doctor and shepherd received the British Empire Medal for their heroism and expertise; Faulks spent eighteen months in hospital, but was able to fly again before the end of the war. A wry footnote to the story – one that sadly only Faulks could justly attest to, after the tragic double loss – is the motto of 519 Squadron: 'Undaunted by the Weather'.

I didn't know any of this as I wandered through the pale wreckage of HP Hampden P2118, metres from my tent, in the gathering dusk of late evening. I certainly didn't know that four people had died here, on this spot, in a stormy night of unimaginable, flame-lit horror almost exactly 70 years ago. That said, it's a good bet that wherever you find air-crash wreckage there will inevitably be an unhappy story. David W. Earl's book *Hell on High Ground* describes many accounts of mountain-crash sites in detail – including the above, sourced from Faulks himself.

As underlined by this and the many other books on the subject, air-crash sites are a startlingly common feature in the British hills. By and large bad weather has been to blame for most; occasionally engine failure or damage, or inexperienced, tragically young and frequently foreign pilots. But more often than not, the aircraft flew into mountains they simply didn't realise were there. Often the wreckage is left as a mark of respect, although it's difficult not to view these universally ugly, bleached remains as unpleasant reminders rather than dignified memorials to the dead. Sometimes you can tell what they used to be; for instance, the enormous wing of a Canberra bomber – complete with blue-and-red bullseye air force roundel – which crashed on Carn an t-Sagairt Mòr in the eastern Cairngorms in 1956 remains on the mountain to this day, along with an assortment of other wreckage from the plane.

But perhaps the most famous crash site in Britain is the wreckage of *Overexposed*, a USAF Photo Reconnaissance Boeing B-29 Superfortress that went down on 3 November 1948 over Bleaklow, a 633-metre moorland summit ten miles to the east of Manchester, whilst ferrying post between Lincolnshire and Cheshire. The crew had been flying by instrument because of low cloud; thinking they had cleared the hills, the aircraft descended, clipping the hilltop and bursting into flames. All thirteen on board were killed. Today the site is a peculiar mix of the moving and the macabre, set against the chilling bleakness of the Derbyshire moors: tiny crosses of wood placed amidst rotting metal, some enlivened with American flags; poppy wreaths fixed to wire-strewn wing-panels and dead engine turbines; crosses of wreckage and rock lying supine against black banks of peat; and everywhere, huge pieces of torn fuselage, rust radiating from pop-rivets like spreading bruises.

On Ben More Assynt in the north-west of Scotland, not that far from where I was now standing, lies a crash site unusual amongst others in that it's also a grave. Six airmen flying a twin-engined Avro Anson through a blizzard were killed on 13 April 1941 when the aircraft's starboard wing glanced a crag and sent the already severely iced-up plane into a spin. That year saw one of the hardest winters Scotland had experienced in living memory, and rescue was impossible in the exposed area in which the plane's wreckage lay, deep snow masking the site of the crash itself. The airmen's bodies were discovered a month later by a local shepherd, the great sadness being that three of them were found wrapped in their parachutes in the fuselage of the plane; a fourth was found nearly half a mile away to the east under a boulder. It would appear that these four had survived the crash, only to later be killed by the cold. The airman under the boulder – Sgt Charles Mitchell – had evidently attempted to try and find help by heading east. Even if he'd been uninjured he'd never have found help in time; little lay that way.

It was thought appropriate on account of the remoteness of the site for the men to be buried on the mountaintop. The six bodies were interred and a cross erected into a cairn. In 1985 this was restored by a group of air cadets; then in 2013 a new granite memorial was placed at the site near the subsidiary top of Beinn an Fhurain by Chinook helicopter. It marks the site of Britain's highest war grave.

The mountain had been particularly dry. I'd hoped to find running water, but hadn't. The surface water I'd found on the mountain had been murky and foetid, its surface a conference of skittering bugs. I was down to my last few fingers of water, but here a small stream was moving significantly enough to trickle near where I'd spotted the crash. I descended into the stream gully to see if I could find anything that looked like a clean flow, perhaps to make a hot chocolate, but to my dismay the stream was choked with wreckage from the aircraft. The passage of 70 years had probably leached out anything harmful, but it didn't feel clever to drink it. It didn't feel *right* to drink it.

As I arrived back at my tent I looked west just in time to see the sun emerging from behind a wafer of horizon cloud, reddened and diffused, its last peep before sinking over the headland. As it lit the door of my tent just fleetingly, I stood and watched the day end, glad to have made it for this last kiss of light on the mountain.

I passed the night dozing and listening idly to the gentle rustle of the tent's nylon shell. Sipping my remaining water at intervals, by the early hours I woke parched, lost my resolve and downed the lot.

As light began to gather around the tent and hearing the faint beginnings of rain I began to stir, determined not to miss the opportunity to pack the tent up in dry weather. By 5.30 I was beginning my descent back towards Cunside, then the car. Ahead lay a long drive across my favourite area of Scotland, and another mountain – hopefully after some much-needed rehydration and a breakfast somewhere. Behind me Ben Loyal poked the occasional buttress out through the lazy dawn mist. Skies crouched heavily to the east. My pace quickened slightly as, far away amongst it, my eyes caught a distant flicker. This was followed by a rumble spreading across the morning sky, like a table pulled across a stone floor.

9 VISION

Heading west, it was 45 minutes before I saw another car. It could have been the early hour, but it probably wasn't.

The roads of Scotland's far north are about as close as you can get in Britain to driving those big American highways you see in the films; grey asphalt unrolling ahead like a cable belt and not a soul on it but you. In an empty place like this you can see objects travelling towards you from miles away, and there's little to give them scale. This kind of thing happens a lot out here. You don't realise how featureless the landscape is until you spot something rising out of it that grabs your attention and holds it. For miles.

As I crossed the causeway out of Tongue I saw something up ahead just off the road. High and commanding, it looked at first like a small power station sporting twin furnace pipes, then a castle turret. As I got close, it turned out to be nothing more than a tiny, roofless croft, the frail apex walls stark against the white sky. The view someone once saw from its skeletal windows must have been stupendous. The dead cottage squares up to Ben Hope and Ben Loyal like a rowboat facing off against two leviathans breaking the surface of a brown sea. Like so many things around here, it stands totally alone.

This morning, to put it rather grandly, I was rounding the cape. My route took me along the tattered northern edge of Britain to the point where the coast meets an obtuse corner and turns south at the storm-flayed pinnacle of Cape Wrath. This place is a collage of deep inlets, silvery tidal lochs, white stripes of sand tracing the shape of a bay and lighthouses glinting in the morning sun atop sloughing headlands. The ten-mile Loch Eriboll slices inland, long a shelter from the storms of the northern coast, its still water hiding a depth that has sheltered ships from the storms of the abrasive northern seas for centuries. Houses speckle its shores like blocks of quartz on a mountainside.

Civilisation can't be taken for granted around here; this area has the lowest population density in the United Kingdom. Sheep walk the roads and hunker behind dry-stone walls, and the radio fades in and out of reception, odd snatches of news coming in through the static: protests in London, a fire somewhere. To me, this morning, it all felt very far away.

In Durness – the only settlement of size since Tongue – I finally managed to get some water. By this point the inside of my mouth felt like it was made from suede, and I went a little over the top, draining an entire two-litre bottle and the first inch of a second, which I'd bought to ensure the same thing didn't happen twice. From Durness I was to amputate the final tip of the country containing Cape Wrath: that final vestige of the wild north is unreachable by normal road, only by foot or ferry, then private bus. I'd never been there, but in a way it was good I didn't have time. It's always good to have a reason to come back to places like this.

I passed little crofting cottages on the road between Durness and Rhiconich, some with peat harvested into neat little piles for drying, and eventually for burning. Through shafts of sunlit cloud and rain I glimpsed the other great mountain of the far north, Foinaven. It looks titanic: a swirl of quartzite ridges and shoulders, most of it a shadow behind boiling mists. Then the road began to dance and climb over tall passes, until eventually – just as it crossed the little Kylesku Bridge – I entered the land of the beautiful freaks.

This place is called Assynt. In the two possible translations from Old Norse it's said to mean both 'rocky ridge' and 'visible from afar'; the first is the more likely but it's the second that you want to believe, as it's quite beautifully apt. The mountains here are like nothing else in Scotland. Indeed, they're like nothing else on earth – and it's not just about how they're made. It's how they stand, how they hold themselves up against the flat landscape. It is, in fact, everything about them.

Assynt has the potential to seduce just about anyone with a pulse, but it is people of a sensitive temperament who have gotten themselves truly flustered here. I say flustered because its charm, for all its spectacle, is peculiar to the point of being unsettling. You might head for the Dales of Yorkshire or the

Cotswolds to immerse yourself in soothing landscapes of comforting comeliness. But here in Assynt, in this far-cast corner of Britain, hardness and beauty become one, breaking the surface and disturbing the horizon with six unique, free-standing mountains, each a delicate geological sculpture of brutal elegance. All are misfits, chucked out like the last bits of junk from a car-boot sale, or pieces of a puzzle that just didn't fit.

The result is a tucked attic of completely unique mountain curiosities, high in the gables of Britain amidst a land thickly dusted with history and atmosphere. It's an utterly extraordinary place.

Quinag is the most muscular, acting like a dramatically ruinous northern wall, isolated and towering to 808 metres above Loch Assynt at the northern gateway to the territory. Slender ligaments of ridgeline are drawn tight between three main summits, from which drape long flanks of ruffled Torridonian sandstone that become vertically striped with fissures of deep shadow when side-lit by the afternoon sun. Seen from above, the massif resembles the letter Y billowing in the breeze, or perhaps a broad-winged gull flying south-west. Quinag is so mighty and so set apart from its neighbours that in these dynamic coastal reaches it makes its own weather, often gathering a cloak of cloud around it even when the mountains nearby are clear. This makes it the least seen, and arguably the least individual, of the Assynt mountains. It's also the most complex and, if awards are given for bulk, the most magnificent.

The bent pyramid of Canisp – perhaps the least noticed peak of Assynt – lies further to the south. It's higher than Quinag, although it doesn't look it. Remote, and home to lingering, rough ascents, it sees few feet. The twins of Cùl Mòr and Cùl Beag are staggeringly steep-looking, their suffixes of 'large' and 'little' respectively quite clearly apt when you see them. Cùl Beag is slight compared with its vulgar northern neighbour, a compact but steep mountain with twin peaks and a small lochan nestled between them. Cùl Mòr is enormous; from above a whirlpool galaxy of contours, from side-on a broad-shouldered hunch tapering upwards to a spacious summit ridge.

Assynt's southern extreme is dominated by the unmistakable Stac Pollaidh, at 612 metres the smallest of Assynt's peaks and one of its most charismatic. From the east it looks like a submarine conning tower, from the south a comb of shattered teeth and from the west a tall, dramatic monolith or the belfry of some Gothic cathedral rising out of a plain. Composed of fractured sandstone weathered into long, reaching fingers, the mountain appears to bristle.

And then the most famous of all: Suilven. All the mountains in Assynt are shapeshifters, altering their pose sufficiently with even subtle variations in your viewing angle that you're convinced you haven't seen the mountain look *quite* like that before. But Suilven manages to be the most fickle of all with its identity, whilst somehow simultaneously remaining the most distinctive.

This is down to it being so striking in the first place. It's not often nature produces a mountain that captivates so effectively from every side. It's tempting to think that whatever sculpting machinations designed most of our peaks, they did so in order that they'd be admired especially from one aspect, like a painting or a dressed stage. The rest is just the messy backdrop. Not so Suilven. It simply looks staggering – and staggeringly different – from all angles, yet it always looks like Suilven. And until you see it, you don't realise how unusual that is.

It's a mountain of two parts: the slightly lower eastern end a difficult series of terraced towers that make the mountain resemble a kind of tusk rising from the landscape when looked at head on. The western half is composed of a massive semicircular buttress, like a disc-saw half-buried in the ground.

The proximity of Suilven to the sea and its distinctive, isolated position amidst a largely flat landscape suggest nautical thoughts from its other angles. From the south-east, the mountain tilts elegantly away, as if it were a yacht on the high seas with its sails tapered by the wind. From other angles it looks like a leviathan, all bulbous head and tapered tail. When viewed directly along its axis from the west, Suilven resembles a massive domed pillar, or the head of some appalling tanker slicing through the land towards you. It's a presence that most will consider striking, indeed from some angles even beautiful. Others will find it strange, intimidating, watchful.

However peculiar it might look, and however contorted it may appear from certain angles – and from some it does actually look like it might roll away or fall over at any moment – the mountain is actually tall, skinny and dead straight in trajectory. It fattens beneath the higher, domed western summit of Caisteal Liath, but nowhere along its mile-long length is the mountain wider than 600 metres. It isn't a giant in terms of height, either.

Despite its charisma and promise of challenge, Suilven is 731 metres tall, half the height of Ben Nevis. Yet these are big-feeling mountains, each wholly adrift and of great presence. More proof, if it were needed, that height is of little value when a peak is worth so much.

Climbing Suilven would therefore be the obvious target for anyone coming to this region, but that was not why I was here. Not that it matters, but I've climbed it before and I'll tell you about it later. What I was seeking instead was a vision of this extraordinary mountain tableau in as close to its entirety as I could manage: a place that showed off Assynt's haunting nature with some semblance of completeness. This isn't arty farty like it sounds. The mountains here seem to be engaged in a permanent game of musical statues in the way they seem to slide in and out of view behind each other; I just wanted a view-point from which I could see it *all* – the single-most expansive vision of this strangest, most visually *other* of all Britain's mountain places.

And there was no way I could get away from it: Suilven had to be in the view – and there was no way of seeing Suilven if I was *standing* on it. Likewise, were I to climb Stac Pollaidh, Stac Pollaidh would be absent from the view, and that just wasn't acceptable. A mountain to the north wouldn't do, either: these isolated hills would then be denied their silhouettes and would simply jumble together against the bigger hills to the south. These, too, offered their own takes on this clutch of hills, but to obtain them would mean having to leave Assynt and look back in, probably from a higher mountain. Something about that just didn't feel right. If this all sounds a bit pedantic, it is – but I knew the right viewpoint would be worth the fuss. The problem was, I had no idea where or how I'd find what I was looking for. And from the looks of the weather, that wasn't going to be the only thing worth worrying about.

The mountains round here are so noteworthy they're given roadside interpre-tation boards, like animals at a zoo. This is thanks to the area's status as Scotland's first Geopark, a UNESCO designation that covers this far-flung chunk of the North-west Highlands and its coast. As the name suggests, this is a kind of geologically focused nature reserve that acknowledges the scien-tific importance of the surface rocks hereabouts.

I stopped to look at the board that overlooks Quinag. The simply worded explanations of the geology, along with annotated images of the view, did a fine job of describing just what was very, very, very slowly going on in front of me. I learned that Quinag was made of a foundation of Lewisian gneiss, a rock that gets geologists particularly excited principally because it's extremely old, bearing the breath-drawing distinction of being 'Precambrian'. Precambrian rock, as you might guess, was formed before the Cambrian period – something that's rather more important than this dry definition suggests. The Cambrian period stretched from about 550 million years ago to about 485 million years ago. During this period, if you happened to be walking around, the dominant form of life you'd encounter would be the trilobite: those peculiar, skeletal-looking aquatic bugs that form the cornerstone of most fossil-hunters' collections. But the *Pre*cambrian stretched from between 550 million years ago to – get this – the *creation of the earth*. That's a period of about four billion years in our planet's four-and-a-half-billion-year history, or around 80 per cent of known geological time. These rocks not only witnessed the dawn of life as we know it; they witnessed the dawn of life itself.

Geologists know relatively little about the Precambrian – it does have a somewhat sweeping catchment – but if you wish to study Precambrian rocks in Britain this corner of north-west Scotland is the place to do so. Named after the Isle of Lewis, which it also underpins, Lewisian gneiss is a particularly characterful rock. Originally volcanic – not unlike granite – gneiss is the result of geological metamorphosis, in this case approximately three billion years of squeezing, folding, heating, buckling, cooling and thrusting. This has left it in a bit of a beautiful mess, as you might expect from a rock very nearly as old as the earth.

Back at the interpretation board and our little roadside science lesson, I was instructed to look at Sàil Gharbh – the 808-metre summit of Quinag – and the distinctive rock layering of broken horizontal steps, like geological rice terraces, that made up much of the mountain's bulk. As the present company attested, mountains exhibiting this bedding tended to be steep, crumbly and dramatic.

It was exactly this intermittently precipitous structure that made my ascent and descent of Beinn Dearg in Torridon last autumn so upsetting. Indeed, the way that mountain, and its neighbours Liathach and Beinn Alligin, so spectacularly displayed it was precisely why this type of rock was named for that very region: Torridonian sandstone.

Unusually, Torridonian sandstone was largely deposited by great rivers.*
Its red hue – which has meant that several hills made of it have been given the
knee-jerk name Beinn Dearg, or 'Red Hill' – comes from tiny fragments of
oxidised iron, whereas most marine sandstones are grey. This process of depo-
sition took around 400 million years, and finished around 800 million years
ago, during and after which a process known as diagenesis turned the sediment into rock. So Torridonian sandstone is pretty venerable, too. It's thought
that deposits of this rock once reached up to 5,000 metres – higher than the
Alps – and the weight of these deposits was so great it actually bowed the
older rocks beneath it into a basin.

The final and perhaps most important constituent of the Assynt hills is a
top layer of Cambrian quartzite. This quartzite is essentially a sandstone
whose marine-deposited sediment has been subjected to considerable tidal
sifting, resulting in a much more uniform composition very high in pure silica,
or sand.† This quartzite was laid down a few hundred million years after the
Torridonian sandstone, during which time the deposits had been covered by
a shallow sea and had lost much of their extensive height. A harder, more
erosion-resistant rock, this quartz formed a protective 'cap' – perhaps more
aptly considered a 'helmet' – which to some degree protected the rock beneath
from being eroded away. It was resilient against the weather, tended to sharpen
rather than crumble, and in all likelihood saved the mountains of Assynt and
elsewhere nearby from fragmenting away to fragile, weathered stubs of sandstone through vast ages of wind and glaciation. Quinag, Cùl Mòr, Canisp, Ben
More Assynt and Foinaven all have such a cap. Poor Stac Pollaidh is a dramatic
example of what happens when a peak lacks or has lost one, and is therefore

---

* Given the immense amount of time involved, it's certain that a degree of tidal action was
also at play at some point, as parts of the area were frequently submerged under shallow
tropical seas.

† Quartzite can be confusing. Much of what is commonly called quartzite is sedimentary
rock that has been metamorphosed, with a silica content of around 80 per cent. Cambrian
quartzite has not been subjected to metamorphosis, and has an even higher proportion of
silica – as much as 99 per cent – probably down to the naturally sifting action of a shallow
sea. It we're being strictly technical we should call this sedimentary rock 'quartzose sandstone', but this obviously hasn't caught on. Anyone interested at all in the specifics should
read Paul Gannon's superb *Rock Trails* series, which explains all this rather better than I can.

exposed to everything the elements can throw at it: a tooth that's lost its crown, then rotted away.

I loved the fact that someone had deemed this landscape important enough to explain it in terms everyone could understand, here at the roadside. Geology as a science has some interminably dull literature, and even those texts that begin with the promise of clarity soon descend into such catacombs of esoteric terminology that readers pretty soon become lost, or are sent into a stupor. This is a shame because it's fascinating stuff; and often just the basics are needed to gain a different level of appreciation, as demonstrated both by the little board I'd found here and others that occasionally furnished the road-sides to the south. Just as I was about to climb back behind the wheel and continue on my way, something else on the board caught my eye. It was a quote from a poem titled 'Moment musical in Assynt', which read:

> A mountain is a sort of music: theme
> And counter theme displaced in air amongst
> Their own variations.

I was happy to see this, as my companion for this leg of the journey, lying newly dog-eared in the passenger footwell, was a weighty book of poems by the man who wrote it: Norman MacCaig.

Every landscape has its laureate, and whilst many artists have attempted to capture Assynt visually, it's the words of MacCaig that render the land-scape's true character most strikingly.

I was new to MacCaig's work (actually, if I'm being honest, I hadn't heard of him at all prior to stumbling across another line from a different poem whilst researching the area before leaving) and therefore was in the fortunate position of discovering his evocations of Assynt whilst moving through it. The line that had hooked me was in the first stanza from his 1959 poem 'High up on Suilven':

> Gulfs of blue air, two lochs like spectacles,
> A frog (this height) and Harris in the Sky
> There are more reasons for hills
> Than being steep and reaching only high.

MacCaig was born in Edinburgh in 1910, and first visited Scalpay in the Outer Hebrides – the island where his mother was born – at the age of 12. He later claimed that this was a pivotal moment in his life, and that his annual visits to the remote island awakened a connection with the tiny community and its environment that ran ancestrally, if not exactly religiously, through him. Later a teacher, MacCaig would proclaim that 'landscape is my religion' – this at a time when his young family had long taken their summer holidays amidst the queer magnificence of Assynt.

Both the climate and the strangeness of this corner of the far north-west pervade MacCaig's poems. These poems do not romanticise the region: what they do is strip it back, interpreting its elemental grandeur in a manner that requires no embellishment. Dozens of vignettes build a tapestry of an area with which the poet enjoyed a tempestuous affair throughout his life. Many of his works are about life in Assynt, of the mountains, and the moments where the two meet. MacCaig's masterpiece, 'A Man in Assynt', is perhaps the most affecting of these works. It begins by uncannily capturing the nature of the landscape:

> Glaciers, grinding West, gouged out
> these valleys, rasping the brown sandstone,
> and left, on the hard rock below –
> the ruffled foreland –
> This frieze of mountains, filed
> on the blue air – Stac Polly,
> Cul Beag, Cul Mor, Suilven,
> Canisp – a frieze and a litany.

It's not just descriptions of landscape that MacCaig loved; a deeper communion is at play, one that speaks of a much more personal interpretation of the mountains. In 'Landscape and I', written in 1972, he even gives Schiehallion a nod:

> This means of course, Schiehallion in my mind
> Is more than a mountain. In it he leaves behind
> A meaning, an idea, like a hind
> Crouched in a corrie.

He ends the poem with a call to action: 'There's a Schiehallion anywhere you go./The thing is, climb it.'

You don't have to know all – or any – of this to be bewitched by Assynt. The place just feels special. It has a smell, a space and electricity that is just *different*, and defies definition. The way the Atlantic storms wash over the area at a swirling clip, the fantastical shapes of the mountains and the way the light hits the shimmering, nebulous lochans that interlock across the flat land between them like wine spilled across a table top: it's as if you're inhabiting some dramatic, impressionistic painting. Someone's vision of a place, rather than the visage of a place itself. It was the distillation of this vision that – in the most physical sense I could – I'd come here looking for. And whilst I didn't know exactly where to find it, I had an idea where to start.

The road to reach the foot of Cùl Beag took me along the southern border of Assynt, where it meets another region – Coigach. This is the name given to the peninsula and coast to the south-west of Assynt. The single-track road that leaves the A835 at Drumrunie passes along the border, and by God it's stunning. Loch Lurgainn sprawls beneath you; Stac Pollaidh's weathered funnel stands ahead; and opening to your left is the sprawling Ben More Coigach – its most attention-snaring feature the spectacular buttress of Sgùrr an Fhidhleir, a sharp triangle, like some Himalayan freak stripped of ice and dropped into the North-west Highlands. I parked the car in a lay-by just where a faint, unsigned path left the road, and began the climb through bracken towards Cùl Beag.

I was trying to see my reasons for deciding to climb this 769-metre mountain as something other than a compromise. None of the other peaks that make up these chapters were compromises – quite the opposite – but I was now making my way up Cùl Beag as it was perhaps the mountain I'd miss least from the view I was looking for, making it a logical place from which to see it. Plus, it looked interesting and little-tackled; apparently no clear paths went up it, so the route to gain its summit would have to be done more or less entirely by instinct.

The initial thicket of trees eased after a few minutes, the skinny path emerging out onto upland, clear and stripped. To my left, Stac Pollaidh punched from the landscape, transient light gilding its rough relief. And ahead, across a wilderness of water and knotty rock, stood Suilven. The intervening ground was all rough, green-furred bedrock, puddled with pale lochs – not flat exactly, but not hilly either. Just hard. Difficult-looking.

Like the Flow Country of Sutherland, this equally distinctive landscape also has a name: 'knock and lochan'. You find it in patches across the Northwest Highlands, where successive glaciers have scoured the sedimentary fat from the land, revealing the ancient gneiss bones beneath. Its evocative name comes from the Gaelic and translates roughly to 'low mounds and small lakes',* which is certainly literal. It does, however, belittle the challenge of navigating it: crossing knock-and-lochan terrain is like negotiating an exhausting labyrinth of impassable stretches of interlocking rivers, bodies of water with squirrelly banks that add hidden miles to your journey, and terrain that swallows you and chokes the view away like rising quicksand.

Of course, from this distance it all looked rather comely. The six or so miles between where I was standing – overlooking tiny Lochan Fhionnlaidh in the crook between Cùl Beag and Stac Pollaidh – to the summit of Suilven and back appeared as if it would take no more than a couple of hours. It was, in fact, an expedition – a day at least, probably more, and exhausting. I looked at the map to remind myself of the names of the reasons why. The organic outline of the massive Loch Sionascaig, weird and frantic, dug into the land like a sap tattoo into tree bark. Loch Veyatie and Fionn Loch tore into the land from the north-west and south-east, joined in the middle by the Uidh Fhearna, a short river. On the map this is drawn using double blue lines with blue fill between: what this means is it's over eight metres across. Rivers between four and eight metres wide are shown as one thick blue line. Less than four metres, a blue squiggle. Details like this are important to remember when planning an expedition. On the scale of the map I held in my hand – 1:50,000 – 1 cm on the map was equivalent to 50,000 cm on the ground. To move 1 mm north on my map I'd have to walk 50 metres, past the little loch, towards Suilven.

The casualty of this relatively small scale – when compared with the 1:10,000 or 1:25:000 large-scale maps – is that landscape features are some-

* Knock, from the Gaelic *cnoc*, meaning hill or mound.

times too small to be conveyed accurately. A glance at an Ordnance Survey map armed with such knowledge will immediately tell you that certain key things on a map of such condensed detail have necessarily been massaged; were every feature totally faithful to this scale, many would barely be visible, let alone useful. Were they to match the indicated scale of 1 mm to 50 metres, the road upon which the car was parked would be dozens of metres across, the little squares marking tiny, isolated crofts would indicate buildings the size of sports stadiums and the wiggly A837 road I'd turned off at Ledmore would be a highway the width of the Thames.

Back to the job in hand, though. I'd been standing there for a while staring at Suilven and Cùl Mòr, trying to imagine how they were going to look from the summit of Cùl Beag, awaiting to my right. The mass of Cùl Mòr was blocking much of Suilven; I judged from the shoulder height of this bigger mountain that this was unlikely to improve, but it might. I'd find out either way once up.

The map indicated no path, but here indeed was one, marked by a small pile of stones. It slinked off through the heather towards the foot of the mountain, although I couldn't see whether or not it continued beyond there. Glancing over at the sky above the bulky, horizon-filling Ben More Coigach behind me, I hesitated for a moment. The top point of Sgùrr an Fhidhleir's 705-metre triangle had disappeared, and now a swiftly moving finger of cloud was reaching across the loch and caressing the highest reaches of Cùl Beag.

Ah yes, the weather. This had been tentatively holding steady for most of the morning. The forecast looked relentlessly depressing but, based on conversations with the few people I'd interacted with – and, of course, our conversations were always about the weather – I'd noticed that nobody placed a lot of faith in it this far north. It seemed the only way to know what the weather was going to be like in an hour's time was to stick your head out of the window, face the wind and see what was coming – more or less what I'd been doing all day, and this was the first time I hadn't liked what I'd seen.

There had been flickers and dark clouds in the distance descending Ben Loyal that morning, but they'd been inland on the eastern horizon. Plus, I'd travelled a long way west since then and I was now just short of paddling in the Atlantic. With its changeable coastal weather systems, wherever that storm was this morning might as well have been a different country. As I'd moved across, however, I couldn't help but feel things were getting worse rather than better. It had been an unusually humid morning, and as the afternoon went on a weird stillness had gathered, broken only by the 'zeeee' of midges that were beginning to fester in the windless air and pester me when I stopped. Mithering the top of Cùl Beag just 500 metres above me, the clouds seemed to be moving at a fair clip, though; and as I looked around with increasing concern both Stac Pollaidh and Cùl Mòr were being intermittently striped by moving yellow light beneath a bruised sky. Something was definitely afoot, and it soon became obvious that my early optimism had been misplaced – possibly foolishly so – and that I wasn't going to escape whatever the weather had in store.

But by the time I realised all of this it was too late. I'd taken the path and pushed on towards the shoulder of Cùl Beag. I then left it to follow the course of a stream across a gently climbing stretch of open ground towards the point where the mountain's northern ridge revealed a chink of weakness in the form of a little shoulder. It looked like a good way up; indeed, it looked like the only way up.

It was just after crossing the 300-metre contour that I knew I'd made the wrong decision. Things happened quickly to confirm this: a double flash, and immediately a concussive crash I felt in my chest that made me reflexively duck. Almost immediately there came another, a stick of lightning bridging the gap between the sky and something in the knock-and-lochan landscape between where I was standing and Suilven. This frightened me: lightning was supposed to strike high things, yet here it was reaching down between the peaks. Hitting things low down. Things like me.

What I should have done was hunker down somewhere secreted, preferably on a convex slope, taking comfort from the fact I had the bulk of a big mountain next to me that should, if theory were to be believed, offer some protection from a lightning strike. But I didn't: I felt exposed, and in danger. Following my gut, I turned and ran.

The closest I'd previously come to being struck by lightning was many years ago, in the company of probably the calmest mountain guide in the world. We'd just descended from a clutch of Munros in Perthshire when lightning started hitting fence-posts on the summit of Carn Mairg – a high, featureless

Munro near Schiehallion – near which we'd been standing not twenty minutes before. Stuart, who's generally an unflappable chap, said something along the lines of 'Perhaps we'd better start making our way down now' to our little group, which – heartened by his apparent lack of concern – began moving earnestly down the valley. A few minutes later (and this is true, honest to God) we saw a bolt of lightning hit the point where, again, we'd just been standing. It was as if it was following us down the mountain. With eyes a-panicked, once again our little group all turned to Stuart, who – with perhaps the *slightest* crinkle of concern – imparted in quiet, almost jovial Perthshire tones that, in his opinion, going down was still the best plan, but perhaps a little more briskly than before.

Well, the six of us must have looked like a Benny Hill sketch. We made it down, mind, with – if I do say so myself – quite admirable self-restraint and no further incident, and eventually the thunderstorm rumbled away. Back at the car I looked at Stuart, who gave me a sheepish grin.

'Bit of a close one back there,' he said.

'So you *were* worried,' I replied.

He shrugged, before imparting the best bit of mountain-crisis advice I've ever heard.

'Situations like that, you've got two choices: you either descend quickly, or you descend quickly in a panic. So why panic?'

It's difficult to imagine what a direct lightning strike is actually like. You hear this most spectacular and uncompromisingly deadly of weather phenomena being compared to all sorts of things, but basically it's a bloody big spark – and in the mountains, where you lack the comfort of shelter, it can be terrifying. In the static fog of a lightning storm, metal-rich rocks can crackle, ice axes can hum and even give off tinsel-like electricity, and your hair can stand to attention – all of which might sound rather jolly, but as all are common precursors to a lightning strike, are actually rather not. Another term for a lightning bolt perhaps helps visualise its final, cataclysmic discharge: it's an 'electrometeor'. This projectile of a billion volts heats the air to around 15,000°C as it burns through it along a pathway of ionised particles towards whatever it has identified as its conductor.

Like a bullet, lightning travelling into you will enter and exit. And, like a bullet, it will leave a hole. Deep wounds, burns and the peculiar, so-called

Lichtenberg scarring – where burst blood vessels form often strangely elegant, tree-like tattoos on the skin – might result around these wounds. If lightning enters your skull, your brain might literally be cooked. Your heart might stop. The moisture in your body will evaporate, desiccating your tissues. Anything metallic on or inside you – piercings, jewellery, or (unthinkably) surgical plates will superheat and contact-fry anything around them.

Even if you're not struck directly, the secondary effects are often just as dire. If you experience what's known as a 'flashover' – where the current doesn't enter your body, just dances over it – your clothing might catch fire, or be blown off, leaving you burned and exposed. Flash discharge can occur when something close to you is struck, and the bolt then jumps sideways, knocking you off your feet or, indeed, off the mountain.

This might all sound bad enough. But if yours is suitably lucky enough – so to speak – to be amongst the 30 per cent of lightning strikes that are witnessed by someone else, you've got an additional problem. Many won't touch the recently struck, fearing they too might get a shock; a common belief, but completely false. Not enough people know this, and as a result potentially lifesaving first aid such as CPR suffers needless delay.

Back in the civilised world, being struck by lightning is the analogy of choice for any rare event, the ultimate yardstick of absurd unlikelihood, against which every other threat is measured and belittled. But assign numbers to the chances and it's a little sobering. It's estimated that a so-called CG (cloud-to-ground) strike in the United Kingdom occurs about 300,000 times a year. Once every 6,000 of these, someone is struck. Every 100,000, someone gets killed.*

In towns you might have little cause for concern. But ironically, the second you leave that congregation of metal and seething civilisation everything changes rather dramatically out of your favour. In urban areas you're one of a million potential conductors; out in the open you're a solitary little bag of salty

---

* All of these numbers vary wildly; a single stormy day in July 1994 produced a record 85,000 ground strikes. In terms of deaths, the worst year on record for the UK was 1982, with fourteen people killed by lightning. Conversely, in 2000 and 2001, there were no lightning deaths reported.

water sticking up from a bare landscape. Basically, you're a walking electrolyte.

It's therefore no accident that you're most likely to be killed by lightning whilst off exploring the world's wilder side. In the United States between 2006 and 2012 lightning killed an average of 40 people per year. A recent study by the US National Weather Service (NOAA) revealed that two-thirds of these people were taking part in what it termed 'leisure activities' when they were struck, and analysis of the results reveals some strangely telling patterns. The day on which you were most likely to be killed was a Saturday in July (it just happened to be a Saturday in July as I was running off Cùl Beag, but I didn't know any of this at the time) and you'd most likely be fishing – the activity during which lightning claimed the lives of 11 per cent of these poor hobby-loving souls. Camping came next, with 10 per cent. Comfortingly, walking accounted for only 4 per cent, whilst golf, long the clichéd activity for lightning risk (probably those jumpers), came a surprising ninth on the list of risky activities, with just 3 per cent.

By comparison, here in Britain up to 60 people a year are struck by lightning, of whom perhaps three or four are killed. But over the years there have been a disproportionate number of people within this comparatively small fatality rate who have been killed whilst wandering in the mountains. Statistically, although you're far more likely to die because you lack proper equipment than be struck by lightning, this hasn't stopped the two dangers from coinciding rather cruelly on occasion. There have been cases when, in their haste to distance themselves from their conductive metal implements, winter walkers have flung axes and crampons off the mountain at the sight of threatening thunderheads. Following the storm's passing, they've then had their relief scuppered by the far more dangerous prospect of descending a treacherous, frozen mountainside without them, something that can be as risky as driving a car with no brakes down the M1.

Just before we move on and get back to Assynt, one further point about lightning – and perhaps the most oddly depressing statistic in the NOAA report. Eighty-two per cent of those killed by lightning were male. It's a statistic that's almost identical for England and Wales, where men accounted for 83 per cent of recorded lightning deaths between 1852 and 1999. The report offers – with thinly veiled damnation – a potential cause for this: 'Possible explanations are that males are unaware of all the dangers associated with lightning ... are unwilling to be inconvenienced by the threat of lightning ... [or] don't react quickly to the lightning threat.'* It basically implies that in the face of devastating peril males have a tendency to be stubborn, macho and a little bit stupid. Which, on reflection, is probably about right.

I didn't get struck by lightning on Cùl Beag, and for this I was immeasurably thankful, if a little disappointed I'd had to bin my climb. I managed to reach the car within twenty minutes, during which time the flashes and the rumbles began to separate, indicating the thunderstorm was moving away. In its place, a pretty severe rainstorm was establishing itself – which meant wherever this elusive view was, it wasn't going to be here and certainly wouldn't appear in the next few minutes. This was made a little easier to take as Cùl Beag would never have delivered exactly what I was looking for, anyway: I'd realised this when I broke out of the trees and saw that from this angle, however high I got on Cùl Beag, the oh-so-important ingredient – Suilven – was going to remain half-blocked by neighbouring Cùl Mòr's colossal west flank. As I sat in the car, morosely watching the spires of Stac Pollaidh disappear behind thickening rain, I made a decision. Starting the engine, I pulled out of the car park and headed for Lochinver.

The founding of Lochinver in 1812 sadly took place under the pall of something less than celebratory. This was known to local people as the 'Fuadach nan Gàidheal' – the expulsion of the Gael – whilst the landlords called the process 'improvement'. The rural people of England had seen this already in the form of the Enclosure Acts, but north of the border history would give them another, less ambiguous and entirely more notorious, name: the Highland Clearances.

Between 1812 and 1821 some 160 families were evicted from their homes in Assynt's glens. The Duke of Sutherland, like other landowners across

* The England and Wales figure for males' tendency to be struck more between 1852 and 1999 is skewed by societal factors, and therefore has a more flattering explanation – more men than women are and, critically, were employed in outdoor work. The figures come from the Tornado and Storm Research Organisation (TORA), based in Oxford, which keeps a record of lightning deaths as recorded on death certificates.

Scotland, had decided to convert the most fertile parts of his land from croft-ing to the more lucrative sheep farming, necessitating the forced removal of the families smallholding upon it.

Even before the Clearances, the turbulent history of Assynt makes for sour reading. The Clan MacLeod had controlled the land since the Vikings were defeated by Alexander of Scotland in 1263 at the Battle of Largs. Reputedly the descendants of a Viking named Leod were permitted to remain in his lands, but not as Vikings; instead, they became Gaelic clansmen, and their name became MacLeod – literally, son of Leod. They would build Ardvreck Castle, now a magnificently ruinous and ancient finger of old stone pointing skywards from the banks of Loch Assynt beneath Quinag. In 1672 the castle and its lands were seized by the Clan Mackenzie of Ross-shire, and after the Mackenzies went bankrupt in 1739, Assynt was acquired by the Duchess-Countess of Sutherland in 1757.

The Clearances of Assynt were less evictions than forced migrations. In order to make way for what would become five enormous sheep pastures, the people were offered an alternative livelihood by the sea – typically kelp-farm-ing, fishing or smallholding on the quaggy coastline. The only inland area to receive an influx of displaced tenants was what is today Knockan and Elphin, where 58 crofts were designated.

It was a desperate existence for many, with starvation a very real prospect. Many of those who once worked the land of Assynt were forced to leave the region altogether and seek better lives in the cities of the south or, in some cases, overseas. In 1817 one Reverend Norman MacLeod left Assynt for Nova Scotia with a sizeable contingent of his flock. Those who left – and for that matter, those who remained – nursed a bitter sadness for the loss of their upland home that often made its way into verse, such as Donnchadh Bàn Mac an t-Saoir's* 'Final Farewell':

---

* I use the name in full Gaelic respectfully, given its context; in English it's Duncan Ban MacIntyre if you wish to seek him out, and you should.

I hardly thought
That the mountain would ever change,
But now it is under sheep,
The world has cheated me.

Today, northern Scotland is amongst the most sparsely populated areas in Europe, and a sadness pervades this serene landscape, the earth itself seeming to mourn for its lost people. The thrust of Norman MacCaig's 'A Man in Assynt' – that poem whose opening so beautifully distils this place – is in fact a lament for those departed, and for those who remained:

Who owns this landscape? –
The millionaire who bought it or
The poacher staggering downhill in the early morning
With a deer on his back?
Who possesses this landscape?
The man who bought it or
I who am possessed by it?

This particular story, however, has a happy ending, and one that gives hope to other areas still suffering the indignity left by the Clearances.

In 1992, after hundreds of years of clan turmoil, eviction and latter-day deed-swapping, slicing, renaming and fragmenting between various super-rich landowners, the crofting community of Assynt stepped up for a fight. Upon hearing the news that the estate on which many lived and worked was to be broken up further and sold yet again without their consultation, the Scottish Crofters Union called an emergency meeting to discuss the viability of purchasing the land themselves. They launched a campaign to raise the necessary funds to make a bid, under the new banner of the Assynt Crofters' Trust. A story appeared in the *Daily Telegraph* under a headline of gleeful irony: 'Crofters gather to plan clearance of landlords'. This was the moment when the tide turned and the traditional land ownership currents of the Highlands began to reverse. Donations flooded in. Supporters all over Britain sent money. Politicians sent money. People now living on other continents whose ancestors were evicted in the Clearances sent money. Even a rock band donated. 'I Support the Assynt Crofters' car stickers were circulated. Grants were given by councils, loans were pledged by Scottish Natural Heritage and Highlands and Islands Enterprise. And the canny discovery of a legal clause from the 1976 Crofting Reform Act stating that a crofter has the right to buy their land for fifteen times the annual rent – meaning the entire area could be bought for just £39,120 – gave the crofters further legal support should a friendly bid fail.

It didn't. A bid for £300,000 was accepted on 8 December, and on 1 February 1993 the Trust took possession of the title deeds to 21,300 acres of land containing thirteen crofting townships. In 2005 the community also bought the Glencanisp Estate, including the mountains of Suilven and Canisp, and the Drumrunie Estate, containing Cùl Mòr and Cùl Beag: a further 44,000 acres. Finally, hundreds of years of unrest and near-feudal rule were over. The land – and anything earned from it – belonged to the people, and the drawbridge was flattened for similar estates to follow suit, and free themselves from absentee landlords. In the years since, many have.

I learned all this from the Tourist Information Centre in Lochinver, which I can highly recommend – and not only for slightly directionless afternoons such as the one I was currently experiencing. Two displays in the building particularly caught my eye. The first, on the top floor, contained a diorama put together by local communities and was dedicated to the fauna of Assynt both living and long dead; the second was a model of the region under heavy glaciation, and this I found particularly captivating. Its ice was a white resin, with crevasses scratched in by the sculptor's knife and then lined further by the countless schoolchildren who have doubtlessly run their fingernails across it over the years. It was a very vivid way of articulating a process that's so ancient and colossal it's almost impossible to visualise.

Imagine a mountain range flooded to its neck with water, then imagine that water freezing and cracking. That gives you a very basic idea of what happened to much of northern Britain following the period of rapid cooling that occurred around 2.4 million years ago. By this time the landscape was – relatively speaking – something that could be called familiar, in that places were more or less geographically where they are today. Continents have been shifting around and tearing themselves apart since the dawn of time, and one of the reasons Scotland in particular is such a geological jigsaw puzzle is that much of it came from elsewhere. Of course, as with most things to do with geology it all happened (and continues to do so) very, very, *very* slowly – but don't mistake lack of speed for lack of violence. If you sped the whole multi-billion-year cycle up it would look like a psychotic dodgems ride, with chunks of vaguely recognisable land mass colliding into pile-ups, ricocheting off each other, and scudding across oceans to various destinies and dooms.

To get an idea of how all of this affected Britain, we'll drop a pin along the timeline of this chaos at roughly 500 million years ago, during the Ordovician period. At this point, Scotland (along with much of Ireland) and England (with the rest of Ireland, and Wales) were looking at each other across an ancient ocean known as Iapetus. The former was part of the ragged coastline of a huge supercontinent known as Laurentia; England was its facing shore, on the 'microplate' of Avalonia.* Over the next hundred million years, Iapetus would close, and England and Scotland would first kiss, then snuggle, then be forced inexorably into each other's personal space by the massive forces of two continental plates colliding. The two land masses made contact rather conveniently along what is today the border between England and Scotland. To geologists the line is called – with a pleasingly surgical note – the Iapetus Suture, and runs roughly along the line of Hadrian's Wall. The actual collision itself is estimated to have occurred 410 million years ago, and caused a period of mountain building that resulted in the Southern Uplands and much of the Highlands – a series of events known as the Caledonian Orogeny.† This produced a mountain range comparable in stature to the Alps. This is, however, an almost embarrassingly slight fragment of the story; Britain still lay south of the Equator, resembled Mongolia and would become part of several further supercontinents in the following few hundred million years, to list just a few

---

* It's a fashionable idea to suggest that the Scottish Highlands were once part of the Appalachian Range in the United States, which is true insofar as they once shared the same land mass, along with much of Canada, Alaska and Greenland; what's less known is that much of England and Wales share their Avalonian ancestor with Nova Scotia (literally, 'New Scotland'), as well as Newfoundland and parts of New England.

† In America, the mountain-building that followed the same collision is known as the Acadian Orogeny, which contributed to the formation of the Appalachian Range and Basin.

minor changes that took place during the intervening period. But at least it was now all in one piece.

Many of the rocks created during this period had what scientists might call plutonic origins: they were erupted. Volcanism and tectonic collisions generally come as a package, and Scotland certainly saw its share. Ben Nevis, the mountains of Glen Coe, and many of the peaks of Snowdonia and northern Britain owe much of their form and character to eruptions during this tumultuous period.

The last volcanism in Britain subsided about 60 million years ago, leaving a blanket of ash on the ground and yielding its youngest rocks, twisted into peaks by time and most dramatically epitomised today by the dark mountains of the Isle of Skye. Today its most eye-snaring range, the Black Cuillin, is all that remains of the old volcano. It remains a sombre and fearsome place.

The ice – when it arrived – therefore had a fair bit to sculpt. The period of major climatic change that gave rise to Britain's glaciation probably began with geologically short, sharp contrasts: 50,000 years of glacial cooling here, 40,000 years of interglacial warming there. Later on, these cooling periods began to lengthen in increasingly unbalanced seesaws of sustained cold followed by brief periods of warmth. The most dramatic of these have been the more recent: the last 750,000 years have seen the greatest smothering of ice grind away at our landscape with the least intervening warmth, the glacial periods lasting up to 90,000 years being punctuated by short periods of melting lasting a mere 10,000 years or so. The most severe of these began 110,000 years ago – a period now known as the Devensian. At its zenith – around 29,000 years ago – the glaciers had risen and joined to form a contiguous ice sheet 1,000 metres high across Scotland and much of northern Britain. Only the very highest peaks could keep their chins above this, and they paid for their temerity by being sharpened and stripped by the scraping ice. The legacy of this survives today in, amongst others, the lacerated ridges of Liathach in Torridon, the northern corries of Ben Nevis, and some of the higher, more jagged features of Snowdonia and the Lake District.

Following a period of heavy melting 14,000 years ago, the great ice sheet of the Devensian glacial period would stutter through short periods of warming and cooling before finally leaving Scotland altogether around 10,000 years ago. What remained is the landscape that we see today: once sprawling, ancient mountains clawed into crumbling relics by ice.

Conjuring a great image that has nothing at all to do with mountains, glaciology calls these isolated peaks that poke their heads through the sea of ice sheets 'nunataks'. But there's an elegant German term – and it's not often those three words are found together – that describes more evocatively what's left behind when everything around a mountain has been stripped away by the receding ice: *Inselberge* or 'inselbergs', literally meaning 'island mountains'. Assynt has several of these, the most flamboyant being Suilven.

And that's not all that the ice left behind. During warmer interglacials and the final melting, parts of a layer of limestone laid down during the Carboniferous were dissolved by the water from the ice, creating a system of caves, the most famous being the Bone Caves of Inchnadamph just down the road. This was the second display that caught my eye in Lochinver's visitor centre: a collection of photos of the caves, as well as an assortment of bones of animals long gone from Scotland – bears, wolves, lynx – discovered deep within the system. Some say the bones were washed in when the glaciers retreated. Others think the bones were carried in. Were this latter to be proven to be the case, the Bone Caves – where, during the Ice Age, Scotland's early human beings evidently eked out a difficult existence of hunting and subsistence, using the caves as shelter – would be Scotland's oldest archaeological site.

Glumly aware that the rain might outlast the daylight, after grateful thank yous to the staff of the tourist office I wandered out into the drizzle.

Lochinver smells great. The air is a nasal soup of thick salt and seaweed, and it's a pleasing place – all the more so in that it's of considerable size for this part of the Highlands. About 600 people live here year-round, and the town swells considerably come summer, yet it's miles from anywhere else. It's still a working port, and has the slightly rough air that seems to come with large, rusting fishing boats, loading ramps and a seafront evidently prioritised for daily use rather than anything chintzy. And there it was, Loch Inver itself: grey and flat, gateway to the Atlantic, the twin headlands of Roe Point and Kirkaig Point pincering the bay, with little Soyea Island in the middle. From that adrift little place looking back to Lochinver, the view of Suilven – head-on and hulking, a monster advancing on this insignificant white stripe of waterfront civilisation – must look almost impossibly surreal. Quite a vision. Which reminded me of what I should have been getting on with.

I set off along the road back towards the mountains, with the plan that if the weather stabilised I'd at least be close to something I could walk up, but still none the wiser about where I should go or what I should climb. With the afternoon slowly slipping away I was beginning to feel a little cross about this, not only because it would be the first stumble on an otherwise fairly lucky few months – I'd at least made it to the top of everything else, after all – but also because it *would* happen in Assynt, amongst the mountains I was most keenly anticipating. Now I was here, they were hiding behind cloud and hurling lightning. Not only that, the view I was seeking remained elusive – and not just because of the weather. I'd staked my hopes on finding it atop Cùl Beag; now that I knew it wasn't to be found there I was slightly lost, and, with the depressing feeling that only comes after two largely sleepless nights, nearly 1,000 miles of driving, two and a half mountains, a lot of rain and some lightning panic, rapidly hitting a motivational wall. I pictured jacking it all in, finding a hearty local inn into which I could fold myself, or perhaps a B&B in a little coastal village. It would be *so* good. And so easy.

In a dark mood I drove south through the wooded coastal glens. The rain was slowly stopping, but a softening at the tops of the trees suggested the cloud had descended almost down to the road. I passed through Badnaban and Inverkirkaig, low-lying, impossibly remote. In spirit and aesthetic, it all seemed far closer to Scandinavia than London. Probably, of course, because it was.

I hadn't yet had a proper meal so I pulled into a café just past Inverkirkaig in the hope of scaring up a toastie and studying my map a little more in my quest for a viewpoint. In areas as remote as this you often end up stopping at places of even mild interest, not because you need anything, but simply because you don't know when the next pocket of life might come along. It could have been a tie-pin shop; I'd have probably stopped to have a peer, and no doubt a small crowd of similar onlookers would have gathered – most likely Germans – had I stayed there long enough. Located up a hill and festooned with a slightly improbable totem pole that inserted yet another woody, distant land into the local bouquet, a sign announced that the café was also a gallery, and what must be a contender for mainland Britain's most remote bookshop.

Achins is a proper bookshop, too; filled with local-interest volumes, guides, photography books the size of flagstones and a number of anthologies of Norman MacCaig's poems. Wandering through to the café, I ordered a ham-and-cheese toastie and a coffee from the lady behind the counter, took a seat and allowed my eyes to drift to the walls, which were hung heavy with water-colours, racks of gift cards, jewellery and other diverting, purchasable paraphernalia. And then, grandly mounted in a metre-long frame above the door, I saw *it*.

'Excuse me, where is that?'

The waitress, having just deposited a toastie on my table, looked where I was pointing, then back at me slightly askance.

'Why, that's *here*, of course. The wee mountains just over the back there. On a nicer day.'

'No, I mean where was it taken from? Exactly where?'

'Oh, I wouldn't know *exactly*. Best you speak to the owner.'

Things were looking up. 'Is he here? Will he *really* know, do you think?'

'Would have thought so. I'm pretty sure his wife took it.'

What we were looking at, of course, was a photograph – but not just any photograph. This panorama was precisely the view I was looking for. For me this *was* Assynt, encapsulating everything that gave its mountain landscape such presence. Dribbling towards each other across the foreground, Loch Buine Mòire, Loch Call an Uidhean, Fionn Loch and the nebulous shores of Loch Sionascaig; and, above them, that astonishing skyline. There they all were, lined up, each of itself and nothing else – like strange topiary in a vast, watery garden.

Moments later, I was standing with Alex the owner over an Ordnance Survey map of Assynt, watching his finger move down the road south from Inverkirkaig, and finally stop.

'There's a pull-in. You've got to climb a bit, but not very far.'

I looked hopefully at the knot of contours at his finger.

'Is it a hill?'

He made a face. 'You *could* call it a hill. But not a very big one. Quite a view, though,' he said, before adding in the endearingly smug way only permitted to a local: 'Obviously.'

I thanked him extravagantly and hurried to the car. The weather was brightening and steam was rising from the road as I drove south, the map sprawled open on the passenger seat. There was no view to the left of the car; instead, bumps of rock and heather banked the roadside, blocking most of what lay beyond, with heavy – but slowly lifting – cloud obscuring the rest.

I found the pull-in without a problem – a flat area of gravel up against a jungle of bracken. Beyond it a break in the skyline along the low crags lining the road led up to a round knoll, a hundred metres or so above the road. It was hardly a mountain. Indeed, it was barely a hill. I didn't care. This was my viewpoint.

It was coming up to 6 p.m. My bag was still packed from last night's camp. I had water, food. If conditions were right I could pitch my tent and sleep up there. I could *own* that view; it could be mine for a whole evening, a night and a morning.

Pulling on gaiters, I set off into the bracken, shuddering as rainwater caught by the branches cascaded over my clothes and pinpricks of cold pierced my trousers. It was boggy and muggy, and within seconds I was breathless. Looking around, I was in a crease between two higher areas; a line of crags to the left, the knoll to the right. This crease was filled with mud and vegetation that flattened out and became boggy in the middle. Squelching through it, I began to climb the slope of short, scraggy heather towards the summit of the knoll.

The top was perfectly flat, covered in springy heather and the size of a squash court. I threw down my pack and wandered out to the eastern edge. They were there; I could see their lower reaches, like feet poking from beneath a curtain. It was oddly pretty. The cloud base had lifted but the mountains each coyly held on to their own shroud of white fluff. The lochs were mirrors filled with the grey sky, the landscape dark for the midsummer month. In the entire view there was not a sliver of colour anywhere, no brush of low sun, no burst of green ground or blue sky. Assynt was monochrome.

But this was the place, all right. And whilst hardly a summit, it felt strangely fitting: a podium, a little island of my own from which to observe these island mountains. As I turned to see to my tent I could still sense them there, watching almost. It felt odd to have them at my back, their presence verging on sentience. I almost expected them to have advanced closer or moved when I turned to look, like that old playground game.

I'd almost finished putting my tent up when the first of my visitors arrived. First a few, then – suddenly – thousands. The atmosphere was still, lacking the heavy tension released by the thunderstorm earlier. Utter silence. No wind. Usually, I'd see this lack of breeze as, if anything, a good thing. As it turns out, when you're outside, in Scotland, during summer, approaching evening and not moving, it isn't. Really isn't.

Little harpies. The Winged Plague. Malhoulakins. Na Chuileagan. Fucking sparrows with great big fucking teeth. No-see-ums. Punkies. Moose-flies. Mugge. Mygge. Mudge. Midgeck. *Culicoides impunctatus.* Goetghebuer. Whichever is your favourite, when something has this many historical and regional definitions – and aggressive terms of address – you know you're facing something pretty formidable. Tonight my time was up. It was probably the light breeze I'd encountered thus far that had saved me from anything more serious than mild irritation. But now that the air was still, I was theirs.

The book I'd brought along with me about this was simply titled *Midges in Scotland*. I thought if I could perhaps mine some background information about the torture I was evidently letting myself in for it would somehow make it more bearable, and in snatched moments flicking through it I'd learned much of the following.

It's only the female midge that bites; her mouthparts are sharp and elongated, and they saw through skin with an action not dissimilar to a pair of scissors. Puncturing capillaries just beneath the skin, blood is released that pools and is sucked up by a straw-like food-tube, which also releases anticoagulant saliva into the wound to prevent clotting. This causes a reaction in the victim; immune cells are scrambled to the site, which cuts off the blood supply to the wound and sets about repair. This repair work causes temporary disruption: swelling, irritation and an overwhelming urge to scratch.

Thirty-five species of biting midge have been identified in Scotland, of which four or five prey on humans, one particularly voraciously: the aforementioned *Culicoides impunctatus*, or Highland midge. It's small by midge standards. Its wings have a span of around 1.4 mm and are distinguished from those of other midges by six dark blotches. A relation of the mosquito, but far smaller, if it manages successfully to feed from you it will escape with around one ten millionth of a litre of your blood.

The biting season extends from June to late August, and midges are especially active in the cool early morning and late evening, and at temperatures between 8 and 18°C; there's no guarantee of this, though, and if it's overcast and damp they can bite all day. Midges don't like very bright light, or any wind, and they're attracted to their victims by a mixture of exhaled carbon dioxide, water vapour, lactic acid and sweat.

The most appalling aspect of all of this also explains why one midge is swiftly joined by thousands: when the pregnant female bites, she releases something called a recruiting pheromone. In short, she signals to other midges that a meal has been found. Scientists don't really know why midges see fit to attract others in this altruistic manner; perhaps it's to subdue, panic or weaken their prey.

And if they do swarm all over you, as they did over me on this particular evening, all of the above insight − however diverting − will give you no comfort whatsoever.

Initially, I wasn't that bothered. I told myself I'd have been disappointed had I come all the way up here and not at least enjoyed a mild taste of the legendary discomfort I'd heard so much about. My hoped-for detachment lasted all of 30 seconds, interrupted by a crawling sensation on my neck, ears, hairline and hands, the slowly intensifying high-sonic hum around me, then the near-simultaneous feeling of hundreds of tickling scrapes across my bare skin. Within minutes, as I struggled to strap down the remaining parts of my tent, I began to tremble with irritation. I was breathing them in, spitting them out; they were crawling up my nose, over my ears, into my eyes, down my open shirt. My movements became stuttered and clumsy. I started to swear. Then, as the tent finally began to take shape, the panic − the *horror* − that overcame me when I realised the door and its midge net were hanging open; somehow this threat of having no escape, no haven, no respite from the little bastards was the most desperate feeling of all. I almost fell over in my panic to zip it closed to seal it from invasion.

You might think this all sounds a bit over the top. I'd have probably agreed with you until I experienced that evening in Assynt, but in the event it was far more intolerable than I'd ever imagined.

One thing you will inevitably learn from *Midges in Scotland* – now, tellingly, in its fifth edition – as you lose yourself in its details is just how much of a scourge midges are, and how much has been put in to trying to understand, avoid and even eliminate them from the Highlands. People don't pile that kind of resource into a cause unless it's pretty bad. You can even put a figure on it: £286 million is the midge's estimated annual cost to the tourism industry in Scotland.

Factor in the midge and you might be inclined to extend a little more respect to some of the already gruelling Highland exploits we've touched on. Remember General Wade, he of the military roads used by Roy and Maskelyne? He had a diarist named Edward Burt who recorded some early observations of the Highland midge during the construction of the roads in the 1730s. 'I have been vexed with a little plague,' he wrote with rather admirable restraint, 'swarms of little flies which the natives call Malhoulakins ... being of a black-ish colour when a number of them settle on the skin, they make it look dirty.' Bonnie Prince Charlie reportedly suffered terribly during his flight from Culloden, scratching his bites to the point where they resembled ulcers. More recent royals haven't escaped, either. Queen Victoria is said to have abandoned a picnic in Sutherland having been 'half devoured' by midges. And in 2012, whilst organising a striking portrait of Queen Elizabeth II in the grounds of Balmoral – the sprawling Highland estate bought by Victoria in 1852 – to mark her 60th year on the throne, author Alastair Bruce encapsulated the midge worries that plagued the shoot, and presumably Her Majesty, with a splendidly pithy soundbite. He said: 'There are two stages of a midge attack. In the first you think you are going to die, in the second you are worried you might not.'

Hillwalking is full of the whispered tactics, suspect unguents and old-wives' remedies for avoiding midges. Historically, tobacco smoke, the exhaust of paraffin lamps and steam were all considered effective counter-measures, although some regional accounts suggest that some of these served to attract midges, rather than repel. Something generally accepted is that wearing dark clothing isn't recommended, because of midges' predilection for shade, whilst their supposed aversion to Vitamin B1 has led some visitors to the Highlands to consume vast quantities of Marmite a month before a summer trip to the hills. Oddly, a moisturising product named Skin So Soft – produced by cosmetics stalwart Avon – seems for many to have mysteriously mastered midge repellency without even trying, and sells considerable volumes each year for this specific purpose. Then there is the widely trusted, highly notorious Diethyl-m-toluamide – DEET – which, in various concentrations, appears in branded repellents. DEET was once used as a pesticide; it's designed to block the ability of insect receptors to detect their prey. Spread it on your skin and it's probably the most effective repelling agent you can buy. But this splendid effectiveness comes with a trade-off. DEET melts plastic, is toxic and is thought to have long-term effects on health that are at best little understood, and so is shunned by many. And whilst repellent is all well and good for avoiding bites, it doesn't prevent the swarming – which can be almost as maddening.

I got into that tent as quickly as I possibly could. During the fifteen seconds or so that it took me to get boots off and body inside, approximately 65,000 midges managed to enter the tent. Immediately, the tent's dark corners became motion-filled; I spent a lively ten minutes thwacking and clapping, before I realised any attempt to clear the tent was futility itself. At least it was sealed. But although I was safe, amidst the building, panicked hum outside, it was difficult to ignore the fact that I was – in the most literal sense – being besieged by an army of millions.

As the evening progressed I sat in my tent and, through the mesh net, watched the insects gathering. Midges swarmed outside the net like silvery static, lanky mosquitoes posed statuesquely upon it and I even saw a fat tick sidle slowly, mechanically, across it. Eventually, as the light began to fade and hunger started to tug at my gut, I made a little opening in the tent's zipped mesh door – big enough to get my hands through – to fish my stove out of my pack, like a nuclear engineer manoeuvring rods of uranium. Half-filling my kettle, I lit the stove. The midges didn't like the steam at all; within seconds of the kettle boiling, they cleared out. Seizing the chance, I left the kettle haemorrhaging steam and leaped outside into the gathering dark and thickening cloud for a pee. Through the gloom, the mountains of Assynt were still hiding.

The night was short but restful. The springy heather atop the knoll made for a fine mattress, and although the tent wasn't short of insect occupants, I'd cinched the sleeping bag tight around my face and this seemed to do the trick. Morning came, and as I prepared to exit the tent I again made a zipped hole in the mesh door and pulled my pack inside. Rooting inside, I groped for my midge counter-measure, something I'd brought along as an emergency, never expecting to have to use it. My fingers found the spongy disc of nylon, I pulled it out and uncoiled it – a flat-brimmed hat, with a fine cowl of mesh fixed to the brim.

I estimated I had about a minute at most once I was outside. The midge net primed by my side, I pushed on my boots and, leaving them unlaced, unzipped the flysheet and staggered out.

And there they were. Lined up, naked of cloud, black in the flat dawn light. The distant, broken-glass spires of Quinag; Suilven, broadside and weird; Cùl Mòr, bulky and hunched; Cùl Beag, sharp and brief; and Stac Pollaidh, a geological salute. For a few moments I stood and absorbed it all. But like so many people, my eyes slowly and automatically slid north to Suilven.

Suilven's highest point lies at the top curve of that skyline wheel. Reaching the top of it seven years ago had been an almost transcendent moment for me. That day in May had started hard, with the mountain frosted, the landscape brown and dead. By afternoon it had all softened. Water had begun to shimmer, turning the landscape into a collage of water grouted with green fur. Up onto the narrow ridge of the mountain I'd walked, marvelling at its deceptive leanness. A golden eagle curled high above. Then the final top, massive and flat, plunging down on all sides. But the summit of Suilven isn't a scary place; you can escape the drops by staying in the middle, where a pyramid of stones marks its top. To the west the land frays: the stripe of the Atlantic, the Minch, the Hebrides, the end of Britain, the beginning of the rest of the world beneath that massive northern sky. I'd stood there, picturing myself atop that strange summit, missing it from the view, but enjoying the feeling of being on the prow of this strange galleon, frozen in its ancient sea.

The little top upon which I'd spent the night doesn't have a name in itself – but on the map it's grouped in with Creag nan Sìthean.* The name means 'Crag of the Ancient Ancestors', and in this it shares etymology with Schiehallion, that 'Hill of the Ancient Ancestors' of the Caledonians. I didn't

---

* Not that it matters, but someone has actually thought to classify this as a hill; it is in fact a TUMP – a hill of Thirty and Upwards Metres Prominence.

know any of this at the time. To me, it was just the Little Hill of the Stupendous View. I had a moment there with the mountains, just enjoying being with them, clear of their veils, peculiar, charismatic, statuesque, beautiful. I even ignored the first tingles around my ear and neck; then, as a high buzz began to build around me and I began to shake, I turned away from the view and dropped the net over my face, watching the view soften behind the tightly hexagonal screen. Then I tightened it around my collar, and set about dismantling my camp.

A long day lay ahead. The last summit of this particular trip beckoned, the source of a long, serrated shadow that for years had excited and frightened me in equal measure. This wasn't the shadow of a mountain feared by casual walkers; most don't even know its name. This was a mountain feared by mountaineers. Lodged in the middle of Scotland's 'Great Wilderness', it's the most unhinged piece of geology on mainland Britain. And, for better or worse, it was next.

10 WILDERNESS

They call the highway between Braemore and Dundonnell the 'Destitution Road'. It's so named because during the Highland potato famine of 1846 starving crofters were recruited to build a rough, coast-bound single-track road across the moor in exchange for rations of oats. With the insult of the Clearances still raw, the famine was the final straw for many highlanders. This exodus even spurned a song, which extended the identity of this statement of sadness to whatever destination awaited. Its chorus:

> But there's no use gettin' frantic,
> It's time tae hump yer load
> Across the wild Atlantic
> On the Destitution Road.

Whatever the political reasoning behind the road, its name is echoed in the many emotions experienced as you travel it. The landscape itself is naked and raw, the pristine road itself – and those occasional, sad little husks of old crofts – the only human mark upon this huge space of grassland and sky. Then you see it: something that shocks the simple lines of the moor with a contrast of startling violence. At the end of the Destitution Road, alone and barbed, stands a monster.

As we've already discovered, mountain names can be complicated things to decode. But Scottish mountain names really are something else. Most of them are disguised to the English ear by successive generations splicing together Old Norse, Gaelic and Scots. But once translated – which often isn't as simple as it appears – they often fall into two parts: a generic name and a specific name.

It's a fascinating study, more so as its pursuit requires earnest inquisitive-ness. It would be so easy just to call the hills by their names and think nothing more of it, as many do. Yet to do so might mean you'd miss an inspiration, resemblance or physical attribute, an old legend, a mysterious character lost to history but clearly important enough at the time to be immortalised in a mountain. In short, you'd miss all the depth that's hidden behind a name in a language barely alive.

The generics – generally nouns – are fairly easy to get the hang of, recurring frequently as they do. You might say that the word for 'mountain' is a specialist commodity for the Scot in the way snow is jokingly said to be for an Inuit, requiring not one but nearly 70 separate terms of address,[*] depending on the physical attribute to which the name is appointed. For instance, for the simple mountain denotation we have *Ben*, but also *Bheinn*, *Beinn*, *Beinne*, *Meall*, *Meallan*, *Meal*, *Mheall*, *Monadh* and *Maolle*, amongst others. More specifically relating to the top of a hill, we have *Bidean* or *Bidein*, *Spidean* and also *Binnein* and *Binnean* – which often relate to rather sharper hills. *Càrn* or *Cairn* is often found, and means what's already familiar as the latter: a pile of stones. How it became common as a generic term for a mountain that patently has no resemblance to such a pile might be for obscure or ancient reasons, possibly dating back as far as the Picts. A crag or cliff is often denoted as *Creag*, a rounded hillock a *Cnoc*, a heap-like eminence a *Cruach*, a rounded top *Mullach*, a sharp summit (as the name seems to suggest) a *Sgùrr*, a pinnacle *Stùc*, a peak *Stob*, a stack *Stac*, a flattening or shelf *Suidhe* and a knoll *Tom*.

Body parts appear frequently and occasionally saucily; *Sron* is a nose, *Maol* a bald head, *Druim* a spine, *Fiacail* a tooth. *Brae* means brow, *Slinnean* shoulder.

---

[*] The *Scottish Mountaineering Club Journal* once published a poem by an 'L.W.H.' wittily(ish) distilling the conundrum thus:

A mountain's a mountain in England, but when
The climber's in Scotland, it may be a Beinn
A Creag or a Meall, a Spidean, a Sgor
A Carn or a Monadh, a Stac, or a Torr.

He's in fact wrong, as evident by the many names in England for a mountain, which we shan't go into here.

Pap, *Cioch* and *Màm* are all meanings for breast or nipple. The Devil's Point in the Cairngorms is a translation from the Gaelic name *Bod an Deamhain*, though for reasons of gentility it's not quite as faithful as it could be; it in fact refers to a particular point on the devil himself, rather than a point where the devil was thought to linger.

In the Borders, Scots is the pervading language of the mountain, with the attribute of 'hill' usually shifted to the back – rather than being a prefix, as is often the case in the Highlands – and varied according to size. Hence, we have in descending order of grandness *Law*, *Coom*, *Dod*, *Craig*, *Rig*, *Edge* and *Knock* appearing as suffixes to various heights in what is generally referred to as the Southern Uplands. As with the Welsh *Fawr* and *Mawr*, and *Fach* and *Bach*, Gaelic features in the frequently suffixed *Mòr* and *Mhòr*, and *Beag* and *Bheag* – meaning 'big' and 'little'.

But these are by no means rules. Fascinating as it is, Scottish mountain toponymy is a fiendishly complicated business, and the above represents the briefest of skips over only its pointiest aspects. There are many, many regional inconsistencies, complicated even further by the fact that many of the most subtle or peculiar corruptions were introduced in the final stages by the imprecise (and often impatient) pen of cartographers as casualties of pronunciation, and thereafter absorbed into the vernacular as they were written. What it does, however, is give us the components to get a feel for the often rather evocative origin of many mountain names, creating a tapestry of a place that is by turns earthy and cultural, and entirely bewitching.

Of the 282 Munros, nearly a quarter have names rooted in the natural world. We have birds in Meall nan Tarmachan ('Hill of the Ptarmigan') and Tom Bad na Speirage ('Tufty Knoll of the Sparrowhawk'); stags, hinds and bucks in Beinn Damh, Sgùrr Èilde Mòr and Sgurr a' Bhuic respectively; a dog in Creag an Leth-choin ('Crag of the Lurcher'); a 'Pinnacle of the Goat' (Stob Ghabhar); horses and parts thereof in Sgùrr an t-Searraich ('Peak of the Horse') and A'Mhuing ('The Mane', referring to a ridge). Tellingly there are also hills named for creatures now departed from the Scottish landscape, such as the boar (An Torc), the elk (Beinn Oss) and the wolf (Sgùrr Fhuaran).

We also have heather (Froach Bheinn), a big peat bog (A' Mhòine Mhòr), moor (A' Chòinneach) and occasional references to geology, with Meall

Gaineimh ('Sand Hill') in the Cairngorms named presumably in reference to the texture of its huge swathes of granite. The often-used *Aonach* refers to a notched profile, and is therefore commonly found in the names of crenellated ridges, such as the famous Aonach Eagach above Glen Coe.

War and weaponry are legion; the mighty Slioch is 'The Spear', despite being rather squat in appearance. Càrn an Fhir-Bhogha means 'Cairn of the Archer', we have a 'Watcher's Knoll' at Cnoc na Faire, and Stob Coire an t-Saighdeir means, roughly, 'Peak of the Valley of the Soldier'.

Mythology, predictably, adds a further layer. We have already seen the 'Fairy Hill' of Schiehallion; the sprite therein may have been corrupted from the term *sìthean* that can also be found in Sìthean na Raplaich on the Morvern peninsula, which employs an additional geological term: 'Fairy Hill of the Screes'. The devil's particulars are mentioned in the aforementioned Bod an Deamhain; the rest of him appears in Assynt, in Meall Diamhain ('Hill of the Devil'). He also has a ridge (on Sgùrr a' Mhaim in the Mamores), as well as a staircase, bite, barn door, cauldron, and many other effects and augmentations across the Highlands and Lowlands. With a similarly lethal tone, Ben Donich near Loch Lomond translates as 'Evil Mountain'. Beinn an t-Seilich is named for a *seilch*, a water monster not dissimilar to Snowdonia's *afanc*, and spectres haunt Sròn an Tàchair ('Nose/Ridge of the Ghost').

We then have a jaunty array of characters and occupations with which to populate this newly furnished natural and mythological backdrop. Sgùrr nan Conbhairean means 'Peak of Those Who Keep the Hounds'. There's a mysterious maiden (A' Mhaighdean), a pair of them in the Mamores' Na Gruagaichean, and a queen in Sròn na Bàn-righ. The famous Cobbler in the Arrochar Alps is properly known as Ben Arthur, although its old Gaelic name is An Greasaiche Crom, meaning 'The Crooked Shoemaker', named for the allegedly footwear-fixer-like shape of its summit rocks.

Càrn an t-Sagairt Mòr is 'Big Cairn of the Priest'. Beinn Mhanach is the 'Hill of the Monk'. Doctors have their own mountain (Meall Lighiche), as do fiddlers (Assynt's spectacularly pointy Sgùrr an Fhidhleir), and there's a locationally specific shepherd standing between Glen Coe and Glen Etive (the famous Buachaille Etive Mòr, literally 'Great Herdsman of Etive'). Occupations need venues, of course. Beinn na h-Eaglaise is the 'Mountain of the Church'.

There's a stonemasons' mountain (Beinn a' Chlachair). And, in Wester Ross, there's the great mountain known as 'The Forge'.*

Some say this final name is literal; that it was so named because its foot was once the site of a blacksmith's furnace. Others have remarked that the mountain's red sandstone when caught by sunset resembles the glow of dying embers, and that mist rising from within its serrated rim resembles steam from a cauldron. The image it evokes is medieval–industrial, woundingly sharp and Gothic. Whatever the origin of the name, it definitely fits: you need only to see it to agree. The Forge stands at the end of the Destitution Road, and if you address it you do so in Gaelic: An Teallach.

An Teallach is colossal. There's nothing on the British mainland that can touch it in terms of spectacle: Torridon tries, but it becomes abundantly clear about halfway along the Destitution Road – sadly bearing the more prosaic label of A832 on today's maps – when it slides into view that you're dealing with an exhibitionist of an altogether higher order. You might well have the sudden urge to stop the car so you can take it in before moving any further towards it.

I'd already stopped that morning for breakfast in Ullapool. Hunkered against the arcing inlet of Loch Broom, Ullapool – for all its isolation – is a splendid, twinkly little place that greets the eye with its handsome, Scandinavian feel. White buildings line the waterfront, fishing boats jostle in the harbour, and the town has just enough of a functional edge to feel like the sort of place where real people might live and work, rather than just visit and look at. I'd certainly live there.

With a newly re-established phone signal, I spent breakfast reassuring my parents that no, I wasn't doing anything silly and yes, I'd seen the forecast had lightning in it and no, I wasn't putting myself in any danger and that yes, I'd call as soon as I was home. I then called my wife. Rachel and I had recently discovered we were expecting our first child – something that gave this trip to the far north a rather harder edge of separation than usual. After establishing

---

* Anyone even vaguely interested in Scottish mountain toponymy needs to acquire a copy of Peter Drummond's splendidly readable book *Scottish Hill Names*, which not only details the generics but breaks the mountains down into the categories by which they are named.

that all was well, I spent just a fraction longer saying goodbye than I usually would. At distance over a telephone, pauses can betray you.

'Are you alright?' she'd asked.

'I'm fine. Just tired.' And bitten.

A pause, this time from her end.

'You're not doing anything dangerous today, are you?'

'Nothing to worry about. Speak to you tonight, all being well,' before quickly adding, 'Phone signals are bad here. You know how it is.'

We'd said our goodbyes and I'd returned to my sausage and egg roll – along with an uneasy feeling that I'd not been entirely honest.

Truth be told, I'd been fascinated by – and fearful of – An Teallach's wild reputation for years. I'd never seen it in its entirety; nothing more than a pinnacle or two held aloft above the hills of Torridon, or its lower flanks descending from the cloud as I'd passed on murk-choked days. I'd seen pictures from up amongst its summits – by all accounts an astonishing view that needed to be earned on foot. But the black, angular thing that slid into view along the Destitution Road still shocked me.

The first thing you notice is its size. Its highest point, Bidein a' Ghlas Thuill, is 1,062 metres above sea level – making An Teallach one of the higher Scottish mountains, if not exactly a giant. But as the ascent begins from the seawater shores of Little Loch Broom, mirroring the scything path of its bigger namesake to the north, you have to climb every centimetre of that height. Also, with nothing around it to jostle for your eye, the mountain stands dominant, visually tyrannical against the sky.

Despite this, it's difficult to imagine what could stand next to An Teallach and equal it aesthetically. Like Snowdon and Cadair Idris, the mountain is a massif rather than a single summit, comprised of many individual tops – *eleven* of them in this case. But it's the massif as a whole that provokes most awe, and An Teallach is therefore generally thought of as one particularly dramatic mountain. And whilst immediately mesmerising, it's a thing of menace, not beauty – an expletive of a mountain, all spikes and hard angles.

The most obvious demonstration of this is to the left of the massif's centre, and appears almost to defy physics when seen from a distance – an enormous radial saw of rock spires that overhangs the precipice beneath as if poised to drop. These are the pinnacles of Corrag Bhuidhe, which bristle between the tops of Sail Liath and Sgùrr Fiòna, from where the mountain dips into a slack *bealach* before climbing to the mountain's true top. These individual names are in fact not as remarkable as the mountain's itself; Sail Liath means 'Grey Heel', Sgùrr Fiòna 'White Peak' and the highest point of Bidein a' Ghlas Thuill the 'Peak of the Grey-Green Hollow'. The dramatic pinnacles themselves have the evocative and faintly odd translation meaning literally 'Pointed Fingers of Gold'.

As for me, An Teallach had long been a seemingly off-limits fascination. It seemed to seethe malevolence: the ultimate expression of Britain's wild, angry north. I had once driven 30 miles out of my way just to get beneath it and feel its bulk above me on an overcast day that held no hope of a view. I was eager to see whether the mountain had the atmosphere I imagined it would, but I was also roundly intimidated by it. You hear a lot about An Teallach; its reputation is as frightening as its appearance. As I parked the car on the shore of the loch in the tentative morning sunshine and dusted the gritty black film of millions of midge corpses off everything (I'm still finding them now), my eyes fell upon the mountain-rescue base adjacent to the car park. Dundonnell Mountain Rescue can rightly claim that on their 770-square-mile patch – close enough to cast a jagged shadow over their HQ – stands the most feared mountain on the mainland. To those with a fear of heights, this thing is the enemy.

Thomas Pennant, the naturalist and traveller whom we met briefly in Wales, described the sight of An Teallach flatteringly in his 1769 *Tour in Scotland* as 'Horrible and awful with all summits broken, sharp and serrated and springing into all terrific forms'. All of this seemed very removed from my early scratchings on the mountain on this particular morning. Storms were forecast, but although the air felt weighty and the very top of the mountain was softened by local cloud, sun was shining on the land to the north and the weather seemed settled for now. I was trying hard not to rush. Every step made in haste wears you out twice as fast – worry burns energy, too – but I was wary of losing the chance of getting high on the mountain before the seemingly inevitable afternoon lightning, a mistake I'd made yesterday.

Leaving the car next to a few others, I could see boot prints in the mud of the path, fresh since the last rain – so chances were good that I wouldn't be alone up there today. With many of these ascents I'd either deliberately or accidentally ended up climbing the mountain at the extreme hours of the day or at night, so seeing other walkers would make a welcome change.

I'd chosen the way up from Dundonnell for a reason besides convenience. If that view of An Teallach from the Destitution Road showed the mountain's bared teeth, the route I was now taking crept up its hindquarters. There was a route that led into Coir' a' Ghiubhsachain, the dark, loch-filled bowl beneath the mountain's spires, but to follow this seemed silly on two levels: one, I'd miss the view to the north, which in the clear morning air penetrated deep into the area I'd been in for the last few days, and two, in all likelihood I'd experience a depressing condition called 'awe exhaustion'. This is when you spend too long in the company of something spectacular, and gradually cease to be amazed by it. It's the same thing you get in museums. You know you should be soaking up every second of the wonderful exhibits displayed in front of you, but you eventually pass saturation point and just can't take any more in. In the mountains, you add to that the rigours of a long ascent and you sometimes even start to resent the spectacular thing you're tackling. It doesn't happen often; but on a big mountain, it can.

Of course, you'd be daft to deliberately ignore the most engaging route up to avoid this condition unless there was a damn good reason to do so. Fortunately, An Teallach – in common with many mountains of this region of the Highlands – had a particular quirk of structure that constituted exactly that. This would come later, however. For now I focused on enjoying the ascent, which, for a mountain that presented such an impenetrable front, was proving surprisingly amenable.

A series of crags hung down a few hundred metres above the green, wriggling path of the steep lower slopes. Once past these, a flattening – and a choice: go left to enter the mouth of the tapering Coir' a' Mhuilinn, or take the skyline slope to the right over the buttress of Meall Garbh. I chose the latter, as would anybody faced with the prospect of a relatively clear view to the north. Climbing into a corrie born down upon by shadow and sharp cliffs just didn't feel like the thing to do. Not this morning.

Yesterday's thunder had made me skittish. I was in the sun, but the sky above the mountain's higher reaches was backlit white from some unseen front approaching from the other side of the mountain. The forecast was

bleak, and I couldn't shake the feeling that conditions would deteriorate into
the predicted rain and lightning before I reached the summit, rather than after.
If I was on the descent, that would be fine, invigorating even. If I was still on
my way up, that wouldn't be fine. The summit of An Teallach is not somewhere
you want to be in any kind of storm. Any chance of lightning up there would
be unthinkable. I'd have to turn around for the second time in two days. And
that would be rubbish.

In the manner of someone recently given cause to distrust the landscape,
I kept hearing things that made me stop and listen. The odd rumble, flat and
without echo – a distant plane perhaps, or the grumbles of moving rock in a
river. But today, everything seemed to sound like thunder.

There were other, less threatening, sounds. Dragonflies were out, and I
could hear the soft hum of their wings as they passed. Streams were stepped
into mini waterfalls lower down in the valley, giving a delicate, distant hiss. I
could still hear the smithy-like clink of someone hammering metal near
Dundonnell, although this was fading now as I began to climb the spacious
slopes of An Teallach's bouldery north-eastern shoulder. It was fantastically
easy walking, following clear ridgelines on good, dry rock, and most enjoyable.
The mountain felt pleasingly huge. Walking up here, looking at the staggered
mountains to the north (I even fancy I saw the distant curve of Suilven's western buttress in amongst the jumble), the feeling was one of intense solitude
amidst enormity. And this was the uninteresting side of the mountain, apparently, although I beg to differ. Spectacle could wait. Spectacle would be the
feeling that would hit when I crested the ridge of this great mountain. Years of
examining pictures of it from every angle had made me wonder what An
Teallach would feel like. Would I feel fear? Exhilaration? An awe that made me
limpet to the rock and sponge away my confidence? I looked up towards the
summit but it was hidden by the intervening ground. A sharp crag – probably
one of the pinnacles – was beginning to move into view to its right. Again I
felt that pang. That primal warning that I probably shouldn't be here, that
nobody should be here. That this thing, this big, sharp, hard thing, wasn't for
people. And any mountain that makes you feel like that needs to be experienced at least once, if only to feel the strange pull of the British wilderness.

*   *   *

We've alighted on 'wilderness' of a sort a couple of times already – beneath the dark skies of the Black Mountain in Chapter 2, for instance – but something about An Teallach perhaps symbolises the concept with rather more bite, and on rather more levels, than any other mountain in Britain.

You could say that simply being in the mountains and exposing yourself to everything this brings is, in a manner of speaking, inexorably linked to the idea of actively seeking an 'uncultivated, uninhabited and inhospitable region' – the basic definition of 'wilderness' as the *Oxford English Dictionary* has it. But the thing about that definition of wilderness is, it isn't *just* that.

Without wanting to get all steeple-fingered and philosophical about this, wilderness – particularly these days – works on lots of different levels. To some it's a place, a physical thing. To others it's the goal of an attitude, the cause of an emotion, or something that lives in the mind as a kind of comforting, distantly medicinal tonic. Scottish emigrant John Muir was a great ponderer of this elusive pull, remarking in his writings that 'Thousands of tired, nerve-shaken, over-civilized people are beginning to find that going to the mountains is going home; that wilderness is a necessity.'

In today's world, society is becoming ever-more connected, vast distances can be covered easily – from a desk, virtually, even – and information flows invisibly through the air: if you'd told John Muir that this would happen less than 100 years after his death, his head would probably have exploded. The world is changing, the way people think is ever-evolving, and our way of moving within our environment is shifting. And wilderness must change with it, or it will be lost.

I'm no great thinker on this (or indeed any) subject, but – whilst it can take a different form in each person's mind – I'd wager that to most people their idea of wilderness probably conforms to one of five interpretations.

The first we'll call *disengagement*. Unless you frequent the mountains, you might not have noticed that these are the last few years in which we, fellow citizens of the United Kingdom, will be able to go to a place where we simply *cannot* talk to another person at the push of a button. Being truly solitary is something that future generations – the ones born into the unconditional embrace of mobile phones, Google Maps and Facebook – will never know. But today in 2014, pockets remain, mainly in the mountains, where mobile phone reception or internet access is non-existent. This won't last. Technology will find a way to penetrate these areas, and in a few years we'll all be sitting around getting nostalgic about it to disbelieving kids. Take a last look at the world before this happens because when it does it will be *huge*. To many it will be a good thing, opening up the wider, wilder world to the nervous or the vulnerable. To the ambivalent majority, it will mean that the experience of wilderness, of detachment, is on our own terms, and to whatever level we're comfortable with. To the rest, it will be the death of self-reliance, and the ability to truly disengage from the hectic world to which mountains are the antidote. For this group, being off the grid will no longer simply be a result of location or activity. You'll have to consciously put yourself there by pressing the 'off' button.

Which leads us on to a second meaning of wilderness: *escape*. Whilst disengagement can be a positive or a negative, escape is always a good thing – to the escapee, at least. Liberation from oppression, imprisonment or control: to many people, this is what a trip to the mountains brings, even if they don't think of it in precisely those terms. It brings a renewed simplicity, a reordering of priorities and a realignment of perspective. Climbing a mountain is the basic act of moving from one place to another and trying not to keel over in the process. It's hard. It's uncomfortable. It's dangerous. But the act itself is as basic as it's ostensibly pointless: get up, get down, survive. Life becomes both very serious and very simple all at once. It's two-faced, but that's what wilderness is: you escape to it, to escape from it.

So where do you go? You go into *the unknown*. Where the wild things are. The hinterland of everything that's everyday, whether that's into the woods you can see from your bedroom window, the dark at the fringes of your town, or the mountains that line the far horizon – however many horizons they may take to reach. In *Arctic Dreams* American writer Barry Lopez remarks of wilderness: 'The edges of any landscape – horizons, the lip of a valley, the bend of a river around a canyon wall – quicken the observer's expectations.'

What you find in this place will really be down to you. But part of what you look for could be *fear*. Fear is a complicated emotion. First of all it's addictive: to face fear and overcome it is an intense physical and psychological high, setting a benchmark that the mind subsequently and subconsciously craves to exceed. Fear is also the justification many have for remaining safely in the outer orbit of wilderness. It's the storm raging outside your battened hatches, or the spook at your window that can't get in. You fear it, but at the same time you kind of *like* the fact that it's there. Some want to conquer it; some just want to be reminded it exists.

Which brings us to wilderness's final meaning: *perspective*. Whatever wilderness might mean to you, the night you return from it you'll experience multiple moments of intense, grateful bliss. You'll enjoy the feeling of eating your dinner that bit more, the sensation of drawing water from a tap rather than a stream, of crawling beneath a feathery duvet, of warmth, of home. You are, however briefly, reborn.

People institutionally urban – particularly those who spend a significant portion of their lives within the noose of the M25 – will tell you that once upon a time there was wilderness in Britain but now there's none. It's gone. Lost.

Well, what crap that is. There's boatloads of it, more than enough for a little human being to have a good physical and philosophical chew on. And the more connected and entangled we all become with each other in our day-to-day lives, the more precious these places are going to become, and the more important – the more vital, indeed – they will be to those who need it. Wilderness is not gone. It's just consumed differently.

So first, get it out of your head that wilderness has to be vast. Size isn't an issue. It can assume any dimensions. So long as it's wilderness to you, it's wilderness – and don't ever let anybody tell you otherwise. Human beings are small and it doesn't take much for us to find a tranquil space. Wilderness is precious, for sure. Smaller in scale than it once was. And it's threatened, too – not by towns, and certainly not by overpopulation. It's threatened by apathy. It's threatened by titanic, stutteringly inefficient wind farms – once described by writer Robert Macfarlane as 'Colgate-white neo forests' – monopolising vast swathes of open wild land. And it's threatened by the very people who want you to believe that there's nothing worth saving here, that Britain's wild places amount to a sort of bonsai garden of ornamental curiosity. It isn't. Britain still has teeth. Whether it's the frozen dawn deep in a valley in the Chilterns, the pathless bank of a Pennine river, or the wind-scarred cliffs of a Hebridean isle, wilderness – both big and small, and equally covetable – still exists.

But if this isn't enough, and you want something altogether less subtle – an aesthetic thing that marries all of these interpretations and flaunts them with an indignant strut – go to Scotland, drive the Destitution Road and climb An Teallach.

At 1 p.m., amidst building storm clouds, I broke over the lip of An Teallach's summit ridge and for the first time saw the true might of the mountain fall into spectacular chaos at my feet.

This, the first sight of Toll an Lochain – the great valley of An Teallach – and the orgasm of sky-scratching towers that stands above it, provokes an absolutely unforgettable feeling. For me it banished even the vaguest notion of my chosen route being some sort of soft touch. The hours of climbing up bare mountainside, traversing its hard shoulder up buttresses of sandstone creased and coloured like elephant hide, are merely the build-up to this one sensational pay-off. No habituation to spectacle, no awe exhaustion. Just bang: *mountain*.

An Teallach is one of the great icons of British wilderness because it does it all. You have the detachment of being all the way out here, way the hell up on Scotland's Atlantic coast, looking out into an area that constitutes some of the most untamed terrain in Britain. You escape here because it's a concentration of elementals, a giant spectacle that makes you recalibrate your internal barometer, reassess your abilities and, finally, wrestle with this seemingly insurmountable place and make it back home – or back to Dundonnell, at least – to tell the tale. And the thing is, you don't know how this thing is going to affect you. How you're going to feel, or cope. The only way is to go and see, to walk into your own personal unknown.

An Teallach does fear, too: the 500-metre fright of exposure beneath the tilting pinnacle of Lord Berkeley's Seat is, I'm reliably informed, absolutely fucking terrifying. The rest of the mountain's long, complex ridge is difficult, too – the pinnacles of Corrag Bhuidhe a fearsome challenge if taken direct, too fearsome for most walkers.

I stood looking at it for a long time, bent in a squat, hands on knees and mouth gaping. After all the years of staring at pictures of this place I couldn't quite believe I was here, both in it and looking at it. I'd wondered so long what it would feel like. And here it was.

My feeling was of elation, mixed with a familiar tension. I'd climbed through cloud to get here. The valley to the north-west, Coire Mòr an Teallaich, was now full of vapour that was swirling upwards into a bank of flat, deepening grey. The crest of the mountain's clawed ridgeline formed the bulwark between the cloud and the mountain's innards, and the truce didn't look like it would hold for long. The air was still and heavy with the tension of unspent humidity. The whole mountain felt like a tightly held breath.

Where the two ridges met, a thin path worn pink to the sandstone eeled up towards me from the right. I was standing on the saddle between the two halves of the massif: to my right, Sgùrr Fiòna and the pinnacles; to my left, Bidein a' Ghlas Thuill – An Teallach's highest point. In front of me, extending south beyond the long, sun-caught blue slick of Loch Toll an Lochain, lay the landscape known as the 'Great Wilderness'. There it was, brushed by cloud and smudgy like a watercolour, fleeing to a horizon of muscular, layered mountains. It's commonly said that amongst it lies the furthest point from a road in all of Britain, on the flank of an obscure, humpy mountain known as Ruadh Stac Beag, which lies seven miles from the nearest metalled road. It isn't. The remotest point from a road is dozens of miles to the south-east in the Grampians south of the Cairngorms between two peaks in an area covered with varicose streams: Carn an Fhidhleir and An Sgarsgoch. It's just under ten miles from a road – 15,558 metres, to be precise.* That's as remote as it gets in Britain. And for a little, supposedly teeming, archipelago, that's not bad going. There are other mountains hereabouts that bear mention, both for their spectacle and remoteness: robust and sharp, A' Mhaighdean to the south-west deep in the heart of the Fannaichs is considered the most difficult of Scotland's big mountains to reach. Slioch, on the fringes of Torridon above storied Loch Maree, stands like a raised fist; Beinn Tarsuinn and Mullach Coire Mhic Fhearchair to the south-east: all burly mountains that see few feet and are spaced by endless heathery hinterland.

The Great Wilderness has another name: the Fisherfield Forest. Stand like I did on the ridge of An Teallach, stare into it and you'll be struck dumb with

---

* Messy argument, this. The key caveat is exactly what constitutes a 'road': some say it's a track, some would say it's something with tarmac on it. For anecdote, the furthest place from a road in England is near the peak of Glendhu Hill in Northumberland, in the Kielder Forest. It is 7,617 metres from a road – almost exactly half the distance of Scotland's wildest point. *Trail Magazine* went to find it once; it's at NY58006587. The Scottish location is NN91618328.

awe. You might also be struck with a question: why do they call something with no trees a forest? The answer is a chapter in the long story of British wilderness you probably don't want to know – but everybody should.

The word for 'wilderness' actually originates from an Old English term, the place of the wildéor – wild beast, or, more specifically, deer. You still hear deer called by the name 'beast' in the Highlands. And in a storybook sense, the natural habitat for a beast is the forest.

So the Great Wilderness's other name is a relic from another era, a name that can still be found amongst the nomenclature of other vast places on the map of Scotland with startling regularity. Within sight of my position on An Teallach lie the Fannaich Forest, the Dundonnell Forest and the Flowerdale Forest. Just yesterday I was on the fringe of the Glencanisp Forest, looking at Suilven. Practically every big space and mountain place in Scotland has it somewhere on its map sheet. But there are hardly any *forests* here; outside the relic woodlands in the Cairngorms and a few others elsewhere, those trees that do fur the 'Forests' hardly merit geographical designation, and are rarely old enough to make it onto the map anyway. There must be some mistake. Nothing this vast, open and conspicuously treeless could, within living memory, have ever been a forest. The word must have some dual meaning. But there's no mistake: or at least, there's no mistake we can reverse. And therein lies the great tragedy of the Great Wood of Caledon.

The destruction of these forests is chilling testimony to man's impact on the British landscape. It's not something I take pleasure in bringing up, as the story is likely to subvert your whole idea about British wilderness and quite possibly leave you feeling rather sour. But hopefully it will also instil in you – as it did in me – a fierce sense of protectiveness over the little that remains of what was once a mighty swathe of forest that stretched across Scotland like a rich, green mane. Out of this, the mountains poked like they once did above the thick ice the trees replaced. The Caledonian Forest was composed initially of dwarf birch and alder, growing on thin post-glacial soils. The forest was soon thickened by the arrival of Scots pine, that broccoli-shaped work of natural art that rises up to nearly 30 metres in beautiful silhouette, and endures on occasion for over 500 years. The Highlands was once a sea of these lovely trees. The Greco-Egyptian geographer Claudius Ptolemy, in his extensive geographical assessment of Europe, coined the term *Caledones* to refer to central Scotland either side of the Great Glen, probably in reference to a tribe that occupied the region. This became the Latin denotation *Caledonia*, fittingly meaning 'wooded heights'. The ancient pinewood – less a pure forest than a sprawling wilderness – was truly a primeval place. Elk, bear and wolf skulked its dark recesses, as did lynx and wildcat.

The Neolithic people made the first dent. Subsistence felling then continued for several thousand years until the Vikings arrived in the 9th century – and the industrial slaughter began. They killed the trees, hunted the occupants of the forest, and harvested the timber for their houses and their boats. Slowly but inexorably the forest was nibbled away from within and without as populations grew. Boars were hunted for their meat, beavers for their coat – Inverness later became a teeming port for the fur trade – and wolves and lynx were killed because they endangered the livestock that was increasingly finding home on the land and grazing the ground where the trees once stood. Stands of trees were burned to flush out the last of the remaining predators, until the 'last wolf' was killed some time in the 18th century.

Then came the railways. Hundreds of miles of sleepers were made out of logs extracted from the forests, and business was so good that wood was exported, using new river-flotation methods to send the felled logs downstream. The Napoleonic Wars increased felling to a record rate; on either side of this conflict, between 1780 and 1890, 300 ships were built at the Moray Firth – the mouth of the Cairngorms-penetrating Spey. Lacking any predators, deer would nibble at the saplings of the ailing forest, scuppering any chance of regeneration. Sporting estates and sprawling farms were set up, populated with deer and sheep that chewed the ground to a grassy scalp. The First World War saw massive stands of native woodland felled all over Britain to make the buttresses and walls for trenches on the Western Front. This had such a devastating impact it spurred the creation of the Forestry Commission in 1919 to manage Britain's dwindling timber reserves and make the country self-sustaining in the event of another war. This saw the planting of huge numbers of fast-growing, non-native conifers such as Norway spruce, Sitka spruce and various firs – the endless carpets of dark, empty 'Christmas tree' forests so common today. When the Second World War started, Canadian lumberjacks were enlisted to clear-fell huge stands of the shrinking forest for the war effort, principally the Battle of the Atlantic. They worked with a predictably horrifying efficiency: 'Canadian mills and lumbermen are turning out 200,000 board feet of Scottish timber a day!' ran a story in the *Edmonton Journal* in September 1941. And it was the mature trees – being of the most useful size – that were the first to be felled. Around half of the remaining Scots pine forest vanished.

Today, the forest that once spread across the Highlands from Loch Lomond in the south to Loch Shin in the far north has been felled, leaving only paltry crumbs in places such as Rothiemurchus, Abernethy, the Black Wood of Rannoch, Glen Affric and Shieldaig – and almost within eyeshot of An Teallach at Loch Maree, in Torridon. The oldest living relic of the great wood is thought to be the old yew in the churchyard at Fortingall in Perthshire. This tree is so ancient – between 1,500 years and 3,000 years old, and probably the most venerable living thing in Britain – locals say that Pontius Pilate played in its shade as a child. These places are now so precious, both to us and to the remaining animals that cling to the vestiges of this ancient forest: great crested tit, Scottish crossbill – the 'parrot of the pinewood' – red squirrel, spotted woodpecker, capercaillie and the secretive, desperately threatened Scottish wildcat. The Highlands are now completely different from the landscape of the pre-Neolithic period. The only things that ancient eyes would recognise are the immovable outlines of the mountains.

As I stood on the shoulder between the two summits of An Teallach I noticed four silhouettes making their way up towards me from the direction of Sgùrr Fiòna and the pinnacles. As they reached me, I nodded hello to the first who arrived. His name was John, a Scot who – at the point we were standing – was precisely between his 199th and 200th Munro. The former was Sgùrr Fiòna; the latter was Bidein a' Ghlas Thuill.

'Big moment,' I said.

'Aye. Eighty-two to go after this.' A slight frown. 'If they don't change the bloody list again.'

We chatted for a few moments – remarking on the weather, and comparing kit and the like – and then slowly, as a group, we began to climb towards the top of Bidein a' Ghlas Thuill, An Teallach's highest point.

This final climb on the mountain is exhilarating: easy, grippy, and all the way with that awesomely primal view for company. The summit is a white trig point horizontally fractured by a thick crack twelve inches above its base and perched on a shelf of bubbled sandstone. I hung back as we neared it, John covering the distance first. As he reached the top he stood alone until one of the group embraced him, the others patting him heartily on his shoulders. I hung back sheepishly, then shook his hand. Seconds later a hip flask of whisky was being passed around. We sat quietly, the highest people on this great mountain – the highest people for hundreds of square miles – in the silent air, watching the tower of cloud continue to grow behind us. It was building at a fair clip.

'Look at that. Got some charge in it,' someone said. I didn't know if he meant its rate of movement or its contents. I didn't ask.

It wasn't long before John and his group were on their feet and on the move. I declined their offer to join them on the descent – they were parked further down the glen – and watched as they began to descend, carefully but steadily, down the east ridge of the mountain.

It was amazing how much better I felt – how much safer, more confident – with other people around. Earlier, as I'd approached the summit, I joined the path. In the dirt were boot prints, fresh since the last rain, and just that – even though it had been only hours since I was on a road, in the car – was comforting.

As they left the summit and I watched them go, another walker was covering the last few steps to the top. He was older, in his sixties at least, and had the lithe stoop of a lifetime walker. He was leathered accordingly, too, but had a look that betrayed a slight desperation – as if he were surprised how hard the ascent had been. Old timers often complain how they can't do what they used to. They don't seem to realise that they can still do something most people half their age would struggle with.

'Afternoon. Not too bad,' he said, possibly to himself, as he arrived at the trig point. He motioned out to the stormy view. 'Wouldn't work with a blue sky, would it?'

'How's that?'

'Wouldn't have the same ...' – he flexed his shoulders, as if suppressing a shiver – '... the same. You know.'

I did know. Shafts of sunlight through broken, grey cloud hit the pinna-cled buttresses of the massif, the grey cloud and the rich yellow afternoon sun

– it made the mountain's bare rock look almost green. He was right. Stripped of this dynamic atmosphere under a flat blue sky, it probably wouldn't work. Not as well, anyway.

'See the goats?' he said.

'No, up here?'

A nod. 'Feral goats. Ancestors of the ones kept by them crofters in the valley,' he swirled a finger down into Toll an Lochain, 'before they got cleared out. They do pretty well up here. Find a ledge or a scary precipice, and I guarantee you'll find some goat shit on it.'

I scanned the mountainside for movement, for the distinctive 'M' of goat horn breaking the ridge's skyline, but saw none. My eyes were stopped, time and again, by the pinnacles.

'Have you been over that lot?' I nodded towards the western half of the mountain, as he sat by the trig point and took a slug from a dented blue bottle.

'Not today.' He tapped his head. 'Can't deal with heights like I used to. Berkeley's Seat, the one that leans over like that ...' He nodded towards it, the most dramatic of the pinnacles, and fixed it with a haunted look. 'Once is enough.'

We stood in contemplative silence long enough for him to catch his breath, then he was off.

'Shouldn't leave it too long,' he said.

I stood alone on the summit for about ten minutes. I liked it, but then I didn't like it; the feeling of being left alone up there, rain-and-God-knows-what-else-heavy clouds building in the corrie behind me. This wasn't some 8,000-metre peak, gradually starving me of life, nor some frigid winter plateau. I just didn't like the feeling of being on top of this sharp, high thing on my own. My brief bit of company up here was now gone, and for some reason I felt more alone than I did on the way up. I loved being here, in this place, on a mountain I'd dreamed about climbing for so long. It just didn't feel like a place to hang about.

I left the summit as the first tendrils of cloud found it. Accompanied by the weird, echoey rasp of my boots on the clean sandstone, I began descending the slope off the edge of the north-east ridge. The broken tower-block shadows of the mountains built around me again behind the cloud and I quickened my pace, within minutes descending below its strafing base to the pass between Ghlas Mheall Mòr and Bidein a' Ghlas Thuill. From here a swift descent into the valley of Coir' a' Mhuillinn – the ramp leading north-east out of An Teallach's inner keep – was possible. Soon I was back in the sunshine and wandering along the edge of a crisp stream of clean water that led back down towards Dundonnell and the road.

What a thrilling day. It had been electric, precarious – the whole deal. For that moment as I walked down the last verdant steps of the mountain towards the road, still dry, still alive and satisfied I'd witnessed the full spectacle of the mountain my nerves would allow, I felt like the luckiest walker alive. But the day's challenges weren't over yet. Not quite.

I had booked a room at the hotel in Dundonnell, an isolated, burgundy-carpeted edifice wedged between Loch Broom and the mountain. It felt a bit decadent, but after three nights sleeping rough and crawling with midges, I felt I deserved it. I reached the door of the hotel just as the storm broke overhead with an almost audible 'crack'. An Teallach was now swaddled in a blanket of cloud and, by the time I'd checked in, rain was hammering furiously on the windows of the hotel, studding deepening puddles on the tarmac outside. It felt amazing to be in a room, with a bed. It had only been three nights but I still felt pretty punched. First order was a shower, followed swiftly by dinner, washed down with plenty of local beer. After dropping my bags on the floor I went into the bathroom, yanked on the light and peeled off my base layer for the first time since Schiehallion. I was bruised around the shoulder from my rucksack, and the angry red swellings of bites traced my hairline, wrists, forearms and neck. But as I brushed bits of fluff and the endless grit of dead midges off my skin, I noticed something else.

I've a good friend who's been walking – and sitting on, lying down and crawling through – the hills for the best part of twenty years. And in all those years he's never had a tick. Having enjoyed a much less intimate relationship with the hills for half that time, before this point I'd had eight. Over the next ten minutes as I sat, quietly aghast in the bathroom of my room in the Dundonnell Hotel, that number would double.

A tick, for many reasons, is something you don't really want to have. An arachnid parasite, it spends its entire existence hanging off vegetation hoping to snare a passing blood-bearing limb, ideally that of a deer, sheep, dog or walker. About the size of a poppy seed, they're so armoured they're tough to dispatch even if you can catch one beetling around you before it latches on. Once aboard, the tick wanders until it finds a quiet, damp and warm part of your anatomy. Then it bites. Its bite attaches it to you, and once attached it begins to feed. You don't notice any of this as it secretes an anaesthetic onto your skin beforehand, and by default tends to occupy areas that escape your immediate attention. The eight I eventually discovered were attached in a row along my belt line, in my armpit and on a patch of skin typically, how shall we say, covered by my underpants.

The rub in all of this is that ticks aren't just a pest. Left alone to do their business they'll swell with your blood, become increasingly repulsive and eventually drop off. You don't want to let them linger – that can cause its own problems – but pull them out with careless abandon and, in an act of natural spite, they can regurgitate the content of their stomach into your bloodstream. That content might contain something really nasty, and in Britain,* nasty no. 1 is a bacterial infection called Lyme borreliosis – Lyme disease. This begins with the sinister signal of a bullseye rash around the area of the bite, which can take weeks to appear or might not appear at all. From there, it's pretty much anyone's guess. You might experience unexplained muscle pain and lethargy, and it might stop there if you're lucky. Or it might progress to swelling of the joints, immobilisation of the facial muscles, difficulty concentrating, loss of short-term memory, bladder disorder, meningitis, depression, changes in heartbeat, and – in extreme cases – brain damage and paralysis. Perhaps the biggest problem with Lyme disease, as if all these aren't enough, is that it's so symptomatically unpredictable and leisurely in its insidious build-up – years in many cases – that it's notoriously difficult to diagnose and little understood. Crusading American physician Dr Edwin Masters, who was one of the leading researchers into 'chronic' Lyme disease, once cannily summed it up: 'First off, they said it was a new disease, which it wasn't. Then it was thought to be viral, but it isn't ... They thought it was easily treated by short courses of antibiotics, which sometimes it isn't.' This 'sometimes' refers

---

* The continent has it worse. European ticks carry the potentially fatal tick-borne encephalitis (TBE), which can cause swelling of the brain and lead to lasting neurological damage. As with Lyme disease, diagnosis is difficult and there's no cure.

to the fact that there's no cure for Lyme disease, swift diagnosis and treatment with antibiotics to prevent the infection developing being really all you can do. It seems the only consistent advice is to not get bitten in the first place – or if you do, get the bastards out, cleanly and quickly.

After staring at the little clutches of embedded creatures in the mirror, I set about doing the latter. Several looked to be 'nymph' ticks – or juveniles – and therefore so small they slipped through the claws of the tick-removal tool I'd taken to carrying in my first-aid kit. A fine pair of needle-nose tweezers took care of most of these except one, which to my dismay broke in half and required painful digging around and much swearing. Breaking a tick as you remove it isn't good, but there was little I could do about it now.

Half an hour later I was finally able to have a bath, after which – the euphoric exhaustion of the day only slightly dulled by my unwelcome passengers – I made my way down to the bar.

A huge amount of food later, with glass of beer in hand, I went outside, wandered over to the shore of Loch Broom and stood, looking out to where the long waterway opened into the Atlantic through a tight natural harbour of embracing, mountainous headlands. It was almost impossibly serene. The clouds had passed, the water was like glass and the sun had set, turning the air pink. There were no midges, the gentle ebb of the breeze at the lochside keeping them at bay, leaving me free to just sit and watch the scene separate into vivid colours and gently fade as one. I looked at my watch; it was after 10.30 p.m. What a way to say goodbye to the Highlands.

Tomorrow I'd leave, back to the normality of home life for a while. And besides the memories I'd take with me, An Teallach would continue to impress itself strongly in my thoughts far longer than it took for its angry silhouette to fade in the rear-view mirror, for two reasons. One, my little run-in with the ticks would mean I'd spend the rest of the summer on precautionary antibiotics. And two, meeting John and his friends on the summit had made me realise I was missing something important that was all too easy to forget.

I'd be on my way back to Scotland in the autumn, when – hopefully – the ticks and midges would have gone. But first, I needed to phone a friend.

PART III

AUTUMN

11 ISLAND

The grey morning air hung heavy with the stink of fish. Punctuated by thin nautical clinks from the surrounding masts, the rough diesel engine of the 15-metre catamaran *Andromeda* sat idling against Mallaig's north pier waiting for the last couple of passengers to stagger down the slipway. One was resplendent with orange dreadlocks and a black Labrador on a rope lead; each was laden with two cases of Tennent's lager. As they lumbered aboard, the pilot turned to his payload of 22, each coddled to varying degrees against the autumn air. 'How many getting off at Kinloch?'

About half those present raised arms, including myself and Jim, who sat opposite me on the stern benches, hunkered beneath a navy woolly hat, dark waterproof and a weary dawn scowl.

The pilot chuffed in mock disgust as he unhitched the boat from the dock. 'God knows why.'

The diesel revved, and the boat swayed away from the pier and launched off into the strait.

It was early October. A few weeks earlier in the soft warmth of late summer Jim and I had stood in his garden in Lincolnshire drinking beer and spidering over maps of the west coast of Scotland, comparing various ferry lines and timetables. The two mountains we were going to climb weren't in dispute, but the fact that they were two of the country's most inaccessible meant some planning was needed. Fiendish logistics notwithstanding, all of this served only to heighten anticipation: within the week we'd set aside, we were heading into the heart of two of Britain's most remarkable – and remarkably seques-tered – mountain places.

* * *

Given the abundance of scenically outstanding islands anchored off the west coast of Scotland – the Hebrides – you'd think choosing one to best exemplify the prickled, mountainous isolation so many share might be difficult. The islands fall into two main geographical groups: Inner and Outer. The former lie on the mainland side of the Hebridean Sea's soft S-curve, and fall into three natural congregations around Skye (Raasay, Scalpay, Rona, and the Small Isles of Rùm, Canna, Muck and Eigg), Islay (Jura and Scarba, Colonsay and Oronsay, Cara and Gigha) and Mull (Iona, Inch, Coll, Tiree and Staffa). Beyond the Minch, the Outer Hebrides of Lewis, Harris and the Uists form a south-tapering arc – a bird's view of a great fish patrolling Scotland's edge.

The mountains on these islands are, by virtue of their isolation, totally unique. Jura, with its three 'Paps'; Arran, with its delicate ridges crowned by Goat Fell; Mull, where lies Ben More, the Munro many leave for last; Eigg, with the Devil's Tower-like monolith of An Sgùrr; and Harris, with the far-flung and sprawling Clisham.

None of these fitted our brief, though. Jura, Arran and Mull seemed too large, too developed. Eigg, for all its dinky charms, had but one mountain. The Clisham was tempting, but loch-spattered Harris and Lewis are actually connected, together making a single large island that it's easy to forget is an island at all.

Then, of course, there's Skye. Skye is separated from the mainland by less than a quarter of a mile, and is today linked by a bridge at Kyle of Lochalsh. It's a nice bridge – but it's a bridge nonetheless. The mountaineer W. H. Murray, who wrote his *Guide to the West Highlands of Scotland* more than twenty years before the bridge was opened in 1995, lamented what was then merely a whispered threat to Syke's truly offshore status, that 'Skye owes much of its fame and attractive power ... to an island magic that any bridge would diminish. It would become another peninsula.'

Essentially made of a jumble of peninsulas already, all radiating messily from a central nucleus, Skye is scenically kaleidoscopic. In the north lie the mossy steps of the Trotternish Ridge and the peculiar, steepled altars of the Storr and Quiraing. The south is riven with inlets and lochs, some of them staggeringly beautiful, such as the freshwater lozenge of Loch Coruisk, Loch Scavaig and the little settlement of Elgol – a viewpoint of particular distinction.

It's the contents of the view from Elgol that capture most of the attention directed at Skye. The island is home to two mountain ranges of opposing character; one is composed of gentle-topped summits of pink scree. The other is a vision of horror.

The infamous Cuillin Ridge – properly the Black Cuillin, to define them against the comelier, slighter Red Cuillin – has a particular malignancy that's inspired and scared mountaineers since they began their exploratory scratches in the 19th century. They're Britain's youngest peaks, spat from a volcanic fissure 60 million years ago and still to succumb to the de-barbing of great age. From many angles, the startling peaks of the Black Cuillin and Blàbheinn (often shortened to Blaven) seem to defy your eyes, appearing like the bristles of a water monster rising from the sea, tilted and serrated, curved in a range that utterly dominates the southern end of the island and violently punctures the horizon.

The Black Cuillin aren't elegant. They're vulgar and frightening, and many are extremely difficult to get up. The string of peaks that forms the ridge represents Britain's greatest mountaineering challenge, in which severe scrambles and one roped climb make the journeys to gain their summits a hazardous, barren multi-day expedition. This is problematic, as twelve of these peaks poke above the 3,000-foot mark with enough independence from each other to merit Munro status, and are therefore on the to-do list of those who attempt this famous 282-mountain itinerary. The Cuillin Munros are considered by baggers to be the 'bad step' of their ticklist: the awkward, dangerous shuffle in the arduous but otherwise reasonably straightforward challenge many make the lifelong focus of their mountain activities. It's an irony that the Inaccessible Pinnacle of Sgùrr Dearg, standing proud of the central ridge like a tilted index finger, was the only Munro Sir Hugh himself failed to reach the top of. Often cited as the most difficult Munro, which may be true, it certainly isn't the most dangerous. Anyone attempting it will generally use a rope and very much want to climb it; to *accidentally* find yourself committed to it isn't really possible. The same cannot be said for the other, less vertiginous but equally difficult, mountains of the Cuillin, which are hard scrambles often tackled without a rope rather than easy climbs usually tackled with one.

Much has been written about Skye's Black Cuillin. But perhaps the most unlikely literature on this singular mountain range comes from a man resolutely associated with another area of upland – and another country – altogether: Alfred Wainwright.

Wainwright was born in Blackburn in 1907. Initially an accountant, his skills as an illustrator were displayed in his seven *Pictorial Guides to the Lakeland Fells* – dense, hand-written, little hardback books that today are as iconic as they are ubiquitous amongst visitors to the Lake District. Wainwright clearly loved his landscape, but to this day not everyone likes Wainwright: the tone of his guidebooks is by turns effortlessly evocative and irritatingly twee, and whilst some admire the intricacy and artistry of his sketches, others are quite bewildered by them.

The popular image of him physically is of the archetypal walking crotchet: plus fours, grey mac, flat cap, white hair and a pipe around which a thick Lancashire drawl would rumble. For all the affection he received during his lifetime, Wainwright was not one to court celebrity. He initially refused to reveal any biographical information in his books, something that even stretched to his first name: for many years his books were authored by 'A. Wainwright', or the enigmatic 'A.W.' He did nothing to promote his guides and, when cornered by a local newspaper into having dinner with whoever bought the millionth copy of a *Pictorial Guide*, Wainwright ensured that it was he himself who bought this symbolic book. His reasoning: 'I don't want to eat with strangers.'

In later life he apparently relaxed. He penned a memoir, relented and allowed himself to be interviewed, and even became a stately TV personality at the age of 80, his motives apparently entirely altruistic: the bulk of his money went to animal charities, with even his own son snubbed in his will.

Regardless, Wainwright – who died in 1991 – is today so synonymous with the fells of the Lake District, that 214 of them collectively bear his name. 'Bagging the Wainwrights' is a challenge all of its own, and the hunger for anything featuring his scrawly signature is seemingly insatiable. The amount of printed material dedicated to the man and his work is quite astonishing: three autobiographies, four biographies, a collection of letters, dozens of spin-offs featuring collations of previously published works, gazetteers and log-books – alongside some 40 guidebooks, sketch collections and memoirs written by the man himself – comprise a canon of close to 100 separate publications. That's not to mention the numerous television programmes, the Wainwright Society and his eponymous animal rescue shelter.

Yet it's Wainwright's enthusiasm for Scotland – a place he viewed with the awe of a visitor rather than the affectionate familiarity of a resident – that's perhaps the most surprisingly realised yet least explored aspect of his otherwise rather overexposed output. Written very late in his life, *Wainwright in Scotland* was the culmination of his final tour of the Highlands, by which time he was an observer rather than a walker. In its lean text he alludes to his introduction to Scotland via a climbing trip to the Isle of Arran on the eve of war in 1939. He describes being 'deeply touched' by a group of villagers who gathered at the pier as his ferry departed Brodick and sang the lament 'Will ye no' come back again?'

His descriptions of the mountains he finds are splendidly vivid. Suilven he cannily describes as a 'grotesque outline ... popping into view unexpectedly and always seeming to be peering inquisitively to see what's happening'. An Teallach is 'imposing in its majesty ... overpowering, intimidating'. But it's Skye's Black Cuillin for which he reserves his most effusive praise: 'Nature's skyscrapers ... the grandest mountains in all Britain ... a scene both compelling and repelling that will never be forgotten. The stuff of which ambitions are made. And dreams. And nightmares.'

Referring to the traverse of the main ridge, Wainwright stresses the need to be an 'equipped and experienced cragsman', recalling an incident in 1954 when he once shirked the last 30 yards of Sgùrr nan Gillean 'in growing apprehension of an instant demise'.

The Cuillin are indeed difficult; their mixed composition of gabbro (grippy, even when wet) and basalt (like soap, especially when wet), and the often unclear distinction between the two, can make simply placing your feet confidently a stressful process. And their satanic profile when seen from anywhere in the coastal West Highlands – particularly the astonishing leaning tooth of Am Bàsteir, which appears along the ridge as a medieval puncture tool and translates as 'The Executioner' – makes the Black Cuillin a prospect of concentrated dread. Sounds good, doesn't it?

You might then wonder why, that morning as we pulled out of Mallaig's rusting harbour, Jim and I weren't going to Skye. The answer's easy: we were going somewhere better.

*   *   *

Jim – that is, James Provost – was, amongst many other things, my next-door neighbour. He'd knocked on my door eighteen months earlier to introduce himself and pass in a spare key (or complain about a smell, I forget), and I noticed his jacket was emblazoned with a brand popular with hillwalkers. I remarked upon it – this happens quite a lot – and we swiftly established a keen shared interest in the mountains. Loose plans were made to climb a few together at some point. Back in September, as we finally nailed these down, we clinked bottles and toasted the trip.

'I'm looking forward to seeing them again,' Jim had said, before adding, 'from ground level, that is.'

Something else about Jim you should probably know is that he has the rare qualification of knowing the British mountains from a viewpoint few others have had the privilege – or skill – to witness. Jim is a former fast-jet pilot for the Royal Air Force. If you've ever been on the side of a mountain and that familiar chalkboard scratch has chased a black arrowhead down a mountain valley: that could have been Jim. His knowledge of the valleys and lochs of Scotland was immense, though from a very different point of view and interpretation. As we'd travelled up in the car from Lincolnshire he'd pointed at things out of the window such as a refinery ('That was useful for target practice'), a narrow valley in the Southern Uplands ('Flying down that is like flying down the Death Star trench at the end of *Star Wars*'), and various obstacles and landmarks that had some terrifying anecdote attached to them ('Let's just say that day I learned once and for all that night flying is for bats and twats'). Following tours of active duty and a stint as squadron leader of the Red Arrows, Jim was now a commercial pilot. In his downtime between long-haul flights he was slowly rediscovering his old aerial playgrounds on foot. The Hebrides in particular stood high on his list.

One island in particular he remembered lay eight miles off the west coast, entirely off on its own. From high above he remembers spotting it and noting it as being compactly robust and heart-shaped, with an extraordinary natural harbour bitten out of the eastern side. This had a particularly lean frosting of civilisation around its edge – just a few buildings – that appeared to be the island's only habitation. The southern part of the island was fringed by extensive cliffs haloed with surf, and contained an extraordinary, sinuous mountain range the shape of an oxbow and linked by thin ridges. Jim had recognised the outline of the island on the map, and as my finger fell on it he made an appreciative noise.

'I remember that. Always thought it looked interesting.'

The island on the map was Rùm. And as the *Andromeda* began its choppy crossing on this particular October morning, Rùm was the dark, knuckled shadow off the port bow towards which it steadily began to turn.

Despite being home to what is widely considered one of the great mountain traverses in Britain, Rùm hasn't enjoyed nearly the same level of fame as its illustrious neighbour Skye – nor even that of Arran, Mull or Jura – for the simple reason that practicality isn't its strong point. That's nonsense, actually; what I meant to say is that practicality *wasn't* its strong point. Until relatively recently, the cost and infrequency of passage to the island was the principal barrier to the mountaineers whose gaze had alighted on the bumpy dash the island and its mountains cut on the horizon. Rùm is what you could bluntly term a 'proper' island. No bridges reach out to it, you're the mercy of ferry schedules and, once there, at no point can you forget you're not on the mainland. With Rùm comes the delicate feeling of balanced existence one gets in a place large enough to support life, but small enough to feel pleasingly cloistered.

W. H. Murray was one of Britain's leading mountaineers just before and after the Second World War, as well as an outstanding writer, who – whilst incarcerated as a POW – had recorded his memories of the Scottish mountains on toilet paper. He'd discovered Rùm in much the same (well, sort of the same) way as Jim had, in that it drew his admiring glance from a distance. It was, he wrote, 'a cluster of dark and secret peaks on a sheet of steel-grey sea ... an unknown island'. In *Undiscovered Scotland* Murray paints an awkward – if enticingly romantic – portrait of the island, noting that in conversation with a veteran mountaineer in 1945 he learned it was necessary 'to raid the island by motor boat from Mallaig at a cost of £5 10s ... then you have to get *off* it again. You can buy no food on it, get no roof over you, and gales may stop you leaving just when you have to. In fact, is it worth it?'

Murray evidently felt it was, because in 1948 – in the company of Mike Ward, later expedition doctor on the successful 1953 Mount Everest expedition and a face in many of the photographs on the wall of the Pen-y-Gwryd

Hotel – he boarded the by-then twice-weekly Outer Hebridean steamer for the more affordable fare of five shillings. Interestingly, Murray's anonymous mountaineer informant had used the word 'raid' – and one of the reasons not much had been written about Rùm's mountains prior to this is that the island lived up to its nickname: the 'Forbidden Isle'. An exotic private shooting reserve until well into the 20th century, whilst 'forbidden' was perhaps an overly strong word, visitors were hardly encouraged by the owners and the island preserved a sense of exclusivity.

Murray, who had rather prudently sought permission from Rùm's steward, Lady Bullough, would later pen an account of the trip titled 'Rock Climbing on Rùm'. As well as being a visceral portrait of a then rather shadowy destination, it amusingly describes the stoic interplay between partners on a climbing expedition in post-war Scotland, with many passages that hint at the extraordinarily optimistic tolerance of discomfort displayed by this generation. Having lost his weighty bag of equipment when it was confused for mail sacks on the steamer, Murray was left with few supplies, and they only had the somewhat utilitarian Ward's inventory to make do with in hard April weather. Refusing Ward's offer of sharing a sleeping bag for warmth (can't you just imagine that conversation?), he instead borrowed his spare jumper, remarking that their first night camped on the shore on the southern edge of the island was 'by no means as bad as I'd expected. The soft and springy leather of climbing boots makes a not uncomfortable pillow, and although cold interfered with sleep I was able to doze.' Of the following night, soaked through and forced to sleep in his wet clothes, he recalls that 'the very dampness of the cloth, perhaps caused by swelling of the fabric, helped to exclude cold air and preserve body heat,' continuing: 'It is a sign of a man's wholeness of mind and body if he can lie out at night and be numbed by cold, then be thawed in the morning and be none the worse.' They don't make many like that anymore.

Murray and Ward had walked six miles along the coast and pitched their tent at Dibidil, a point on the southern flank of the island where a ruined cottage stood along with the remains of a croft.

As Jim and I sat on the ferry, our rucksacks bulged with overnight supplies. Our plan was to re-trace Murray and Ward's steps to Dibidil, spend the night at this isolated spot, then walk up the glen to the foot of the mountain – whose north-west buttress the pair had been the first to climb. As the boat slid towards the island, the eastern horizon began to glow with the sunrise, light-ing the grey sky above like hammered tin catching firelight. And ahead, hack-sawing through the cloud shrouding Rùm, we saw Askival.

At 812 metres, Askival is the taller peak on the two-headed ridge it shares with its neighbour, 722-metre Hallival. Their angular Scandinavian names are from Old Norse,* the language that also spawned the name of the range they inhabit – which, like Skye, bears the name of Cuillin. This probably comes from *kiolen*, or 'rocky mountains'. Whilst Skye's mountains bear predomi-nantly Gaelic names, some peaks only being named by early ascentionists,† many of Rùm's mountains have evidently much older names, probably of Viking origin. Peaks such as Trollaval, Hallival, Ainshval, Barkeval – all tall and aggressively steep volcanic mountains that dominate the southern half of Rùm – conjure images straight out of Norse mythology. Askival – 'Spear Hill' or 'Hill of the Ashwood', nobody's really sure – was our mountain. And what a mountain it is.

Rùm's Cuillin – like Skye's – look like they've been burnt. With their charred ridgelines and crisped, blackened edges, both islands wear their volcanic past with similar pride. But whilst many of Skye's mountains are out of bounds to the walker, Rùm's are *just* within their reach – not that you'd know to look at them. Askival's profile from Kinloch makes it look, if not completely insurmountable, then at best an alarming proposition. Jim suggested as much as we entered the inlet of Loch Scresort and the sharp mountain began to shed its cloud cover with increasing abandon.

'*Bit* scared if that's it.'

Eyes fixed on the mountain, we barely noticed as the *Andromeda* swayed up to the slipway, the young attendant lashing the boat to the dock with a deft knot then stepping aside to let the dozen or so passengers off.

---

* The Norwegian word for mountain is *fjell*, which on Rùm has taken on the regionalised corruption *-val*. This is also the source word of the much-used 'fell' of the Lake District and elsewhere.

† One of these was the influential climber Professor Norman Collie, who gave several peaks on Skye their names. These include the island's highest peak, Sgùrr Alasdair, named after the man who in 1873 made the first ascent, Sheriff Alexander Nicolson. The north top of Sgùrr na Banachdaich – Sgùrr Thormaid – was named after a modified version of Collie's first name.

'So, what time do we need to be here tomorrow?' I asked the captain.

'Same time,' he replied.

It was just after 9 a.m. I could swear I'd read the sailing was at 11.

'What, 9 a.m.?'

'Like I say, we usually pick up here at the same time each day.'

I took a deep breath. 'The same time as what?'

He fixed me with a look. 'Same time we get here each day.'

'And what time is that?'

He threw his hands up. '*You* should know that. You bought the ticket!'

My ticket was an open, five-day pass, no times. 'So ... 11 a.m. then?'

'Sounds about right, I think. Yeah.'

'Right.'

I left him shaking his head, evidently bemused at my awkward line of questioning, and proceeded up the slipway where Jim was waiting, pack on.

Being left on an island – and let's not forget, a *proper* island – isn't something many people experience these days. To actually cut yourself off from your car, shops and roads to a point that not even your legs can get you home is a feeling that is both exciting and novel. There's no mountain rescue on Rùm – a few local volunteers patch the gap left by 'official', long-range volunteers – so whilst this is a wonderland for the adventurous, it comes with some serious commitments, too. We watched the boat as it pulled out and began its chug towards the next island on its route. As its engine faded and the sounds of the island took over, Jim and I began to get used to the idea that we were here until tomorrow whether we liked it or not.

If I'm making out that Rùm is in some way totally barren, it isn't; but as the small isles go it's certainly close. Just over twenty people live here year-round, equating to just over one person per two square miles. Of course, as tends to happen in such outposts, nearly everyone lives close together, leaving the rest of the island almost entirely devoid of people. And as we wandered towards the path that would take us along the coast to Dibidil, the silent, traffic-free track took us past the places they lived. A tiny schoolhouse; a cabin museum filled with display cabinets; several scattered houses, each with at least one wall stacked high with logs being seasoned for winter; the estate office, a handsome, whitewashed building. And all of this set along a track intermittently ducking between the shore and tall stands of russet-trunked Scots pine dappling the path with shadow in the watery sun.

We found the path, signed to Dibidil, and walked out of the trees onto the rising, open hillside. The morning was starting to get warm, and we soon stopped to discard the jackets and hats we'd worn on the crossing. Ahead of us to the south, the land was beginning to rise into mountains, their peaks poking above the skyline like faces over a wall. To the north, the loch, the jetty, Rùm's clutch of buildings and its low-lying northern edge. Around us autumn was beginning to deepen. The island was the colour of rust.

The path to Dibidil is dreadful. It's not that it's scenically awful or follows a bad line across the island; quite the contrary. It's just incredibly boggy. Rare is the occasion where no path at all would probably facilitate passage more easily than one that exists; but this path, which cuts to the east coast of Rùm then makes a rising traverse towards the southern end of the island, would certainly come close. Perhaps it was the recent rain, but every few steps either Jim or I would sink to our knees, point darkly to a spot for the other to avoid, before repeating the process further down the path. Six miles of this with an overnight pack can get wearing, and soon – despite long trousers, gaiters and supposedly waterproof boots – I was soaked to the thighs and every step sounded with a cold squelch.

This notwithstanding, it's a damn impressive place for a path. Rùm's position offers some stupendous views of the charismatic Inner Hebrides and the surrounding sea. The most striking view is of Eigg – the kidney-shaped, largely low-lying island with the profile of a capsized speedboat, the pinnacle of An Sgùrr the hoisted tiller. Eigg is smaller than Rùm by a thick half, yet hosts a population four times greater than its more mountainous neighbour. Like many far-flung regions of Scotland, this delicate little place has its horror stories, too. Today home to, and owned by, its 80-odd residents, the entire population of Eigg was massacred in the 16th century during a clan feud between the MacDonalds and the MacLeods – the former by the latter after a squabble over advances towards the island's women. The story goes that a group of MacLeods were cast adrift into the sea in punishment for this behaviour; they subsequently returned with a revenge force and found the MacDonalds hiding in a cave on the island's rugged south coast. Four hundred of them were asphyxiated by the smoke from fires the MacLeods lit at its mouth. Today it's known as Massacre Cave. An earlier massacre occurred on Eigg during the time of the Christian missionaries in around AD 617, when St Donnan founded a religious community on the isle. Donnan's fate is given in two differing stories: either he and his 52 followers were executed by thieves following a Mass (Donnan apparently requested he be able to finish the rite before his beheading), or the entire contingent was burned alive by a pagan from Arisaig who took a dislike to his activities. What desperate tales for such a small isle.*

The coast of Rùm becomes ever more dramatic the further you inch towards Dibidil. Hallival and the great, serrated fin of Askival soon emerge to the right, fighting for your attention with the sea far below to the left and – perhaps more pressingly – the treacherously slippery path underfoot. Every now and again the path is sliced by burns cascading from the mountains. One of these has cut into the land above the path and carved itself a little natural cave, where a waterfall pours into a grotto beyond a slit-door visible as we walked by. The sun glinted off the clear water within, making the whole scene look tropical and coolly beautiful.

Then the ground tilts dramatically and you find yourself perilously high above the sea, walking a grassy balustrade. Slip, and you'd die.

Jim, ahead, says it's like walking one half of a knife-edge. There are hoof prints in the mud. Amazing to think some of the island's ponies have ended up on this drastic path – and terrifying to think they might actually have had people riding them.

Eventually you near the end of the trail, and your payoff. You round the headland to see a mountain-rimmed valley descending from the right, flattening out where it meets the island's southern tip. Nestled against the mountain side on the other side of the valley's wriggling stream, half a mile distant, is a small, twin-chimneyed cottage, squat and proud, occupying what must be one of the most covetable coastal locations in Britain – a place only the committed

---

* In a move inspired by the Assynt purchase of 1993, Eigg was sold to its residents by the landowners in 1997. The former Laird of Eigg once memorably – and one suspects unfairly – described the island's residents as 'drunken, ungrateful, dangerous and barmy chancers'. Said folk are today successfully piloting one of Britain's most progressive environmentally sustainable communities.

can reach. The reward for those few is shelter, and unattended overnight accommodation, as the ruined cottage Ward and Murray slept in at Dibidil is today a bothy.

This basic breed of wild shelter is something many of Britain's furthest flung places have in common, and if our hundred or so mountain bothies were to have an ideal yardstick against which to measure themselves, Dibidil would probably be it.

The very existence of bothies amidst the British mountain landscape is quite wonderfully miraculous. In Scotland, they offer the tiniest twitch of light in rural lands left suddenly dark by the Clearances, then darker still in the century that followed. Typically, homesteads and farmhouses that had been left to ruin gradually became known to walkers and climbers in the years following the Second World War, when recreational hillwalking started to become immensely popular. Some of these buildings were ancient ruins; others had only recently been vacated by farmers, who – thanks to the invention of the all-terrain vehicle, and because returning soldiers wanted to work in greater comfort – began to house their staff in less remote locations. Because a large number of outlying buildings were simply too far from the rest of the farm for the landowner to maintain, and with huge swathes of land no longer used for hill farming coming under the control of the Forestry Commission, many huts and cottages fell into disrepair.

Some of the buildings' itinerant residents began to leave logbooks in the rotting ruins so others could record their passage. From this, participation in a growing trend known as 'bothying' grew. By the 1960s many of the buildings – which by their very nature occupied areas subject to extremes of weather – were in such a poor state that they barely offered any shelter at all. Legend has it that a comment made in the logbook of the forbidding-sounding Backhill of Bush bothy, suggesting that a club should be dedicated to the upkeep of these buildings, was the inspiration behind the formation of the Mountain Bothies Association (MBA) in 1965. Its original aim, remarkably selfless given the work involved, is still upheld today: 'To maintain simple unlocked shelters in remote country for the use and benefit of all who love wild and lonely places.'

The first official bothy was a Galloway farmhouse at Tunskeen, restored by a group led by Bernard Heath, who would become the first secretary of the

MBA. Heath was foremost in promoting the altruistic message of this embryonic association, stating that its members' only reward 'will be the knowledge that their efforts have helped save some bothy from ruin'.

In 1968 Sandy Cousins, a member of the Scottish Mountaineering Council, identified what would be the MBA's first major challenge when he curled up for the night in the lean ruins of a cottage on the southern tip of Rùm. Dibidil was then a particularly sad wreck; no roof, no windows, no door, and walls that were barely standing. It had been built in 1849 to house a shepherd family when the island, like much of the rest of the Highlands, was cleared of its then thriving population to make way for sheep. Originally comprising three rooms and a cellar, its last known resident, John MacDonald – who, for mysterious reasons, went by the name 'Johnny Come Over' – had vacated the cottage almost exactly a century earlier.

Cousins was moved by the stupendous location of the cottage. He noted its importance as a base for those attempting the Cuillin, and the fact that, like Murray, Ward and countless others, he had bedded down rudely within its ruined walls to escape the foul weather billowing off the Atlantic. For there to be only *half* a shelter in such a place – well, it seemed a damn shame. Cousins would later describe how he'd clambered 'into the ruin, thinking of the bygone days ... the joys and the sadnesses of the voices that must have been heard within'. He then penned a paragraph that sums up the lure of mountain bothies better than any other I've read: 'There should again be flickering shadows on these rough walls; they should again hear voices – the cheerful chatter of those who come because they love the wild places.'

Romantic as all this was, if Dibidil were to be brought back to life as a mountain bothy somebody was going to have to organise the revival, and it was a monstrous logistical task to transport both personnel and supplies to the battered, inaccessible tip of a largely unpopulated isle. The man tasked to do it was the MBA's newly installed project manager: a Yorkshire-born customs and excise civil servant named Irvine Butterfield.

We've briefly met Butterfield in these pages, thanks to his vivid 1986 guidebook *The High Mountains of Britain and Ireland*. Dibidil's eventual restoration would be a vindication for both Butterfield and the MBA, but it wasn't easy. After the overwhelmed project manager found the cottage in 'dismal remains', Bernard Heath would enlist the Royal Navy to ship in supplies, create a makeshift army of helpers from packs of university 'student sherpas' and Manchester schoolchildren who would brave midges, snow and tents wrecked by wind. But for all the hardship involved, the whole experience was suffused with good-natured striving for a common goal and no small amount of camaraderie. The team even composed a 21-verse song to the island, and carpenter Bill Mejery wrote a poem, simply titled 'Dibidil', opening with the lines:

> Dies the sun; and long shadows run across the slopes down the
>   rocky shore.
> There by the burn, a lonely Làrach stands, a roofless ruin with an
>   earthen floor.*

Butterfield's own summary would be characteristically humble, yet full of satisfaction in the group's feat: 'A modest achievement of the ordinary man and woman who – because of their sincere belief in the ideals they set out to achieve – win over others in their cause to find final victory: a modest shelter called Dibidil on the Isle of Rùm in the Hebrides.' His first book – *A Hebridean Adventure* – was his account of the restoration, and it ends with the simple line: 'I'm glad I volunteered.'

Today Dibidil is a proud monument to the early days of the MBA, and Jim and I arrived to find that the bothy had recently been given a solidly fitted new door, a new roof and a lick of paint. Pushing the door open, we were greeted by that familiar bothy smell of damp, wood smoke and generations of relieved exhaustion. The weak light from the window lit its dark innards: wood-panelled walls and sketchy, rag-tag furniture (bench, burnt-topped table, chair), an ash-choked fireplace haloed with the silvery discs of tea lights, and spent, candle-stuffed bottles of – naturally – rum. On the walls were various signs imploring visitors to be thoughtful to both the bothy and its surroundings, a few words of caution relating to some surface fissures a hundred metres from the door that it would be quite possible to disappear into if you were stumbling around in the dark, and a copy of the bothy code. Also present were two abandoned paperbacks – a Wilbur Smith and *Carry Me Down* by

---

* Làrach, in this context, means a ruin.

M. J. Hyland, in case you were curious – a logbook and, for delicate personal matters, a shovel.

We took the room to the right of the door; by the scattered possessions present, the left room was already occupied. More thorough explorations would have to wait until later as we had a mountain to climb. After depositing our heavier supplies – emergency tent, sleeping bag, a pouch of wine – and with stripped-down bags, we set off towards the mouth of Glen Dibidil, and the slopes of Askival.

Askival is another one of those mountains – like Cnicht – that looks pretty lethal from a distance. The difference between Askival and Cnicht in this respect is that whereas Cnicht yields with approach, Askival doesn't. Sheer and snub-nosed, it remained daunting all the way up Glen Dibidil as Jim and I made our way ever-hesitantly towards it.

The glen itself is a revelation, although it's necessarily bypassed by those making the full traverse of Rùm's Cuillin. Walking up the broad, green-carpeted glen, however, offers the finest perspective on the extraordinary horseshoe of the island's highest peaks. Most eye-grabbing is Trollabhal – predictably but splendidly the 'Mountain of the Trolls' – a Chinese pavilion of rock that rises at the end of the valley, fluted and scorched, as if made from vented iron.

The Rùm Cuillin are the modern remains of an ancient volcanic caldera, their peaks representing the shards of a broken rim around a long-spent vase of magma. The distinctive layering of igneous rocks – which you could be forgiven for mistaking as the bedding of sedimentary rocks, such is their stepped appearance – is the result of the volcano repeatedly expelling deep material that cyclically built and collapsed in on itself, like the rising and sinking of a poorly – and endlessly – baked loaf. These are what geologists call 'ultramafic deposits', essentially the spat foundations of the volcano's magma chamber, and the quality of those found on Rùm has made the site of particular scientific importance.

Although volcanoes formed these mountains, it was ice that gave them their fractured appearance. It's likely that Rùm's summits remained above the glaciers during the Ice Age – remember nunataks? – whilst the shallower coastal ice scoured valleys such as Glen Dibidil. Frost-shattering brittled their ridges, and they continue to crumble to this day.

What struck me was just how awesomely mountainous the glen felt. To our left stood Sgùrr nan Gillean and Ainshval, awesomely complex, spectacular examples of everything a mountain should be: difficult, high, steep, filled with hanging valleys and with waterfalls slung down them like lines of frayed rope. Their eastern scoops have fantastic monikers – the Nameless Corrie and the Forgotten Corrie – and the peaks themselves stand forbiddingly tall. *What* a place.

We decided the best line of attack would be to walk up the glen to the point where the ridge between Askival and its craggy southern neighbour, Beinn nan Stac, flattened to a *bealach*. To reach it meant a stiff ascent up grass; as I followed Jim up the glen I could see him looking up to the right for the best line.

We'd hoped as we'd left the bothy that the steepness of the glen's grassy eastern slopes was a trick of the angle, and that they would tip in our favour as we got closer. Now we were climbing the glen they looked every bit as steep as they did at the valley's head.

'Doesn't look as steep, does it?' Jim shouted back at me.

'Sorry?'

'I think we should head straight up here.'

He pointed a hand directly up the slope where, after a long, grassy ramp, a snake of grass slunk through a band of crags to reach the summit ridge.

'Perhaps a little further along ... Might catch us out at the top.'

Jim looked back to the slope and waggled his head as if appraising the idea.

'OK.' He didn't sound convinced, but continued on.

I was enjoying the feeling of walking with someone else again. The familiar bits of banter, groans of discomfort, remarks about the weather – and the general division of every emotion, from uncertainty to awe, fear to joy – these are all the things you miss when walking alone. I was even enjoying the little, unspoken competition that goes on between walkers – generally male walkers, it has to be said – of not wanting to fall too far behind or show weakness too obviously. Hillwalking is quite an intense way of getting to know someone. Jim and I might have lived next door to each other, but we'd never made decisions on a mountain together, and those can be really quite important –especially when the mountain in question has little in the way of paths, an element of complexity and something of a snarl. All of a sudden you're making decisions that, if unwise, could have dangerous consequences.

You also notice each other's strengths fairly quickly and – I love this about hillwalking – completely wordlessly and automatically award responsibility accordingly. We seemed to have fairly quickly fallen into our respective roles. Jim seemed to be a pretty handy navigator with a fondness for working out timing legs – probably a pilot thing – and also had a fitness edge, so was usually to be found a hundred metres or so up ahead. As for me, despite being without doubt far more proficient at heavy breathing and deciding when we should stop for rests, I was fairly confident that, from experience, I was also better at visually assessing routes up dodgy-looking mountains that turned out to be less dodgy up close. This last one was a qualification I was beginning to wonder about, as when we were halfway up the glen Askival was still looking pretty mean and I could sense Jim looking uneasily back towards me as we closed on the mountain.

'Are you sure we can do this? Still looks gnarly.'

'It'll look better up close. I'm sure it will.'

Soon we were beginning to freelance our way up the grassy ramp towards the ridge. As it turned out, overall this slope wasn't as steep as it seemed, but cruelly got steeper the higher we went. When climbing a grassy slope you don't really concentrate on what's happening behind and below you; you just get your head down and crack on with it. It's sometimes a surprise, therefore, when you turn round, look down, and are shocked by the realisation that should you slip it would be quite a long time before you stopped.

I was following Jim, who seemed to be making a good job of finding the easiest route, when I turned around to appraise our rising perspective on the glen and breathe heavily for a while. It was then that I saw it: there, lazily cruising up the valley below us, wings barely flexing, the sun catching a chocolate brown back slimming to a fan of brilliant white, was an absolutely enormous bird.

I shrieked up to Jim and pointed. This was one of Rùm's more recent and elusive additions: the white-tailed eagle. I'd hoped to see one but didn't really think I would.

Often called the sea eagle, it's one in a sad list of grand birds hunted out of existence in Britain during the early 20th century. With a wingspan of over two metres, a body the size of a German shepherd, a hooked yellow beak and claws made for dismemberment, it's Britain's largest bird of prey and is thought to be the eagle with the largest wingspan in the world. Its eyes – as big as a man's – are capable of spotting fish below the surface of coastal waters as it swoops to snatch them. It's a magnificent animal, and a rare sight.

Thanks to poison-baiting farmers, gun-wielding fishermen and Victorian trophy hunters, the white-tailed eagle – like its cousin the golden eagle in England, and the poor, beautiful red kite* – was persecuted out of existence during the 18th and 19th centuries. The last breeding pair on Rùm died in 1907, with the final indigenous pair – on Skye – succumbing less than a decade later. After 60 years of coastal skies devoid of the bird, a reintroduction programme took place on Rùm, spearheaded by the Scottish Conservancy Council.

Between 1975 and 1985, 82 young eagles – sweetly known as 'eaglets' – were imported from Scandinavia and, after being reared to fledging age in captivity, released onto the island. Their eventual breeding success was made all the more impressive in that these first juveniles had no parental guidance – no birds from which to learn the skills needed for survival. But they thrived, establishing eyries on Rùm and neighbouring Mull. Three more reintroduction programmes took place in subsequent years, taking the total number of white-tailed eagles reintroduced to various areas of coastal Scotland since 1975 to 226. And they appear to be happy. In 2010, 52 pairs of eagles raised 46 fledglings, and the numbers are increasing every year. And how splendid that it all started right here, on the mountainous little Isle of Rùm.

As we watched the eagle fly towards the crags at the head of the valley, I wondered where this particular bird's story began and what it was up to. Maybe it was carrying food to its own screeching fledglings in the nest. Or maybe it was keeping an eye on the two strange creatures – one of them breathing very heavily – currently making their way towards a stronghold of

---

* In all of these cases, whilst landowners and gamekeepers didn't help, decimation of the birds' habitat didn't either. Red kites are currently enjoying a successful resurgence in England thanks to a reintroduction programme; alas, England's golden eagle population numbers just one single, presumably deeply lonely, male, which haunts the crags beside Haweswater in the Lake District.

a favoured prey. This, the Manx shearwater, is another bird that favours Rùm in particular. During its breeding season the cliffs around the island once hosted a third of the world's population of this small relative of the albatross, whose maudlin cries gave rise to the local superstition that they were the souls of lost sailors. But indicative of the island's delicate ecosystem, predation by the non-indigenous brown rat – as well as just about anything else which hunts on Rùm (ground evasion is not this bird's strongest suit) – has seen numbers fall.

Every now and again, as Jim and I ascended further, a crook of rock, burrow or a hollow littered with tattered, greasy feathers revealed the now-vacated nest of a 'Manxie', most of which had departed from the island until the following spring.

Askival still wasn't looking any more welcoming by the time we crested the skyline and took our first steps along the walkway linking it to Beinn nan Stac, but views over the Sound of Rùm to Eigg and the mainland suddenly greeted us. After the tiring rigging-climb of the grass it was an electrifying reward, like walking the broad yardarm of a ship at sea.

It had turned into a glorious day. High cloud the texture of beach ripples had burned off over the course of the morning, giving way to a sky of thinly diffused white sun. Across the valley, bulky Sgùrr nan Gillean and Ainshval stood back-lit. Everything was sharp and silvered, with just a hint of autumnal chill on the wind.

We were almost there, although the leisurely saunter along the ridge wasn't something either of us wanted to rush. Ahead, drawing ever nearer, the blunt nose of Askival was at least now close enough to appear a possible, if not exactly straightforward, way up. The south buttress appeared to be a collapsed wall of grey gabbro, grippy and dry, but steep and composed of blocks big enough to make a reach awkward and a fall unthinkable. To the side a chute of rock seemed to offer an easier – if slightly looser – passage to the summit, which appeared to lie just beyond it.

Jim was assessing the map when I caught up with him, and looking with a creased brow across the valley towards Ainshval and Sgùrr nan Gillean.

'Askival is the highest on Rùm?'

I nodded.

'Which means it's higher than those?'

He pointed across the valley to the two mountains opposite. I followed his gaze and quickly understood. Even compensating for unreliable eyeline comparisons, we were nowhere near the same height as them, let alone above them.

'You know, I don't think we're anywhere near the top. I think this,' he said, indicating the buttress ahead, 'is a false top. We still have a few hundred metres of ascent to find from somewhere.'

I looked up at the buttress. I'd been preparing to suggest we give it a go, but now it appeared that it might only be the first in a series of unseen obstacles hidden by perspective, this didn't seem like such a clever idea. The map didn't give much away at this scale; I pulled out my camera and found a photograph I'd taken of Askival from the bothy, and zoomed in to the summit. Sure enough, its intimidating appearance from a distance was not because of this buttress; there was a series of rock steps beyond this one. We still had a way to go.

Given we didn't know what lay beyond, we opted to bypass the buttress and make a rising traverse over the steep, boulder-littered flank of Askival's summit cone. In truth it probably wasn't any less treacherous, but it wasn't frightening either. The boulders were sound and grippy, and there were some magnificent volcanic textures to be found within them. Jim went first initially, then I took over, and we continued to leap-frog one another as we picked our way ever upwards, ever more steeply, up the side of the pathless mountain's highest reaches. The ground angled steeply down, but it wasn't so bad. I remarked to Jim halfway up how curious it was that a slope made up of sharp, wounding boulders felt a lot less frightening than one made of friendly grass. Boulders gave you comfort – you could cling to them and, however painfully, they'd stop you if you slipped. With steep grass you had nothing to grab, nothing to grip. Slip, and you'd just keep going.

The last section was a blast. When eventually we reached the edge of the west ridge we were almost on the summit. The northern side of Askival is probably the most spectacular part of the mountain, as Jim and I discovered when we looked over the edge of the west ridge. The good news was that visually we were certainly in the best place to appreciate that. The drop is sheer, and immediately upon looking over it my legs became light and lively with the jangle of adrenaline. From where we stood we could see a few people walking along the grassy skywalk leading to Hallival, far below us. Tall fingers of rock poking from the skin of the mountain and drops of hundreds of metres separated us from them. As we watched, two little sticks of red far below on the ridge began to make their way away from us towards the tilted, terrace-patterned wedge of Askival's 722-metre neighbour. It would certainly seem we had taken the less-travelled route on the peak. Aesthetically better? Perhaps not. More satisfying? Certainly.

Together we scrambled up the last few metres to the top, marked by a trig point cemented from the native stone. The summit was large, unthreatening and deserted, and although the view wasn't as commanding as I'd thought it would be, it would be a lie to say it wasn't awesome. The wall of mountains on the other side of the glen blocked out much of the view of Rùm's western edge, but the peaks themselves more than made up for this loss. We could see a minute figure making the final few steps to the summit of Ainshval, directly opposite – a tiny moving splinter on the mountain's black skyline. It reached the summit, barely broke stride and continued with my eyes. I followed the dauntingly steep route down from Ainshval's top into the crease between it and Trollabhal. Then another massive ascent up difficult-looking rocks. It seemed a long, hard way for such a tiny thing. I expect we looked little different to whomever it was, standing atop the bristling Askival. Our peak had looked similarly daunting hours earlier.

We spent a while on the summit, enjoying the maritime air and the views to Eigg and the cloud-shrouded mainland. Then, at a mutual nod, wordlessly we began to make our way towards our agreed way down – the west ridge. The descent was challenging and steep, but not perilous. Time and again we met bands of crags we couldn't descend, necessitating a detour. The little roof of Dibidil bothy, tacked onto its little platform where the valley met the sea, never left our sight, taunting us down. Then, as we reached the floor of the glen, it became ever larger with our growing tiredness. By the time we crossed the Dibidil River, we were close enough to make out the door, and the figure standing outside it.

This is how bothying works: you don't need permission. You can't book; there's no fee; the buildings stand open. You need exactly the same things you'd take if you were camping, apart from a tent. But you do still need to take a tent – or some form of shelter – because although there's every chance you might have these atmospheric little places to yourself, in high season many bothies beneath popular mountains become full. If you want a modicum of comfort in this circumstance, you're better off outside. Whatever happens, there's no guarantee you'll be alone. And whilst this is usually to be welcomed, sometimes – well, sometimes, *this* happens.

We arrived back at the bothy to find a group of three in residence, who we'd earlier – correctly – assumed were occupying the left-hand room of the building. Mick, the tall one we'd spotted standing outside the bothy, seemed the most talkative. We chatted for a while, along the typical lines of the weather and each other's gear, the beauty of the island and the outstanding position of the bothy. Turns out they were staying for a couple of nights, and had lugged in a considerable amount of firewood, some of which they kindly offered to us should we need it.

After a while we made our excuses and wandered inside, eager to remove damp boots and gaiters, and get some food on the go. We were preparing the stove on the table of the bothy when Mick stuck his head round the door and announced that he was going to have a wash outside, and jokingly mentioned that if we were of a sensitive disposition to exercise caution, as there might be some flesh on show. Jim and I both agreed this was very courteous, thanked him and carried on making dinner.

Jim was tending the stove in the weakening light from the window when a few minutes later – like the moon eclipsing the sun – Mick's bare arse swayed past the window and, the rest of him similarly unadorned, swaggered down the path towards the sea.

'Bloody hell, he's going to be *cold*,' said Jim, spotting him. 'He hasn't even got a towel.' His face darkened. 'Hey, do you think he knows about those fissures? Imagine if he fell down one.'

We both watched him go – a little smear of milky white – as he approached the shore. After a chuckle and a head-shake we carried on cooking.

Around half an hour later we were sitting outside chatting to Colin – another member of their group – in the waning sun, when Mick came back. Mick still wasn't wearing a towel.

Now, I don't have a problem with liberation, natural refreshment, skinny dipping and all that. If Mick had pootled past, grabbed a towel – dammit, a thong even – off the washing line he and his group had comprehensively requisitioned, it would probably only be a colourful footnote in our memory of Dibidil. But he didn't. He joined the conversation. He sashayed around our makeshift dinner area naked as a chimp, at one point gesticulating a point so hard that all kinds of things wobbled. At this, I saw Jim's eyes widen and immediately bury themselves in his food packet. I concentrated on the ground. It was a good ten minutes before anything was covered up.

So to conclude our lesson in bothy conduct: be courteous; sweep up after yourself; don't leave so much as pocket lint behind. And something I find is always a useful litmus test of etiquette when sharing a communal sleeping place is this: if anyone should have cause to start a conversation with the line 'Hey, you're naked!,' you may have crossed a social line.

Later that evening Colin, Mick and the third member of their party – we didn't get his name – lit a fire in their end of the bothy without opening the chimney vent. The room Jim and I were sharing was soon enveloped in thickening, eye-stinging smoke whilst, next door, sounds of confusion and hilarity gradually intensified. After a while Jim's patience broke.

'Hell with this. I'm going outside. Where's the wine?'

Smoked out of the bothy, at the mercy of the few remaining midges of the season, that was that for us. It wasn't bad. Actually, it was rather good as it goes – we'd brought plenty of warm gear, it was a clear night and the wine certainly helped. We sat down on a rock by the shoreline watching a depthless sky of stars traversed by the mist of the Milky Way emerge above. In the absence of a moon and light pollution of any kind, the darkness was totally black. It was a spectacular sight.

A couple of hours later the bothy had fallen quiet and into darkness, and we decided to make our way back. Jim staggered up and switched on his head torch, before turning to me.

'Hey – this was my first bothy experience.' He thought about this for a second before adding: 'Interesting.'

I considered apologising – after all, nobody else had – and reassuring him it wasn't usually like this. But I didn't. We were here for free, we'd be gone tomorrow and at any rate it had certainly been memorable. Who were we to judge people's eccentricities, anyway? We climbed mountains.

* * *

On the subject of eccentricity, we couldn't leave Rùm without paying our respects to a man for whom being colourful was a way of life. His name was Sir George Bullough – and it was he who was responsible for building Rùm's most distinctive human structure. You can see it as you arrive into Loch Scresort and climb the slopes out of Kinloch towards the Cuillin. Made from brown sandstone and nestling amongst trees at the head of the inlet, this is the unique and singularly bonkers Kinloch Castle.

Bullough's father, John, was a canny textile industrialist who in 1887 had bought Rùm to use as his own private hunting estate. John was only able to enjoy his part-time purchase for four years, dying from the effects of smog inhalation in 1891. Rùm then fell into the hands of his flamboyant youngest son – a man firmly committed to the pursuit of 'purposeful idleness', and who six years later set about constructing the monument to his family's wealth that stands to this day.

Knighted in 1901 by Edward VII for donating his 221-foot yacht *Rhouma* to the Boer War effort, Sir George married Monique Lily de la Pasture, and the couple began hosting opulent shooting tours on the island, turning away those who were not there by specific invitation. Rùm's reputation as a 'forbidden isle' probably developed during this period, although the island had long been used for game hunting (and before that subsistence, which had seen the island's native deer wiped out).

The island's population reached its peak of 400 in 1795 but Rùm didn't escape the Clearances. Its entire population was shipped off to Nova Scotia in 1826 to make way for 8,000 head of sheep* and a number of families to manage them. Sheep-farming continued throughout much of the 19th century,

---

* Concerning Scottish islands and sheep: whilst roundly scorned for association with the Clearances, the little woolies haven't always had it that easy, either. In 1942, amidst fears of a biochemical attack from Germany, a flock of sheep on Gruinard Island – near Loch Broom in the north-west Highlands – was intentionally wiped out by anthrax, a desperately horrible bacterium that effects the skin, heart, lungs and digestive system. The island was contaminated so comprehensively it was out of bounds for half a century. After a cleanup in 1986, a flock of sheep was again introduced to prove it was successful. Thankfully for all – not least the sheep – it was.

and cottages were built at Dibidil, the bay of Harris, Papadil and Guirdil* –
where there's another bothy – to house the shepherds.

Rùm has in fact been inhabited since about 8,000 BC. A Mesolithic settlement yielding thousands of artefacts was discovered north of Kinloch, and is
considered one of the oldest human settlements in Scotland. Carved crosses
mark the passage of Christian hermits in the 9th century, and crofters and
fishermen lived on the island in the intervening years. Kinloch Castle, however,
doesn't possess a single ancient wall; it's more stylised palace than castle,
standing amidst vivid green lawns and flaunting turrets and towers like a
Gothic film set – 'bizarre, battlemented and pseudo baronial', as one historian
has put it. But it's all rather nicely done, and both the castle and its contents
are an enduring statement to Sir George Bullough's eccentricities and the
seemingly limitless excesses of industrial wealth.

Some of Sir George's additions were peculiar, although probably the sort
of thing that seemed savvy purchases at the time. One of these is an odd
Victorian instrument called the Imhof & Mukle Orchestrion, which by all
accounts was a sort of early home entertainment system. The orchestrion's big
idea was that it had an actual instrument automatically play a predefined
sequence of music, as opposed to just amplifying a recording, as on a gramo-
phone. The machine read the music off a perforated spool, which instructed
the built-in organ and an array of percussion instruments what to play and
when. Huge – it would take up a sizeable chunk of anyone's house – and
desperately clever for the time, it was intended to give the illusion of a live
band classily playing away in your private domicile. It completely failed in this
(sounding instead like a Wurlitzer player slumped dead against the keys
whilst a nearby drum kit fell down a flight of stairs, underwater), but as show-
pieces went, it was a whopper.† The orchestrion remains in the castle to this
day, as do an early 1900 Steinway concert grand piano, a selection of animal
rugs, strange artistic tokens from the Far East (the Bulloughs were personal

---

* *Dil* is a Norse word meaning valley or vale. It's the root of the word 'dale' so frequently
found in upland areas of northern England.

† Only three orchestrions exist today. Whilst my description of its sound is perhaps a little
cruel, according to the castle's literature the one in Kinloch Castle is the only one that still
works.

friends of the Emperor of Japan) and many other things decidedly out of place on a small, thinly populated Hebridean island. The most impressive room – the hall – has been lovingly preserved, and today appears as if momentarily vacated. As the castle guide rather nicely puts it: 'Nothing has gone except the people.'

Sir George also changed the island's name to Rhum (he was worried the title 'Laird of Rùm' might strike quite the wrong note), and as well as making Kinloch Castle the first electrified private house in Scotland, he had a basic type of air conditioning fitted in the billiard room and filled the gardens with all manner of creatures, including hummingbirds and alligators, all of which no doubt impressed his well-to-do guests. Sadly, the inhabitants of this ambitious menagerie – somewhat inevitably – met sticky ends: the hummingbirds fell victim to a failure of the early-model central heating, and the alligators escaped and were later shot under the alarming justification of 'interfering with the comfort of the guests'.

For a number of years the Bulloughs' lifestyle maintained its opulent stride, but the arrival of war in 1914 marked the beginning of the end. The estate's able-bodied workers went off to fight in the trenches; only two came back. The castle, left vacant for the duration of the war, fell into disrepair, and whilst the Bulloughs did return, the glamour of their idyll had faded.

Sir George Bullough died in 1939, golfing. His widow, Lady Monica, returned to Rùm on occasion until her death aged 98 in 1967, at some point granting permission to W. H. Murray for his climbing trip. The Bulloughs – all of them – are buried in a Doric-style mausoleum in the bay of Harris, on the island's west coast.

To her eternal credit, ten years before her death Lady Monica sold Rùm to the Nature Conservancy Council with the understanding that it would be preserved as a nature reserve. Included in the sum – £20,000, roughly £1 an acre – was the castle and its contents, with the understanding it be maintained 'as far as may be practical'.

Today, the whole island is a national nature reserve. The sheep are gone and, thanks to their reintroduction by Lord Salisbury in the 19th century, red deer are thriving. Otters play in its waters and two species of eagle nest in its mountains. The people living on Rùm are mostly employees of Scottish Natural Heritage, together with their families and a schoolteacher. A community trust launched in 2007 ensures that the 22-strong population of Rùm owns itself and its assets. The castle is immaculate, although being entirely reliant on Scottish Natural Heritage and tourism – and something of a pain to maintain – its future is uncertain. But the impression you get here is of an island gradually returning to a near-natural state – with assistance, where necessary – beneath the watch of that singularly dramatic mountain range. It's a beautiful thing to see.

In the morning sun Jim and I sat quietly, boots off, in front of the castle, looking out across Loch Scresort. After an eventually peaceful night in the mercifully smoke-free bothy, we'd woken to a crimson dawn beautifully fracturing the sky above Eigg. Mindful of both the muddy path and the somewhat vague repatriation instructions regarding the ferry, we'd set off at a fair clip not long after.

Reaching Kinloch at 10 a.m., we took the opportunity to poke around the achingly serene buildings at the head of the loch, before settling on the emerald grass of the castle's lawn. Idly in and out of Jim's hands was one of the two grim relics we'd discovered on the walk out: a small antler, broken and bloodied at the hilt. Not far away from it on the hillside I'd found a spent .270 rifle cartridge case, bright brass against the heather.

Eventually, as 11 a.m. approached, we dragged ourselves to our feet, put our boots back on and made our way along the shore to the slipway. Just over two hours later, the ferry left for Mallaig.

12 LIFE

The room is golden with lamplight on wood. The windows are black. It's 12.15 a.m. and Kenny sits at the bar of the Old Forge in Inverie. Born on Harris, he has lived here for over 50 years, since his father took an estate job stalking deer on the mountains. His first language is Gaelic. This lends his English a textured, lengthening burr, tapered even further by the fact that he's clearly been in the pub for a while.

'The names of the lochs to the north and the south ...' he begins. 'You know, Loch Hourn means "Loch Hell". Loch Nevis is "Loch Heaven". So here in Knoydart,' he paws a line along the table between two empty beer glasses, 'you're between heaven ... and hell.'

Kenny tells us about a valley to the north amongst the high mountains of the Knoydart peninsula, Coire Dhorrcail. He says that even amongst Scottish glens the valley is notable for its extraordinary beauty. And when the mountain from which it was scraped comes into the conversation his chest swells, and for a moment I think he's going to stand and climb onto his chair.

'This hill is a finer hill than Ben Nevis. When I was a boy I was told by my father it was the loveliest in Scotland.'

He nods solemnly, before enunciating the two Gaelic words that comprise the name of the mountain as one purring syllable: '*Larrrven.*'

The day had begun early – as many do hereabouts – in Mallaig, waiting for a boat. Over-sharpened by coffee, Jim and I were standing to the side of the main harbour when a tall man of maturing years strode towards us with the stoop of a beanpole teenager. Wearing a cable-knit sweater, bent baseball cap and a US Navy parka and wellies (amongst other things), he introduced himself as John and indicated the small front-loading boat jostling below us against the jetty wall.

'Reckon you're it. So whenever you're ready.'

John lived in Inverie. He pointed out his house to us as the boat began inching out into the sound where the asphalt-coloured mouth of Loch Nevis met the sea under a sky of white, high cloud. The house at the bottom of that valley was his, he said, indicating it with a point. His accent missed the t's off 'bottom'. He definitely wasn't Scottish.

'Oh, Hertfordshire, originally,' he confirmed cheerily when asked.

I wondered what route brought him from the Home Counties to navigating the ferry between Mallaig and the most remote village in Britain. At this he grinned and shrugged.

'Chance.'

As we buffeted across the water, catching the odd, invigorating burst of spray, the tiny, dotted white stripe of Inverie appeared straight ahead. Behind it, layered back to the horizon and sprawling down to the head of Loch Nevis, the mountains of Knoydart stood like a battalion of tanks. Against them, the buildings of Inverie – mainland Britain's most remote village – looked pitifully tiny. Nestled delicately between the water and the mountains like a salty tide mark, it looked as if a hearty slosh from the loch might wash it away.

The boat comprised an open loading bay the size of a Land Rover, a dropleaf bow and a bridge at the back. Presumably it was used for ferrying supplies across to the 70 souls who inhabit Inverie, as well as the odd foot passenger or 4x4. There were no seats. Salt water splashed around our feet. The engine roared in our ears. The whole thing just felt fantastically utilitarian. I looked over at Jim on the other side of the loading bay, his coat zipped to the neck. I gave him a thumbs-up, and he shouted something back.

'Feels like D-Day.'

Travelling by boat to the village of Inverie isn't some needless contrivance to lend your arrival extra occasion. Despite being part of the mainland, you can only get to Inverie by two ways: half an hour on a boat, or eight hours on foot – and even then, only from a road-head tortuously removed from anything else. Both have merits, and this way had two for us: one, John and his boat got us there with time to spare, and two, we arrived with spare energy. You see, Knoydart isn't quite like other mountain places in Britain. It really isn't quite like them at all.

* * *

'A knuckled fist of land rooted in the long arm of Glen Garry,' is how W. H. Murray rather brilliantly described Knoydart. He added that it was 'the only big peninsula of the West Highlands to retain to the present day its ancient isolation'. That was in 1968, and nothing has changed. In fact – like many of the places we've seen – Knoydart is emptier today than it has ever been.

The place has a particular resonance to mountain walkers that echoes deep. Those who know of Knoydart but have never been, crave it; those who have, speak of it with reverence, dread or that implacable mix of the two you encounter so often in this world.

Its location helps, of course. Approach from the east and Knoydart is an ever-distant hinterland of sharp, very high summits, sprawling but densely clutched. From the coast these constitute the most westerly high mountains of the Scottish mainland. If they look distant and inaccessible, that's because they are – they're bruisers to even get to the bottom of, let alone climb.

And this is the next bouquet of intrigue that helps affirm Knoydart as uniquely tucked away: very few paths trouble its capacious interior. Within the 85 square miles that make up the peninsula proper, you can count the official paths and tracks that sidle through it on a single hand. None of them makes any proper headway over the mountains; there are skeletal lines of passage that can be detected over the highest points of the highest peaks, but nothing approaching a find-and-stick-to handrail. Given the proclivity of the area to hold on to blinding cloud, this would make finding your way difficult in itself for all but the most competent navigators, but Knoydart has even more up its sleeve to bewilder the intrepid.

First, the rock that makes up its mountains contains intermittently high volumes of iron ore. Iron ore is magnetic; so are compass needles. In the worst cases, at sufficiently close proximity, this ground iron can send your navigational needle into worried, inaccurate spasms. Whilst this is likely to be local- ised to the rock beneath you and thus easily solved (walk a few paces then try again), what it does leave you with is a general sense of distrust about any navigational decisions committed to on the hill.

And even if you're blessed with clear conditions, navigational pauses will be frequent. Knoydart's other name is the Rough Bounds, and it's apt. The term isn't restricted to Knoydart; technically, the Rough Bounds also include neighbouring Moidart, Arisaig and Morar as far south as Loch Shiel. But it's in Knoydart that some of the most complex, geologically jumbled and indecisive terrain in Britain holds sway. It's as if a massive, long-ridged, elegant mountain once stood here that has since collapsed to rubble and been grouted with heather, forest and river.

Knoydart is therefore a perplexing foe to hillwalkers. The mountains don't join up like they're supposed to, making multi-summit traverses difficult and energy-sapping. There are thirteen separate mountains on the Knoydart peninsula,* highest of all of them being Sgùrr na Ciche – 'Peak of the Breast' – which greedily snares your attention when it slides into view from whichever angle you approach. It's almost conical, and makes for a dramatic outline at the head of Loch Nevis. So striking and raked is its form that little hides amongst it for subsequent discovery, the mountain being quite featureless. The most remarkable thing about it is its shape.

The second-highest, however, is different. Ladhar Bheinn (pronounced *Larven* – silent *dh* and a *v* for the *bh*) is undoubtedly one of the great mountains of Scotland. It's certainly the greatest in Knoydart.

You'd think the whole area has been preserved in this wild way conscientiously, as some sort of epitaph to a more unwieldy, unhinged Britain. But it hasn't. Knoydart's history is as tumultuous as its skyline. Whilst recent years have seen a revolution in its fortunes, the truth is that throughout its troubled, violent past, Knoydart has deftly managed to put off, scare away or appear off limits to anyone who has ventured an exploratory limb across its borders. Filling the pages of its history have been outlaws, cattle rustlers, gangsters, political deviants, religious outcasts, hated aristocrats and land raiders, all of them playing out their dramas against a backdrop of astonishing geology, heavy weather and a wild natural habitat of extraordinary fecundity. It's like a cross between the Wild West and *Jurassic Park*.

Today, people call Knoydart Britain's 'last wilderness'. Dramatic as this sounds, in reality it sells the place rather short. If you're looking for a big,

---

* Thorny issue again, but as with any other such cases, this number is according to the rule laid out by Alan Dawson in *The Relative Hills of Britain*: that is to say, a hill or mountain is considered by its height relative to everything around it, rather than simply its bare elevation above sea level. Dawson's list is the best, as it quite simply has more in it, isn't snobbish about height and is much more inclusive of smaller, charismatic hills.

empty place, it's no more a wilderness than the 'Great Wilderness' we saw from the summit of An Teallach, and by comparison there's nothing about Knoydart that marks it out as being particularly slow on the uptake or comparatively dwindling.

Wilderness, as we've seen, is a misleading term for a landscape that, in mankind's living memory – before woodcutters and sheep got to work – resembled something really quite different. But Knoydart is rare and unique in and of itself; and if this is true of the land, it's also true of the life that resides here. The human life in particular.

This is the final lure. Today, Knoydart is perhaps the most irresistible mountain place in Britain not for its lack of life, but because of the life it has. The idea that nestled on the edge of Loch Nevis, completely cut off from the mainland road system, accessible only by foot or by boat, lies a tiny, twinkling village of 70 souls, whose lives revolve around each other, and the mountains and the loch and the animals who dwell there. And, of course, the place where they all meet and swap tales after a hard day battered by the Rough Bounds: one of the most gleefully infamous pubs in the Scottish Highlands. Now really; who could resist that?

As the boat pulled up the pier at Inverie, and John began tossing ropes and doing violent things with levers, a grinning young boy on a BMX bike skidded to a halt near the trees at the top of the slipway. Emblazoned on the front of his handlebars on a blue and grey sign was one word: POLICE.

The lady with him was his mum, Jackie Robertson. She waved hello as John cut the boat's engine and silence descended on the little jetty. Inverie has no public roads – just a rough-surfaced track, up and down which a few Land Rovers occasionally pootle – so there's no traffic noise. All Jim and I heard as we stepped off John's ferry was the sound of the water, wind through the trees, birds, nautical clinks and human voices. It was like stepping out of a gale into shelter.

Jackie and her husband Ian were veterans of Inverie, having moved to the village twenty years ago. Much of that time had been spent running the aforementioned pub, the Old Forge, steadily turning it not only into a local institution but a national treasure, and one that would always retain its raffish intimacy by the very nature of its location. The pub's slogan reads: 'Walkers, yachties, trampers, dogs, kids, landlubbers, musicians, anarchists and politicians welcome. Impromptu ceilidhs – bring your own instruments, or use ours.' They'd sold the pub eighteen months earlier to focus on their accommodation business, but – and this is something you tend to find here – their involvement hadn't stopped. In a place as small and isolated as Inverie, everybody is involved in everything.

I'd been to Inverie once before, and remember being oddly moved by it. Part of the reason for this is probably because, to anyone who walks across Knoydart – as we had, on this occasion – the amber lights of Inverie peeping through the rainy gloom after twenty miles of rough track and mountain come as a flood of intense relief. The people we found were far from being social outcasts; they were friendly, funny, interesting and welcoming in the unconditional way that can take people used to the collective cold shoulder of urban living quite by surprise. We ended up in the pub and, after vowing to take it easy, became ensnared in an impromptu sing-along. We got really quite drunk. Then, the following day we walked all the way back with painful heads, out through Knoydart, back to the rest of the world.

Jackie and Ian were still running the pub on that first visit three years ago; I'd got back in touch and they'd very kindly offered to put Jim and me up in their home for the night. Sitting in the living room of their spacious house overlooking the loch, watching their clever, happy children running around, snatching up musical instruments, darting in and out of the house – no traffic to worry about in a place with no roads, after all – I again began to feel deep admiration and the stirrings of mild envy. Probably I was guilty, like so many, of focusing too heavily on what might be lost by living in a remote place like Inverie: supermarkets, takeaways of every flavour, a seamless connection to the rest of the country. But you don't sense loss in the people here. All you see is what you gain: a willingness to chat, a sense of community, a feeling of belonging and a freedom from the fears of the rest of the mainland. Life wasn't all that different. People in Inverie just relied that little bit more on things running smoothly. For you and me, if the weather's bad it might mean not sitting out in the garden. For people in Inverie it might mean they don't make an appointment, do the shopping, see a relative, get to work. They adapt, because they have to. That's what you need to do to live in such a place – somewhere with one of the most rugged mountain regions of Britain as your backyard.

The first time I came to Inverie was in 2011 for *Trail*, and it rained. My God, it rained. Approaching the peninsula from the land is a different experience altogether to approaching it from the sea. After driving upcountry beneath Ben Nevis, you leave the main A87 road at Loch Garry, and enter a hard place of grey hillside and brooding skylines occasionally interrupted by lines of pylons and the antlers of wandering deer. The road goes on for over twenty miles – leaving Loch Garry, entering a hinterland then picking up the sinuous beginnings of Loch Quoich, shaped on the map like a road-killed fox, paws to the sky, supine in shock.

The area between Loch Garry and Loch Hourn is a difficult place to find *beautiful*, but it certainly stirs awe. Perhaps it was just the monochromatic conditions, but I remember finding this vast, empty place slung wide between the skylines of mossy ridges around the road intimidating, and the atmosphere singularly oppressive. The road itself – in places just a shallow river of rainwater runoff, its edges crumbling in the rain, which falls more heavily and in greater abundance here than anywhere else in the Highlands – kept on, a spindly tape of watery tarmac. It then dropped, dropped and dropped again to a clutch of buildings at the head of a far grander loch, whose extent on this particular evening was masked by a blanket of cloud. This settlement is Kinloch* Hourn – the beginning of Knoydart, and the end of the road.

Loch Hourn is astonishing. The view that greets you as you step onto the shore-hugging path leading to the natural anchorage at Barrisdale – roughly halfway to Inverie – is extraordinary for Britain. As you walk along the south shore, occasionally festooned with stands of old Scots pine, their bark a russet so vivid it looks like it's bleeding, you look across the loch to its northern shore, beyond which is a line of mountains, some dropping from heights of almost a thousand metres to sea level in much less than one horizontal mile. Further along, frayed stripes of waterfalls fall into the loch.

---

* 'Kinloch' is a word found throughout the Highlands and Islands, typically at significant points of watery settlement or anchorage. The word is actually a corrupted combination of Gaelic words – *ceann* and *loch* – which means 'head of loch'. Place names can mean simply that – such as Kinloch on Rùm – or have a specific as a suffix, as in Kinloch Hourn: 'head of Loch Hourn'.

The loch itself, with its elegant, petalled edge, widens and curves as it draws the eye along its length, becoming mighty as it approaches the Sound of Sleet, where it meets the sea. It's one of the most spectacular, powerful natural visions in the land, but its isolation means nobody really knows it. Show someone a picture of it and they would immediately think it was Norway, New Zealand or Iceland here, hugged into the affray of our own West Highlands, is a fjord. This fact, as is often the case in Scotland, is hiding in plain sight within the name 'Knoydart'. In it, not only do we have a fjord, but one named by a visiting Viking: Knut's fjord. W. H. Murray acknowledged the forbidding peculiarity of Loch Hourn in his description of it in *The West Highlands of Scotland*. 'Loch Hourn is sombre even on days of sun ... no sun shines on the Knoydart shore for five months of winter.'

That day we walked a tenth of Scotland's breadth to get to Inverie. It was one of the hardest days I'd ever had in the mountains, but I can't recommend it highly enough. It gives you the flipside to the seaward approach to Knoydart, and any augmentation to a single way in to this kaleidoscopic place should be eagerly seized. You can never really say you know Knoydart unless you've approached it from all sides; the same can be said about many mountains, too, but few more so than Ladhar Bheinn.

Jim and I left Jackie at the top of the track that leads north from Inverie and we dived into a patch of wood plunging east into Knoydart's interior. As we entered the trees the crackle of raindrops on leaves filled our ears. Ahead, between parallel bars of barbed pine, the grey banner of sky was cut by a ridgeline. It didn't look sharp, but it looked high and far away. We stared at it in silence, turned to each other with raised eyebrows, then pressed on.

Soon the track left the woods and joined the lively course of the Allt Coire Torr an Asgaill, the river named for the corrie into which the track arced, then eventually petered out. Our target was the *folach* – a roofless ruined building on the edge of a heart-shaped patch of trees that marked the ascent route onto the southern flanks of the mountain.

Nothing comes easy in Knoydart. Distances are stretched, approaches swallow up hours, and then you've still got the mountains themselves to tackle. Ladhar Bheinn is perhaps least intimidating from the south, but it's still high. The mountain stands with its guts out to the north-east, where deeply gouged corries face Loch Hourn and several lean ridges ascend from the water's edge like the ribs of a starving dog. From the south, the mountain is a long, largely featureless slope, terminating in round shoulders and a flat, short summit ridge. Our approach – like most made from Inverie – aimed for the left shoulder between Ladhar Bheinn and its intimidating-looking 700-metre outlier, An Dìollaid.

It had been An Dìollaid's top we'd seen through the trees. Jim gave a little cry of anguish when he looked at the map and realised the top of this seemingly giant peak was a full 300 metres lower than our own objective.

By the time we reached the skeletal *folach* the rain had eased, but the top third of Ladhar Bheinn was still covered by low cloud. Rounding the edge of the wood, Jim and I began to make our way through the thick heather alongside a stream that descended in stepped falls from the mountainside. Gradually, the incline began to rake, and we started to climb. It was relentless, but in Britain steep slopes are by their nature mostly brief. Within half an hour, and with intermittent stops, we emerged onto the broad, grassy *bealach* between An Dìollaid and Ladhar Bheinn. We were on the very edge of the cloud; instead of an expansive reveal of the landscape, all we could see were mist-softened ridgelines, the flanks of the hills to the north and absolutely nothing of Ladhar Bheinn's summit. We were in a silent world of soft green and grey. To our right, grass led steeply up into the murk.

Things look bigger and harder in mist, the lack of visibility twisting your sense of perspective and robbing your eyes of intervening detail. Because you can only see the outline of the hill and not the way up it, your brain can only interpret what it's got to work with and therefore hits the warning button. But the truth is, if you're walking in mist, anything you see ahead of you must by definition be close. Sure enough, as you get nearer to it, the seemingly distant skyline you've been working towards is suddenly upon you and a lot more surmountable than you originally thought.

This was pretty much how it went for Jim and me as we approached the summit ridge of Ladhar Bheinn. We'd looked at the map at the *bealach* and attempted to mentally log the changes in terrain that were coming – steep, less steep, a bend to the left, steepening again, a narrowing top. I'd turned on my phone's map, put it in my pocket and the pair of us had proceeded by sight up the ridge, eager to feel our way with our senses if we could. It's a big ridge at first, with plenty of space and unthreatening slopes. We moved over to the left as we worked up it, and then things changed. The ridge ends in a grassy step that falls steeply into the northern chasm of Coire na Dìollaide. It was filled with grey clag, a slope descending into nothing.

We were in what was becoming our normal formation – Jim ahead, me fifty metres or so back. A couple of times he'd edged towards the limit of my visibility as we climbed, and I called for him to wait; as the ridge began to narrow we walked together. Navigation was no longer an issue when the ridge straightened and thinned, as there was clearly only one way to go. After a hundred metres or so it flattened, and something appeared ahead.

Ladhar Bheinn hits its roof in twin, often-confused tops at 1,010 and 1,020 metres. The first is the most grandly celebrated on the ground, but unusually it's the lower of the two. This is rather cruel; many stop and turn here, thinking they've reached the mountain's highest point, when in fact the true top lies a couple of hundred metres further along the ridge.

This first top is marked by a fittingly brutal monolith. Most Ordnance Survey trig points are thick-bottomed, angular trapezoids, but on higher, more remote Scottish peaks many are circular tubes called Vanessa Pillars. Nobody's really sure who Vanessa was, but her pillars are a favourite of trig-point builders as she's easy to construct. Ladhar Bheinn's trig point is – was – a Vanessa, and it's seen better days. As with many broken pillars on high mountains, the story goes that multiple lightning strikes have reduced Trig Point S9806 to its current wrecked state. At some point, however, someone has picked up a huge, sharp shard of native rock and stabbed it into the top of the pillar, creating a rather gruesome sculpture of nature versus culture in the process.

But what Vanessa very much isn't is the top of the mountain. That's marked by a small pile of stones further along the ridge. Jim and I arrived, shook hands, and stood for a few moments in the mist. We were at this point a long way from anywhere, and it felt as much, despite – or perhaps because of – the weather. One of the great views of the Highlands lurked behind us. We'd see none of it today.

We stayed awhile, eating and drinking, listening to the silence. Then Jim pulled out the map and we both converged on it.

The way down from Ladhar Bheinn – unless you want to retrace your steps – is a complicated series of wriggles between a steep slope and a deep cliff. At the eastern end of the mountain's summit ridge the way splits: the name 'Ladhar Bheinn' means 'Forked Mountain', and it could well be this very divergence that gave the mountain its name. It's imperative you take the correct fork; they might be split by 90 degrees but in the confusion of thick mist it's a lot easier than you'd think to make an error. It's in fact the difference between a treacherous descent towards Barrisdale Bay and Loch Hourn, and turning back towards civilisation at Inverie – and correcting one back to the other is impossible without retracing your steps. Confident we'd made the right call, Jim and I began descending the complexity that is Ladhar Bheinn's south-east ridge. Ahead of us the mist was filled with strange shapes.

The first thing that's unusual about this ridge is that it's green. From a distance to the north, Ladhar Bheinn looks sharp and dark, but closer inspection reveals that much of its top is covered with bulbous tumours of springy coral-like vegetation, a mixture of grasses and sphagnum moss that hangs over the lips of cliffs like velvet loosened from an antler. It's unusual for a mountain this high and dramatic to have such verdant higher reaches, as if the mountain itself is alive.

The ground beneath this vegetative pelt descends in steps, like the edge of a collapsing causeway. As Jim and I made our way down the ridge the drop to our left became vertical, and the narrow path we'd joined took a line that carried us out onto huge blocks overhanging the drop. I watched as Jim – fifty metres or so ahead – walked out onto a block the size of an upended bus. The lower edge of the block cut back in towards the cliff-face; beneath that, mist-filled emptiness. I waited until he was off it before I told him that he'd practically been standing over fresh air.

Every now and then we'd meet something tricky – a down-climb, or a chimney that needed care. The rock was very slippery in the water-saturated air and progress was slow. That, and the constant twists and turns of the terrain, made it impossible to get any kind of consistent pace in a direction in which we had confidence.

The rock on the path had a shimmer to it. The mineral that causes this is mica, which flakes off, sticks to your boots and for days afterwards glitters on your clothing. Where there were sizeable outcrops of rock, often they were inlaid with fascinating metamorphic patterns, a legacy of pressures, thrusts and fractures over tens of millions of years. I stopped to admire one, exquisitely layered; a crumbling onion of metalled rock covered in lichen.

Conditions seemed to be improving, but visibility wasn't. Occasionally through the cloud we caught a glimpse of Sgùrr na Ciche's spired top or the silvery drizzle of Loch Hourn to the north-east – the 'reveal' of the other half of Knoydart, and something I was keen for Jim to see. They amounted to little more than snatches, however. Knoydart remained coy.

Our turn off the ridge was at a spot height at 707 metres, where a low-point nick is reached and offers a line of descent back into Coire Torr an Asgaill at a spot beyond the dangers of hidden cliffs and crags. Beyond this the ridge begins to climb again and becomes the strange, twin-crested Aonach Sgoilte. Jim and I had been gently considering this, but the wet rock and bad visibility had fatally dented our ambition to tackle it.

As we reached the nick a noise made us stop. An animal sound, deep and rough, rose from the mist to the left. Now still, we listened in silence for another. Again it came, and my neck hairs stood vertical. It was like a cross between a cow's *moo* and the bellow of an ape. A long roar, followed by several punctuated barks echoed around the corrie, then silence descended again. I looked at Jim, just as his eyebrows un-knotted and raised hopefully.

'Stag?'

I exhaled.

'Let's bloody hope so.'

One of the great things about walking wild in Britain is that you don't have to worry about what walks with you. Not any more, anyway. This should give the skittish a lot of comfort when settling down for the night on a mountainside or within a shadow-filled forest; there really aren't many wild places that share Britain's enviable absence of threatening wildlife.

It wasn't always so. Depending on how far back you go, the animals that used to roam these areas of the Highlands included key players in the what's-what of alarming things you'd really rather not encounter whilst walking in remote country. Perhaps the most fearful animal to walkers in the Americas and wilder parts of Europe – the brown bear – was once a fixture of the British ecosystem. Deforestation and aggressive hunting during early medieval times depleted Britain's population of Eurasian brown bears, and the last one vanished from Scotland's wilderness sometime between AD 500 and 1000.

Disappearing from the British food chain at around the same time – though in any meaningful way much earlier – was another superb predator: the Eurasian lynx. A creature of rare beauty, the lynx is the size of a golden retriever, with paws as large as a human hand, and is about as secretive as they come. Ecologists estimate there were once in the region of 7,000 lynx roaming the length of Britain. Feeding largely on woodland deer, deforestation for farming in the early Middle Ages forced the few remaining lynx into the open, where they took to killing livestock. Then, naturally, farmers took to killing the lynx.

These days the lynx is considered by many wild-land organisations to be the most viable carnivore for reintroduction to Britain – a popular idea at the moment under the blanket term 're-wilding' – its love of seclusion meaning that it's considered highly unlikely to cause problems to human settlements. Many don't like the idea, worried that the odd lynx will lay catastrophic waste to grouse-shooting grounds, compromise private deer stocks and wreak untold other havoc in the rural economy. Others think that Britain is simply too far from its original wild state to support large predators. If a reintroduction programme were to start, it would almost certainly be somewhere in the West Highlands, probably not far from where Jim and I were right now. Scottish Natural Heritage has the final say, and discussions continue.

If the lynx is facing opposition to its reintroduction, this is nothing compared with the most controversial Old World predator of them all: the wolf. The grey wolf was once the most hated and feared animal in Britain. The Saxons, then inhabiting a Britain still covered in the dark forests of the Middle Ages – including Caledon in Scotland – referred to the month of January as the 'wolf month', no doubt because the scarcity of food emboldened the animals, forcing them into contact with people far more than at other times of the year.

So many were there, and so dangerous were they considered to be, that systematic hunting of the animal took place by royal decree for centuries. Monarch after monarch attempted to rid England completely of wolves, often awarding a bounty to anyone producing tongues or pelts as proof of a kill. This was, as you would expect, wildly successful – there are few references to wolves in England later than the 15th century, with wolves in Wales probably all but extinct by the 12th.

In Scotland, however, wolves remained part of the wilderness until possibly well into the 18th century, conceivably even later. Here the animal was viewed as even more of a hazard to the rural traveller, the wilderness areas of the Highlands being home to the shrinking vestiges of the forests and therefore the greatest number of wolves. In his *Chronicles*, the Elizabethan writer Holinshed makes reference to shelters that were erected along roads as refuges for travellers overtaken by darkness. These shelters – known as *spitals* – were located in particular in the wild-forested areas of Perthshire and Atholl, where wolves were known to hunt after nightfall. Today a trace of this can be found in the names of the places that stand where these wild shelters once did, such as Spittal of Glenmuick and Spittal of Glenshee.

Even the dead didn't escape. The graveyard for the Sutherland community of Eddrachillis had to be sited on the Island of Handa because wolves would habitually dig up the graves. The same is true for the Isle of St Munda on Loch Leven, and the Holy Isle of Innishail – the 'Isle of Peace' – on Loch Awe, amongst doubtless others. In the Forest of Atholl bodies were buried in coffins made from flagstones to prevent scavenging wolves feeding from the dead within. Mary, Queen of Scots, is believed to have hunted wolves in Atholl in the second half of the 16th century, a time when wolf populations in Scotland were at their peak.

There is little that needs to be said regarding this animal's role as a human foe: if there was ever a creature irrevocably immortalised as such – in fairy tales, etchings, horror stories and the campaign that finally eradicated it entirely from British forests and mountains – it's the wolf. How much it deserved this title depends on your point of view, but as far as recorded history of such things goes, wolf attacks on people could never be called common. It's more likely that stories of 'mad wolves' – such as the one alleged to have killed 22 people in 1166, as recorded in the *Annales Cambriae* (Chronicle of Wales) – were either exaggerated or invented to provoke hatred of the animal.

The saga of exactly who shot the last wolf in Scotland – how you could possibly know yours was the *last* one is surely a question worth asking – rumbles on, but the wolf shot in Perthshire by Sir Ewen Cameron in 1680, or the wolf shot in Sutherland by 'the hunter Polson' in 1700, or indeed the one shot in Moray on the lands of the Laird of MacKintosh in 1743 seem to be strong contenders. Either way, Thomas Pennant – the roving naturalist who pops up seemingly everywhere around this period – concluded after presumably *very* considerable investigation that by 1769 British wolves were extinct.

That these 'last' animals were killed many years apart – and there are reports of wolves seen in the Highlands as late as the 1800s – lends weight to the argument that nobody really knows when wolves finally howled their last in Scotland. All we really know is that at some point between then and now, they did. And with them, the natural balance of the Highland food chain collapsed.

Today, the apex mountain predator in Scotland is the golden eagle. Apart from man, nothing can kill it and it will kill anything it can, often with astonishing calculation. The poor, confusing wildcat – which resembles a particularly robust, hairy tabby with a bushy tail – has fallen foul of interbreeding with domestic cats, and the few that are left in the wild are of uncertain genetic purity. They're still out there but are so difficult to observe and so secretive that it's nearly impossible to estimate their numbers accurately. The omnivorous badger and the red fox, as well as stoats, weasels and other small carnivores, do their bit to pick up the predation slack left by the wolves, lynxes and bears, but there's little escaping the fact that today we're a nation of large, wild herbivores that have nothing to keep their populations down.

All this means that these days, Britain is an extremely safe place for anything of human size and above to wander through the wild. Unless you have a spectacular reaction to an adder bite or annoy a particularly violent badger, there's nothing you'll meet that's capable of killing you. Unfortunately, there's also nothing to kill deer. And for the well-being of mountain places like Knoydart, that's a big problem.

With the death of the wolf came, in the minds of many ecologists, the death of the wilderness in Scotland. Knoydart – although it may seem unspoilt to the human eye – is not as it should be in nature's plan. Deer that once lived beneath trees here and were hustled from place to place by packs of wolves have now moved into the open and see no reason to move on. Their populations thrive, and as a result of their habit of nibbling saplings, the regeneration of any species of tree is made impossible except on inaccessible cliffs. The introduction of sheep after the Clearances made the problem much worse, and today the landscape – once covered with dense forests of Scots pine, filled with predators and nurturing a healthy natural cycle of death and rebirth – whilst lively enough on the surface, is in reality perilously unbalanced.

As Jim and I began our descent into the corrie and dropped below the bluster-line of the wind, we heard beneath us the low sound of many hoofed feet striking heather. Like a wheeling flock of birds, red deer – dozens of them – emerged from below and darted across our view, their pogo-prance carrying them under the skyline and out of sight. It's a stirring thing to witness. Exhilarating, even. But natural? Difficult to say.

The sun emerged as we walked far beneath the summit ridge of Ladhar Bheinn and the wet mountainside above us caught steel light along its cragged dents. Ahead, the valley offered us a respite from the complex terrain of the ridge. Far ahead I could see the black smudge of the *folach*, from where we'd be back on ground trodden with our own prints that morning.

I stopped to show Jim the base of a butterwort, its unpleasant Latin name – *Pinguicula vulgaris* – rightly suggesting that this fleshy little plant, with its splayed banana skin of leaves sprouting a purple flower in summer, harbours something sinister. Its flower acts as a lure, drawing insects in to the plant's sticky leaves, which consume them with a digestive enzyme. In ancient times the plant was thought to ward off witchcraft; charms made from it under its earthier name of 'bog violet' were said to ensure safe travel when carried in bunches of nine. Another carnivorous plant in Scotland – the alarming-looking sundew – perhaps more obviously fits the stereotype, being composed of nebulous, round leaves studded with spines. Both plants can be found across Scotland's boggier mountain environments; I'd only ever seen them in the same place in Knoydart, so to me plants that bite are indelibly associated with this place. Nearby, the clawed handprints of an otter padded the mud. My own boot prints joined it.

As we walked, the sun lit up more and more of the valley. Stands of birch, colour drained from their leaves, shimmered like silver chandeliers against the riverbank. An hour later we reached the *folach* and the bridge, and rejoined our outward path. Ours were the only prints we met in the mud, stamping an opposing return journey next to them as we retraced them back through the wood, out of the valley and onto the rough-shod track to Inverie.

* * *

As if mirroring the complexity of its mountain landscape, Knoydart's human history has been one of particular brutality and tumult. Agriculturally poor and so packed with mountains that areas upon which to settle are limited, it's unsurprising that Knoydart has little prehistoric record, save for one coastal fort at Doune, which dates from the Iron Age. Place names tell of visitations by the Norse; the aforementioned *Knut's fjord* gave its name to the region as a whole,* and it's worth noting that the typical word order of Gaelic – a generic followed by a specific – remains in the Norse-flavoured order in several of Knoydart's mountain names. Hence we have Ladhar Bheinn rather than Bheinn Ladhar, and Luinne Bheinn rather than the reverse.

Things really got cooking in the time of the Jacobites. Knoydart had not been penetrated by Generals Wade nor Caulfeild in their industrious period of road building, so to a large extent the peninsula remained very much off the map. As such, Knoydart's isolation made it a hotbed of radicalism, ruled by clan chiefs who were staunch Jacobites. This overt political leaning therefore meant their destinies and the destinies of crofters who lived on their lands were – whether they liked it or not – entwined with that of the uprising.

It didn't help their cause that Knoydart and its people were already notorious by the time of the Jacobite Rebellion. They were viewed as violent thieves by neighbouring clans, and one name in particular crops up again and again both in historic accounts and on the modern map of the region: Barrisdale.

Coll Macdonald of Barrisdale – as with so many accounts of prominent people during a time of what was effectively civil war – is seen as both good and bad in histories of the area. To some he was a common thug who stole cattle, terrorised Knoydart's neighbours and kept a set of stocks and a peculiar instrument of torture outside his palatial dwelling, from which he ran what was effectively a protection racket across neighbouring settlements. To others he was an educated figure of considerable gravitas who inspired respect from all under his sway. In *Voyage to the Hebrides*, Thomas Pennant wrote of Barrisdale and his legendary skills as a thief, referring to 'the celebrated Barrisdale ... who carried the arts to the highest pitch of perfection'. In the days before the Battle of Culloden in 1746, the Barrisdales and the Scottos

---

* Which is odd, as the name *Knut's fjord* was obviously intended to apply to either Loch Nevis or Loch Hourn, not the peninsula between them.

– another Knoydart family under the sway of the Jacobite Glengarry clan – were sent to fight.

Barrisdale never made the battle, but several of the Scottos were killed and others were later transported to the colonies. Barrisdale joined a contingent of clansmen intent on prolonging the uprising, but the war was lost. He returned to Knoydart a fugitive later that year, to find that the Duke of Cumberland's 'punishment parties' had robbed him of his cattle. Worse was to come in the shape of Captain John Ferguson of *The Furnace*, a government ship that was cruising the west coast in the name of retribution for the uprisings. Ferguson recorded the destruction of Barrisdale's house with some brevity in his log of the incident: 'Firid 48 guns to beat the house down and Sett the Town on fire.'

Although Knoydart was viewed as one of the last bastions of resistance, hardship and poverty eventually wore the region to the bone. Coll Barrisdale was captured in 1749 and died a year later in Edinburgh Castle, but it was the common people who bore most of the punishment; whichever account you believe, in Barrisdale they'd lost one dictator and thanks to his allegiances gained a much crueller one in his stead. Loss of homes, loss of possessions, loss of livelihood, the inability to steal cattle as they once did: after Culloden, the people of Knoydart suffered.

In 1755 the lands under Barrisdale's control were forfeited. For the following 30 years the estate remained under governmental control, until the forfeiture was lifted in 1784 and developments in the region were made in the all-too-familiar name of 'improvement'. Sheep arrived in Knoydart that year; the population, which had swelled to over 1,000 people, was intermittently cleared from grazing land; major emigrations and evictions took place in 1786, 1802, 1815 and many times in between as the already meagre land was slowly given over to grazing.

Then, in 1853, came what historian Denis Rixson, in his definitive book *Knoydart: A History*, describes as the 'last spasm in a conflict which occurred because landowner and tenant no longer shared economic or social interests'. In short, it would be the final and most brutal of all the Highland Clearances.

MacDonell of Glengarry, the landowner at the time, had died in 1852. His descendants, deep in debt, had come to the conclusion that a land cleared of tenants was more attractive to a potential buyer and set about emptying

Knoydart of its occupants with considerable enthusiasm. Reported upon by Donald Ross in *The Glengarry Evictions* – a slim volume of enormous power – the 1853 Knoydart clearance by Josephine MacDonell was a singularly shameful act. Following the mass deportation of over 300 people to Canada, the families who remained on marked land were forcibly evicted and made to watch their houses be torn down or burned. Those who attempted to erect shelters following the demolition of their dwellings had them ripped down, sometimes repeatedly, forcing the desperate residents to live amongst the rocks on the shore. Some of the evictees were elderly; at least two were pregnant, one of whom suffered a miscarriage, the other contracting consumption; many were forced to survive beneath basic shelters for several years. They had, quite simply, nothing of their own and nowhere else to go.

Knoydart would see further hardship. After the Clearances, sheep farming would boom, then bust, then the Victorian craze for Highland stalking began. Large estates such as Knoydart became the playground for the paying gunman, who would come to shoot deer and return home with their severed trophies. Throughout the late 19th and the beginning of the 20th centuries the land passed from one owner to another: the Bairds in 1857, the Bowlbys in 1893, and – most notoriously – the Brockets, in 1933.

For all the distasteful things that had already taken place by the time Lord Brocket took ownership of the land, you would scarcely imagine that the Nazis would make a guest appearance in Knoydart's history; but sure enough, they do. Brocket – properly Arthur Ronald Nall-Cain, 2nd Baron Brocket – was a supporter of National Socialism and a member of the Anglo-German Fellowship at a time when it was a more than dubious organisation. Brocket famously attended Hitler's 50th birthday party in 1939, and even following the outbreak of war continued to engage with senior Nazis, possibly attempting to broker a negotiated peace deal that would have seen Germany retain control of Poland and Czechoslovakia, something completely unacceptable to the British government.

Whatever his political leanings, Brocket was deeply unpopular as a landowner, being for many the very epitome of the over-privileged landlord that had caused so much despair for so long. Rarely present on the estate, he saw Knoydart as a toy for his amusement, for entertaining guests and for occasional recreational pleasure. Under his ownership the population of Knoydart dwindled to just over 140 in the late 1930s. The situation reached boiling point in 1948 when seven returning soldiers staged a land raid on Knoydart in defiance of Brocket, attempting to claim the right to own smallholdings on his estate. It was a publicity stunt as much as it was a statement of land reform; the raiders were photographed during their siege and stories appeared in *The Scotsman* in the days that followed, until finally Brocket acquired a court eviction order and the men reluctantly agreed to withdraw.

Whilst ultimately unsuccessful, the land raiders* garnered considerable public support on account of both their cause and their foe (by all accounts Brocket wasn't difficult to dislike), entering folklore as the Seven Men of Knoydart. Today they're commemorated as rebels against injustice, and are frequently cited in proposals for land reform. Brocket sold the land soon after; both he and the Seven Men have monuments to them in Knoydart – the latter in Inverie, the former a Gothic cross some way outside of it.

After another 50 years of squabbling, Knoydart's happy turning point finally came in 1997 with the establishment of the Knoydart Foundation, which enabled control of the estate to pass to the community who lived there. With echoes of Assynt, in 1999 a partnership between the John Muir Trust, the Chris Brasher Trust, the Highland Council and the Knoydart community saw the purchase of this wild, contested place for £750,000. Knoydart is now in the attentive hands of its full-time residents. Long may it remain so.

Later in the evening, Jim and I are in the Old Forge on the south side of a palatial meal and several drinks. Kenny is telling us about Knoydart, Harris and his love of the Hebrides. He tells us a little Small Isles ditty: 'Go to Rùm, drink rum; go to Eigg, eat egg; then go and get buried in Muck.' We laugh; it's not funny. But it's been that kind of night. And it's that kind of place.

The Old Forge has been lively all night; now only a few of us remain in the bar, none of us in a hurry to leave. Earlier Jim and I had been people-watching from our table. In particular, we'd been intrigued by a table of big, tweed-clad men in flat caps with dark expressions and a weariness that seemed to seep

---

* The seven were Alexander MacPhee, Donald MacPhee, Duncan MacPhail, Henry MacAskill, Jack MacHardy, Archibald MacDonald and William Quinn. There was originally supposed to be an eighth – Archibald MacDougall – but he was on military service at the time.

from them. They didn't seem to be talking to anyone, nor catching the infectious revelry. They were just sitting, and drinking.

It's later now, and after talking to Kenny, Jim and I start a conversation with two men sitting at the bar, also in tweed and woollens, also visibly knackered, although seemingly much chattier. Introduced as Ian and Max, both bear an unmistakable rich odour. It wasn't necessary to ask what they did; these men, and the different men we'd been watching earlier, are the modern predators of Knoydart.

There are few rational arguments against the need to cull deer. If we didn't, they'd eventually overpopulate, strip the land of grazing and starve to death, taking goodness knows what else along with them. It's down to Ian and Max, and other deer stalkers, to fill the vacuum left by the wolf.

Thanks to the removal of natural predators it's now estimated there are 1.5 million deer in Britain. Ecologists are worried that this is already far too many; but for the time being it's the stalkers employed by estates such as Knoydart who control deer numbers. Stalking operates on the principle that the old, the weak and the sick are taken. If no such animal presents itself, no shots are fired. As Max puts it, 'Better a blank day than to come down off the hill with the wrong beast.'

Ian is English, originally from London. His hair is pulled back in a straggly ponytail, and he wears a fine tweed jacket he lets me try on. Max is also English. He wears a flat cap and a dark woollen V-neck. He looks very tired. Both have been out all day on the slopes of Ladhar Bheinn.

It would be naïve to say that there aren't other aspects to their work besides population control; after all, people pay to come and take part in a stalk. It serves a purpose, but it also brings in money. I ask Ian how hard it is to ensure the stags don't suffer, particularly at the hands of an amateur marksman.

'A professional shot goes through the neck,' he says, pointing to his carotid artery. 'But you don't want to get that shot wrong. So you instruct the client to aim for the engine room, an area about the size of a sheet of A4 paper between the shoulder and the neck. Anywhere inside that sheet, the animal's going down.'

The deer are butchered on site, then trussed and dragged off. Max tells us he once carried a stag weighing seventeen stone down the slopes of Ladhar Bheinn. Ian describes being so hot and dry on the mountain that he took to squeezing clumps of moss into his mouth. His typical sustenance for a day stalking, he tells us, is two sandwiches – one in each pocket of his tweed jacket – and a Mars bar. He inclines a finger for emphasis. 'And I usually don't need the Mars bar.'

Jim and I, still in our mountain gear, suddenly feel overdressed and over-serious. Here was a different way of being on the mountain than our own – totally different. I suddenly have the urge to go out with them on a stalk, to see what it's like, but we can't. Our ferry leaves first thing for Mallaig.

The night goes on. Kenny stumbles out, back home. Max, by his own reck-oning, is 'bollocksed' from his day on the mountain. He buys us a drink then begins to nod where he sits. Ian becomes ever more animated and impas-sioned as today becomes tomorrow. He's worried about something, though. Perhaps he's worried that – like many outsiders who judge this place by urban values – we don't understand the cycle of life here in Knoydart. Before we leave he beckons me outside, and we stand in the cold whilst Ian smokes a rolled cigarette.

'You know, I'm just like a farmer, only I do my job through binoculars and a rifle sight. I don't create life to kill it. These animals aren't born to be hunted.'

He spits smoke into the air. My own breath smokes in the cold.

'It's pure selective management, what we're doing. The replacement of a natural predator within the UK. The wolf, the bear, the lynx ... gone. Man's eyes,' he scissors his fingers towards his, 'are on the front of his head. We're the predators now. I wouldn't be doing what I was doing if man hadn't fucked it all up in the first place. You climbed the mountain today. I work *for* the mountain.'

With that, Ian is off. Just before he drags Max up and the two disappear out of the door, I ask him what the weeks ahead hold. He says they're busy. The stag selection is one part of their job; the other is the cull of female deer and the young. No ceremony, no foreign clients. Pure population control.

'A hundred and fifty hinds this year,' he says. 'Plus calves.' He puts his jacket on and, just for a second, looks desperately sad. 'Calves are hard.'

Jim and I finish our drinks, then stumble out into the black night towards Jackie's. There are no streetlights in Inverie. Free from light bleed, the autumn stars burn brightly. Across Loch Nevis the dark shapes of the mountains slice the sky into diagonal divisions of blackness: stars, no stars, stars.

13 ART

Nobody can really pinpoint the exact moment it happened, but at some time around the late 18th century mountains shifted from being universally reviled to becoming just about the most inspiring things on earth. Simply put, the monsters became muses – and an entire artistic movement was born. This movement became a love affair, the love affair became an obsession, and gradually but surely, obsession turned into lifestyle as mountains were stitched into the fabric of the British cultural tapestry.

What it was that triggered this evolution in the perception of the mountains is difficult to pin down, but there's little argument over *where* it happened.

Located in the county of Cumbria, within the Lake District National Park's 885 square miles, there lies, as its name suggests, quite a lot of water. England's largest and deepest lakes can be found here – Windermere and Wastwater, respectively – but you could very easily have named the area after its other rather more abundant geographical features. The highest mountains of England – and all the land above 3,000 feet in the country – lie in the Lake District, the latter culminating in the country's four highest summits. All of this would fit with a squeeze inside the M25, but is instead crowded thick onto a pronounced platform of land jutting out into the Irish Sea. The watery word may have won in the end, but this could have easily been called England's Mountain District.

Really, with the exception of the most muscular sections of the Pennines (including, if you were to really squint, the Peak District), when you're looking for a raw, genuine mountain landscape in England, the Lake District is the only place you're going to find it. But once you're within its borders, it's everywhere. It's as if someone has heaped the country's entire quota of mountains together, shoved it into one corner and fenced it off.

The result is something fairly unique amongst mountain landscapes in general: true convenience. Nothing is too far away from anything else, valleys and ridgelines flow into each other with an ease that at times suggests conscious design, and an elegantly arranged windmill of lakes and numerous villages of dark stone fills the spaces that are left. Even the mountains themselves seem intended to offer pocket-sized versions of other wild places, yet remain entirely of their own character.

The northernmost slice of the Lakes is scraped and lean, the area beyond the sentinel peaks of Blencathra and Skiddaw more reminiscent of Scotland's Southern Uplands than northern England. Geographically, that makes some sense, as parts of this region lie closer to the border than they do to other parts of the Lake District.

Likewise, parts of the Southern Lakes – with its dark rock, its quarries and splintery ridgelines – have a sniff of Snowdonia to them, whereas the flowing eastern summits merge almost seamlessly with the Pennines beyond, when seen from afar. But whilst comparisons like this might lead you to think the Lake District is some kind of British mountain zoo, it's really all just part of what makes this region perfect for the mountain lover. It's like a sculpture depicting some kind of utopian mountain landscape – a geological 'best-of' – and it's this grandeur together with the proximity of everything that makes the place so exquisite. People will tell you this causes its own problems, as the 20 million visitors every year, in addition to the 50,000-odd folk who live and work within the national park itself, need to be put somewhere, after all. But no matter what anyone tells you, the exorbitant praise for the Lake District's scenery is entirely justified.

And it's lovely that in a place made up of landscapes so readily reminiscent of elsewhere, its central nucleus – the place most responsible for drawing gaping travellers here in the first place – really couldn't be confused with anywhere else.

Grasmere's popularity these days as Lakeland's quintessential heart is such that it has an unofficial nickname: Gras Vegas. This is largely nonsense. Yes, Grasmere *does* get exceptionally busy if you happen to be caught up in the throngs on a sunny bank holiday. But if nothing else, let's be thankful that what's been a small and pretty village for hundreds of years remains a small and pretty village, when it so easily could have sprawled into some tat-infested vulgarity. You can walk around it in about twenty minutes. It's geared for tourists, there's no doubt about that – the entire place seems made of confectionery outlets, gift shops and cafés – but it still feels like a *place*, not just the gaudy ghost of one. Wander through the village on a quiet, snow-silenced winter's day, and it's charm in a box.

A lot of this has to do with its situation. Grasmere feels crowded in on all sides by a keep of compact, rugged hills. These – together with the woody-shored lake of Grasmere itself and the toytown-like houses built from a chipped-grey spectrum of Lakeland slate – make the village an achingly picturesque prospect, if you're that way inclined. These days it would appear a lot of people are, and because it's not far from the bigger, more practical towns of Ambleside and Keswick to the south and north, Grasmere sees many hundreds of thousands of visitors every year from all over the world.

Of course, before the 20th century, tourist brochures and websites didn't exist; depictions of the Lake District, its quaint villages and compact natural drama needed to be spread in other ways. And it would be one man's evocations of this landscape in particular that would fire a fascination with England's most artistically potent mountain place that has gathered an ever-diversifying pace ever since.

On the day the clocks went back in 2006, Cumbria Tourism launched something called the Lake District Escape Line. The idea was that people would be able to beat the winter blues triggered by late October darkness by picking up the phone and listening to a comforting series of quintessentially Lakeland sounds. The national park quietens down at this time of year as the landscape physically and visually hardens and tourists go elsewhere. It was thought the scheme might tempt people back to the area with an audible reminder of the region's year-round charms.

The sounds that were chosen were these: the water of Windermere lapping against a jetty, the gush of Aira Force, wind rushing across Scafell Pike, the crunch of autumn leaves underfoot, birdsong in a valley, the sizzle of Cumberland sausages in a pan (one can only imagine how appetising that would have sounded over a phone line) and, finally, a reading of 'Daffodils' – a poem written in 1804 by William Wordsworth.

The opening line of 'Daffodils' (and also the title Wordsworth originally gave the poem*) has become curiously synonymous with the emotion of recreational walking in Lakeland, or anywhere else for that matter. It reads:

> I wandered lonely as a cloud
> That floats on high o'er vales and hills,
> When all at once I saw a crowd,
> A host of golden daffodils;
> Beside the lake, beneath the trees,
> Fluttering and dancing in the breeze.

Written about a particular moment when the poet and his sister Dorothy came upon a ribbon of daffodils near Glencoyne Bay on the shores of Ullswater, this poem has endured more than most as a tribute to the serenity that can be found in the Lakes. But it's just one example of the powerful literary and artistic awakening spurred by the landscape amongst which Wordsworth – and the contemporaries who would collectively become known as the 'Lake Poets' – would draw their inspiration.

The usual place where many ponder the Lake District's literary canon – alongside a great many who don't – is Wordsworth's resting place, which lies in the branch-shrouded graveyard of St Oswald's church in the centre of the village.

I arrived in Grasmere on one of those days of change you tend to get in the Lakes in late autumn. The roads were plastered with rust-coloured leaves, the air lively on a wind packed with seasonally youthful chill. Squalls of rain stalked the hills around the village, occasionally dropping angled veils of grey on their summits. The weather was warming up for the cold.

'We' had become 'me' again. Jim was off doing something important like flying a plane, and whilst I felt strangely bereft to be on my own once more –

---

* 'Daffodils' has become the name by which many know the poem, mainly because the original title 'I Wandered Lonely as a Cloud' – thought to have been given because of the standard practice of naming a poem after its first line – was thought misleadingly maudlin, betraying the work's rather brighter central theme. Wordsworth would possibly have had something to say on the matter but was no longer around to share his thoughts.

especially with the cold weather beginning to bite – I was looking forward to exploring the Lakes on my own terms.

Walking past the handsome, boxy structure of the church, I found the Wordsworth family graves, and stood for a moment watching a lean procession of American tourists shuffling by and photographing the headstone beneath which the poet's 80-year-old body was interred in 1850. The gravestone and memorial were, surprisingly, barely legible beneath the jungle of algae and lichen that favoured their shaded aspect under a yew that Wordsworth himself had planted when he lived in the village. The popular notion and the source of much of his enduring fame is that the poet 'started' Lakeland tourism. But whilst he certainly contributed to it, he definitely didn't invent it, as we shall see.

I'd come to Grasmere not to look at graves, but to find and climb a mountain – or a 'fell', to use the vernacular – which would exemplify and provide a podium to best appreciate the landscape that inspired this explosion of artistic creativity. Wordsworth lived in Grasmere, as too did several of his contemporaries, such as Thomas De Quincey and Samuel Taylor Coleridge – about the latter of whom much more will come. In the years since, many other artists and writers have also made this little village the centre of their activities and meditations. Whatever your thoughts on modern-day 'Gras Vegas' and the inspirational power supposedly to be found in the landscape, high above it was one thing – possibly the only thing – that would be as naturally potent now as it had been then.

There are many great things about Loughrigg Fell, but the best thing about it is that it's just *there*. It's tiny, even as Lake District mountains go – 335 metres at its highest point – but this is immaterial as there's no other hill nearby that so deftly and conveniently illustrates both the context of the surrounding mountains and the swift shift in feel between valley and fell.

Loughrigg was perhaps an obvious choice, but then again also not so obvious. Grasmere's most dramatic mountain neighbour is probably Helm Crag. Itself hardly a giant at 405 metres, this outlier of the Easedale horseshoe is topped with a clutch of exposed andesite pinnacles standing proud of the fell's otherwise dumpy profile like a raised middle finger. Given that it's within sight of the village, this little outcrop has earned itself many nicknames, most of which reflect the way it appears in silhouette: variously, it's called the Lion and the Lamb, the Lion Couchant, the amusingly imaginative Old Woman Playing the Organ and the Howitzer. The last is the most apt at close quarters, as the most prominent rock does indeed resemble a great cannon tilted out over a sickening drop. It also represents the final five-metre shimmy to the fell's true summit, and is a tricky prospect for the nervous. Alfred Wainwright – who, despite his wonderful evocations of Scotland, will always be associated most closely with the Lake District – failed to climb to the very top of the Howitzer, earning Helm Crag the distinction of becoming the only 'Wainwright' summit Wainwright himself never reached.

But whilst Loughrigg might not be able to compete in terms of vital statistics or attendant rites of passage, it does offer something that Helm Crag doesn't: Loughrigg is unashamedly for everyone. Small, convenient and well tracked, getting to the very top doesn't require you to prove a damn thing. And therein lies something rather important.

I left Grasmere by Red Bank, intending to approach the summit of Loughrigg from its quieter western side. Red Bank is the old, steep road that links Grasmere with Great Langdale, and immediately on leaving the village the modest throngs of daytrippers disappeared, replaced with an intimate, tree-lined lane where windows cut in the deep foliage offered snatches of a view down a beautiful valley jigsawed with dry-stone walls.

The path to Loughrigg from this direction is direct. You leave the road, walk momentarily beneath trees and through sloping, nibbled fields where sheep watch you. Then, after a gate emblazoned with the oak leaf of the National Trust, you're out of the shade and onto the fell.

I was impressed how quiet it felt around here. Grasmere was just over the brow of the hill – it had taken me five minutes to drive to Red Bank from the village – yet there was nobody about as I started my ascent of arguably the most amenable and conveniently located fell in the Lakes. Perhaps the weather was to blame, although in that respect Grasmere and its immediate surrounds seemed to be escaping what the rest of the Lake District evidently wasn't. I'd pulled on a fleece and thrown a waterproof over it as I was sure at some point I was going to get wet, but as I rose above the trees and the views began to unfurl around me, it was as if Loughrigg stood in the dry eye of a sodden vortex.

It really is astounding how quickly you start getting really great views in the Lakes. Loughrigg isn't high, but its position as the hub from which several valleys radiate means it's a great spot from which to watch the scenery unrolling around you. It's a fine example of a small effort being rewarded with a big payoff – and as far as mountain walking goes, that's the key to the Lake District's success. Whether the hordes of people you see trotting about trussed up in walking apparel would still be here if the mountains were twice as far apart and an average of 500 metres higher is worth considering; maybe there wouldn't be as many, or maybe there would be more – but either way, you can't contest the fact that a central part of its appeal is that its mountains can be enjoyed no matter who you are.

Architecturally, Loughrigg initially appears sprawling and quite nondescript. It's actually quite a complex little hill, though never dauntingly so. There are crags, but not big ones. There are some caves in the north-east corner, and a squid of paths that ascend not only from Grasmere but from Ambleside and Rydal, each backing onto a different side of the fell. From below it seemed a warty dome of grey rock flooded with brown autumnal bracken, and it would have been a slog if there were no clear line of passage through it. Ascending from Red Bank I immediately felt was a good choice. Within moments of setting off, I could see right into the mouth of Langdale, the famously picturesque valley above which rose the jumbled, charismatic pikes of the same name. Cloud obscured their tops; all I could see was the shadow of their bulk.

The path crossed streams and clambered up the pale rock, before entering a shallow gully and giving way to felty, close-chewed grass. The path vanished, and soon I was approaching Loughrigg's extraordinary summit.

The relationship between art and mountains has been an odd one. It's also been the unlikely source of much intellectual meandering, some of it actually interesting. Before the 18th century, people tended to be horrified by mountains, particularly the privileged classes who were more inclined to record their thoughts. The most obvious explanation for this reaction is probably simple habit. They viewed the wild outdoors from the point of view of practical or commercial value, and on this scale the mountains ranked low. Consequently they were seen as uselessly barren, a place through which passage had to be forged, often traumatically. That's not to say mountains were universally avoided by all; as we've seen, there are records of 'curiosity men' (enthusiasts of botany or geology, mostly) being escorted up mountains in North Wales, particularly Snowdon and Cadair Idris, by the 18th century if not a little earlier, and there were enough of them to warrant a mini-industry of local guides for the purpose. It's just that the idea of actually experiencing mountains for *enjoyment's sake* was as perplexing as, say, going coal mining or setting up a picnic in a ruined car park would be to us. Back then, anyone inclined to look at the outdoors for enjoyment tended to restrict their attention to gardens or places with views of pretty architecture.

Mountains were therefore either ignored – remember Paul Sandby omitting Schiehallion in his *View near Loch Rannoch** – or became scratching posts for stridently harsh language in the literature of the time, with which they were brutalised with histrionic glee.

Throughout much of the 18th century mountains were rarely mentioned except in term of disdain for their visual outrage, which occasionally crossed the line into outright fear. They certainly seemed to have scared the life out of Daniel Defoe, who travelled extensively throughout Britain and wrote prolifically of his movements in a series of letters, which together comprise some of the first travel literature of its kind. In his voluminous *A tour thro' the whole island of Great Britain, divided into circuits or journies* from 1724, he picks his descriptions of the many mountains he met from what appears to be a very limited pot of adjectives, all of them negative. Scotland in general he describes as 'frightful', Ben Nevis and Lochaber as 'a frightful country full of hideous desert mountains, and unpassable'. He compares the mountains of South Wales to the Alps and the Andes, before exclaiming that these mountains – probably the Brecon Beacons – rose straight from the valley to their highest points, which made them look 'horrid and frightful, even worse than those mountains abroad'. The prospect of Snowdonia seems to have deeply traumatised him: 'I have seen the Alps ... have gone under some of the most frightful passes in the country of the Grisons and the mountains of the Tirol ... [and] never believ'd there was any thing in this island of

---

* This could of course have been for propaganda; the message that Sandby was probably intending to promote to the folks back home was one of earnest industry and indomitable progress, not a hopelessly tiny band of figures attempting to map a landscape filled with mountains.

Britain that came near, much less that exceeded those hills, in the terror of their aspect; but certainly, if they are out done any where in the world, it is here.' When it came to the Lakes, Defoe describes the region as 'the wildest, most barren and frightful place' he had ever seen, adding: 'Nor were these hills high and formidable only, but they had a kind of an unhospitable terror in them.'

Before Defoe came Celia Fiennes, whose *Through England on a Side Saddle in the Time of William and Mary*, a travel diary of a two-decade tour, didn't find its way into print until 1888 despite being completed well over a whole century earlier. In it she nicely conveys the feelings of the genteel classes towards the upland, describing areas of North Yorkshire as 'rough all over and unpleasant to see, with craggy stones, hanging rocks and rugged ways.' The Lake District predictably comes off no better, as 'desert and barren' and full of 'very terrible' mountains.

Equally appalled by the uplands was Dr Samuel Johnson, who commented on the upsetting view presented by the Grampian mountains in his *Journey to the Western Islands* of 1775. 'An eye accustomed to flowery pastures and waving harvests,' he wrote, 'is astonished and repelled by this wide extent of hopeless sterility.' And at least one writer even made the point of praising a more comely county as being agreeable because it *lacked* the horrors of mountain places. In 1712 John Morton said of Northamptonshire: 'Here are no naked and craggy rocks, no rugged and unsightly mountains, or vast solitary woods to dampen and intercept the view.'

William Gilpin, in a 1786 treatise whose title is sufficiently rambling to require a footnote,* said of sighting the prospect towards Dunmail Raise – which I could see if I turned my head from where I was now standing on Loughrigg Fell – that 'the whole view is entirely of the horrid kind. Not a tree appeared to add the least chearfulness to it.'

It's therefore perhaps surprising to learn it was eventually Gilpin who would be instrumental in opening up the whole idea of mountains as Jolly Inspiring Things for a variety of artistic endeavours, signalling the beginning of a

---

* *Observations, relative chiefly to picturesque beauty, made in the year 1772, on several parts of England; particularly the mountains, and lakes of Cumberland, and Westmoreland.*

generation of artists and writers who would become collectively known, rather oddly, as the Romantics.

You could say that Romanticism, at least in part, began when people attempted to rationalise the potent feelings that mountains – and other similarly disorderly, inhumane natural phenomena – stirred in the observer. Young men of the leisured classes at the time would embark upon the 'Grand Tour', a cultural excursion to Europe enabling them to immerse themselves in the culture of classical antiquity in places such as Rome, Florence and Venice. These journeys meant that they usually had to cross the Alps.

One of these Grand Tourists was poet and essayist Joseph Addison, who described his first sight of these mountains with a contradiction of terms that would have great resonance in the years to come. He said of the Alps that 'they fill the mind with an agreeable kind of horror.' In this he had touched on the peculiar dichotomy between fascination and fear that many writers had suggested when writing of these 'frightful' natural abominations: whilst many were bluntly scornful of mountains, others were clearly slightly excited by them.

Addison went on to expand and rationalise this idea in *The Spectator** in 1712: 'By Greatness, I do not only mean the Bulk of any single Object but the Largeness of a whole View ... Such are the Prospects of ... a vast uncultivated Desart, of Huge Heaps of Mountains, high Rocks and Precipeces, or wide Expanse of Waters, where we are not struck with the Novelty or Beauty of the Sight, but with that rude kind of Magnificence which appears in many of these stupendous Works of Nature.' He then goes on to say: 'Our Imaginations loves to be filled with an Object, or to grasp at any thing that is too big for its Capacity. We are flung into pleasing Astonishment at such unbounded Views, and feel a delightful Stillness and Amazement in the Soul at the Apprehension of them.'

In 1756 Addison's ideas were developed by the philosopher Edmund Burke, who introduced and explained (in *great* detail) the idea of the 'sublime', and how it relates to the 'beautiful'. His work, whilst somewhat wordy to the modern reader, was enormously influential. He argued that the *sublime* – something of

---

* This short-lived publication, which ran from 1711 to 1712, is not to be confused with the modern *Spectator* magazine, which, whilst venerable and no doubt taking its title from the earlier publication, did not appear until over a century later.

chaotic, fearful form and almost incalculable greatness – and the more benign, delicate features inherent in the *beautiful* were mutually exclusive qualities, but could often be found together, and triggered an accordingly juxtaposed emotional response in the observer. 'In the infinite variety of natural combinations,' he wrote, in a *Philosophical Enquiry into the Origin of Our Ideas of the Sublime and the Beautiful* (1756), 'we must expect to find qualities of things the most remote imaginable from each other united in the same object.' Hence what he called 'not pleasure, but a sort of delightful horror ... tranquility tinged with terror.' Not only that, but both sides of this duality had the potential to produce positive emotion as the sublime object – whilst stimulating feelings rooted in self-preservation – posed no immediate physical threat to the observer.

Whilst this idea that something visually intimidating could also possess aesthetic qualities might seem fairly elementary these days, back then it was big stuff. It would give rise to a term still in casual use today, however improperly: *picturesque*.

This is where William Gilpin re-enters the frame, so to speak. A cleric who was born in Carlisle, Gilpin became the most articulate theorist on the emerging idea of the *picturesque* – a type of landscape which, by its very nature, mixed the sublime and the beautiful to produce an effect that was artistically pleasing or, in Gilpin's words, 'would look well in a picture'. It was Gilpin who argued that the traveller needn't embark upon the Grand Tour to find the sublime, and that, to those attuned to their virtues, the landscapes of wild Britain could stimulate just as much excitement as the Alps.

Gilpin's writings were packed with theories about how certain landscapes conform to picturesque principles, and if they didn't, *why* they didn't – and what the observer could do to rectify nature's clumsy compositional errors. His most influential work to this end* was what you might call an instructional manual to assist the reader in viewing the Lakeland landscape in a correctly picturesque manner. Sketches accompanying the commentary as he moves through the Lake District indicate how the elements of a particular scene should be arranged to conform to his principles.

---

* *The aforementioned observations, relative chiefly to picturesque beauty, made in the year 1772, on several parts of England; particularly the mountains, and lakes of Cumberland, and Westmoreland* (1786). Succinct titles were clearly not in fashion in the 18th century.

When it came to mountains, Gilpin was particularly adamant. He describes – with illustrative sketches – the beauty of a mountain in resting in 'great measure upon the line it traces along the horizon'. He goes on to insist that 'mountains rising [either] in regular, mathematical lines or whimsical, grotesque forms are displeasing', citing several examples – one of which is the famous Lakeland peak Blencathra, here appearing under its other name, Saddleback, in reference to its shape when seen from certain angles – which form 'disagreeable lines'. He speaks of the spired peaks of the Alps constituting objects more of 'singularity, than beauty', and that forms suggesting a 'lumpish heaviness are disgusting ... round, swelling forms without any break to discumber them of their weight.'

He therefore gently suggests modifications to rectify such subjects into 'pleasing' forms. The result is what Gilpin called 'the embellished scene' – a delicate balance of the faithful and the fiddled. He explains that 'this beautiful mode of composition is oftner aimed at than attained. Its double alliance with art and nature is rarely observed with perfect impartiality: ambitious ornaments take the lead, and nature is often left behind.'

Key inspirations for the picturesque movement were the French neo-Classical landscape painters Gaspar Dughet (then known as Poussin, after his more illustrious teacher), Claude Lorrain and Salvator Rosa, and much delight was found in describing Lakeland scenes after the manner in which these 17th-century artists might have treated them. In 1753, Dr John Brown – one of the first to write specifically of the Lake District in picturesque terms – famously described the vision of Keswick as requiring 'the united powers of Claude, Salvator and Poussin. The first should throw his delicate sunshine over the cultivated vales. The second should dash out the horror of the rugged cliffs, the steeps, the hanging woods and the foaming waterfalls; whilst the grand pencil of Poussin should crown the whole with the majesty of the impending mountains.'

In comparison with the original scenes, the interpretations of the many who followed picturesque principles were, at best, gently augmented or stylised: figures, ruins, an altered line of a ridge or a fortified vertical were introduced where none existed in reality. At worst they were exaggerated, clumsily theatrical visions of intricate drama, a notable – and very early – example being *A View of Derwentwater, Towards Borrowdale* by William Bellers, painted in 1752.

Although Gilpin's articulation of picturesque ideals was considered to be overly prescriptive and his suggestions somewhat clinical – which you would imagine contradicted the very nature of art – in places he writes most evocatively about landscape. In the introduction to his *Observations* he quite beautifully describes the changing forms the mountains take amidst the swivelling light of day and the dynamic weather. Such passages conjure a vivid image of the mountains as fascinating, changing things that are not horrifying but alluring. 'In a warm sunshine the purple hills may skirt the horizon and appear broken into numerous pleasing forms; but under a sullen sky, a total change may be produced: the distant mountains, and all the beautiful projections may disappear, and their place be occupied by a dead flat.'

Gilpin's *Observations* not only encouraged artists but became an inadvertent travel brochure. Picturesque tourism became fashionable and the Lake District its most revered destination, and many crowded into the area if only to see what on earth all the fuss was about. They arrived armed with two things: a somewhat preconceived idea of how the landscape should affect them, and a device that would help them to actually 'see' a scene. This was called a 'Claude glass', a folding instrument not unlike an oversized make-up mirror. Inside was a convex reflective surface which, when mirroring a landscape, corralled and darkened the vision to a sepia or brown tone and, in Gilpin's words, 'gave the object of nature a soft, mellow tinge like the colouring of that Master'. It's no small irony that the observer who had travelled so far to witness the landscape then had to literally turn their back on it to view the Claude glass's reimagining of it. Predictably the device, the entire idea behind it and Gilpin himself were ridiculed,* but as Jonathan Bate notes in *The Song*

---

* Most notably in 1809 in the satirical *The Tour of Dr. Syntax: In Search of the Picturesque*. Twentieth-century poet Norman Nicholson would later ask:

> What if I listen? What if I learn?
> What if I break the glass and turn
> And face the objective Lake and see
> The wide-eyed stranger skyline look at me?

Comparisons have been made to the manipulation of digital images using computer software, even to the emerging phenomenon of stylised mobile-phone photography, with the Claude glass being the '18th-century version of Instagram'.

of the Earth, tourists wielding a Claude glass were in no way dissimilar to modern sightseers with cameras stopping to capture a fine view. 'If we stop and think about the procedure,' Bate notes, 'this is a rather strange thing to do.'

The poet Thomas Gray had been on the Grand Tour, and after visiting the Highlands – of which he would make the telling remark, 'The mountains are ecstatic ... none but ... God know how to join so much beauty with so much horror' – in 1769 he journeyed to the Lake District, Claude glass in pocket. He was probably drawn there as an early picturesque tourist, although the novelty of the idea at the time meant his observations were only subtly influenced by the ideas that Gilpin would later make fashionable. *Thomas Gray's Journal* is therefore an interesting document not just for Gray's appealing eye for detail, but because it's an original, aesthetically flattering account of the Lake District written before such a thing became commonplace. Gilpin himself spoke warmly of Gray: 'No man was a greater admirer of nature than Mr Gray; nor admired it with better taste.'

Day four of Gray's journey features an anatomical metaphor of Borrowdale that has survived in descriptions to this day. 'To the left the *jaws of Borodale*, with that turbulent Chaos of mountain upon mountain roll'd in confusion.' He describes rocks in the valley 'hanging loose and nodding forwards ... the place reminds me of those passes in the Alps, where the guides tell you to move with speed and say nothing.' Gray also visited Grasmere, describing the view of the little lake from Dunmail Raise as 'one of the sweetest landscapes that art ever attempted to imitate ... all is peace, rusticity and happy poverty, in its neatest, most becoming attire.'

A later settler in the village would praise Gray's prose for its 'distinctness and unaffected simplicity'. This was William Wordsworth, and – in the wake of these earlier pioneers – he began his own contribution to Lakeland literature at precisely the right time.

By the time Wordsworth began publishing his poetry in 1793, the Lakes had been an artistic and tourist destination for nearly half a century. There had been Addison's 'agreeable horror', Burke's explorations of the sublime, Gilpin's picturesque and the soulful descriptions of Gray's *Journal*. There had even been the first guidebook to the Lakes, written by Jesuit priest Thomas West in 1778.

And by 1789, with the French Revolution making travel on the continent dicey, erstwhile Grand Tourists were turning more and more to the Lake District in search of the mountainous landscapes that were now resolutely in vogue. It was against this backdrop that Wordsworth, together with his fellow Lake Poets Robert Southey and Samuel Taylor Coleridge, began to write the work that, in its seamless combination of landscape and mood driven by feeling, many would regard as the definitive poetic interpretation of Lakeland – and of Romanticism at its peak.

As I reached the top of Loughrigg it became clear I'd taken by far the quietest route up. The top of this little hill is unique because its true summit is merely the proudest of many, dotted like little turrets around a grassy plateau approached by several paths. I just happened to have picked the path that started in the most inconvenient place, which is why I'd had it to myself. At the tall, stone trig point I could see that even in the squally, heavy weather there were lots of others on the hill with me. I stood in the beginnings of a rain shower on the summit and watched the crouched, broken line of people beetle up from Rydal towards me, some using poles and leaning against the wind, all trussed up in colourful waterproofs. Hearing a gathering commotion between gusts of wind, I turned to look towards Grasmere, and saw a group of no fewer than 30 schoolchildren and several harassed-looking supervisors appearing over the brow. Despite the weather, the children – clearly out for a school daytrip – were full of it.

I stepped back from the trig point and watched the two streams of people steadily converge on the top in a babble of chatter. When one of the schoolchildren heard one of the elderly walkers' accent I heard him pleading at London volume with the bemused man to say 'something else … anything!' The gruff response was: 'You don't often hear that about the Cumbrian accent.'

More people arrived, others departed, and the weather continued to blow and intermittently dump rain on the little summit, cloud just glancing the top. I walked around it for about an hour. The many little knolls forming the top are fun to scramble up and down, and are arranged so you can easily turn your back on any crowds and occupy your own little, private summit. I managed to find one at each of the four cardinal points, offering views deep into the Lakes. This really is a superb vantage point from which to get a feel for the place; on a clear day it probably ranks amongst the very best in the district, simply for the way the landscape around you shifts as you wander the hummocky tops.

'It is not likely that a mountain will be ascended without disappointment, if a wide-range of prospect be the object,' Wordsworth once wrote. 'But he is the most fortunate adventurer who chances to be involved in the vapours which open and let in an extent of the country partially, or, dispersing suddenly, reveal the whole region from centre to circumference.'

He could have written this passage for Loughrigg, on an indecisive day like today. As I bumbled round the little knolls, sometimes using my hands to grab the hillside for assistance, the clouds moved across the landscape around me, occasionally opening windows through which I could see clutches of layered mountains. To almost all of these something previously expressed in poetry, captured in literature or immortalised in paint could have been appended.

To the north, beyond Helm Crag, was the bruised saddle of Dunmail Raise, the pass that led into the northern Lakes, the view upon which Gilpin poured scorn and from which Gray eulogised perfection. Rotating the aspect east lay the shrouded shoulders of the Helvellyn massif – one of the most popular mountains in England, a kind of Lakeland equivalent of Snowdon. Two tapering ridges just the agreeable side of frightening prove a popular test of nerves: Striding Edge and Swirral Edge. It was from the former that in 1805 a young tourist of the picturesque from Manchester, Charles Gough, lost his footing in falling snow and fell 200 metres to the foot of Red Tarn Cove. His skeleton, still guarded by his Irish terrier, was found there by a shepherd three months after he was last seen. His hat had been split in two by the fall, and he carried two Claude glasses in his pocket. Gough was a Romantic who'd died in his adventurous pursuit of a vision, and he was duly eulogised by many of his fellows, including Wordsworth, who wrote the poem 'Fidelity' about the tragedy. In it, Wordsworth describes the harsh area of Helvellyn in which Gough's remains were found:

> It was a Cove, a huge Recess,
> That keeps till June December's snow;
> A lofty Precipice in front,
> A silent Tarn below!

Continuing to the east, beyond the lazy pyramid of Red Screes was the Kirkstone Pass, which in 1803 Coleridge climbed in a storm. 'The farther I ascend from animated nature, from men and cattle and the common birds of the woods and fields,' he would write of the experience, 'the greater becomes in me the intensity of the feeling of life.' Further south, the mountains lower in altitude, and the view was dominated by the great silver tongue of Windermere, frosted on its northern reaches by the white buildings of Ambleside and Bowness. Overlooking the shores of Windermere, Beatrix Potter bred Herdwick sheep, drew scientifically important illustrations of fungi and – rather more famously – wrote stories about small animals fond of frilly dress that continue to be an international sensation.

To the south-west rose the bulky Coniston fells, the highest of which – the Old Man of Coniston, its peculiar name thought to relate to the silhouette of its sizeable summit cairn – provided the inspiration for the mystical mountain of 'Kanchenjunga'* in *Swallowdale*, Arthur Ransome's sequel to *Swallows and Amazons*. The author had a house on the shores of Coniston Water itself, and many of the locations in both books can be traced to landmarks on or around the lake. Also on the lakeside lies Brantwood, the home of John Ruskin, a philanthropic multi-talented figure in the world of art theory, and a fine painter himself.

Further west and the mountains stack up into layered heaps, the high, knuckled crag of Harrison Stickle signalling the position of the Langdale Pikes, beyond which under a stripe of orange light lay the highest mountains in the land: the Scafell massif. Of the former, countless paintings and sketches have been made by the likes of Turner and Holroyd – and Coleridge has notorious form with the latter, as we shall see in the next chapter. Lying between my vantage point on the felltop and the Langdale Pikes was heart-shaped Loughrigg Tarn, the miniature lake that Wordsworth singled out as being 'the most beautiful example' of the type.

Wordsworth's effusive love of the region is of course revealed in his poetry; but, surprisingly, it's perhaps more fully displayed in his *Guide to the Lakes*, a book first published anonymously in 1810, then in a definitively revised form

---

* Named, presumably, for the existing mystical mountain of Kangchenjunga in the Indian Himalaya, which we encountered in Chapter 3. That Ransome's spelling omits the 'g' is just another instance of the somewhat elastic spelling of just about every mountain on earth.

in 1835. It's an absolute treat, testimony to Wordsworth's uncanny connection with the landscape he revered, and full of learned, semi-practical but always evocative descriptions far above anything of its kind previously committed to print. In it, he describes the fells of the Lakes:

> In magnitude or grandeur they are individually inferior to the most celebrated of these in some other parts of this island; but in the combinations they make, towering above each other, or lifting themselves in ridges like the waves of a tumultuous sea ... they are surpassed by none.

As a result of the efforts of the Lake Poets, during the 19th century almost every prolific painter and writer felt obliged to offer their own take on mountains. What had previously been little more than irritations of landscape, or objects of fear and awe, were now a fashionable immersive experience for the creative mind, offering a concentrated mix of hardship, exhilaration, terror and beauty that was apparently a creative catalyst of the highest order. And what was so earnestly forged in the Lake District was soon propagated to other British mountain places. John Keats would stand upon the summit of Ben Nevis 'blind in mist', and write of heaven and hell; Lord Byron's 'Dark Lochnagar' is a fine mountain in Scotland's Grampians – and is indeed a place of 'crags that are wild and majestic' and 'steep frowning glories'. Felicia Hemans – writer of *The Rock of Cader Idris*, and admired by Wordsworth – also wrote *Mountaineer Song*, a love letter to the Grand Tour:

> Blow, mountain-breeze! all wild, like thee,
> Unfetter'd as thy wing, I rove;
> With airy step and spirit free,
> From snowy cliff, to shadowy grove!

Not everyone was inspired; Queen Victoria herself would climb Lochnagar from the newly acquired royal estate of Balmoral, pronouncing its summit 'cold, wet and cheerless, and ... blowing a hurricane'. And early in the next century, D. H. Lawrence had a moment of high temper when he described mountains in a letter to Cynthia Asquith as 'always in the way, and so stupid ... never moving and never doing anything but obtrude themselves'.

I looked back towards the summit of Loughrigg, thickly wigged with children, their supervisors pointing out landmarks as and when the cloud allowed it. Doubtless the same would be true for them. Not all of them would be enjoying this. Quite a large proportion were probably wet, sore and wishing they were back in Grasmere. It wasn't the *best* day to be up here, but if the landscape was going to get you, it would still get you. And maybe – just as it ever was for those who have stood here and looked at that – within the damp crowd, gazing out towards a horizon of layered hills beneath a sky beginning to ember in the autumn afternoon, there might be the soft but certain glow of a lifelong spark igniting.

The descent towards Grasmere would be a different way down, with a different view. Many words had been inspired by that view. But, of course, words are only one means of artistic expression.

It was dark and raining by the time I arrived in Cockermouth, north-west of the border of the Lake District, and knocked on the door of Julian Cooper.

Julian is a working mountain artist, and one of particular distinction. I had contacted him before heading for the Lakes hoping he might agree to meet me and perhaps help define what it was about the mountains that for him, and indeed for others, seemed to carry such potent creative fuel. If anyone was able to help me, it was him; that much I could see in his painting, but also in something he'd written about one of his own exhibitions, something that to me felt like his own interpretation of the mountain places: 'When a piece of land inclines toward the vertical, our relationship towards it changes. We can no longer walk on it and it cannot grow food for us. So we either ignore it, or it becomes an aesthetic object in itself, akin to a work of art.'

Julian's work often focuses on abstract detail pulled from massive rock faces, which he then translates onto enormous canvases to spectacularly defined textural effect. Send him to the north face of the Eiger, and he doesn't come back with a painting of the north face of the Eiger; he produces a three-metre-high canvas of one specific part of it. It doesn't sound like it should work. But it does. And it's terrifying.

'It had never really been done that way before in painting,' he says, as we drink tea in his living room. 'Treating the mountain as this kind of big arena, but with no edges, and no sky. It loses its silhouette. Once you cut the top off, it enriches it. You can concentrate on the goings on, the structure of the mountain. The workings.' He smiles. 'The guts.'

There was another reason I wanted to get Julian's take on mountain art. For him, being a truly original contemporary mountain painter carries particular weight given his lineage. Brought up in Grasmere, his single-barrelled surname masks the fact that he's in fact the third generation of a family famous for painting the scenic drama of the Lakeland upland. His grandfather was Alfred Heaton Cooper; his father William Heaton Cooper. All three were – or are – versatile, highly individual painters, but as their preferred subject all have chosen mountains. When I ask Julian why, he winces just a little.

'With my dad and my grandfather and me, there's a continuity there,' he says. 'But then again, in some ways there isn't. You know, we all look at things differently. Each generation has its own way of taking things in.'

The contrast between these three generations of mountain painters is striking. Alfred's images drew heavily on the influence of Turner and Constable, both of whom visited the Lakes in the late 18th and early 19th centuries, and produced work notable for its luminous, semi-impressionistic atmosphere, something that would infuse the later work of Turner in particular.

'My granddad, working as a Victorian, was very much producing paintings of his time. But did you know,' Julian continues, 'that Alfred was really the first painter who went up onto the high ground to paint? Most of the other Victorian painters just did the valley scenes, the lakes, a nice mountain stream. Turner and Constable might have climbed a pass once or twice, but they weren't actually up on the tops. You get that from my grandfather, that visceral enjoyment of being outdoors, and dealing with what he's looking at instead of this kind of formula. He's got a sort of *bite* to him.'

Alfred's painting certainly didn't shy away from the menace inherent in the mountain places of the Lake District: the mist-wreathed crags suffused with a burst of sunlight in his *Pillar Rock, Ennerdale* is a masterpiece of mood. Alfred's son William – Julian's late father – developed his own interpretation of the mountains surrounding him. His paintings emphasise the naked architecture of the fells with vivid colour, crisp contrast and spare lines. The images are sharper yet at the same time more impressionistic than the work of his father before him.

'My dad, when he was young, was more of the modern-art type of painter you might get in the 1920s and 1930s. When he returned to the Lakes from London when Alfred died, he started painting the Lake District, and became a bit of a throwback. He wasn't really doing the sort of painting his generation was producing on the whole, but he knew all about it. He was far from naïve.'

William Heaton Cooper's revolutionary techniques for mass production – and the consequent demand for his more tourist-friendly Lakeland scenes – provoked much criticism of his ideals and accusations of painting stereo-typical scenes for the tourists. Regardless of this, his finest work ranks amongst the most visually striking mountain art ever created, covering as wide a spectrum of atmospheres as the mountains themselves. As a point of comparison, *East Face of the Pillar* hits the eye as a starker, darker homage to Alfred's earlier depiction of the same rock, whilst his painting of *Scafell Pike from Eskdale* portrays a glowing cavity of peaks that both beckons and repels. Indeed, a continuity. But then again, not quite.

Julian's work shifts style yet again, differing from both his father and grandfather's work far more than they differ from each other – in terms of subject, portrayal and medium. Whilst Alfred and William's paintings were *of* mountains, Julian's, in a manner of speaking, *are* mountains.

'My sort of painting is very much to do with the surface of the canvas itself,' he explains. 'Vertical rock faces and mountain faces seem a natural subject when you're physically building this thing up on the surface of the canvas. It makes a bit of a statement that this canvas is an object, as well as an image of something else. Painting and mountain at the same time.'

For about twenty years mountains didn't figure in Julian's art. Instead he based himself in London, firstly working with abstract landscapes, then concentrating on narrative figurative work. He was very good at it, too, 'but after a bit, there was still this thing hankering away,' he says. 'So I came back with my wife, to live in Cumbria.'

He describes his influences as evolving from 'my dad, as a kid', to the New York abstract expressionist movement of the 1940s, 'people like Jackson Pollock and de Kooning, with the big canvases. I've never lost that. I think if you could do paintings of mountains with that same energy and power ... I still probably think like that, but I'm trying to make all these subtle shapes of rock, the way the light hits it, and the shadow. Working in an abstract way, but it's real at the same time.'

I ask him if there's other mountain art he admires, and he pulls down a book by the late 19th-century Swiss artist Ferdinand Hodler. 'He was about the same time as Cézanne, who also had a big influence on me. He really gets to grips with the form ... he's doing things to do with how it really feels to be there, not some formula, some script of painting that's been reiterated a million times before. Now *that*,' he points over my shoulder to a page dominated largely by sky, a shark's tooth of a peak occupying the bottom third, 'is a beautiful one. The Breithorn. It's beautiful in real life, but that proportion of sky. It just feels right, don't you think?'

Given his family tree and growing up in the Lake District, and having subsequently immersed himself in the Alps and Himalaya, I expect Julian to be ... not cynical about the Lake District exactly, but jaded perhaps.

'Since moving to Cockermouth, I think I prefer the north and western mountains better than the South Lakes. There, the hills are all, sort of little-wooded and intimate and ...' He makes a motion with his fingers as if inspecting a head of hair for nits, before trailing off. 'Here, as soon as you go over Dunmail Raise, suddenly there's swooping shapes and you've got Crummock Water, Ennerdale, Buttermere, Wasdale. It feels totally different, very Scottish-feeling. When you're up on Scafell or Great Gable, or the rocky, higher areas here in Cumbria, you're on the same sort of terrain as you are on a rocky ridge in the Alps. It's just a matter of scale. Once you get to a certain level around here, you're in semi-wilderness. You flit your eye, and it goes from suburban, to pastures and fields, then you get to the top – it's 90 per cent influenced by nature, which is a definition of wilderness, I'd have thought.'

We finish our tea and Julian nods towards the back door. 'Anyway. Do you want to go and have a look in the studio? Get a real idea of what it's all about?'

The thing that hits you immediately as you walk into the place where Julian makes his mountains is the spirit. It's not an unpleasant smell but it's strong.

'It's what kind of gets me going in the morning, the turps,' he says, as he turns on the lights, illuminating rows of brushes, photographs and a floor spattered thick with multi-coloured barnacles of paint, edges frayed from their energetic impact. And on the far wall, a large, half-finished canvas of a red-hued rock buttress, split and deep-furrowed.

'This is a copper mine in Australia,' he says. 'I went there a few years ago, then returned to the same place last year to find this big chunk of rock had sheared out of the face. On contact with the air it becomes brittle and just falls out. See this cavity, this gap, this feeling of ...'

His easy composure slips a little as he steps forward, indicating the broken edge of the buttress, before moving back from the image again. 'There's something a bit brutal about it.'

Julian's work – like most good art – is all about feeling and reaction. Everything that repelled, intrigued, confused and inspired those early travellers, people like Gray, and those who theorised about the sublime and the picturesque, the Lake Poets, Turner, Constable – this landscape did *something* to them. Standing in Julian Cooper's studio, it's here. The fear, the visceral clench of an image or a word, or words creating an image, whatever catches you – the mountains had it, they have it still. It continues to be potent.

'Oh yeah, I like a bit of fear,' he chuckles. 'This rock face – I want to communicate the feeling of being in front of it. You see it, and you want to climb it. But ...' – he points at the dark, angular cavity – 'there's nothing to hold onto.'

Moments later he disappears into a storage area and I hear the sound of large objects being slid around.

'Like this. Here's another bit of "fear".' He pulls out a massive canvas depicting an abstract mountain face of pale rock – only this one contains a huge, angular door. 'This is in Carrara in Italy, where they have these great marble quarries. It's a sort of giant portal into the mountain. Inside there's all these chambers and passages, these great halls ... It's like an Egyptian temple cut into the mountain. You want to go in, but you wonder what's in there.'

He picks up a small chunk of white rock the size of a shelf ornament from his work bench. 'This is Carrara marble. This is what the mountains are made of.' It's shaped like a mountain, triangular, a scything ridge bisecting the fragment into two textural halves on the axis of its peak. 'You see the way it's cut. That extreme contrast.'

On one side of this miniature ridge is a smooth, machined face. On the other is the raw rock, rough and pitted. I turn the fragment in my hand, a miniature, marble mountain. One half elegant, beautiful. One half rugged, sublime.

'That shape, that mountain shape,' he says as I pass it back. 'There's something instinctual in a human being's response to it. It's repeated in architecture. It's probably got some deep, primal resonance. Don't you think?'

An hour later I'm driving back into the Lakes over Dunmail Raise.

This pass was once the border between England and Scotland. It was said to be the scene of a battle between Dunmail, King of Cumberland, and Edmund of Scotland in around AD 945. Dunmail was killed, and his followers took the crown of Cumberland to Grisedale Tarn near Helvellyn and tossed it into the waters. Today a large pile of rocks is said to mark the spot where Dunmail was buried. Wordsworth wrote of it in *The Waggoner*:

> ... that pile of stones,
> Heaped over brave King Dunmail's bones;
> He who had once supreme command,
> Last king of rocky Cumberland ...'

Nobody really knows if the story's true. But when the road was widened the stones were left undisturbed. They're still here. I don't see them as I drive over the black pass, wind rocking the car.

We'll leave this part of the journey with a more contemporary Lakeland poet, who wrote of the mountains, of mountain poetry, and of Wordsworth in his *Five Rivers* collection. His name was Norman Nicholson, and the following passage comes from 'To the River Duddon', written in 1944. The Duddon Valley was a favourite haunt of Wordsworth: a secluded cul-de-sac rimmed by little-travelled mountains. You don't find many tourists there. All you find is the Lake District, stripped bare.

> Not the radical, the poet and heretic,
> To whom the water-forces shouted and the fells
> Were like a blackboard for the scrawls of God,
> But the old man, inarticulate and humble,
> Knew that eternity flows in a mountain beck.

Static envelops the radio, and as the road narrows and begins its descent back towards Grasmere, a few thick splotches of snow join the rain on the windscreen. They sit there just long enough to be seen before being swiped away.

14 SPORT

To the west the Lake District hardens. Angles take a steep rake, the skyline leans over you and crags pierce the grass-pelted slopes like fractured bones through skin. All of a sudden the cuddly landscape of the lower, greener fells chills down and frowns, and you enter a very different place. It's a shift that happens on a more local scale all over the Lake District, a mountain dichotomy Wordsworth noted in the introduction to his *Guide to the Lakes*: 'Their forms are endlessly diversified, sweeping easily or boldly in simple majesty, abrupt and precipitous, or soft and elegant.'

If you were going to pinpoint an exact place to appreciate this transition, it would be in Borrowdale, the deepening valley south of Keswick. As we've seen, Thomas Gray's reaction to the place has lingered in local vernacular: 'The *jaws* of Borodale, with that turbulent Chaos of mountain behind mountain roll'd in confusion.' Gray obviously felt intimidated rather than enchanted; you don't enter the 'jaws' of something and expect a happy time.

This might of course have had something to do with the weather. The oft-deployed word 'brooding' when used to describe mountains is usually a fancy way of saying it's 'cloudy', and in this attribute Borrowdale excels: it's the wettest part of the wettest county in England. The agricultural hamlet of Seathwaite – which, to thrash the metaphor to its last, could be said to lie in Borrowdale's 'throat' – holds the dubious top spot of the settlement that sees the most rain in the entire country, with an average of three metres falling in a year. A single 24-hour period in November 2009 gave a record 314 milli-metres of precipitation.

This bleak accolade means there must therefore be strong lures for those who come into Borrowdale with mountains on their mind, and in this the valley certainly doesn't disappoint. Seathwaite is often used as a springboard into the 'chaos' at the head of this deep, rocky trench, which includes within it England's highest twins, Scafell and Scafell Pike. Whilst the status of this massif draws the numbers, there are many other redoubtable objectives here, too. Great End, Ill Crag and Lingmell circle the Scafell massif like watchtowers around an inner keep, all bustled shoulders and grinning buttresses.

And then there is another, less lofty but more distinguished, peak. Small but kaleidoscopic in character and filled with far more intrigue than befits a mountain of its size, this is of course Great Gable. And whilst some mountains are bastions of science, of art or of legend, Gable is the hard rest upon which the strange and troubled game of rock climbing lays its spiritual head.

The cold was definitely coming. Autumn's fire was fading from most of the Lake District, but from Borrowdale it had vanished. The entire valley looked desaturated and tired. It would probably be another month or so before the fell tops began to gleam with winter's first sneeze of snow, but for now the landscape was in a limbo of monochrome, backlit by the westering sun.

I'd spent the previous night amidst the steep, rain-mirrored streets of Ambleside, first at a tucked-away pub called the Unicorn, then a cheap but comfortable B&B. The pub was pleasingly local-feeling, all cluttered walls beneath low beams and the sort of place where a local gent walking his dogs would wobble in for a no-doubt nightly constitutional half Guinness, then wobble out again all in the space of ten minutes.

Optimistically taking with me several books on the history of rock climbing, in the end I only made it through half of one, spending most of the time cross-referencing the extraordinary place names it churned up back to the map and attempting to plot a logical route through them.

Probably the most disappointing description of Great Gable is the one that the majority of people will unfortunately end up reading. Alfred Wainwright (he of the ubiquitous, evocatively written and scratchily drawn guidebooks) does the mountain the most extraordinary disservice in its entry in Book Seven of his *Pictorial Guide to the Lakeland Fells*. 'The failing of Great Gable,' he claims, 'is that it holds few mysteries, all its wares being openly displayed.'

Perhaps when Wainwright wrote this of Great Gable in 1966, such was the reverence towards the mountain within the climbing and hillwalking communities that it was rather unfashionable to gush about it. Maybe he felt enough had been said, and enough was known, or maybe the mountain just didn't tickle his personal cockles. And although the book's descriptions aren't *rude* towards the mountain, you just get the sense that he was a little annoyed by it. The compliments he gives it feel conciliatory at best and begrudging at worst; he bemoans it has 'no cavernous recesses, no hidden tarns, no combes, no waterfalls', and his choice of descriptions – 'excrecence of crags', 'desert of stones', 'petrified rivers' – paints an image of a dull mountain whose virtues have been oversold.

Well, excuse me for challenging a Lakeland cultural statesman, but I feel I need to set the record straight and emphatically state that this is nonsense to the point of lunacy. Great Gable is absolutely magnificent, the perfect articulation of everything a British mountain should be: grand, charismatic, by turns spectacularly intimidating yet achievably diminutive, its summit a pedestal, its flanks a catacomb of exciting and at times unsavoury history swaddled in an atmosphere so thick you could punch it. Even its height – an untidy 899 metres – suggests a rascally nonconformism.

The first proof of this magnificence is its shape. They call it Great Gable on account of its appearance from the secluded valley of Wasdale to the south-west. Whilst from Borrowdale it's hidden and shapeless behind Brandreth's high ridgeline, from Wasdale the mountain stands as a proud, rakishly flinched pyramid that is indeed quite reminiscent of the structural apex that gives it – as these things go – its comparatively straightforward name.*

I'd chosen to approach Great Gable this afternoon from Borrowdale, first for convenience (however blissful Wasdale's isolation is once you're there, it's logistically very awkward to reach when you're not), and second because there was something awfully special about catching the first glimpse of the fabled Wasdale from high on the mountain, having earned it on foot. It would also give me the opportunity to approach the mountain from its eastern aspect for the first time, via the high pass that holds the wriggly-shored Sprinkling Tarn.

---

* If you're interested in the etymology, 'gable' as a term for an architectural apex or house-end comes from the Old Norse *gafl*.

The odd thing about Great Gable's shape is that it's equally distinctive from wherever you look at it – but it's distinctive in very different ways. Some will know the mountain best as that photogenic pyramid at the head of Wasdale, but from every other angle it resembles a kind of domed bulge, which, whilst full of character, is anything but pointy. From the north the eye hits the great wall of Gable Crag, deep-slashed and footed with slopes of scree. Gable Crag looks like the cut edge of a mountain sliced in half to expose its core, but is in fact just the scarp of a sliver that's been calved off by hard time. The west and east offer softer slopes, with each face edged by ridges – like a pyramid – that offer logical routes to the top.

Lastly, there's the south face. The top half of this huge triangular chunk of mountain side is a thicket of mean-looking crags, bristling out of the mountain like stone conifers. Within its labyrinth of buttresses, ridges and gullies lie some of the most distinctive pieces of rock in Britain, amongst features given names that make this side of Great Gable sound a menacing place indeed. Three major groups of crags are exposed here, separated by two huge scree chutes that descend from the mountain's top. Beginning at the eastern end, the first of these as you weave through on the indistinct path known as the 'Climber's Traverse' are the Kern Knotts, split by a huge crack. The tongue of angled scree that's soon reached is known as Great Hell Gate, beyond which begins the next and grandest arena of crags: the complex, broken warren known as the Great Napes. The Great Napes are geological Gothic, and amongst the names of its more charismatic features we even see a rather dark instance of ancient Hebrew. Within this forest of rock you can find Arrowhead Gully, the Sphinx Rock, Tophet Bastion,* Hell Gate Pillar and, most famously of all, Napes Needle. There's then another steep chute of scree – Little Hell Gate – before the final swathe of crags is reached: the White Napes. It's all very big-feeling, particularly for a mountain that's in actual fact very compact. The whole rocky pyramid, and all the interest within it, is corralled into considerably less than a single square mile.

---

* A peculiar name, not least for its old biblical connotations which, like everything else on this side of the mountain it seems, are somewhat bleak in nature. In the Hebrew Bible Tophet was a place in the Valley of Hinnom, near Jerusalem, said to be where children were burned alive in sacrifice. To Christians the name became synonymous with 'hell', a term evidently already overused in the toponymy of Great Gable by the time this particular feature – actually a tall, brutal-looking pillar – was named.

This was to be my second time climbing Great Gable. The first had been several years ago, by way of exploring the crags of the Napes by the Climber's Traverse. Whether or not the name refers to it being a traverse to enable rock climbers to access the many darkly named objectives on this side of the mountain, or that you need to be a climber to traverse it is a question worth asking, but it's certainly the most unpredictably entertaining way of getting up Great Gable – and one, for us, that very nearly ended in quite serious mishap.

It was May, and bursts of brilliant sunshine had lit the southern slopes of the mountain, illuminating the green curve of crinkled felt that formed the downward sweep into Wasdale. The day was blustery, though, and the high summits were being stalked by unpredictable, powerful gusts of wind. My cousin Steve and I had spent most of the afternoon exploring the sheltered crags of the Great Napes, weaving in and out of the cold shadow draped by the overhangs and leaning blocks of rock. It's a real labyrinth in there; we got lost several times, and were forced to backtrack upon meeting obstacles that were too steep to climb up or down. It was tremendous fun – exploratory, absorbing and satisfying.

This southern slingshot of the mountain is a visual treasure hunt, containing not one but two of Britain's uncanniest pieces of rock. The easiest to spot has two weirdly complementary names, depending on the angle from which you approach. From a distance across the Great Napes it's Cat Rock, and does quite resemble a seated feline, looking back over its shoulder at you in that aloof way that cats have. (Don't look for a tail; Wainwright's addition of one in his illustration was artistic cheek, nothing more.) Up close and viewed side on, the six-metre rock is a striking human face in side profile. The strong features, pronounced chin and topknot-style protrusion from its crown faintly suggest a Native American chief, one of the Easter Island *moai*, or an ancient Egyptian rendering of a face – hence its second, also coincidentally feline, name: Sphinx Rock. Stoic like an impassive sentry, from high on Great Gable this charismatic face looks down into Wasdale.

The other of Great Gable's most enduring features is a superstar. It's famous to the degree that it's even had its image seedily misappropriated and – on one occasion – has been threatened with assassination. It's certainly statuesque, from one angle in particular resembling a fractured church spire fissured with diagonal cracks, and capped with a sickeningly overhanging top block. This block looks top-heavy from almost every angle except one, where perspective grants it a slight sharpening that sits nicely with the overall taper of the pinnacle.

In the early 20th century a now famous photograph of this gaunt ziggurat appeared on a tourist postcard in the Alps, cheekily pinched and attributed to a fictional feature – the 'Aiguille du Nuque' – suggesting it lay amongst the mountains above Chamonix. The translation was slightly muddled ('nuque' means 'neck' in French) but in the right anatomical area. It's called Napes Needle, and it's the closest Britain has to a rock-climbing head of state. But we'll come back to that.

That afternoon Steve and I had rested in the shape made by the crags between Napes Needle and Sphinx Rock, looking down into Wasdale, stroked with crisp spring sunshine and enjoying the feeling of sitting slap-bang in the middle of one distinctive mountain silhouette and between two others. Eventually the gradual shiver of inactivity crept into our bones, spurring us into getting a move on up the mountain. Extracting ourselves from the crags of the Great Napes, it wasn't long before we found ourselves on the precipitous flanks of Little Hell Gate.

Little Hell Gate – despite its cheerful name – is a pretty monstrous proposition to ascend. It's essentially a thick ribbon of loose rock descending at an angle of repose nudging 40 degrees, which may or may not decide to shift about when you try and climb up it. Imagine walking up an escalator the wrong way with no handrail and you're in the right sort of area; you just need to factor in a couple of hundred thousand tonnes of loose rubble and a long slide down a mountain. You're also walking up into a snaggle of dramatically pitched crags, doubtless the 'gate' of its name, beyond which the top of the mountain lurks.

As we moved out of the shelter of the crags the wind hit us hard. May is usually a lovely time to be in the mountains but the air can still chill you down rapidly if you let it. Ten minutes of stooped climbing into the wind, legs slipping downwards with every step, splayed arms occasionally grasping the few solid holds for support, and we were exhausted.

Scree is a magnificent visual feature. Once dislodged from a buttress, a little piece of rock continues to be at the mercy of the laws of physics. Add in a few million other pieces of rock, and the resulting slope can be surprisingly elegant: the spoil of the mountain, a snapshot of its natural breakdown, gradually sieving and eroding over the millennia to an ever-finer constituent, eventually carried off by a river somewhere, dumped on a sea bed and one day forming part of some other mountain somewhere else. From a distance scree *en masse* can fan out into flared triangular cones as it splays, form an oscillating valance of granular buttresses or just sit as a beautifully uniform, level sweep filling the gaps and acting as a contrast to the shriller features of its parent peak. Sometimes scree is the key physical feature of the mountain, dominating its visual appearance. Gaze towards Wasdale from the side of Great Gable and you can see in the distance a slope that descends from the south-east into the lake as straight as a tipped table top. This north-west-facing flank takes its very name from this arresting attribute and is called, simply, the Screes.

The scree of Little Hell Gate is a lot more broken up but just as troublesome. As we sat, breathing heavily and buttressing ourselves against the wind amidst the plate-sized fragments, I felt a soft impact to my right. About six inches from my hip – the place you might naturally rest a lunchbox or a flask – a rock the size of a human head had appeared. I knew it had only just appeared there as the cord from my jacket and one of my rucksack straps were now pinned between it and the ground. Steve had noticed, too, and was looking from the rock up the slope with round eyes and draining skin.

'Wind doesn't blow rocks off mountains. Does it?'

'Think it just did,' he replied.

'Maybe it came down on its own ...'

Steve was already on his feet and moving across to the other side of the scree chute as I said this, and I quickly followed him. The rest of our ascent of Little Hell Gate was spent using its frayed, craggy edge as a banister. High up at the top of the gully a faint path led across the Gate at its highest point. The view down into Wasdale from here was sensational, but on a windy day it's a precarious crossing. One at a time we crossed the steep, unstable slope to the relative safety of the summit crags above.

And that had been that for our exploration of the Great Napes and Little Hell Gate. We'd rushed down the mountain with barely a glimpse of Great Gable's summit – I don't think we even stopped for a cursory acknowledgement. But I'd never forget being amongst the weird panoramic claustrophobia of the Great Napes. And whilst to me Little Hell Gate would always be the place where the wind blew rocks at you, I was looking forward to revisiting the summit by another route and spending time on a quite exceptional English mountain landmark. But first, we need to go back in time.

Stand between Sphinx Rock and Napes Needle and look south-west, and you'll see Wasdale, floored by Wastwater and home to the tiny village of Wasdale Head. You'll see the steep wedge of Scafell and Scafell Pike high to the left. Over the bulk of Kirk Fell in the middle right, you'll see a high pass that leads into Ennerdale. Within this narrow field of view – just 90 degrees between south and west, requiring the slightest of head turns – and in the chill of the Great Napes at your back, lies much of the history of rock climbing.

There in the high left of the view from Great Gable, on a clear day, is a long, elegantly concave snout tapering languidly up from Wastwater to a high point. Here, at a pincer of rock pinnacles, it drops into a deep cleft. The skyline then begins to rise again, rather bumpily, towards a less shapely but fractionally higher top. This duo of peaks comprises the highest ground in England: the summits of 964-metre Scafell and 978-metre Scafell Pike, respectively. The bite between them is known as Mickledore. And most discussions concerning the origin of rock climbing as a pursuit focus around a rock buttress that forms the right wall of this high gap: a series of oversized, tilted rock steps known as Broad Stand. It was down this that on 5 August 1802 a slightly chubby, flustered man slithered fractiously into Mickledore, and in so doing made what most people consider to be the first recorded rock climb.

Broad Stand is notorious today, sometimes fatally so. It still catches out unwary walkers who, descending from Scafell, try to take the deceptively direct-looking route into Mickledore by way of this lethal staircase and slip, falling several metres and typically landing on the same small patch of ground – nicknamed grimly by the local mountain rescue as the 'crash mat'. There has been at least one occasion during which a mountain rescue team has been tending one casualty on this spot only for a second unlucky adventurer to loudly and quite literally land on top of the first. Both suffered broken bones. Both were very lucky.

Back in 1802, however, the high mountains above Eskdale and Wasdale were little explored by tourists. At this time William Wordsworth was settling in at Grasmere, enthusiasm for the picturesque and the sublime was well into its stride, and another of the Lakes Poets – 29-year-old Samuel Taylor Coleridge – had taken to the high fells of Lakeland for a nine-day 'solitary tour'.

Coleridge was something of a troubled soul – it has been suggested he was bipolar, a little-understood affliction at the time – and evidently a personality of maddening turbulence, warmly described as a 'rotten drunkard' and 'absolute nuisance' by even his closest friends. In later years he enthusiastically medicated his flakiness with tincture of opium, known as laudanum – the culmination of all manner of addictions throughout his life. But he was, however, undoubtedly a poet of genius. He gave us important works such as *The Rime of the Ancient Mariner* – from which the concept of an 'albatross' round one's neck originated, as well as the phrase 'water, water everywhere, nor any drop to drink' – and, with his friend Wordsworth, the *Lyrical Ballads*, the publication that contained the aforementioned masterpiece. It put both poets on the literary map and was the first blossoming of the Romantic movement in Britain.

As recorded in his notebooks and letters,* Coleridge left Keswick on 1 August in possession of a 'shirt, cravat, 2 pair of Stockings ... my night cap, packed up in my natty green oilskin ... and the Knap-sack on my back'. He also carried a 'besom stick', essentially a broom handle he'd acquired from his kitchen, much to the dismay of his wife and housemaid, not least because he'd left the rest of the broom scattered all over the floor.

As Coleridge wandered the Lakes, his letters carry weighty descriptions of the scenery he encountered, particularly extolling the 'wildness of the mountains, their Coves, and long arm-shaped & elbow-shaped ridges'. He took considerable pleasure in describing the hills of Buttermere and Ennerdale, then, on 2 August, Coleridge spied the mountains at the head of

---

* It should probably be noted that the 'Sca'Fell letters', which contain many of the descriptions above, were addressed to a 'Sara' who was clearly in Coleridge's high esteem, despite most certainly not being the Sarah he was married to. The former was Sara Hutchinson, Wordsworth's future sister-in-law, with whom Coleridge was infatuated.

Wasdale. He noted the shift in their character and the darkening of the scenery here, calling the mountains at the head of the lake the 'Monsters of the Country, bare bleak heads, evermore doing deeds of Darkness ... in the clouds'.

The poet identified the trio of peaks at the head of Wastwater as 'Yewbarrow, Sca'Fell and the great Gavel' ('gavel' being the bridge between the Old Norse *gafl* and the modern 'gable'). After a detour to the coast, Coleridge returned to Wasdale and, on the morning of 5 August, climbed up into the pass between Scafell and the Screes, turning north-east towards the summit of Scafell.

'O my God! What enormous Mountains these are close by me, & yet below the Hill I stand on,' he wrote. As he climbed he also noted that local shepherds, typically the only folk to wander the high fells back then, suspected – rightly – that Scafell was higher than Helvellyn and Skiddaw. Coleridge found a hollow on the summit of Scafell with a 'nice stone table' upon which he wrote his letter – 'surely the first Letter ever written from the Top' – commenting on the deteriorating, thundery weather and that should he wish to, he could remain, warm but hungry, until morning. Coleridge decided to push on, however. Hurriedly signing off his letter – 'I have wafers in my inkhorn' – he left his place of 'lounding'* towards the most 'sublime Crag-summit, that seemed to outdo Sca'Fell ... in height, & to outdo it in fierceness'.

He was talking about what we now call Scafell Pike. Between him and it lay Mickledore and, unbeknownst to him, Broad Stand. His journey towards the former via the latter would, in a strange kind of way, make history.

Much has been written about and credited to Coleridge's experience on Broad Stand in the two centuries since. It's curious that whilst climbing by its very nature focuses on ascent, what he actually did that day was make a *descent* – and thus he wasn't climbing but downclimbing. This is immaterial. Whatever you want to call what he undertook on Broad Stand, it's the way in which the ever-articulate (and dramatic) Coleridge himself described the experience – and the cathartic sequence of emotions he clearly worked through during his descent – that marks it out as being so significant in the

*   Coleridge often used the Cumbrian word *lounded*, meaning 'sheltered'.

history of mountain adventure. Quite simply, in modern parlance, even though it scared the crap out of him, it also gave him a buzz. And although he wasn't the first to have experienced such a thing, he was certainly the first to articulate it in such style.

'There is one sort of Gambling, to which I am much addicted,' he continued in his letter the following day. 'When I find it convenient to descend from a mountain, I am too confident & too indolent to look round about & wind about 'til I find a track or some symptom of safety ... where it is first possible to descend, there I go – relying upon fortune for how far down this possibility will continue.'

So it was that, under the threat of treacherous weather, Coleridge left the summit of Scafell and encountered Broad Stand. His descriptions of the descent are highly detailed and entertaining, describing a series of 'little precipices' he descended with 'tolerable ease' before one particular drop 'put my whole limbs atremble'. He was fairly sure he'd descended something he could not re-climb (he actually uses the term 'crag-fast') and therefore had little choice but to go on.

'Every drop increased the Palsy of my Limbs ... I shook all over, heaven known without the least influence of Fear.' In shaking like this Coleridge was probably experiencing lactic acid exhaustion caused by muscle fatigue, as well as surges of adrenaline: that fight-or-flight response so common in precarious places. Faced with the prospect of two more rock ledges, he noted that the first of these 'was tremendous, it was twice my own height,' floored with a ledge so narrow 'that if I dropped down upon it I must of necessity have fallen backwards & of course killed myself'. His reaction to this peril was to lie down to recover from his fatigue and attempt to regain clarity of thought. This, it seems, he achieved, as he stated that 'I know not how to proceed, not how to return, but I am calm & fearless & confident.'

So gathering himself, he noticed one of the rocks beneath the ledge on which he was lying was cracked in such a manner that he could wedge himself into it and descend. Coming across a rotting sheep on a rock towards which a shepherd had ramped stones in an effort – unsuccessfully, evidently – to give the creature an escape route, Coleridge managed to reach safety in Mickledore, reclaim his besom stick, which he'd thrown down ahead, then resume his walk. He could scarcely have imagined that – however modest – his account of his escape on Broad Stand would inadvertently become the first piece of edge-of-your-seat mountaineering literature.*

Back to our perch on the Great Napes, and the imposing pinnacle of Napes Needle. It was upon the top of the Needle's overhanging top block that, in 1886, Oxford graduate Walter Parry Haskett Smith left his handkerchief fluttering, having made the audacious first ascent, alone and unroped. In his account of the climb, Haskett Smith described the crags of the Great Napes as being hitherto viewed as 'dangerously rotten' by climbers; this was the reason he was able to claim the first ascent of the Needle, which from his first sighting of it some years earlier had become something of an ambition for him. Although only 22 metres or so from top to bottom, it's an incredibly awesome and exposed prospect even from its base, let alone the top. Shouldered out over the steep screes of the Napes, the feeling of height is quite sensational. The top block itself looks precarious, too; not only is it obviously loose† – as shown by the crack that separates it from the Needle's slender neck – it's also overhanging, and from beneath it's difficult to estimate how accommodating the top block would be for a climber.

Haskett Smith reportedly tossed some small stones up onto the top to see whether any would stay put, indicating a flat surface. It's difficult to decide which is the more horrifying: the fact that he decided that only one out of three stones staying put on the top was sufficient to commit himself to a potentially fatal ascent, or the fact that a piece of ground large enough to accommodate a palm-sized fragment of rock signified a surface that would be large enough to accommodate a swaying, adrenaline-soaked climber. Either way, he committed himself – like a 'mouse climbing a milestone' – reached the top, left his handkerchief behind as proof, then wondered how the hell he was going to get

---

* Anyone who reads Coleridge's account might notice that although he confused some of the place names – he mentions Bowfell, for instance, which lies a considerable distance away – it's agreed by all who have studied the account that he was most certainly on Broad Stand.

† It's said that four climbers sitting around the top block of the Needle can actually rock it. Before you ask what type of climber would do such an appalling thing, consider the type of climber prepared to be one of *four* who would share that tiny pedestal, and both answers will probably present themselves.

down again. That he lived long enough and in sufficient health to repeat the climb for its 50th anniversary in 1936 shows he eventually figured it out.

So iconic did Napes Needle become for Lakeland climbing in later years that a plan was hatched in the late 20th century to blow the top block off using dynamite. It's believed this ludicrously dangerous – not to mention stupid – plan was devised by a group of competitive rock climbers from the Peak District who were determined to bruise the nose of the Lake District climbing fraternity. Happily, the plan never came to fruition, and Napes Needle remains the wholly intact symbol of the Fell and Rock Climbing Club to this day.

It's often written that Haskett Smith's ascent of Napes Needle was the first such climb of its type – that is to say, a climb for climbing's sake, and therefore the 'birth' of the sport. This isn't the case. What Haskett Smith actually did – apart from make a highly daring and audacious ascent, which his most certainly was – was to epitomise it, in effect becoming rock climbing's first celebrity. By finding and tackling the talismanic pinnacle of Napes Needle, something that seemed to embody the challenge of rock climbing so fittingly, he captured the imagination of an entire generation. Haskett Smith's ascent was, quite simply, stylish: the most electrifying single articulation of a dangerous sport in its infancy.

Between Coleridge's buzzy descent of Broad Stand and Haskett Smith's tour de force on Napes Needle, we cannot tell who actually made the very first British rock climb with sport as its express object – but we do know which was the first *recorded* pre-meditated ascent. And this was also in the vicinity of Great Gable, though not precisely on it.

Lakeland sheep can be deft and fearless climbers but give little consideration to descent, and shepherds had been climbing the frowning crags of the western Lake District to retrieve them for years; as we've seen, Coleridge found evidence of a shepherd trying to pile stones into a ramp to aid the rotting sheep he encountered on Broad Stand prior to its untimely end. It was inevitable – given the cocktail of physical responses rock climbing triggers – that one of these hardy men would detect a glimmer of pleasure or challenge in the pursuit. And it was one of these shepherds who made the first recorded ascent of a high buttress of rock, the size of a small block of flats, hanging free of its parent summit above the deep valley of Ennerdale, the head of which is just visible from the Great Napes to the far right of the view down into Wasdale.

The buttress's name is Pillar Rock, and if you're looking for a place to pinpoint exactly where the first sporting climb that we know of took place, this would be it. The climber was a shepherd from Croftfoot in Ennerdale by the name of John Atkinson. The year was 1826, almost exactly 60 years to the day before Haskett Smith's ascent of Napes Needle.

It's around Pillar Rock – as has a tendency to happen in the Lake District – that many threads coalesce. Wordsworth and Coleridge passed this way on a 1799 tour of the Lake District. In Ennerdale they heard the tale of a shepherd, James Bowman, who was sleeping on top of a crag near Pillar Rock when he walked in his sleep, fell from the crag and broke his neck. As Coleridge would write in his notebook entry for 12 November 1799, his 'pike staff, struck midway, stayed there until it rotted away'. The story would form the loose foundation of Wordsworth's celebrated poem 'The Brothers'. He transposes the location of the crag from which Bowman fell – Proud Knott – to a rather more prominent object:

> You see yon precipice – it almost looks
> Like some vast building made of many crags,
> And in the midst is one particular rock
> That rises like a column from the vale,
> Whence by our Shepherds it is call'd, the Pillar.

This passage would influence Alfred Heaton Cooper's atmospheric 1908 painting of Pillar Rock from Ennerdale, which features a shepherd tending his flock in front of a savage backdrop punctured by the gothically rendered Pillar Rock. Physically, Pillar Rock is no Napes Needle; where the latter is shapely, sharp and hidden, the former is muscular and unsubtle, and is certainly extremely impressive when seen from verdant Ennerdale.

It's said that Atkinson's ascent of the rock was born of a challenge amongst local shepherds to counter the emphatic lines in John Otley's 1823 guide *The Geology of the Lake District* that told its readers the 'Pillar Stone' was 'unclimbable'. The awkward suggestion here is that to label something *unclimbable* strongly indicates the author was aware of comparable eminences that were *climbable*, which seems to cast doubt on whether Atkinson's ascent was indeed the first of its kind. In addition, local newspaper coverage of the shepherd's feat – which reputedly followed what is now known as the Old West Route – proposed that his was the first successful bid of 'thousands' to climb the rock, again hinting at other objects nearby of surmountable difficulty. After all, you don't generally attempt Mount Everest without climbing something smaller first.

But Atkinson's climb was certainly a physical landmark worth noticing and it marked a change in attitude towards endeavour in the mountains. No longer did climbing simply involve reaching the top of a mountain; it was reaching any summit, ledge or pointy bit by a deliberately difficult route. The climb itself had become the object, not the high point at the end of it. Mountaintops – if they were a feature of a rock climb at all – were just ceremonial elevational endstops, and quite often ignored by climbers. This fundamental difference between rock climbing and hillwalking may seem over-subtle to the outsider, but, then as now, the two activities are quite different.

Atkinson's climb made local headlines, and inspired a litany of visiting imitators, all of which means that Haskett Smith – an Oxford-educated barrister – can't even be called the first tourist rock climber in the Lake District. In the intervening years before his ascent of Napes Needle, Pillar Rock was climbed by, amongst many others, a lieutenant in the Royal Navy, several women – one of whom, in 1873, was Mary Westmorland, climbing with her brothers, of which more anon – and a vicar. The latter, the colourful Reverend James Jackson, was even nicknamed the 'Patriarch of the Pillarites', having made his first ascent of Pillar Rock in 1875 at the age of 79. He made a second, at 80. Having headed out for a third attempt, at 82, he failed to return; his body was found three days later, having seemingly fallen as he approached the start of the route. Between 1826 and 1875 there were at least 119 ascents of Pillar Rock. In 1881, five years before his Napes Needle climb, even Haskett Smith himself put up a new route on it, with his brother Edmund. At one point during this period there was said to be a bottle on the top containing a log of the names of those who'd reached this redoubtable high point.

Whilst Pillar Rock clearly received niche attention long before Napes Needle captured the nation's, the reason rock climbing didn't take off in Britain as quickly as you might have expected was that, quite simply, there were grander, rather more glorious objectives to bag abroad. And through the middle decades of the 19th century a generation of classically educated men and women emerged – with a profoundly different and entirely more practical attitude towards mountains than previous generations – who proceeded to do just that.

These intervening decades between 1826 and 1886 saw an exodus of British tourists and adventurers into the higher Alpine regions on a latter-day Grand Tour in search of ever-more sublime terror. Many used the freedom granted by the Empire's extensive influence to explore and in some cases mountaineer, thereby taking part in what's called 'the Golden Age' of Alpine mountaineering. Despite the vogue for ascending unclimbed peaks, this period saw many of its most successful protagonists continue to insist they were in the mountains for far more noble reasons than simply climbing them, as if unwilling to admit to some peculiar fetish. Some, such as the Irish physicist John Tyndall – who made the first ascent of Switzerland's formidable Weisshorn in 1861 – and geologist James Forbes, continued to travel to the mountains under the auspices of science, although Forbes in particular made no secret of the fact that he enjoyed the experience of mountaineering, describing it as a 'satisfaction and a freedom from restraint'. Forever famous amongst glaciologists, as pleasing collateral he's also considered one of the founding fathers of British mountaineering.

Switzerland in particular was so rife with a certain class of leisured British traveller in the 1850s and 1860s that, as put drily in the *Alpine Journal*, if you 'met a man in the Alps, it was ten to one that he was a university man, eight to one that he was a Cambridge man, and about even betting that he was a fellow of his college'. Many prized continental objectives were first trodden by these Grand Tourists, typically in the company of local mountain guides. The Eiger was climbed for the first time by Irishman Charles Barrington in 1856, Italy's Gran Paradiso in 1861 by Englishmen Cowell and Dundas, the Schreckhorn in 1861 by Leslie Stephen, the father of Virginia Woolf. The coveted first ascent of the Matterhorn – by London-born Edward Whymper – came in 1865. On that July day, as the last, great unclimbed summit of the Alps fell, so too did four of the seven-strong party when their rope snapped on the descent. It was a tragic full-stop to the Golden Age of Alpine mountaineering.

With most of the high peaks of the continent conquered, and most – though not quite all – native peaks trodden, the lure of the Alps began to subside and attention turned to smaller-scale objectives closer to home: the rocks, the cliffs, the pinnacles. The ascent of Napes Needle would electrify the generation who'd carve the foundation of the sport from the bedrock laid by those early pioneers on Pillar Rock. It would be a generation suffused by brilliance and – ultimately – almost unimaginable tragedy. And again, it would be the crags of the western Lake District, the very landscape that wheels around the hub of Great Gable, where their greatest games would be played out and be both immortalised and memorialised.

However fond most of my memories of that day spent beneath the Great Napes were, I'd no desire to repeat the route in the gloom of a late-autumn afternoon. The edges of the seasons bleed into each other the higher up you get at this time of year, and whilst it could still be autumnal in the valley, winter's teeth might already be sharpened up top. I had to catch the light whilst it was still lit, and deep-dug in the crags of the south face was not the place to do it. Besides, I was keen to see a different side to Great Gable, one that was the complete antithesis of the craggy Napes and presented the mountain's less intimidating, more inclusive side.

So, having climbed up from Seathwaite, I made the approach from Sprinkling Tarn, a tucked-away miniature lake high above the head of Borrowdale beneath the deep-fissured crags of Great End. This pleasant way up the mountain doesn't give you an impression of Great Gable's pyramid – only Wasdale gives you that – but of a rough-edged dome with a deep bite out of the high left, sharpened by the bristles of the Napes. Closer, I could see this bite was actually the scree fan of Great Hell Gate, its purply-tinted chute smooth and veined amidst the chaotic, blocky ground it cut. I edged around the tarn and wandered across the boggy pass, stepping over rivulets and puddles, their surfaces fish-scaled by the breeze, and began the descent to Sty Head, where Great Gable began.

The landscape was dusky. Half an hour earlier I'd watched a stripe of brilliant sunlight trace across the flanks of Glaramara, then watched it snuff against Allen Crags as the short day began to wane. If I was lucky I'd catch the final gasp of the light from Great Gable's summit. The evening was calm, with only the trickle of water and wind funnelling through distant crags augmenting the dull clump of my boots on the rock. There didn't seem to be anyone else up here at all.

Great Gable at first looks like it might be made of the same purple-brown sandstone as the mountains of Torridon, but it isn't. Like most British geology, the story of its rocks is a fiercely convoluted one. The closure of the Iapetus Ocean around 400 million years ago joined England to Scotland, and the violent volcanism and mountain-building that ensued gave rise to many of northern Britain's mountain ranges. A large number of the Lake District's highest, most rugged mountains are built of volcanic rock, spat explosively from the earth's crust in deposits that in places were over 8,000 metres thick – as deep as the very tallest mountains on the planet today are high. Many of the rest are made up of rocks dredged up from the sea floor and compressed into slate during the same continental collision. This sandwich of ancient rocks was then worn down by the ocean and later by ice, leaving its scoured remnants behind. The mountains made from volcanics are notable for their dark, tough rock and their craggy appearance, and include the Scafells, Great Gable and the Helvellyn range; the rock is named the Borrowdale Volcanic Group, after the valley.

The mountains made from the older slates tend to be smoother, although they've often been enlivened by river-cut gorges and arêtes carved by glaciation. This rock is named for the mountain that best embodies it, standing regally at the end of Derwentwater: Skiddaw Slate. The join between these two major rock groups can be seen on nearby Fleetwith Pike, long quarried for its Honister green slate.

One of Borrowdale's claims to lucrative fame is that it was the original source of graphite in Britain – then known as wadd, 'plumbago' or black lead. Graphite is almost pure carbon, and during the Napoleonic Wars this was an extremely precious commodity both for its lubricating qualities and its role as a cannonball mould. It's said that the term 'black market' was coined by smugglers of wadd on account of the dark smears it left on anyone who handled it, and high amongst the rafters of Gable Crag was the habitation of one who did: an enterprising crook by the name of Moses Rigg. Moses has been accused of many things – from using his hut for the distillation and trafficking of illegal whisky to smuggling wadd from the heavily guarded quarries at Seathwaite over Gable Crag via a tucked-away retreat; nefarious, occupational rock climbing in action twenty years before Coleridge muscled in on the act. Up amongst the crags there still exist the vague remains of a hut, in a place inaccessible to the walker and elusive to the climber, unless you know exactly where to look. A path now bears Moses' name, and leads up from Wasdale to Great Gable.

A long wooden box emblazoned with the seal of Wasdale Mountain Rescue stands at the final junction of paths before you step off the pass of Sty Head and onto the rocks of Great Gable itself. As its unsubtle black letters point out, it's a stretcher box, but it's also a landmark and has no doubt functioned as a claustrophobic but necessary makeshift shelter in dire conditions. There's another on Scafell Pike not far from the spot where Coleridge made his inadvertently historic descent. Stretcher boxes have the habit of popping up in black-spot areas.

From here the path splits: bear left for the Climber's Traverse and the Napes, or straight ahead for the walker's path up the south-east flank – a way known as the Breast Route. I took the latter.

It climbed rapidly, occasional backward glances revealing a splendid but darkening view back to high-tucked Sprinkling Tarn and the grey arrowhead of Styhead Tarn in the pass below. William Heaton Cooper described tarns as the 'eyes of the mountains', a great image, and from here particularly apt.

With distance and height, Great End was no longer just a pile of crags but now resembled a mountain, almost rent in two by the deep, black scratch of Skew Gill. The path slacked off in a few places as it ascended grass and loose stones, the steep falls of crags never far away to the left, the opening space beyond them to Wasdale implicit yet invisible over the skyline. The clouds had dissipated in the cooling evening and stars were softly beginning to prick the sky overhead. I stopped to pull on my puffy top and looked up towards the summit to see a sky of deepening, pink-blushed blue. It was nearly 4 p.m.; the sun would be dropping into the sea west of St Bees any second.

The top came quite quickly. The climb from Sty Head is a little over 400 metres, but it takes only half a mile through craggy ground so at no point do you forget you're climbing a mountain. But while the built path lessened the effort, I'd still expected the climb to be more arduous. The gradient lessens long before the top, and you enter a wasteland of lichen-whitened boulders. It's quite a big summit, the top crowned with a natural topknot of bedrock sprinkled with unnatural, human-laid cairn stones. I saw it but didn't visit it. Not just yet. Instead I walked to the edge of the south face, where the mountain collapsed into crags and a large wigwam cairn presided over a quite exceptional view.

In 2007 the vista looking up steep-sided Wasdale towards Great Gable was voted by viewers of a British TV channel as Britain's favourite view. If only more could see the reverse of that view – from the point of Great Gable's pyramid where I was now standing – they'd realise that the far more famous, ground-level aspect is at very most a runner-up. From the summit it's a similar view to that from the Napes, but far more commanding, and lacking the claustrophobic bulk of a mountain at your back. The perspective is immediate. Wordsworth once said that Great Gable was the centre of a wheel of valleys radiating from it like spokes, and it certainly feels like it. From its top you can see Crummock Water filling a distant crook of hills, peer down into Ennerdale and even – as a horn on its bulky parent fell – make out Pillar Rock.

It was an intensely beautiful sight. The sun had gone, diffused beyond sea fog ribboned across the horizon, but the clouds above were just catching its last warmth. As their daylight colours faded, every stone, blade of grass and patch of sky momentarily took on a fleeting tint of lilac. Only a few precious seconds would look like this today; how lucky I was to be there, just then, to see one of those moments that you never really forget. But then, in the mountains, that happens a lot. You get to see stuff like this. That's why these places are so special; here, any spectacle has the volume turned up.

The pile of stones marking this spot is known as the Westmorland Cairn. You'd assume the cairn's name would be to do with the old county of Westmorland, but Great Gable was never in Westmorland; its ancient county was Cumberland. You might recall an earlier mention of one Mary Westmorland, who climbed Pillar Rock with her brothers around 1873; it was these brothers – Thomas and Edward – who built the Westmorland Cairn three years later to mark the point they considered to possess the best view in the district. They're still right.

From their newly crowned perch, the brothers had a commanding view of Wastwater, and the valley that was then, more correctly, known as Wastdale. No doubt they knew well of the inn there, which in the years to follow would become the epicentre of rock climbing's elite.

* * *

Were you to buy a beer at the bar of what was in 1880 called the Wastwater Hotel and linger there for 35 years or so, you'd have been treated to a conveyor belt of rock climbing's most influential and notorious stars. Wasdale's remoteness at the time meant it required great commitment to reach the valley, and simply being there seemed to enroll you in a sort of club that was in turn convivial and chaotic. It was a point of pilgrimage, as many of these far-flung hostelries were and remain, for adventurers, eccentrics and isolationists. A grand, whitewashed building with the bold word 'INN' emblazoned on its side, the Wasdale Head Inn is still a seductive relief for any traveller who attains this sequestered part of the Lake District, dug in at the end of a valley that goes nowhere but into mountains.

During this period, rock climbing began to create athletes the like of which had never been seen before. Many of these were intellectuals, who by their nature and social persuasion philosophised at some length about their dangerous yet ostensibly pointless pursuit. By day the rooms of the inn would stand empty; by night the bar would be filled with chatter of the day's sport, and talk of culture and politics. The air would hang heavy with the smell of wet tweed and pipe smoke, and the hallway would habitually be piled deep with nailed boots. And as the century came to a close and climbers became younger and more numerous, the Wasdale Head Inn became a rather more anarchic, booze-powered proving ground for gymnastic prowess. One popular game centred on the billiard room – and more specifically the billiard table – where a rite of passage was to clear a corner of it with a single leap. Another popular game was to climb around the room and over the table without touching the floor, a pastime unofficially transposed in more recent years to the dormitories of bunkhouses and hostels. Yet another would be the 'barn door traverse', which took place on the rough walls of the adjacent stables. A sadly anonymous person was overheard here by a journal-writing climber named Lehman Oppenheimer sniffily deriding these brash displays as 'men struggling to degenerate into apes', before adding that 'the anthropoid ... in man tends to disappear, but those fellows at the Hotel won't let it die.'

Many climbers came and went from Wasdale Head, and some are remembered more than others. There was Haskett Smith, of course, as well as his finely named contemporary Cecil Slingsby. The aforementioned Manchester-born engineer Oppenheimer was a regular, as was Oscar Eckenstein, who would later refine crampon and ice-axe design to basic principles that continue to this day. Eckenstein often climbed in the company of an asthmatic young climber named Aleister Crowley. Crowley is perhaps the most well known of these early climbers, not for his prowess on rock, which was considerable, but for the peculiar course his life would take. We'll get to that, but in his day he was quite a formidable cragsman; one of the early and notable climbs made from the Wasdale base was his casual pioneering of a new route on Napes Needle in 1893 that still bears his name.

Crowley, in a memoir, recounts a climb with a young physics master by the name of Owen Glynne Jones. It did not go well: 'I was only once on a rope with Jones. It was on Great Gable; the rocks were plastered with ice and a bitter wind was blowing. I looked up to [him] ... and saw to my horror that he was maintaining his equilibrium by a sort of savage war dance ... I have no idea how we got to the bottom undamaged; but when we did, I promptly took off the rope and walked home, utterly disgusted with the vanity which had endangered the party.'

However Crowley felt about Jones, history would remember the bespectacled – and apparently brusque – Welshman as one of the first rock athletes, possessed of awesome talent and seemingly reckless arrogance, which would gain him both respect and disdain from his fellow climbers.

Jones was also one of the first climbers to be spectacularly photographed taking part in his sport, typically in images taken by Keswick photographers George and Ashley Abraham, whose ability to wield enormous plate cameras around the high crags of Britain ranks as remarkable in itself. The Abraham Brothers' record of now iconic Lake District landmarks such as Napes Needle, Scafell Pinnacle, Kern Knotts and the Wasdale Head Inn itself would introduce images of a young climber dramatically excelling in this exciting new sport to a much wider audience. Ashley Abraham would in 1906 become the first president of the Fell and Rock Climbing Club, which endures to this day.

Crowley had been a student at Trinity College, Cambridge, where (ironically, given what followed) he studied Moral Science. Whilst at Trinity he briefly befriended a fellow student by the name of Geoffrey Winthrop Young. Young, as well as being a poet and intellectual, was also a climber – and pioneered the night-time assaults on the university spires (the 'college Alps'), an illicit practice now known as stegophily or 'buildering'. He even wrote a book about it in 1899 – under the pseudonym A. Climber – titled *The Roof-Climber's Guide to Trinity*.

Winthrop Young is perhaps the most important figure in the early British mountaineering scene. A regular winter visitor to Wasdale, where he would hope for days when the 'sky stayed steel blue and the rocks were all draped with dull ivory ice', Winthrop Young, who would later become a master at Eton and a prolific Alpine mountaineer, exerted a kind of gravitational pull on talented young climbers. His gatherings at Pen-y-Pass beneath Snowdon and Crib Goch would invariably be oversubscribed, and often by those inhabiting the higher altitudes of society such as was typical of climbers of the time. Early devotees included Geoffrey Keynes – brother of Maynard, the economist – and 'Cottie' Sanders, who would later become a prolific novelist under the pseudonym Ann Bridge.

One photograph, taken in 1912 by Winthrop Young, pictures two of the fiercest young talents of the infant century casually reclining against the wall of what is now the Pen-y-Pass youth hostel. The snow-frosted arête of Crib Goch rising behind them, the pair had just completed a difficult traverse on Y Lliwedd in full winter conditions. In the photograph one absently rests a foot on a bucket and smokes a pipe; the other looks humourlessly into the distance. The former was 21-year-old Siegfried Herford, a climber who'd trained on the coarse gritstone of the Peak District, and in two years would put up what was regarded for many years as the hardest rock climb in the country, 'Central Buttress' on Scafell Crag. The latter, a 26-year-old Cambridge graduate and son of a Cheshire vicar, would go on to become one of the most famous mountaineers in history: George Mallory.

Young and Mallory had climbed together in the Alps in 1909, where Young was simultaneously both awed and horrified by Mallory's astonishing talent and seemingly reckless lapses of forgetfulness. In one instance, Young spotted Mallory on a tiny, ice-covered ledge above a 2,000-metre drop on the south ridge of the Finsteraarhorn in Switzerland having neglected to rope up for a pitch. Young was so terrified of startling Mallory into a slip he had to whisper a warning to him. 'My panic was unnecessary,' he later wrote, 'because the reassurance of a rope never meant anything to Mallory, who was as sure-footed and as agile in recovery as the proverbial chamois.'

By these early years of the 20th century it seemed that Britain's love affair with the mountains was reaching something of a climax. The love of the sublime and picturesque had drawn people's gaze up to the mountaintops; the highest peaks of the Alps had felt the boots of the mountaineers; focus had returned to difficult, small-scale technical objectives on the crags and pinnacles of the Lake District; and now the quest for mountain summits and the technical minutiae of rock climbing were combining. Big, difficult unclimbed mountains in the mystical greater ranges of Asia were the next frontier. To this young, hungry generation of rock climber–mountaineers, the Himalaya were beckoning.

Then, on 28 July 1914, everything changed.

After the sun had died, I walked from the Westmorland Cairn to the summit of Great Gable. Pulling on an extra coat on the darkening summit, I spent a moment enjoying the emergence of the stars above, then went to look for something important. It took me a few moments to find it: a small bronze plaque, greened by age, recessed into a fractured boulder beneath the summit. In the gloaming I could just read the inscription. Having done so, I stood there with it for a quiet moment, then began my descent down towards Windy Gap, back to Seathwaite, then back home – home, to wait for winter.

Hemingway once famously said that there were only 'three true sports: bullfighting, motor racing and mountaineering. The rest are mere games.' However drenched in machismo this is, any sport that pushes people to dangerous extremes can claim a price, and sometimes escapades in the mountains go wrong. The tiny church in Wasdale – St Olaf's – hosts the mortal remains of many who have been unlucky on the hills that circle the graveyard. Within the church there's a stained-glass window featuring a tiny image of Napes Needle above an inscription, paraphrased from Psalm 121: a Song of Ascents.* It reads: *I will lift up mine eyes unto the hills from whence cometh my strength.*

---

* The New International Bible has these lines in Psalm 121:1 as *I lift up my eyes to the mountains – where does my help come from?* The King James Bible of 1611 translates them as *I will lift vp mine eyes vnto the hilles: from whence commeth my helpe.* The substitution of 'help' for 'strength' seems to be a later hymnal addition, but it's certainly fitting in the context.

Owen Glynne Jones was killed in 1899, aged 32, following a fall on the Dent Blanche in Switzerland. Albert 'Fred' Mummery, whilst attempting to be the first to climb an 8,000-metre peak, was killed in 1895 by an avalanche on an expedition to the hazard-riddled Nanga Parbat in the Himalaya. Oscar Eckenstein and Aleister Crowley attempted K2 in a disastrous expedition that descended into acrimony when Crowley pulled a gun on fellow expedition member Guy Knowles. Crowley's transformation into the man history would remember as the 'Great Beast' had already begun; besides his notably unsympathetic attitude to the deaths of various contemporaries, by the 1890s Crowley had become known for dabbling in the dark arts, taking huge amounts of opiates and bending the morals of the age for his own amusement, as and when the whim took him. His obscene poetry, sexual depravity and the occult societies he formed made him notorious, dubbed by the press the 'wickedest man in the world'. In the face of such infamy, by his death in 1947 his mountaineering achievements had understandably been forgotten, and he's possibly best remembered for a series of frightening photographs and his appearance as the strikingly bald head on the cover of *Sgt. Pepper's Lonely Hearts Club Band*.

These events aside, it would be the outbreak of war in Europe that would leave the most lasting scar on the brilliant, cursed first generation of British rock climbers. Many did not return from the trenches; and most who did were never the same again.

On 8 June 1924 a 48-year-old man with a limp left Borrowdale and began to climb falteringly towards the summit of Great Gable.

The previous year, the deeds to 3,000 acres of the Lake District had been handed over by their new owner, the Fell and Rock Climbing Club, to the National Trust. They'd bought the mountains that had become their playground – Lingmell, Great Gable, Green Gable and Kirk Fell, amongst others – and donated them to posterity. In 1919 Scafell Pike had been bought by Lord Leconfield and similarly presented to the Trust, in whose hands now rested a huge clutch of English mountaineering's most revered peaks. The debt anyone who walks these hills owes to these gifts is immeasurable. But on this particular June day, the mountains had another part to play: they were about to be dedicated as an enormous war memorial.

The small party, led by the limping but determined Geoffrey Winthrop Young, continued up Great Gable, joined, quietly and solemnly, by a huge crowd of walkers and climbers converging on the summit from the valleys below. Cloaked in a union flag, a bronze memorial bore the names of the lost, amongst them Siegfried Herford, killed by a grenade in the Flanders trenches in 1915 (his ghost is said to haunt Hollow Stones beneath his beloved Scafell); Lehman Oppenheimer, who wrote *The Heart of Lakeland*, killed the same year; and H. L. Slingsby, son of Cecil and a promising climber himself, killed in 1918. Winthrop Young limped because his left leg had been amputated after an injury suffered during the battle of Monte San Gabriele in 1917. After the formal dedication of the plaque, Winthrop Young delivered a solid eulogy:

> We dedicate this space of hills to freedom. Upon this rock are set the
> names of our men – our brothers ... who surrendered their part in the
> fellowship of hill, and wind, and sunshine, that the freedom of this
> land, the freedom of our spirit, should endure.

The plaque, still there, carries this message beneath a sculpture of the mountains that frosts white in winter:

> In glorious and happy memory of those whose names inscribed below
> – members of this club who died for their country in the European war
> 1914–1918. These fells were acquired by their fellow members and by
> them vested in the National Trust for the use and enjoyment of the
> people of our land, for all time.

One climber who'd also returned from the Great War had joined an expedition to Mount Everest in 1921, with Winthrop Young's encouragement. From the ridge that marked the border between Tibet and the forbidden kingdom of Nepal he'd spied a great valley that he named the Western Cwm, in honour of the great Welsh valleys of Snowdon where he'd cut his climbing teeth. He'd return twice again to Mount Everest, and although Winthrop Young didn't know it at the time, this great hope of British mountaineering would soon also be lost. On that day in 1924 – the very day the assembled crowd on the summit of Great Gable listened to the bugle call in the fog and remembered

their dead — 4,000 miles to the east, George Mallory and his climbing partner Andrew Irvine walked into the clouds swirling around the summit ridge
of Mount Everest. Into the clouds, into silence and into mountaineering
legend.

According to Noel Odell, who saw this final, fateful vision, they were
'going strong' for the top. Whether or not they made it there, we'll probably
never know; all we do know is that they didn't make it back. And of all the men
whose boots walked both these hills and the world's highest mountains, theirs
are the ones history will be the last to forget.

PART IV

WINTER

15 TERROR

Bulbous and benign as they may look under summer skies, in winter Scotland's Cairngorms can be truly murderous. This massive slab of glacier-chewed granite landlocked in the Highlands' girthy east is the largest piece of really high ground in Britain. Physically, the Cairngorms range is a gritty 427-million-year-old rock cap that heaves above the 1,200-metre contour, gouged in several places by valleys deeper than much of the Lake District is tall. It's big, hard and blank. And from it poke the summits of five of Britain's six highest mountains: all scraped, all sprawling and each requiring long, demanding walks in summer to surmount.

Some would say these walks are drawn out and monotonous, and that this large and empty place lacks the charisma and sharp drama of less subtle parts of the Scottish Highlands. But then autumn takes its lurch into darkness, the mountains freeze tight, snow begins to layer relentlessly onto heights where it will lie for months, and the Cairngorms begin to shift skin into something altogether more malignant. In the short, choppy days of the year's extremities, a walk through them becomes an expedition into mountains capable of producing the cruellest conditions these otherwise mild-mannered isles can muster. In winter the Cairngorms become Britain's deep freeze.

High ground is not in short supply here. The Cairngorms lie inside a formidably huge 1,748-square-mile national park into which you could drop Luxembourg, Singapore and Andorra and still have room to wriggle. If the size of the park is somewhat surprising – it's by far Britain's biggest – what's perhaps more so is that the Cairngorms represent one of only two national parks in Scotland. Loch Lomond and the Trossachs is the other, leaving a huge amount of notably sensational Highland bereft of this illustrious endorse-ment. Glen Coe, the wild Southern Uplands, Ben Nevis and the Lochaber

mountains, and Torridon and Applecross are but a few examples of undesig-
nated areas.*

Within the park lie 55 summits over 900 metres, with 36 per cent of the
park lying above the 800-metre contour. Geographically speaking, the
national park's boundaries stretch down to Blair Atholl and extend east
beyond Ballater, but the biggest peaks of the Cairngorm mountains lie within
a triangle dangled from Aviemore, with its lower points splayed to
Newtonmore and Braemar.

The position, bulk and elevation of these mountains make them a natural
windbreak for the cold polar maritime weather systems invading Britain from
the north. In winter the Cairngorms become the super-cooled link between
here and there: an extension of the Arctic. At their heart is an exposed area of
high ground across which wind can accelerate with gleeful abandon, blasting
summits that lie a committing distance from help, all within some confusingly blank topography. This is the Cairngorm plateau, and in the depths of
winter it's one of the most dangerous places in Britain – the true dark heart of
Scotland's winter mountain places.

Predictably, then, many stories of tragedy litter the Cairngorms' long
history. Unwary travellers cut down by blizzards or perishing through hypothermia and exposure, devastating avalanches, falls through snow cornices
onto invisible and sheer cliffs, disorientation in white-outs: this vast range
seems to have suffered more than its fair share of the typical – although thankfully fairly rare – incidents of misadventure in Britain's winter mountains.

The reason for this could be the illusion of safety. These aren't the sharp
monuments to visual menace you might find on Skye or in the heights of An
Teallach. Most are apparently dumpy, bare and gentle in profile. There's even a
train that goes up one of them and ski slopes that come back down again. But
up close, things change. The distances reveal themselves to be daunting, those

---

* Not everyone likes national parks. Whilst there's little argument about the ethos of wilderness protection and its recreational benefits – nor the fact that they bring in a huge amount
of tourist revenue – many argue that national park status restricts development, increases
property prices and causes overcrowding. Plans to create Britain's first coastal and marine
national park covering the Outer Hebrides were recently considered, the Isle of Harris having
sought the status as a way of slowing down its depopulation. These plans were subsequently
put on ice.

amenable slopes become endless, intimidating sweeps, and the many hidden valleys and corries that punch into the plateau – the Lairig Ghru's deep slash, the crag-ringed Coire Etchachan and the perma-shadowed Northern Corries, to name but three – all inflate the range's seemingly comely appearance into something unnervingly immense.

The skiing infrastructure to the north also makes the Cairngorms rather more accessible than many Scottish mountains, as the car park takes a 630-metre bite out of the ascent required to reach the range's highest places. For the prepared this is a quick ticket into the hills; for others it's an equally swift ticket into colder, wilder weather that in places without such easy access is usually gradually climbed into. The conditions up there can consequently come as quite a shock.

Perhaps it's the confusing terrain, the frequent sight-stealing mists or the light conditions that cause the white sky to merge with the snowy ground. Or maybe it's the plummeting nocturnal temperatures after a day dripping with hypothermic damp that make a winter's day in these mountains so unexpectedly committing.

But in addition to all of these quite rational reasons to be wary of the winter Cairngorms, these mountains harbour something else: something implacably, deeply frightening. This weird landscape of climatic extremity, of bare heights seething with featureless slopes haunted by the ghosts of the unwary and the unlucky has been known to stir feelings that sit entirely apart from the simply explainable factors of terrain or conditions. Feelings that have turned otherwise stoically rational folk decidedly irrational. And in such a place, a shift like this is far from welcome.

These feelings are invariably pinned to one mountain in particular, one vaunted for its isolation, sprawling structure and great height. A mountain – as successive generations of walkers have attested to varying degrees of hysteria – that certainly seems to have something *unsettling* about it. One writer summed this up as 'that fear without a name, that intense dread of the unknown'. The mountain also happens to be Britain's second highest: Ben Macdui.

*   *   *

Nearly four months after we'd been packing our bags beneath the oceanic blue skies of late summer, Jim and I stood in my yard, our breath smoking in the winter air beneath the sharp beam of a security light. Above us, a yellow moon was riding low over the rooftops. And laid out at our feet was a very different arsenal to that which we'd been assessing before heading for the Isle of Rùm – one that had doubled in size and gained the glint of tarnished metal.

Heading for the mountains in winter requires far deeper consideration than in summer. An unexpected night on the hill after a balmy day in July or August usually isn't life-threatening, provided you haven't broken a body part, eaten a suspect mushroom, run out of water, snapped your bootlaces* or something equally nigglesome – but in winter you're jousting with a whole new set of variables that must be accounted for. First, there's the obvious: cold.

The coldest temperature ever recorded in Britain happened to be in the Cairngorms, just outside Braemar on 11 February 1895. The temperature was logged at −27.2°C at a weather station 339 metres above sea level, a figure that – remarkably – was precisely repeated at the same weather station in January 1980. Something called the lapse rate normally ensures a temperature drop in dry air of about 6°C for every 1,000 metres ascended, so – whilst this is a variable science and it's unlikely (however possible) that the mountains above Braemar that night were pushing a Himalayan −35°C – it's certainly likely that sheltered spots high on Ben Macdui or Lochnagar were several degrees colder than the figures recorded by Braemar's weather station. That's not just cold for Britain; that's cold for anywhere.

But cold in itself isn't that hard to deal with. Puffy jackets filled with goose down, woollen underlayers, warm hats, thick gloves, and boots that don't leak when encased in snow are a few basics that will go a long way to keeping you warm on a day's walk. Factor in a night spent out, however, and the pile of kit at your feet has to get a little bigger. Walking all day, even in winter, produces sweat. When you stop, your body cools and your sweat starts to feel cold against your skin. And as your body loses heat through damp layers of clothing at a much more rapid rate than through dry layers, if you're intending to

---

* You may laugh, but this can be serious. Consider driving a car home down several miles of bad road without tyres on it and you have a sniff of what it might be like to walk home with a boot you can't keep on.

stop outdoors for a long time – such as overnight – a fresh set of thermals along with a spare warm jacket is probably a good idea.

That's the wet that you produce yourself. The next problem is the wet you don't. Scotland's climate isn't like the Himalaya or the Alps; it's far worse. The first concept to get your head around is that there are two different types of cold. Dry cold is deeply freezing weather that stays as such throughout both day and night. Snow doesn't melt, ice stays as ice and the only moisture you really have to worry about is sweat, which your spare set of thermals should help you tackle. Wet cold is more of a menace, as everything you wear can become soaked by melting water, wet snow and even rain during the day. Then at night, the moisture you've collected throughout the day – soaked up by clothing no longer attached to a warm human being – turns to ice. Ice is not ideal insulation. Therefore the prudent camper on a committing expedition packs spares of everything: fleecy top, fresh socks, puffy jacket – if something keeps you warm, pack a spare.

The pile's getting big now but we're not done yet. The next winter element we have to tackle is perhaps the most lethal, and one responsible for many of Cairngorms' tragedies: wind.

Wind chill is a killer. The term is given to the effect that air moving swiftly over exposed skin has on heat loss, and it's at its most dramatic when that skin is wet. The canniest way of demonstrating this is still to lick your finger on a chilly day, stick it in the air and feel how much more quickly the moist side chills down. Now imagine your licked finger is in fact an entirely damp you, high on a mountain with no gloves and no hat, the chilly day is actually a bracing –10°C, and that gentle breeze is a 40 mph gale relentlessly barrelling into you. You won't, I'm afraid, be lasting long out there. 40 mph winds in air temperatures of –10°C will strip the heat from your body as if it were –25°C. Exposed flesh will start to freeze within 30 minutes, beyond which frostbite of the ears, nose, fingers and toes is a real possibility as your body draws blood away from the extremities to feed the body's chilling core with warmth-bearing blood, like an army falling back from a castle's outer walls to protect the inner keep. You'll sense the heat leaving your body and then you'll start to go hypothermic. You'll feel thoroughly beaten, appalled and overcome by the elements. You might get angry, confused, frustrated, mumbly. You'll shake, then you won't shake. You might get tired, you might feel like stopping, then you might feel like you want to go to sleep. And then you'll die. So spare gloves, spare hat and something windproof should find its way onto that pile, please.

Lastly, most heavily and probably most dramatically is your means of actually staying upright. And for the slightly pugilistic, it's probably the bit that makes it all worthwhile.

'Axes? Really?'

Jim was examining with a mixture of curiosity and trepidation one of two long-shafted ice axes I'd dragged from the garage and slung on our ever-deepening pile of gear. In truth, as we were taking strong trekking poles and crampons – crampons being metal spikes that fit to stiffened boots and bite into the ice – I suspected these pugilistic additions may turn out to be unnecessary on a bulky mountain like Ben Macdui, where the need to slam the sharp end of an axe into the ground for any reason would probably be minimal. But again, winter has a funny way of throwing surprises at you. And if there's one place you don't want to be ill-equipped to deal with surprises, it's winter in the Cairngorms. Be careless enough to take a slide on a steep slope and your ice axe is just about the only thing that's likely to stop you.

'We might not need them but, hey, better safe than ... Well, you know.'

Anyone who's been to the Cairngorms in winter knows all too well. Better safe than dead.

Over the past few days Jim and I had been watching the weather reports as if preparing an assault on the summit of Mount Everest. With Christmas close enough for every shop window to resemble the inside of a Kleenex box and free time getting more precious, we'd nailed our Scottish winter hopes to four days of lean daylight. Everything had been looking tentatively superb up until that morning – the day before we were due to set off. Then an area of low pressure had slid in from the north earlier than expected, and the forecasts began to light up with the bright colours of severe weather warnings.

The forecast I'd downloaded that evening read like a what's what of angry weather, some of it quite lethal. 'Northerly winds in the range of 50 to 70 mph, gusts up to 90 mph,' it began. 'Considerable buffeting even at lower levels. Higher up, any mobility very difficult indeed. Severe wind chill.' Jim's eager face had stumbled on the first line.

'70 mph? That's 60 knots,' he'd said, as if its presentation as an aeronautical speed* made it sound even more serious than it already did.

'Oh, there's more. "Frequent hail and snow. Risk of thunder. Threat of the showers merging one into another in some areas, giving almost constant snow. Whiteout."'

This last word describes perhaps the most frightening of all weather conditions to winter mountain walkers. A whiteout is what happens when the contrast between the pale, snow-heavy sky and the pale, snow-covered ground ceases to exist, creating a world where you can't see where one ends and the other begins. Sometimes the diffused light through heavy cloud cover is so severe it swallows any surface texture, making it impossible to see even the ground in front of you. It's like floating inside a bright white box. Snowy mountains bring worries even in perfect visibility – but imagine travelling over terrain festooned with cornices, loaded snow slopes ready to avalanche and 300-metre crags whilst wearing what is effectively a blindfold and you'll start to understand why whiteouts reduce seasoned mountaineers to sobs. One often-adopted tactic if you find yourself impaired to such a degree is to toss a snowball a metre or so ahead of you; if it appears to float in midair, you're climbing a slope. If it sits in front of your feet, you're walking level. If it appears to settle downslope or disappears entirely, think carefully about your next step as you might be following it. Now, seriously – how unfathomably desperate must things have become for you to have to employ a tactic like that?

Understandably, then, a whiteout was something neither of us was keen to experience. But as we stood in my yard piling up layer upon layer of elements-staving clothing, a grim resignation was settling on us that over the next four days we were probably going to need every single bit of it.

It was early afternoon by the time we drew up in the high car park at Coire Cas, five miles south-east of Aviemore. Already the sun was low. Stretching

---

* Quite correctly, too. Whilst a knot doesn't really mean a lot to most of us, pilots and boat skippers know it as the speed one has to travel in order to cover one minute of latitude in one minute of time. For this reason it's the preferred unit of meteorological measurement, although for those of us familiar with our car speedometers the unit popularly used is typically is either mph or kmh. One knot is equivalent to 1.151 mph.

the stiffness of a nine-hour drive out of our legs and stamping our feet on the tarmac in the sub-zero cold, we began to layer up for the mountains. Around us the plunging lines of the hillsides looked, as per the vernacular, in pretty good winter nick; that's to say snow was in no short supply. That we could see them at all was a surprise, given the apocalyptic forecast.

The car park is actually the car park to the ski centre at Cairn Gorm – the range's namesake mountain, which has sacrificed its northern slopes to the messy, overbearing infrastructure such things demand. On top of this, it also hosts a funicular railway and a restaurant near the mountain's domed, 1,245-metre summit. Unless you have a fondness for draglifts and miles of reedy fencing, it's a bit of a mess, although thankfully restricted to this northern slope. In the interests of taking the positives where we could find them, its car park does offer a quick way high into the hills when daylight is in short supply.

The drive up to Coire Cas seemed to straddle two seasons – autumn to the left of the road, winter to the right – but now we had a view out to the sunlit north, we could see exactly where the winter turned the burnished gold heather of the lowland brown, then mucky, black-pitted grey, then a bleached white. The white was winning.

To the south, beyond the mountains into which we'd soon be ascending, the sun had vanished, replaced by a layer of dim cloud that softened the rounded top of Cairn Gorm. Not perfect weather, yet far from the meteorological cataclysm promised by the forecast. But as we left the car park and began to negotiate the paths at the bottom of the ski slopes towards the open hillside, one concern played on both of our minds: although the weather might be holding now, where would *we* be when it broke? On a committing, overnight route into the heart of Britain's coldest mountain range with a forecast of high winds, blizzards and whiteout, should we seize the unexpectedly comely weather or were we being lured into a trap? As Jim and I trudged off the tarmac onto the snow-dusted path, it was with an uneasy feeling, although one not without a slight sense of irony. Because on this mountain, the unease really wasn't supposed to come until later.

In his exciting book *The British Highlands with Rope and Rucksack*, published in 1924, Ernest A. Baker evoked the contrast between the Cairngorms and other mountainous areas of the Highlands by observing that 'the chief impression is not of towering heights, but of unfathomable depths.' The region was to challenge Baker's otherwise robust narrative composure, which over the course of his ascent of Britain's second-highest mountain would slip a little. Baker set off to climb 'Ben Muich Dhui', as he had it, in much the same way Jim and I had – that is to say unexpectedly late, and with a camp in mind. Caught out by darkness, Baker referred to the feeling of 'solitude amidst shapes so suggestive of latent power' spurring an 'overwhelming sense of one's personal helplessness and insignificance'. He described the darkening mountains as 'watching ... with invisible eyes' and being filled with the sense of 'some unknown presence ... an instinctive dread, as if we denizens of a lower world had no right of entry to this region of calm, this abode of sleeping terrors.'

To augment this, Baker quoted from John Campbell Shairp's 1876 poem *Glen Dessery*:

In the deep of noon, mysterious dread
Fell on me in that glimmering glen
Till, as from haunted ground, I fled
Back to the kindly homes of men.

From this it's clear Baker wasn't wholly comfortable high in the Cairngorms on a gloomy night. But then comes the bit that really sticks out: by way of anecdote, Baker speaks of a 'hard-headed man' he knew who, in no uncertain terms, told him that 'nothing would induce him to be alone on the top of Ben Muich Dhui, even in broad daylight.' This man apparently told Baker he once ran five miles without stopping from high on the mountain down to Rothiemurchus Forest in what he describes as 'mortal panic'.

Baker's description would hardly have been noticed were it not for a descriptively serendipitous incident in an Aberdeen hotel the following year, involving a man named Norman Collie.

We've met Collie already. As we noted, his pioneering climbs in Skye's Cuillin were honoured when one of the peaks in the range was named Sgùrr Thormaid, *Thormaid* being the Gaelic for 'Norman'. As befits someone after whom mountains are named, Collie was extremely highly thought of by his fellows. A tall man of strong, cadaverous features, Collie was once described as being a man 'sardonic and dry as dust in manner' who had 'climbed most of the peaks in the Rockies and named half of them'. These exploratory forays, coupled with expeditions to the Alps and Himalaya, marked Collie as one of the most prolifically adventurous mountaineers of Victorian Britain.* It was also Collie who put a full stop of sorts on domestic mountain exploration, when he made the ascent of the last unclimbed peak in Britain – Skye's Sgùrr Coire an Lochain – in 1896.

Collie was also a highly reputable man of science. As Professor of Organic Chemistry at University College London, he's credited not only with the discovery of neon and the demonstration of its uses but also, on being presented with a nurse who had a fragment of a needle in her thumb, took what was almost certainly the first medical X-ray. All this is merely to highlight how surprising it was when Collie – evidently a man of steady mind and scientific rigour – stood up to make a hesitant after-dinner speech following the Cairngorm Club Dinner of 1925 and, with apparent conviction but no small amount of reluctance, told the tale of something that had happened to him whilst alone on Ben Macdui 34 years earlier. What was remarkable about this is that it was, effectively, a ghost story.

The professor's story has been told many times since, but it bears repeating. Collie described how, after visiting the 1,309-metre summit cairn, he walked through the mist towards his descent route and had the overwhelming feeling that he wasn't alone:

> I began to feel I could hear something else other than merely the sound of my own footsteps. For every few steps I took I heard a crunch, and then another crunch as if someone was walking after me but taking steps three or four times the length of my own.

Collie stopped, at this point convinced he was imagining the sound. It ceased with him, but as he began to move again the sound returned:

---

* He was also present, tragically, when his principal rival for this title – Albert Mummery – was killed by an avalanche on Nanga Parbat.

As I walked on and the eerie crunch, crunch, sounded behind me, I was seized with terror and took to my heels, staggering blindly amongst the boulders for four or five miles nearly down to Rothiemurchus Forest.

Collie ended his story with simple conviction:

There is something very queer about the top of Ben Macdui and I will not go back there again by myself, I know.

A later account had Collie's words as: 'No power on earth will ever take me up Ben MacDhui again.' Apparently, to his death in 1942, it never did.

Collie's words that night have entered folklore as the first formal acknowledgement of a strange presence that reputedly stalks the Cairngorms' highest mountain. Despite numerous erroneous retellings over the years, the professor never *saw* anything – it was the noise of something approaching from behind that spooked him. And whilst it's been speculated that his 'eerie crunch, crunch' sound was a phenomenon caused by recently trodden-in or melting snow, Collie – a man of many days spent in snowy mountains – would certainly have known the sonic quirks of snow and ice.

In the years following Collie's revelation – like hands rising one by one in a reticent crowd – other accounts of peculiar happenings on Ben Macdui began to surface. Many were from sources equally as credible as the professor, people who'd also remained uneasily silent about their experiences through fear of ridicule. And it's perhaps understandable that many of the panic-littered accounts that followed Collie's 'confession' that night in Aberdeen were kept tightly under wraps, because an inexplicable loss of nervous control is probably not something to which a supposedly hardened mountaineer would find it easy to confess.

Some of these stories were, perhaps inevitably in the noise of sensation, far more outlandish and luridly detailed than Collie's. One bizarre early experience was told by naturalist Wendy Wood, who described being in the Lairig Ghru in the early 1920s and hearing an 'underground voice of gigantic resonance' speaking in Gaelic. She, too, heard the strange, out-of-step 'footfalls' described by Collie.

Of the more fantastical tales that emerged, one was from a mountaineer named Alexander Kellas – who coincidentally, like Collie, was also a chemist of considerable standing. He'd been excavating for crystals near the summit of Ben Macdui with his brother Henry on a June evening around 1900. The two were resting some way apart when Alexander observed a figure ascending from the deep trench of the Lairig Ghru, circle the summit cairn and his brother, then disappear from view. The figure's head drew level with the height of the summit cairn, which meant it was around three metres tall. Rejoining his brother, Alexander found Henry to be entirely oblivious to what had just occurred. Whilst Alexander Kellas never recorded his story, he and Collie are believed to have confided in one another about their experiences on the mountain;* Kellas died in the Himalaya in 1921 and was buried within sight of Mount Everest by, amongst others, George Mallory – and so was long gone by the time Collie first publicly spoke of his incident.

Another version of this particular tale, as later told by Henry Kellas to W. G. Robertson in an account printed in the Aberdeen *Press and Journal* in 1925, suggested that Henry Kellas *did* in fact see something, 'a giant figure coming down the hill towards them'. It passed out of sight into a gully, upon which they were possessed by an acute terror and fled at some speed into Coire Etchachan. It's worth noting that in Robertson's letter, the 'figure' had a name: *Ferla Mhor*.

In the years since, the exact point at which this name entered discussions of the 'presence' that haunts Ben Macdui has become a matter of controversy. Perhaps the most telling appearance of the term comes from another tale of terror from the mountain, this time by Hugh Welsh, who with his brother spent several nights in a high camp in 1904 whilst collecting botanical specimens for Aberdeen University. Several times they remember hearing noises they couldn't explain – 'pacing ... slurring footsteps, as if someone was walking slowly through water-saturated gravel'. Welsh also spoke of a feeling of

---

* There's some controversy here over exactly how and when this happened. Some writers refer to Kellas stumbling across a news story that appeared in a New Zealand local paper some twenty years before Collie's speech in Aberdeen, titled 'A Professor's Panic', which apparently contained a tale told by a visiting British professor to some friends. There's some doubt over whether this story ever existed, or whether Collie had even been to New Zealand – where a branch of his family settled – before the 1930s.

'apprehension ... of "something" near us'. Returning to Derry Lodge, the pair told their story to head stalker John Mackintosh, and asked him if it could have been deer. The stalker shook his head, telling them, 'That would have been the *Fear Liath Mòr* you heard.'

Ferlie Mor, *Ferla Mhor*, *Fear Liath Mòr* — these terms are obviously linked etymologically, and were the source of today's general term for the 'ghost' that stalks Macdui. The latter, translated from the Gaelic, means 'Big Grey Man'.

Any investigation into the Big Grey Man begins – if not ends – with Affleck Gray, who wrote a meandering but compulsive account of the phenomenon titled simply *The Big Grey Man of Ben MacDhui*. Many other stories are recounted in the book, including a number of personal accounts given to Gray by people who'd come across the ghost. Some, as well as the usual footsteps, involve actual creatures, notably Tom Crowley's from the 1920s of an 'undefined, misty figure with pointed ears, long legs and feet with talons that appeared to be more like fingers than toes' (clearly not *that* undefined, then), which made him flee down the Lairig Ghru.

Other accounts are highly articulate renderings of a nameless, inexplicable fear. Peter Densham, a forester who'd assisted in the recovery of air crashes in the Cairngorms during the Second World War, spoke of feeling a cold pressure on his neck when near the summit of Ben Macdui in 1945 and subsequently hearing what was by then the infamous sound of crunching footfalls. Remembering the tale of the Grey Man as told by Collie – and firmly disbelieving that there was anything supernatural about it – Densham went to investigate. He managed to get within a few feet of the sound's source whilst remaining 'not the least bit frightened', when suddenly he was 'overcome by a feeling of apprehension ... [and an] overpowering wish to get off the mountain. I found myself running at an incredible pace, and then realised I was running in the direction of Lurcher's Crag. I tried to stop myself and found this extremely difficult to do, as if someone was pushing me.' Densham apparently considered the nature of his experiences on Ben Macdui as being of a psychic nature – something Gray called the 'effect on his consciousness of undefined properties of the mountain'. Densham is quoted as saying Macdui was 'the most mysterious mountain he has ever been on'.

Also reprinted in Gray's book is a poem titled 'Ferla Mòr' by one A. G. Duthie, who reported feeling – though not seeing or hearing – something that made him turn and look back far more often than he would have normally. Its first lines read:

> What is this thing,
> Which haunts the cold grey mists
> Above MacDhui's frowning cliffs?

And its last:

> No one knows,
> The secret is kept
> In the bosom of the hills.

So what indeed *is* this secret the hills keep? Seemingly without exception – even the earliest accounts, which could not have been even unconsciously influenced by the tale Collie would make famous – all share the confusing vagueness of terror: this sudden, seemingly irrational loss of nerve and a feeling of overbearing fear, followed by the compulsion to get down off the mountain as quickly as possible.

Many explanations have been presented, most of them wholly inadequate given the solidly empirical minds of many of those who have encountered the Grey Man in modern times. One is that the creature is actually a Brocken spectre, an optical quirk caused by the backlighting of a walker's shadow onto mist or valley cloud, resulting in a tall, grey, long-limbed shadow often topped with a rainbow halo or 'glory'. However spectacular and convincingly spook-like the Brocken spectre can be, it's a phenomenon known to climbers since the 18th century – and having been lucky enough to see my own twice (once in Snowdonia, once in the Lakes), I can humbly add my own testimony that it behaves in the familiar way that a shadow does: it moves when you do.

Many of the early accounts of terror on Macdui, however, almost certainly do relate to a vision of the Brocken spectre. Poet James Hogg – the 'Ettrick Shepherd' – wrote of seeing a huge, dark figure with a halo high on the mountain in 1791. 'Struck powerless with astonishment and terror', he nonetheless found the energy to turn tail and run, intending to run home 'and hide ...

below the blankets with the Bible'. The following day the same phenomenon occurred, and Hogg realised the source of his fear was in fact a Brocken spectre. When considering such accounts it's easy to understand why this optical phenomenon has been blamed as the source of the feelings of panic on Ben Macdui – especially given that Hogg's reaction was to swiftly escape down the mountain in much the same manner as Collie and Kellas. It's unlikely a mountain would harbour multiple causes for such a reaction; yet, everything considered, it would seem that this one does.

Some mountaineers have described feeling a presence on high mountains in situations that have become difficult or life-threatening. Adventurers and explorers such as Charles Lindbergh, Ernest Shackleton and Ann Bancroft, and mountaineers Reinhold Messner and F. S. Smythe, have reported this with varying degrees of lucidity. But the 'Third Man' syndrome, as it's called, is almost invariably benevolent, and seems more attached to the person and situation than to the place. Many have likened it to the concept of the guardian angel, suggesting that in the absence of an assisting force the mind simply invents one to fill the gap. Others simply accept that there are forces we do not understand that come into play in situations of dire misadventure.

Perversely, it's also possible that a physical Big Grey Man is *also* a scapegoat – that he's actually a metaphor for something far more insidious, something too enigmatic to deserve such a conventionally sensational explanation as 'monster' or 'ghost'. And whilst everyone loves a good spook story, this is in a way a lot more fascinating. It seems to suggest that – behind the ghost story it's been hijacked by – there's something intrinsically frightening about the very atmosphere on the summit of Ben Macdui. As if somehow its height, topography, queer mists and extreme elements coalesce to cause a fundamental shift in the composure of those who reach the top, so that their nerves crack and slide briskly towards blind terror. That's something spooky even sceptics can get excited about.

Looking back at the accounts, the most common and plausible motifs are those that concern feelings and sudden urges, not some creepy figure or Gaelic chant. There's something seemingly tied to this particular place that, for whatever reason, induces panic. Collie himself acknowledged this, writing some years before his speech at the Cairngorm Club that 'there are places that one dreads, when one trembles and is afraid, one not knows why and fears stand in the way.' Considered like this, it would seem Ben Macdui isn't the only such place.

In a superb article written in 1998,* researcher Andy Roberts quotes the experience of a water-company surveyor named Clive Elliot, who in 1954 was walking in the north of the Isle of Skye when he experienced what Roberts defines as a 'mountain panic'. Leaping a stream in Glen Sneosdal, Elliot described landing on the other side as being '... as if I'd stepped into another world. My mind just went to pieces ... I cannot describe the feeling, one of total, blind terror.' Elliot fled up the hill and the feeling subsided. Roberts also cites a 1965 tale of a man walking in South Wales on the slopes of Foel Feddau who claimed that suddenly a 'curtain had fallen, all about him changed completely and he felt the raw edge of fear ... That evil, invisible eyes were upon him.' Like so many, he turned and fled.

Skye's north coast was memorably touched on in Otta Swire's *Skye: The Island and Its Legends*. Swire described the dramatically volcanic, spire-topped amphitheatre of the Quiraing as having 'an atmosphere that can never be captured ... best summed up by saying that it is as if the terror that walketh in darkness, here walks by day.' Swire also quotes hillwalkers who described the hills around the Quiraing as having this 'same feeling of potent, living evil'.

It's worth considering that the root of the word 'panic' is the Greek nature god Pan. Alexander Murray wrote in *Who's Who in Mythology* that Pan was the cause of 'the feeling of solitude and lonesomeness which weighs upon travellers in wild mountain places ... and thus anxiety and alarm, arising from no visible or intangible cause, came to be called "panic fear", such fear as is produced by the agitating presence of Pan.'

So, regardless of whether we're tackling a monster, a spook, our own psychological frailty in a world of unnerving, primordial intimidation or an ancient Greek god who amused himself by making people fret – there's certainly *something* here. Something that walks the story-book woods of Rothiemurchus Forest, treads the snows atop Ben Macdui and climbs through the mists that so frequently settle on its summit. Even if we only carry it with us in our own minds as some sort of frightening antithesis to 'being at one

---

* Entitled *The Big Grey Man of Ben MacDhui and Other Mountain Panics*, this piece surpasses Affleck Gray's for lucidity and draws some fascinating conclusions.

with nature', it made for an interesting backdrop to a darkening winter walk up Britain's second-highest mountain – and a night camped out beneath a spot fabled for its menacing atmosphere.

Of course, I didn't tell Jim any of this. Given our preoccupation with the weather, our principal exchange on the subject of Ben Macdui's more sinister qualities had been pretty brief and took place in the car on the drive north. It had gone something like this:

'So you said there was a story about this mountain?'

'Oh, not really. Old folk tale, nothing to get worried about.'

'I'm not worried.'

'I didn't say you were worried.'

'So what's the story?'

'Do you believe in the supernatural?'

A snort. 'None of that crap.'

'You'll be fine then. It's kind of a ghost story.'

'Oh, great.'

'Well it's not really a *ghost* story. More about psychological terror.'

'Oh, *great*.'

'Do you want to know or not?'

'Tell me when we get back.'

And that was pretty much it, until the darkness started to close in on us just over an hour after leaving the car.

Our original plan – the plan we were working to with a poor forecast in hand – was to follow the languid ridgeline of Miadan Creag an Leth-choin, which ascended south onto the Cairngorm plateau to the 1,000-metre mark and would probably expose us to sensational winds laden with sleet, snow, thunder, God knows what. We'd then plug into the Feith Buidhe stream, and descend east between some steep crags known as Hell's Lum down to the shore of Loch Avon (locally called Loch A'an) for the night. That was the bad-weather plan.

Trouble was, the bad weather we were walking into wasn't exactly the bad weather we were expecting. As the light playing out over the blanching mountains began to deepen to a queer glow – soft pink, then ominous mauve – the crags ahead of us began to soften with the lowering cloud. These top ramparts overlooked the glacial scoop of Coire an Lochain, a frieze of frosted iron, black and repulsively cold-looking. This and its neighbouring valley, Coire an t'Sneachda, collectively known as the Northern Corries – or the 'Norries' to those in a rush – are accessible magnets for novice winter climbers and, being north-facing and perennially shadowed, harboured deceptively brutal conditions. In 2007, five climbers died in Coire an t'Sneachda in four separate accidents over two months. Four of the five were under the age of thirty. Two of them were killed by a winter storm earlier in the year to now. This is, in every sense, a mean place.

In addition to the trickster Northern Corries, also notoriously shape-shifting are the Cairngorm mists. In *The Living Mountain* Nan Shepherd speaks of being atop Ben Macdui on a June day and seeing 'a thousand summits at once, clear and sparkling', then turning to behold a wall of cloud approaching from the south that 'rolled on swiftly, blocking out a hundred summits a minute'. The mist soon arrived on Macdui's summit, Shepherd stating that 'the whole business, from my first glimpse of the cloud to the moment it washed over me, occupied less than four minutes.' As Jim and I walked up into these mists, I made a quiet inventory. Compass, map, GPS. We each had a phone. Jim and I agreed we'd turn one off to save the battery; I took the first shift 'on'.

Gathering mists aside, though, things weren't looking half as bad as we'd been expecting. I fancied the occasional glimpse of an emerging star through the silken cloud above us, and the air was reasonably still and certainly empty of the gales that had been forecast. As we walked up into the gloaming making steady progress over the frozen ground, it occurred to me that perhaps our original course of action wasn't, in light of these conditions, the best.

'You feeling strong?' I asked.

'After nine hours in the car, I'm just happy to be standing up.'

'Why don't we knock it off tonight?'

Jim looked up towards the plateau, pulled out his map and ran a gloved finger over the route. It would be a longer walk, and would take us on a far more circuitous route. But it made sense. If conditions deteriorated during the night the last thing we'd want to be doing was fighting our way up or down the rest of the mountain in inadvisable conditions. This way, it would be all done and dusted before bedtime. A mutual nod, a purposeful tightening of straps and that was that. We were on our way to the top of Ben Macdui.

We reached the Cairngorm plateau at a position marked on the map with a spot height of 1,083 metres. We were now a tower block higher than anything in England and, if we'd raised an arm, equal with the height of Snowdon. We passed a cairn, frosted with icicles elongating into the oncoming wind, then proceeded south, feeling the powerful first tugs of chill upon us.

This plateau, in the darkness of a misty winter evening, is like a black and white photograph of an alien world. Once the path runs out or becomes obscured by the thickening snow, your whole existence just becomes a horizontal line, broken where it meets the sky by the crumpled outline of granite boulders. It's like walking on the moon. You start to understand why it would be unnerving to be here alone and unsure. I could see Jim, four-legged with his poles out, hunched ahead in his storm clothes, certainly battling something. As I approached I heard the brittle 'pock' of Jim's walking pole breaking through ice.

'Stream here,' he said, as he tentatively traversed the resinous surface beneath his feet. As he made his way across I looked around. In the darkening air the mist had stayed at bay to a radius of about half a mile. We couldn't see a lot of what was around us – just the dark shapes of the valley and the hint of a steady incline ahead – but we could see enough to make progress. One thing was obvious, however: we were definitively alone.

It was now very dark and I could feel the cold beginning to chew the bare skin of my face. We had resisted putting on head torches, trying to preserve our night vision in the hope that the residual reflected light from the snow might give us enough illumination to walk by. Steepening ground beneath our feet falling downwards towards the deep cleft of the Lairig Ghru had caused us some alarm and had forced a map check; we were off course and descending towards perilous ground. Jim and I had been passing time and attempting to take our minds off the building cold by talking about various films – *An American Werewolf in London*, the movies of John Wayne – and we'd clearly gone off track. A correction and a refocus, and we were soon climbing through ice-slick boulders towards a dark skyline where, all being well, we'd meet the path we'd long since lost. We were getting close to the top now.

Then the moon came up. The mist had reduced the glow of the diffused pre-lunar dawn to a weak smear of yellow, but when the moon itself rose above Ben Macdui's eastern flank, everything changed. I saw Jim silhouetted against the skyline just as the moon broke above it, watched the ground around him turn from white to gold and the long shadow of his earnestly ascending figure stretch almost as far as my boots. To darkness-accustomed eyes a shadow cast by the moon is novel. In a setting such as this it was ethereal.

The top of Ben Macdui is crowned by a large, built-up platform of rock adorned with a typical white concrete trig point. Before the mountain was surveyed – officially by the Ordnance Survey in 1847, unofficially by barometer enthusiast and first recorded ascender the Reverend Dr George Keith in 1810 – it was thought that at 1,309 metres it might be the highest mountain in Britain. When it was found that it was tantalisingly shy of the height of Ben Nevis, the owner of the peak planned to build himself a tomb on the summit – a massive, 30-metre stone pyramid that would, structurally at least, make Ben Macdui the highest eminence in the land.*

Mercifully, his plan was never realised. The architect at the time, and the owner of the peak, was the Thane of Fife, whose family had acquired the mountain after the Jacobite Rebellion. One theory has it that the mountain is named for this family – the title of 'Thane of Fife' having been made familiar by Shakespeare's *Macbeth* in the character of Macduff. Some hold that the name Ben Macdui – expanded fully to *Beinn Mac Duibh* – is a corrupted translation of 'Hill of the Sons of Duff'. Another rather less romantic and sadly more likely translation is 'Hill of the Black Pig', which would put Ben Macdui more in line with other Scottish hills in being named for its appearance, though to liken its lumpy, oddly anonymous profile to anything – let alone a creature – requires a stretch of the imagination.

As Jim and I arrived at the top in the brightening night, the view opened up dimly to the south in silvered monochrome. I could see the snow-topped wedge of the Angel's Peak – its sweeping form the most visually dramatic mountain in the Cairngorms, with the possible exception of the neatly inverse Devil's Point, hidden by mist opposite on the other side of the Lairig Ghru. The Devil's Point, as mentioned in Chapter 10, has the Gaelic name *Bod an Deamhain*, which actually means 'the Devil's Dick'. It's said that its more

---

* Later improvements in surveying would reveal that even a 30-metre tower would be maddeningly insufficient; Ben Nevis's accepted height today is 1,344 metres, whilst Ben MacDui's is 1,309 metres – a difference of 35 metres.

acceptable name was given by John Brown, who disguised its translation to avoid flustering Queen Victoria.

Head torches remained off as Jim and I congratulated each other and expelled sharp breaths in the summit breeze. In the three hours it had taken us to reach the top, the cloud above us had lost its weight and was now little more than thin scarves of cirrus through which stars were beginning to pierce. We stopped moving for a few moments just to absorb the silence and enjoy being, quite probably, the highest people in the land. Someone would have to be standing on the summit of Ben Nevis 50 miles to the west to surpass us. With a forecast like today's, that was unlikely. But being suddenly still meant we soon felt the cold, which was crushing. I removed a glove to take a picture and my fingers quickly began to numb.

I had the vague sense that I should be uncomfortable here, given all I'd read – or perhaps I ought to have been listening for footsteps or trying to imagine Collie's state of mind when he took flight near this very spot. But I felt quite relaxed. I'd have expected to have been disappointed at this, given that we were standing on the fabled haunted mountain of the Cairngorms on a winter's night in transient mist, but there was nothing about the moment that could be described as underwhelming in any way. Despite being fiercely cold, it was magnificent being up here; and it was getting better with every strengthening degree that the full moon climbed into the sky.

By the time we began to descend south-east towards Coire Etchachan – the same direction in which the Kellas brothers 'fled' – the scene was becoming stupendous. The eastern flank of Ben Macdui tips in a long descent towards a jumble of peaks and corries, and tonight they were all frozen white and lit by the moon. Once we'd dropped below the skyline, the wind dropped and we were in a white, moonlit world of our own crunching footsteps – and only our own, alas! – the easy walking aided by our poles. In this endless, empty landscape we could have been in the Arctic, Greenland – anywhere but the allegedly hugger-mugger confines of densely packed little Britain. No wilderness left? Anyone who says so has never seen this.

A small pile of stones poking from the snowdrifts provoked a whinnie of recognition from me as we passed. From reading I knew this must be the ruined remains of the Sappers' Bothy, a relic of the survey in 1847 when the hardy souls of the Royal Engineers – the 'Sappers' – were conducting survey measurements as an extension of the first great trigonometrical survey of Scotland. William Roy had laid the groundwork with his magnificent 'military sketch' – these were the boys who were filling in the blanks and the numbers. It was probably from this vulgar little hut, most likely covered with canvas, that red-coated, industrious surveyors triangulated many of the Cairngorm peaks.

We continued descending east until a cliff edge became defined beneath the moonlight ahead as a long, dark strip. At this point we turned north-east, using the cliff as a navigational banister for our descent towards Coire Etchachan. Some of the slopes we crossed needed caution; once or twice I backed off a couple of the steeper ones, visually tracing the slide trajectories were either of us to lose our balance. Some of those trajectories were long; some went over cliffs. The snow wasn't the powdery sort you could dig your legs into and land in a heap with a grin. In the night air it was turning rock hard – if you fell on it you'd bruise and if you slipped you wouldn't stop.

Just as I paused for a second time to consider unclipping and deploying my ice axe, Jim pointed towards the shoulder where a black slick made its way over the skyline. That was the stream that dropped down into the corrie. Next to the stream was a path.

Soon we were surrounded by the orchestral gurgling of running water beneath the snow as we forded the ice-clogged watercourse. The path we picked up would lead us between tall, snow-streaked crags and along the edges of the two highest bodies of water of comparable size in the country, Loch Etchachan and then Loch A'an, whose bank we'd follow to its south-western tip, into the innermost citadel of the Cairngorms.

This last part of our journey, the bit that would take us to its most remote point, was also the most difficult. I'd never been more grateful for moonlight during the times it emerged from behind the cloud steadily building from the north, but when cloud obscured it the blindness was crippling – and sections of that final descent to Loch A'an were steep enough to cause worry, even in daylight. Then, as we rejoined the path, it began to snow.

The final task of the night was to find our accommodation. In daylight I didn't imagine this would be much of a challenge; I discovered too late that in darkness, unless you knew where to look, it was nigh on impossible. The slopes building up from the south-western nub of Loch A'an are flung about with boulders: many are huge, all are made of the same rock and, in the building static of a snowstorm, they aren't that easy to distinguish from each other. Normally this wouldn't be a problem. But then normally you wouldn't be trying to find a very specific one – one it was possible to sleep beneath.

The rock they call the 'Shelter Stone' is famous. A chunk of spat granite about the size of a small country cottage and weighing around 2,000 tonnes, the *Clach Dian* – as it was known when Gaelic was still the first language here-abouts – has, by trick of circumstance, a highly habitable chamber beneath it that's very well protected from the harsh elements. It's been used as such for hundreds of years, and has harboured walkers, hunters, soldiers, fugitives and assorted scallywags since its highly convenient quirk was first discovered. Said discovery was apparently impressively venerable, too. As related in *The Life and Times of the Black Pig*, Ronald Turnbull's quirky biography of Ben Macdui, it's said that the first alleged Shelter Stone dweller was Alexander Stewart, son of King Robert II, and known to prosperity as the 'Wolf of Badenoch'. A man of cruelty and darkness – amongst his more distinguished achievements was the destruction of Elgin Cathedral – the 'Wolf' is believed to have slept beneath the Shelter Stone at some point in the late 13th century. The stone itself is certainly described in, and used by, the protagonists of Sir Thomas Lauder's 1886 novel *The Wolf of Badenoch*, in which, between the animal skins, knife fights, fires of gathered heather and bodies of dispatched enemies, lies a description of this 'curious natural habitation ... the space within dry and warm ... partially lighted by one or two small apertures between the stones ... the roof, formed of the base of the great mass of rock ... perfectly even and horizontal. It presented a most inviting place of shelter.'

Inviting it may be, and dry and warm – but first Jim and I had to find it. The Shelter Stone is, alas, not *exactly* where it's marked on the map. In daylight, and by the glow of the night's weakening moonlight, the first landmark is the enormous Shelter Stone Crag – an almost vertical wall of rock that looks like the bow of an oncoming cruise liner. That will get you in the right vicinity, but to find the actual stone amongst the rockery of similar boulders was proving tricky. The weather was becoming quite desperate, too – thickening falls of snow, the wind descending into a foul temper – and our own rapidly thinning patience was making every stone that had an even vaguely human-sized crack beneath it look inviting. Hence a few false alarms.

'This must be it. Look, I can sort of get under here.'

'That's not it.'

'How about this one? It's huge.'

'We'll know for sure when it's the right one.'

I knew this was no exposed sill we were looking for; I'd seen pictures of people reclining, snug and smiling, in something resembling dried-out Roman baths, with a stove on the go and no trace of the outside world visible. But I also knew I'd been remiss in not studying photographs of it more closely before leaving. The apparent difficulty of trying to find a very specific part of a mountain in a blizzard in the dark just hadn't occurred to me.

We peered over the map and agreed to give it five more minutes of searching before admitting defeat and unrolling the emergency shelter we'd brought for a survivable – if terribly uncomfortable – night out. Jim continued along the faint path on the sound theory that it would probably lead to *something* fairly well used, which the Shelter Stone was. Meanwhile I'd caught sight of something large and vaguely familiar-looking in the distance up to the left that I felt deserved investigation.

A few minutes of scrabbling over car-sized rocks and I heard a shout from below. Jim thought he was onto something. Realising I had no way of knowing where he now was, I slid off my backpack and rummaged in the top pocket for my head torch, which I pulled out and turned on, hoping Jim would see the light and follow suit, giving me something to aim for. Just as I did so, the beam caught a streak of orange from the direction of the big boulder; that unmistakable, lifeboat orange. Leaving my backpack on the ground and suddenly nimble with the lack of burden, I climbed the boulder and saw a small throat of rock about two metres long leading beneath it. My heart quickening, I saw that the streak of orange was in fact an old survival bag poking out of the tunnel. I followed it and – with a small yell – discovered it was one of two, laid out and left inside a totally enclosed chamber big enough for five or six. Retreating back out into the snow, I shouted down to Jim, who now had his torch on, too. I stood at the entrance whilst his little light bobbed steadily up the rocks. The light flinched when the beam of my own torch found it.

'*Ow.* Bloody bright.'

'Sorry. Just checking it was you.'

'Who else would it be?' He shivered as he stopped beside me. 'So – is this it?'

Finding the Shelter Stone was, to us, truly a relief – and it had come not a second too soon. The night outside was becoming increasingly fierce, and although it wasn't even 9 p.m. more than four hours had passed since darkness had taken hold and the temperature had long since plummeted. The Stone's a wonderful little place: formed entirely from pink granite, it's sealed mostly by nature but augmented by weighty boulders buttressed into its entrance corridor, thereby possessing all the attributes of a cave but without the gaping opening. Much like the shelter on Cadair Idris's summit and the bothy at Dibidil, it holds that smell of dry must and solace common to all outdoor–indoor places. Two ancient plastic survival bags discarded by a previous occupant have been sliced and folded out like a kind of PVC carpet. You can't quite stand up, and its wedge-shaped cavity tapers, but just to be in here and to think of the decades – centuries – of people who'd climbed into this place seeking the same thing as us was intensely affecting.

I made one more foray outside to fetch some water from the outflow of the loch, and whilst Jim busied himself tending the stove I started pulling soft, fluffy items of clothing from both of our rucksacks. For all our thankfulness for the shelter, it was like a freezer in there – we needed to stay warm, and before long we were wearing just about every dry item of clothing we'd brought. Lying in our sleeping bags listening to the hiss of crack-strained wind and swollen streams from outside, we ate, drank cold red wine and leafed through the logbook, sealed in a plastic bag within a box. So many people, so many nights under here – every few days or so there was a new entry, some from as far afield as Canada, Australia, the US and Switzerland, or as close as Aviemore and Grantown-on-Spey. Many complained of bad weather; some of midges in the summer, or snow in the winter, or rain just about every time else. One person painted a cosy picture ('Sat listening to *Fantastic Mr Fox* with a glass of rum, whilst escaping from the weather – great night's sleep!'), another an informatively transient one ('Stopped on the way back from Ben Macdui, tempted to stay the night but will push on') and many expressed just basic gratitude ('Shelter from the incessant winds and rain of Scotland – much appreciated!'). How nice – how *strangely* nice – that something so simple and basic can engender such community in this wild place. Jim and I registered our presence, sealed up the book and turned off our torches.

The night was extremely cold. Judging by the speed at which everything even slightly moist froze – the litres of collected water, the pan, the sweat on the inside of our dangling jackets and even the dregs of the red wine – the temperature must have been pushing –15°C. Granite has a tendency to hold whatever temperature is winning on the outside – it can be lovely and warm to the touch on a summer day, but can seethe cold on a winter night – and that night I felt like I'd been inserted into an icebox. My feet began to numb, and terrified about the risk of frostbite I spent a mostly restless night rubbing them against each other. I couldn't have slept for more than an hour and woke up aching with cold from the knees down. Sporadically, I'd feel a chill on my face – a tickling draught, I assumed – and could hear the sound of running water from somewhere inside the Stone's cavity. It was only when dawn began to break softly outside that I realised what was going on. Two small circles of pink, no bigger than spectacle lenses, were brightening in the crevice of rock not far above the top of my head. As I lay, transfixed with tired eyes, Jim stirred.

'Were you hot last night? I think I was a little too hot.'

I turned to look at him as he fumbled with his torch.

'Pardon?'

'Had to strip down to my boxers. Was getting sweaty.'

I was about to say 'pardon' again when Jim's head torch fell on my sleeping bag and he started to laugh.

'Shit! What happened to you? You look like Christmas.'

I freed my arms from out of the sleeping bag and turned over to look. My sleeping mat, aside from a mummy-shaped lozenge where I'd been lying, was covered with a well-established layer of snow. Everything lying around me – head torch, gloves, phone – wore a hat of fluffy white, which spread like a fading stain from my side of the shelter and petered out as it approached Jim.

'Well, I guess I picked the right side,' Jim said, pulling on his jacket.

I looked up at the two little apertures of daylight above me. That wasn't a draught I was feeling in the night; it was flakes of snow being pushed through these holes by the wind. The sound of rushing water had been the snow hitting the plastic. No wonder I'd been cold. I'd been getting bloody snowed on.

It took a long time to warm up my stiff joints, and almost as long for my jacket and gaiters – frozen hard as chipboard during the night – to begin to feel like clothes again. Both the corrie and the frozen surface of Loch A'an had suffered quite a dump of snow in the night, but our progress wasn't impeded by it. And within an hour it started to snow again, the sky white above the amphitheatre of rock that walled in around us.

To get out we had to climb up a break in the slopes of Coire Raibeirt – hardly a valley, more a steep chink in the otherwise relentless walls above the loch. From there we'd regain the plateau, climb over Cairn Gorm, then descend back to the car.

Progress was initially slow but steady as we climbed against the course of the Allt Coire Raibeirt. The snow made things interesting, but it was only when we reached an impressive waterfall halfway up that interesting became hair-raising. In summer conditions the waterfall is crossed by a path, which, whilst precarious, is probably not overly hazardous. On this particular morning, however, the path was invisible beneath a raked bank of snow tilted nastily towards a drop of about twenty metres, where the swollen falls dropped into a pool full of churning, glacially grey water.

Jim and I stood for some time looking at this little problem. There seemed no way around it that didn't take us over even more threatening slabs of snow; this was clearly the way across, but a slip was unthinkable. The fall would be serious enough, but to land in a pool of frozen water after a night out, with low energy levels and an ambient temperature well below freezing most likely would be fatal – if not straight away, then certainly from the hypothermia that would grip you within minutes of dragging yourself from the frigid water. Even spare clothes probably wouldn't save you.

We strapped on our crampons, all the while trying not to focus too hard on the gushing blue drop beneath our now clinking feet. Boots clawed, I traversed out a little way towards the 'crux' move – a long reach that, with a pack on your back and snow on the ground, could easily cause momentary unbalance, a panicked flap and little hope of steadying yourself. Suppressing a little shake in my knee, I pulled back. Then I remembered. Collapsing the walking poles that had seen me through the last two days, I slid them into the side of my pack and pulled out my axe. Again traversing onto the snow-banked ledge, holding the axe by its long shaft I swung it out and slammed the pick into the snow ahead at a point level with my shoulders. There was nothing but vegetation beneath the snow, and the axe wobbled out. Swinging again, I aimed higher up and the pick bit solidly into the snow, finding purchase between two rocks beneath. Good enough.

Supplied now with a solid hold, I took a breath and pulled myself over, my crampons finding a solid ledge on the other side of the fall. I was across. Leaving the axe *in situ*, I discarded my pack and offered a hand to Jim, who grasped it with one hand and the axe with the other and pulled himself over. Releasing the pick from the ice, I tapped the shaft of the axe on my boot to dust off the powder.

'Worth bringing after all.'

The rest of the ascent posed no similar challenges. We reached the plateau in a barrage of wind and eddying snow devils, its blast hitting us like a truck and forcing us to don ski goggles and cinch every piece of clothing tightly inward. The wind pushed against us as we reached the summit of Cairn Gorm, its peculiar weather station mummified by a thick blanket of ice with daggers of ice pointing out in all directions. It was like the Antarctic. Lingering long enough only to shake hands on our second winter 4,000-foot peak in as many days, we turned to descend. Before us, the Cairngorms appeared bleached beneath the first really heavy snowfall of the winter. The dark forest of Rothiemurchus, the storied dells of the glens and the high plateau of the Grey Man were this morning smothered by a rug of fresh, virgin white. Our skin stinging from the wind of the plateau, we began to descend northwards into the skiing infrastructure of Cairn Gorm and slowly re-entered civilisation. Through the white mist ahead, two walkers passed us up the fenced path towards the summit of Cairn Gorm. Neither even lifted their head to acknowledge us. That never would have happened in the remote corries we'd come from; now we were back in the world of fences and ski lifts it seemed people had no reason to be civil.

We took our goggles off and loosened our hoods as we passed the Ptarmigan Restaurant at the top of Cairn Gorm's funicular railway – the highest building in Britain. We didn't stop.

'Cairngorm plateau in winter. You know, that's about as extreme as it gets,' I said to Jim as, with the steady drop in height, the weather calmed down around us.

This is true. It's *about* as extreme as it gets. But in fact there's one other mountain place – a small, irregularly shaped bit fifty miles to the west – that can outdo it. And whilst we didn't yet know it, Jim and I were about to attempt it in some of the worst weather of the year.

16 SUMMIT

There's a quote – one of those quotes rescued from obscurity and subsequently attributed to just about everyone who ever laid a finger to their chin – that goes something like this: 'It's good to have an end to journey towards; but it's the journey that matters, in the end.' Like all good quotes* this means different things to different people, but the most obvious interpretation is probably that the reward to be found in the cumulative experience of the journey towards a particular goal often eclipses the rewards of the goal itself.

The act of climbing a mountain has, by its very nature, an ambiguous end point. The temptation would be to say the end is the summit, but in fact the summit only marks the exact halfway point of the journey. Put all of your physical and mental resources into getting there, and obviously you won't have anything left to get you home. This catches people out all the time. Those who allow ambition to eclipse reason and climb beyond the point where they should turn back are said to have succumbed to 'summit fever'. On big mountains this can be a killer.

Rock climbing is a good example of the journey itself being the goal: the removal of the summit from the equation altogether is key to the ethos of climbing a small but important piece of rock just for the sake of so doing and the sport of the route itself. And whilst there are many rock climbs that finish on mountain summits, there are many that finish on a nondescript skyline that is far from the highest thing around. Physical summit or just the summit

---

* And this one, incidentally, came from the pen of Ursula K. Le Guin in her 1969 novel *The Left Hand of Darkness*, a science fiction think-piece that rather fittingly involves a long trek across a frozen wasteland.

of a journey, there will still be a moment on the mountain when you stop, then turn for home.

And so our little journey through the mountain places of Great Britain is also reaching its end. When I started out just over a year earlier, the summits of these mountains themselves felt like the goal to me. But now, at the cold, thin end of the wedge, I was beginning to realise that their actual summits represented only a small part of the whole experience – minor memories amidst the tapestry of just being witness to these extraordinary places and the unique quality that has made each one so special.

But as Jim and I drove west through the winter night in deteriorating weather, I began uneasily to realise that one particular summit in this journey really did matter – and, rather more than most, this one mattered *because* of its summit.

Maybe because we were approaching journey's end, or maybe it was because with every speed-spread bomb of furry white that hit the windscreen, we knew this one was probably going to be by far the hardest to win. Or maybe it was just because this particular storm-hammered top has been so important on so many levels, to so many, for so long. But as Jim and I approached Scotland's west coast through the heavy snow, the mountains invisible in the black outside, the knots of trepidation were tightening in my gut. Perhaps in this weather, at this time of year, what we were about to do had crossed the line between being ambitious and being stupid. We'd been lucky on Ben Macdui. The chances of luck shining on us twice in Scotland's winter mountains – somewhere it's in generally short supply – were, however, slim. But still we kept driving west into the night towards Scotland's Atlantic coast, towards Lochaber – and Britain's highest mountain.

It had been quite a journey. And it *would* be the journey that mattered the most, in the end. But sooner or later, just like ours, every journey through the mountain places of Britain has to lead to Ben Nevis.

W. H. Murray once wrote, 'No man will ever know Ben Nevis. And no man has *ever* known Ben Nevis.' Murray's comment – that of a mountaineer who, by his own reckoning at that point, had climbed Ben Nevis a 'mere 37 times' – is typical of those who've habitually got involved with Britain's highest mountain. The more you visit, the more you find and the less you feel you know this colossal, fiercely contradictory place. It seems a little too neat, but it's difficult to counter. Given all the history acted out on and beneath Ben Nevis's massive shoulders over the years and its inexhaustible fascination, Britain's highest mountain is also quite indisputably its greatest.

That it was the highest took quite a while to establish, though. Until quite recently, determining the precise height of a mountain wasn't all that easy and many mountains were considered to be the highest in the land before Ben Nevis was found to usurp them all: Ben Cruachan in the West Highlands, Cadair Idris in Snowdonia and many other impressive, locally esteemed peaks have all been suggested as possible contenders for the ultimate mantle at some point.

Our inescapable naturalist friend Thomas Pennant spied Ben Nevis (or 'Benevish', as he called it) on his exhaustive tour in 1772 and had this to say: 'As an ancient Briton, I lament the disgrace of Snowdon; once esteemed the highest hill in this land, but now must yield the palm to the Caledonian mountain.'

A 1794 map of Scotland also decisively pointed out 'Ben Nivis – 4,370 feet high – the Highest Mountain in Great Britain', although it's unknown how such an accurate height and so confident a geographical status were able to be assigned so long ago. But these notwithstanding, Ben Nevis was far from accepted as the nation's high point until relatively recently. The principal challenger to Ben Nevis's title in this was Ben Macdui, which, for a long period in the mid 19th century, was considered a fairly safe bet despite these historic challenges to the contrary. The efforts of Reverend Dr George Keith, an enterprising amateur, were also seemingly unassimilated into the national consciousness when in 1810 he concluded Ben Nevis was the higher of the two mountains by 50 feet, having measured both with a barometer. It seemed the matter wasn't settled until government officials passed judgement – and even then it took a while.

We've a written witness to the 'official' 1847 measurement of Ben Nevis in John Hill Burton, whose 1864 book *The Cairngorm Mountains* opens with his ascent of Ben Nevis and the strange sight he found when he reached the top:

> It was neither more nor less than a crowd of soldiers ... Yes, there they were, British troops, with their red coats, dark-grey trousers, and fatigue caps ... A very short sentence from the good-humoured-looking

young fellow who received our first breathless and perplexed inquiry, solved the mystery, – 'Did you never hear of the Ordnance Survey?'

Before taking up residence on Ben Nevis, the 'sappers' had apparently been conducting similar measurements on Ben Macdui, and that 'competition had of late run very close between them'. But this was evidently not the settlement of the matter: at the time of Burton's meeting with the surveyors in 1847, Ben Macdui was 'some twenty feet ahead'. It wasn't until 1864 – coincidentally the year Burton's book was published – that the news was officially in. As reported by the *Inverness Advertiser* of 9 August 1864 under the headline 'An Old Dispute Settled', the Cairngorm peak had been re-measured and found to be higher than Ben Nevis, which itself had then to be re-measured using the same techniques for consistency. Ben Nevis was found to be 72 feet higher – with modern equipment the figure is, as noted in the previous chapter, 114 feet (or 35 metres) – and thus the *Advertiser* concluded that 'the supremacy of Ben Nevis as the loftiest mountain in Britain is established.'

'I freely confess to a preference for Ben Muich Dhui, which the recent decision against him has not mitigated,' Burton wrote rather bitterly of the news. 'Indeed, one is always bound to back one's favourite the more warmly if he is unfortunate, and driven from the eminence to which he has been deemed entitled.' Today the precise height of the highest ground in Britain stands at 1,343.7 metres – or 4,408 feet and six inches. Mountain heights are usually rounded down, but this one is rounded up from 1,343 to 1,344 metres.*

But whilst height might matter on this mountain more than most, as we know all too well by now it's not *really* the height that matters most; it's the mountain beneath it. And in this case it's a lot of mountain.

When Ben Nevis is considered on a map two things become immediately evident. First, it's genuinely huge: the Nevis massif accounts for almost fifteen and a half square miles of Lochaber, rising in one great heave from the zero contour at the point Loch Linnhe spears into the mainland from the Atlantic and begins a trajectory that slices Scotland's head clean off along the Great

---

* In a moment of curious indecision, the current Ordnance Survey map gives both metric heights, the lower one in parentheses. This is often done with mountains of significant elevation status.

Glen. The mountain itself has a diameter north to south of over five miles, and it would take around 560 typical domestic staircases to climb to the summit. If there were such a thing as a vertical road upon which you could drive a car, at 30 mph it would take you over two minutes to cover the distance between the summit and sea level. This isn't simply a bulky mountain for Britain; it's a bulky mountain, full stop.

The second thing the map will tell you is that structurally Ben Nevis is a trick. To anyone passing by beneath it or viewing from a distance the mountain is a massive, shapeless lump. Seen from Loch Eil it possesses at best a dubious elegance, appearing as something very burly, curled in sleep. It certainly doesn't have anything approaching a peak, its summit instead appearing to occupy an indistinct part of an extensive flat plateau. But look at a map and you'll see that this isn't so. Those uneventful, steep outer flanks that circle the mountain to the south and west are the mere rump of a much toothier, inner face, to which only the committed can get up close. Put simply, Ben Nevis is like a smashed jack-o'-lantern: from one angle round and smooth, from the other a sinister, grinning mess.

It's the messy side of Ben Nevis – the side that leers down at you from the inner citadel of Coire Leis, bisected by the Allt a' Mhuillinn – that has made it famous. To climbers, the north face reads like a great stone book of the longest rock routes in Britain and some of its most difficult winter climbs. To the walker, unencumbered by eyes that instinctively crawl the lines and buttresses of the northern cliffs for objectives, it's simply a staggering sight.

From this angle Ben Nevis is unyieldingly savage. It has the spired muscle of something ripped from the Alps and dropped incongruously into the West Highlands, yet it also possesses a kind of aged stateliness. Geologically, the whole mountain is a freak. It's all that's left of a sizeable volcano with a hard doughnut of pink granite surrounding its summit, the entire mountain probably having collapsed in on itself at some point in the distant past. But whilst the top is a desert of boulders, the andesite rock of the colossal two-mile north face puckers in and out of deep gullies and looks wrinkled, like the bark of an old tree. From these cliffs – some of which free-fall a clear 500 metres from the summit in horrible, stomach-choking drops – ridges project and deep trenches are sliced, tongue and groove-like. The names of the features on this side range from the evocative (Orion Face, Tower Ridge, Tower Gully,

Observatory Ridge, Castle Ridge, Trident Buttress) to the personal (Douglas Boulder, Cousin's Buttress, Raeburn's Buttress) to the curiously mathematical (Point Five Gully, Minus Face, First Platform, Number Two Buttress, Zero Gully) to the simply odd (Indicator Wall, Gardyloo Gully), but all are important in the landscape of rock and winter climbing on Ben Nevis – which basically means the landscape of rock climbing, full stop. The most impressive of all of these is the extraordinary North-East Buttress. From Coire Leis – and anywhere in the mountains to the east – this powerful, angular piece of rock to the extreme left of the north face dominates one's vision of Ben Nevis, and gives it a different character altogether. Put simply, it gives Ben Nevis a peak, and a terrifying-looking sharkfin of a peak at that – something unthinkable from just about any other angle on the mountain.

But again there's illusion at play. It's a privilege of a highest mountain to never be looked straight in the eye; were you to do so you'd see that how this buttress appears is a trick of perspective. It's only a 'peak' from below. What the North-East Buttress actually marks is something just as lethal: a sharp sideways projection from a quite flat summit plateau, which collapses suddenly and vertically into the corrie far below. Far from being a leisurely saunter, this plateau is a tilted shelf of gully-toothed mountaintop – from above shaped like a side-laid tyrannosaur's jawbone. Dubbed the 'plateau of storms' by our old weatherman friend Clement Wragge, this is, in winter, probably the most insidiously hazardous place in Britain.

One thing was obvious: Jim and I weren't going to be sleeping out on the summit of Ben Nevis that night, as had been our ambitious plan. However prepared we were for foul weather, trying to camp in this kind of lively airborne sludge would have been serious folly. Even with the sternest resolve, the highest we could hope to get in this weather would be the halfway lochan beneath Meall an t-Suidhe. Even then we'd be soaked by the time we set up camp and would spend the night shivering. If we were lucky we'd emerge in the morning with aching limbs and torpedoed morale for what would probably be a still arduous trudge to the top. As we passed through the amber-washed streets of Fort William, pressed upon from above by the invisible presence of the mountain, we made the decision we both knew was the only sensible one: find an inn, gather our thoughts and wait until morning.

Heading past Fort William along the gale-bashed coastal road, we entered the north-western mouth of Glen Coe, then, as the dark sides of the valley rose around us, turned off down a sinuous lane leading to the Clachaig Inn.

To the weary walker, the Clachaig is a vision. Like the Old Forge, the Pen-y-Gwryd and the Wasdale Head Inn, this old pub is a warm ember of hostelry dug in amongst the mountains into which exhausted mountaineers have unravelled into boozy relief for generations. The Clachaig's door handle is an ice axe, and the wooden walls of the climbers' bar are hung heavy with images from mountaineering's past – walls that have probably sponged up more damp and panic than any other, sitting as it does in the very crease of one of Britain's most hallowed climbers' playgrounds. Doubtless for many, the seductive thought of defrosting in front of the Clachaig's fire and drinking beer by the gallon is what has spurred them on through the toughest parts of winter descents from Bidean nam Bian, Buachaille Etive Mòr and the notoriously committing Aonach Eagach, the descent from which ends just metres from the front door. Conversely, for the unlucky – a few of whom there will always be every year in these beautiful, dangerous mountains – the Clachaig's is undoubtedly the last doorway they ever walked out of.

Jim and I arrived in leaden spirits. The weather forecast for the morning was truly awful: upland gales gusting to 90 mph, snow, hail, whiteout conditions and desperate wind-chill adding to already bone-splitting temperatures: it was a list of just about everything potentially lethal to the walker. Weary from our cold night beneath the Shelter Stone, we sat grim-faced in the firelit bar, a finger occasionally sliding over the touchscreen of a phone for an updated forecast during long gaps in conversation. Hoping for some sort of miracle by morning – and glumly mindful of the fact that we'd already had one of those this week on Ben Macdui – we retreated to our rooms. I thought I'd sleep like the dead. Listening to the wind shoulder-barging the window, I didn't.

Whilst I wanted to climb Ben Nevis in winter to reach the fabled 'plateau of storms', the most extreme point in Britain at its toughest time of year – and I *really* did want to – I was also quietly hoping the weather didn't improve. Truth be told, Ben Nevis quite simply scared the hell out of me.

* * *

On the evening of 11 September 1898 a 30-year-old telephonist named Duncan Macgillivray was climbing back to the meteorological observatory on the summit of Ben Nevis after taking part in a shooting competition in Fort William. Macgillivray's job was manning the telephone that had recently been installed at the observatory, a building which, by this point, as described in Chapter 6, had been braving the gruelling summit conditions for sixteen years. He was not expected back at his post that night, and so when he didn't arrive nobody thought to go looking for him.

The following day a visitor to the summit came across something lying just off the path, near the top of a sheer-sided slice into the summit plateau known as Gardyloo Gully.* On closer inspection – and no doubt to considerable fright – the object revealed itself to be a body, that of the young Macgillivray. He had cuts to his hands and his face, and was lying so close to the observatory that a robust shout would probably have roused attention from within. He was thought to have become lost in cloud and succumbed to exposure in the night. The sad irony here is that had Macgillivary telephoned ahead to the observatory, where his call would have been taken on the equipment he was responsible for, a lookout would have been set up for his arrival.

Macgillivray's lonely death on Ben Nevis so long ago is only one of many tragic cautionary tales that have occurred over the years. The mean annual temperature on the summit is −0.5°C, so it isn't surprising that conditions were cruel enough in September to have claimed the young telephonist's life; the chill on much lower mountains has claimed life in warmer months than this. This is simply because many people don't realise not only how bad it can get up there, but critically, how *different* it can be to sea level. Fort William – less than four miles from the summit – has an average annual temperature nearly 10°C higher and receives less than half as much rainfall as the four metres a year that falls on the highest reaches of the mountain. (London, by comparison, is over 13°C balmier on average and receives an eighth of the

* They called it Gardyloo Gully after a well-known contemporary French street cry – *Gardez l'eau!*, meaning 'watch out for water' – that had been adopted in Edinburgh to warn of airborne slop descending from an upper tier. The gully was so named as the observatory used it as a waste chute.

rain.) But of course these averages become meaningless when the chocks are pulled out and the weather turns really extreme.

Imagine for a moment what the summit plateau of Ben Nevis would be like when things seem properly desperate at sea level. The problem is that not everybody spares that moment, so every year people get into trouble because they underestimate the severity of the conditions high on the mountain. Popular summits such as Snowdon and Scafell Pike suffer badly on such occasions because of the number of people who venture up them with inadequate clothing, equipment and experience to bag a national high point – but even amongst the high summits of Britain, Ben Nevis ranks as a particularly special case. On account of its position as the first and biggest thing hit by weather systems blowing in off the North Atlantic, there's simply no other mountain in these isles that encounters such conditions. Weather and outlook change notoriously quickly here, particularly in winter, with weather systems frequently arriving from one of two turbulent origins: polar cold from the frozen north and stormy westerlies from the Atlantic.

In keeping with this rather inexact climate, Ben Nevis's name has been a source of endless debate – and its proposed meanings are quite in keeping with its bipolar reputation. Nevis could be from the Old Irish *neamhaise* ('terrible') or the Gaelic *neamh* ('heaven'). Also suggested have been the startlingly negative *nimheil* ('evil'), *uamhais* ('dread'), *ni-mhaise* ('no beauty') and *neimh* ('poison or bitterness'). Finally, and rather wistfully, there's *Beinn Neimh Bhathais* ('The Mountain with Its Head in the Clouds'). As Ken Crocket drily notes in *Ben Nevis: Britain's Highest Mountain*, 'Failing new evidence, choose what feels right for the day.' The usual alternative adopted by climbers in a verbal doff-of-the-cap to the mountain's singular status amongst many is, simply, 'The Ben'.

Being the highest of all, Ben Nevis – like Snowdon – is sadly doomed to be a vehicle for weird feats, often for charity, sometimes for PR stunts and occasionally just for kicks. Things that have made it to the summit of Ben Nevis include a Ford Model T in 1911, an ascent that took five days and much preparatory work; a wheelbarrow; barrels of beer; a replica of a Travelodge hotel room, complete with carpet, walls, bed and bedding; the rock band Cream for an impromptu photo-shoot that made it into the sleeve notes of their classic 1967 album *Disraeli Gears*; the mortal remains of several hundred people, complete with urns and memorials;* and a pole dancer replete with portable pole.

Perhaps most bizarre were the events that followed the discovery of the skeletal remains of a piano beneath a cairn amongst the mountain's summit rocks in 2006. At first it was thought to have belonged to Kenny Campbell, a woodcutter who'd carried a piano to the top of the mountain 35 years earlier. Campbell had spent four days taking it up, then played 'Scotland the Brave' on the summit whilst several Norwegian climbers danced nearby. But the piano Campbell had carried up was not a piano at all, but an organ – quite different to the remains in question. These turned out to be those of *another* instrument, carried up for a charity stunt in 1986 by a group of Dundee removal men who were too exhausted to take it back down. All of which means that if it wasn't improbable enough to find a piano on the summit of Ben Nevis, there is in all likelihood still an organ buried up there somewhere, too.

Such light interludes, however, shouldn't give the impression that the mountain is a pushover. Ben Nevis can bite with fearsome and cruel unpredictability. The most shocking recent tragedy might be that of a 22-year-old French tourist who in May 2011 had just passed the halfway point up the mountain when he began to feel unwell. After he lost consciousness his companion made a rapid descent to raise the alarm. Two mountain rescue teams headed up and a helicopter was scrambled, but by the time they reached him he was already suffering from severe hypothermia and he lost his fight for life later that night. Here was a young man, described as being 'reasonably prepared', who had frozen to death in a snowdrift on the slopes of Ben Nevis just three weeks from midsummer.

The previous January a walker wearing jeans and T-shirt had fallen down the south side of the mountain having lost his way during a sudden blizzard. A video camera found near his body contained footage of the twenty-year-old

---

* In 2006 a nationwide appeal was launched for the 'owners' of over 50 memorials placed on the summit – to climbers, non-climbers and even pets – to reclaim them before they were relocated to a new garden at the foot of the mountain. Whilst the scheme was met with angry reactions from the bereaved, a former member of Lochaber Mountain Rescue, who opened the garden, pithily summed up the situation: 'People go to the summit of Ben Nevis … It's going to be one of the achievements of their lives. And those people don't want to be walking in what might be termed a cemetery.'

reaching the summit in near zero visibility. Then, a walker from Brighton was climbing the mountain a month later in perfect winter conditions when his legs began to cramp at close to 900 metres. Soon he was vomiting and weakening rapidly, and so sure he was going to die he took a photograph of himself, convinced it would be his last. Half-crawling with numb limbs back down the mountain, he heard the noise of a helicopter above. Sure he was about to be rescued, he was understandably appalled when it flew past and continued towards the summit. He later learned the helicopter was going to the aid of two climbers with whom he'd shared a conversation about the weather earlier that day who'd fallen 300 metres down Zero Gully on the north face whilst roped together. One died; the other – miraculously – survived. But that day could quite easily have claimed all three in two separate tragedies. Make no mistake, and ignore what you hear to the contrary: in winter, summer and everything in between, Ben Nevis is serious stuff.

So now you know what kept me awake in the Clachaig. The following morning dawned cloudy and breezy above Glen Coe. Throwing open the curtains with breath held, the dim sight outside was neither as bad as expected, nor as good as hoped.

Over breakfast and coffee Jim and I once again assessed the forecast, which remained unchanged from the previous evening. A bad forecast should be heeded; it's the first step of prudence, right before packing for all conditions and leaving a written plan of intent with someone who can raise an alarm if you don't turn up back at the ranch by a certain time. There was a lot to be said for going to the foot of the mountain and assessing it from there. But this might just be delaying the obvious, depressing ourselves further and adding 26 miles onto what was already going to be a nine-hour drive home. By the time our coffee cups were refilled we'd come to the conclusion that it probably wasn't worth it, and that we probably should go home. That was the best plan. The clever thing to do. The sensible option with all the facts in hand. After a third coffee we decided to go and give it a go.

Well, it seemed rude to be this close and not at least have a look at it. At the end of the day we were both pretty experienced, well equipped and knew enough horror stories and cautionary tales to be able to keep an eye on each other with something approaching an attuned eye. And besides, sooner or later you need to test yourself a little. We expected snow, and cold wasn't a problem, but as ever the critical thing was wind; strength-sapping frozen gales that were strong enough to blow snow into unstable cornices, and us clean off the hill. Anything over 40 mph was of serious concern, and the forecast predicted gusts more than double that.

I kept a close eye on the liveliness of the trees as we drove the thirteen miles to Fort William then took the road into Glen Nevis. The wind was up, but not strong enough to scupper us. As we reached the foot of Ben Nevis, I could see the top two-thirds of the mountain were plastered white – and not the pleasing white of Swiss chocolate boxes. The tops merged seamlessly with the cloud above and what little detail I could see in the cloud was moving. This meant there was wind up there. It also meant whiteout conditions.

Our original plan had been to climb the mountain by arguably its finest walkers' route: the sharp ridge slung between the shoulder of the North-East Buttress and the neighbouring peak of Carn Mòr Dearg – a route known as the Carn Mòr Dearg Arête. In light of the conditions, to attempt this would, to employ an old-timer hillwalking expression, be taking the piss.

The only realistic route was by the track that was made to service the observatory, which zigzagged up the mountainside by its west flank. This route up the mountain has been scorned by 'serious' mountaineers ever since it was built; they've called it the Pony Track or the Tourist Path – neither name particularly suggests severity, and rescue teams like to refer to it as the 'Mountain Track' for that reason.

Ours was the only car by the roadside at Achintee, the cluster of buildings at the head of Glen Nevis, when we arrived a little after 10 a.m. It seemed to be still getting light. As Jim killed the engine the two of us sat in silence for a few moments, gazing vacantly at the grey and white tableau outside the windows.

'Well.'

'Yeah.'

Silently we nodded at one another and got out into cold. Unloading our kit from the car, we began to fill our packs, stuffing them with almost every piece of warm kit we had. As I threw in my emergency shelter – a kind of bubble of nylon with a drawcord – Jim spoke up.

'Are you packing a sleeping bag?'

'Seriously? Jim, if we get to the point where we need a sleeping bag ...'

He held my gaze for a second as my sentence trailed off, and wordlessly I turned back to the car, pulled one out and shoved it into my bag. As had recently become a mutual motto, better safe than dead.

The path from Achintee is well built. It needs to be. Nearly 150,000 people climb Ben Nevis each year, the vast majority in summer, and most of them start from here. Clement Wragge, climbing the mountain daily to make his meteorological observations during the summer of 1881, wouldn't have done so, as this path was not to exist for another two years. His route would probably have been from Banavie to the north, and most likely atop a horse for almost half of the distance. Still, considering he climbed to the summit every day in all weathers outside of winter, you could hardly hold that against him.

We were sheltered to start with. Our boots made a thick, rhythmic scrape as we wandered up the easy path, and although I could hear gales kicking around far above us, the air was sufficiently still for me to hear something squeaking in Jim's pack with every step he took – a crampon perhaps. As the path crossed the valance-like hillside towards the white mass ahead, it occurred to me how much I'd been thinking about being here. I'd climbed Ben Nevis twice before, but never in winter. Both times I'd been blessed with one of the ten totally cloud-free days the summit enjoys on average each year, and both were in the middle of August heatwaves. Even then the summit was chilly. I couldn't believe just how different it felt now. Where there were green trees, dry, brown stone and chatting day walkers in summer, today there were only the naked skeletons of silver birches, acres of winter-browned heather, oily rock and not another soul.

Nobody, that was, until we reached the halfway lochan beneath the rounded hill of Meall an t-Suidhe, which sits on the north-west flank of Ben Nevis's muscular foundations. The track rises steeply but easily up to the lip of this largish lake in the slouch between Ben Nevis's summit dome and the surrounding upland. Its water was today the colour of iron, its edges laced with delicate ice. The lochan lay exactly on the snowline, and as we broke over the top of the pass that cradled it we relinquished shelter and the wind began to assert itself. The name of the lochan – Lochan Meall an t-Suidhe – means, fittingly, 'Lochan of the Hill of the Stormy Blast'.

On its far side were three figures standing together with heads bent, as if they were studying a map. They were New Zealanders, all girls in their early twenties. They looked wet and cold, their shiny jackets matte with windblown snow.

'I suppose you think we're crazy,' one said, as we approached.

'How's that?' I replied.

'You look like you know what you're doing. And we're in trainers.'

'I guess that depends how high you're looking to go,' I said, trying hard to sound casual rather than concerned. The lochan represented the end of the easy stuff terrain-wise, and they didn't *look* like they were in trouble; but any higher, and that would probably change.

'I think we're going down,' another said, with a note of firmness seemingly directed more to the rest of her group than us. 'We just went out for a walk and ended up here.'

'Probably wise,' Jim said. 'Do you have food? A map?'

They nodded glumly at the former and shook their head at the latter.

'It's cool, we're just going to go back the way we came,' replied the first.

We said our cheerios and watched them move off, back down the path in the direction of Achintee.

'Difficult to know what to do there,' Jim said, as we rounded the lochan. 'I thought we were going have to make an intervention or something.'

'I think they knew the score,' I said. 'Sometimes you've got to let people make their own mistakes.' On hearing how that sounded, I immediately felt wrong for saying it. 'I don't mean ...'

Jim waved a hand. 'I know. I know you wouldn't have left them to die or anything.'

I laughed. 'Do you ever get that feeling ...?' I gestured down at my clothing. I was wearing, in total, four layers – with another two on standby. There was two days' worth of food in my rucksack. An ice axe was strapped to its side, along with my poles. Goggles were wedged on top of my head. I'd two pairs of gloves on, leggings under waterproof trousers and spares of everything warm. I was wearing boots that didn't bend, and about my person had a map, compass, emergency GPS, phone loaded with mapping software, spare battery, shelter, sleeping bag – basically everything I'd carried on every one of these mountains throughout the year was with me, right now. Five minutes ago we'd been standing in the same place as a group of girls wearing tracksuits.

'... the feeling that, you know, we take this too seriously?'

Jim looked at me steadily, then turned his gaze up towards the white ramp that led up into the cloud, up towards the top of the mountain, towards the highest point in Britain. Beyond it, there wasn't a single footprint, just virgin white ground. From here on up, we were alone on Ben Nevis. Or, put another way, we were the only ones dumb enough to go any higher. Looking back at me, he deadpanned a single, steady syllable.

'No.'

Ben Nevis is unusual amongst British mountains in that it has a well-documented 'first ascent' — by James Robertson, botanist, on 17 August 1771. Whilst at the time climbing hills for fun was yet to become popular, there will always be a modicum of doubt when it comes to deciding who was the first person to wander up any prominent mountain that can be had by what's effectively a tough walk.

Robertson's ascent is no exception. A description in *Memoirs of Sir Ewen Cameron of Locheil* — collated by a Jacobite named John Drummond in around 1737, around 20 years after Cameron's death — contains a passage referring to *Beniviss*, 'the huge mountain of prodigious height ... its ascent is pretty steep, though smooth. The top of the summit is plain, covered with perpetual snow, and darkened with thick clouds.' Although possible, it's rather unlikely that such a rendering of the mountain's high plateau could be gotten by simply looking at it from sea level. Cameron, you may recall, was said to have killed the last wolf in Scotland in or around 1680. He was also the onetime owner of Ben Nevis.

There's an even older story that speaks of local peasants being sent up the mountain with bales of straw by Cameron to prevent the snow on the summit from melting. The motive seems to be an old statute — or superstition — that should the last of the winter's snow melt on Ben Nevis the land would be forfeited. True or not as these stories may be, Robertson was certainly the first to officially record his ascent. It's a shame, for such a momentous act, that he seems to have said nothing of great significance. The most colourful description reads simply: 'A third part of the hill ... is entirely naked, resembling a heap

of stones thrown together confusedly.' This could be because he wasn't particularly interested in the mountain itself. Typically for the time, both this first
recorded ascent, and the second – by mineral prospector John Williams in 1773
– had principally scientific motives: Robertson, a rival of Thomas Pennant, was
collecting plant specimens for Edinburgh's College Museum, and Williams was
on the lookout for anything of mineralogical value.

The mountain's most illustrious early visitor was probably the Romantic
poet John Keats, who came sighteeing in August 1818. Keats by this point had
made the acquaintance of Coleridge and had at least met Wordsworth: two
men who, as we've seen, had an intimate affinity with both nature and the
mountains, and whose work Keats greatly admired. Four months after taking
a walk with Coleridge on Hampstead Heath, Keats found himself on the
summit of Ben Nevis as part of a giant walking tour of Scotland, the Lake
District and Ireland in the company of his contemporary Charles Armitage
Brown. Keats would complete less than half of this tour, and by the time he
climbed Ben Nevis he was already suffering the early stages of the condition
that would eventually kill him; following his ascent he went home, and his
health was never quite the same until his death from tuberculosis less than
three years later.

Whatever the physical effects of his climb, the mountain clearly left an
impression upon the young poet. His description of the ascent refers to 'large
dome curtains' and 'cloud veils', these phrases reminiscent of lines in his
unfinished epic *Hyperion*, which he began just a month after returning from
Ben Nevis. He wrote what are probably the most famous lines inspired by the
mountain whilst sitting amongst its summit stones:

> Read me a lesson, Muse, and speak it loud
> Upon the top of Nevis, blind in mist!
> I look into the chasms, and a shroud
> Vapourous doth hide them – just so much I wist
> Mankind do know of hell; I look o'erhead,
> And there is sullen mist, – even so much
> Mankind can tell of heaven; mist is spread
> Before the earth, beneath me, – even such,
> Even so vague is man's sight of himself!

Here are the craggy stones beneath my feet, –
Thus much I know that, a poor witless elf,
I tread on them, – that all my eye doth meet
Is mist and crag, not only on this height,
But in the world of thought and mental might!*

Keats said of the ascent that it was like climbing 'ten St Paul's without the convenience of a staircase'† and it was 'not so cold as I expected – but cold enough for a glass of Whiskey now and then'.

It's probable that the first party to climb Ben Nevis without the help of a guide – a fairly big deal at the time – was led by Willie Naismith, celebrated as one of the great pioneers of Scottish climbing and the creator of 'Naismith's Rule', a calculation used to this day to determine how long a particular walk will take.‡ The ascent took place in May 1880, and Naismith and his party found themselves struggling across the plateau in knee-deep snow to the buried summit, narrowly avoiding plunging off the corniced gullies to their doom when an incorrect bearing was struck. The summit was so thickly plastered by snow and indistinct that only a bottle, left behind on the summit stuffed with a paper record of those who'd been there before, gave physical confirmation that they'd made it to the top of Britain. Their ascent was headline news in the *Glasgow Herald*.

Naismith once described the sight of Ben Nevis's northern cliffs as being 'much more savage' than even the Cuillin of Skye, and would leave the scratches of his hobnails on many of the mountain's most famous routes. Naismith, together with Hugh Munro, was amongst the founders of the Scottish Mountaineering Club in 1889, a club that Norman Collie would join

---

* It's often forgotten that, in contrast to the gravitas of this poem, Keats also wrote another somewhat bouncier work, a kind of dialogue between Ben Nevis and a 'Mrs. C' – Mrs Cameron, the fattest woman in all Inverness-shire – beginning with the line, 'Upon my Life, Sir Nevis, I am Piqued!' and in which Keats personifies the mountain's summit as a 'bald pate'.

† It's actually equivalent to about 12.

‡ Five kilometres per hour as a general rule, to which one minute should be added for every ten metres ascended.

two years later. Yet another familiar face pops up in an 1897 report from one of the observatory staff, who witnessed three climbers making the first ascent of Tower Gully on the north face. One of them turned out to be none other than Walter Parry Haskett Smith, the pioneer climber of Napes Needle. Clearly, climbing mountains for pleasure alone was still at this point the preserve of a somewhat small community.

The 'pleasure' part of it is perhaps more readily understandable in summer than winter, when what can be called physically hostile conditions – as Jim and I were about to find out – are generally endured by anyone climbing a hill. Put simply, a heavy winter is the point at which walking becomes mountain-eering, whether one likes it or not. Naismith himself tackled the subject in the *Scottish Mountaineering Club Journal* of 1893 with an article titled 'Scottish Snow Craft' in which he details typical winter mountain hazards such as cornices, snow-filled gullies, ice-glazed rocks and other horrors the mountaineer can expect to find. 'Let us suppose you get caught in a storm, or that, despising "sage advices" you deliberately sally forth to do battle with the elements,' reads one passage. 'You find yourself in the midst of a howling tempest ... a level snowstorm tearing along as though it were the wind made visible; "Where does the pleasure come in?" somebody asks. *It's all pleasure!*'

Soon after setting off up the slope leading from the lochan, the 'pleasure' began for Jim and me. At first it was just snow; as soon as we began to venture above the snowline a thickening carpet of fine, fresh powder replaced the positive, ratchet-tooth footholds of the path. Concentration now became crucial, as invisible beneath the snow were the sharp switchbacks of the mountain-track zigzags. These legs get shorter the higher up the mountain's west flank you go; miss the corner of a zig or a zag, and in weather like this we could walk off into steep ground above Glen Nevis from which the conse-quences of a slide would escalate from serious to potentially fatal the higher we got. The opening to the right that grows ever deeper as you ascend is called Five Finger Gully from its resemblance to a fanned hand. Wander into this by accident, as many have, and a fatal accident can follow.

Initially, the snow was drifting to ankle height – no big deal. A light kick was all it took to re-establish the path beneath it but, as we climbed, the white blanket got thicker and the wind became truly mighty. It was blowing from the north-west, which meant it was largely on our backs as we 'zigged' on a perfect trajectory for it to blow us down the slope. Then, as we turned to 'zag', it blew blinding tacks of snow straight into our faces. It's liable to cause panic, this sort of weather; the sense that your face is beginning to lose mobility and the weather has far more stamina than you have, and the knowledge that you simply cannot remain static in this environment. That if you stopped you'd eventually die. Everything you were, are and would ever be – snuffed out by the cold; your body and tracks swiftly covered with snow like the inconsequential little particle you are; and the mountain carrying on as if you'd never been there in the first place. It's a frightening feeling.

Luckily for us, all we had to worry about was our judgement. We'd come well equipped, and gradually most of the kit we'd brought for the worst eventualities began to surface. First walking poles were unclipped and extended. Then jackets were battened down and hoods went up. Anything that flapped or whipped was tied in, and eventually goggles were donned. We were totally encased in our own little weather-proof world.

What comes next everyone deals with differently. Sealed from the sharper claws of the elements, I settled into a rhythm, the rasp of my own breath pressing on me in the gaps between the deafening gusts hitting my body. Ahead, the world was a tipped white line left to right, the emptiness beyond it plunging, dauntingly high – the view from a skyscraper. Everything was smoked with violently strafing snow. Then, as we turned each increasingly indistinct corner, it all flipped round the other way. A tune – an old TV tune, something loosened from the recesses of memory – began to seep into my breathing. I started to count my double steps; every ten I looked back and saw Jim as a smear of yellow a few metres behind me, locked in an identical, mechanical plod. As we got higher I caught occasional glimpses of the south-west buttress of the mountain clawing the cloud above us, then steadily drawing level, spat with grey but overwhelmingly white. We were getting into the rafters of the mountain. The weather was worsening but we were progressing. Everything was under control.

The highest ground in Great Britain – Clement Wragge's 'plateau of storms' – begins inauspiciously. You feel a gradual lessening of the gradient, then a bald crescent cutting the sky above you signifies the beginning of the plateau.

Were you to be blessed with hard snow, clear air and the confidence to know a cornice before you step on one, you might take your focus from the east, the place where the summit will eventually appear ahead, and go north to the top of Carn Dearg. From here you'd get a different perspective, gazing up towards the top of the mountain and seeing the astonishing ribs of the north face, flaked and laddered, beneath the white stripe of the summit plateau – far from flat, instead curling upwards like a shallow spiral stair.

Instead you push on, white underfoot, navy overhead. It's still; you hear the deep crunch of your boots on a hard metre of snow, snow that will thicken to a depth of two or even three metres before you reach the highest point of the mountain. You start to notice the snow is torn and folded where it meets the sky to the left; to the right, the ground tips on a long convex slope. It's here the plateau is pinched thin, with the drop of No. 2 Gully to the left, Five Finger Gully to the right. You can see them, and you don't go near them; cornices lip out over the north face, mantled and vertical. You've been warned about these, so you keep back.

A slope comes underfoot; it has a name, MacLean's Steep. Stay focused here. Slopes can betray you and sway your course. You clear the Steep and see a jumble of objects on a stepped cliff high to your left, the lip of a cavernous corrie. A squat funnel of white, warted with frost, the highest thing on the mountain. Once this was the tower of the observatory; beneath the snow there are walls, the old grate of the stove, wooden trestles, even Clement Wragge's old instrument cage. There's also a memorial to the dead of the two world wars – the Peace Cairn. Many have come here and scattered the ashes of their own dead in times past. If the snow were lower, this would appear like some strange henge of ruinous stones; but beneath the heavy white of winter, only the tower protrudes – now home to a desperate metal emergency shelter – and the nearby trig point. Normally it stands on a platform of stones, but just the top half of the trig sits proud of the drifts. It's further away than it looks, but you're going to get there. A line of stumpy cairns, built as navigational aids and poking through the snow, interrupts the white desert through which you're walking. You smile as the view – the view no other place in Britain has the loftiness to match – begins to define itself around you. An ocean of mountains ripples to the south: the Mamores, smooth but cut by sharp ridges; the mountains of Glen Coe; the symmetrical thorn of Schiehallion, distant but distinct;

then in the sea to the north-west, the Cuillin of Rùm and of Skye, more islands, more sea. You're higher than everything. Higher than everything for tens of thousands of square miles. You need to get down, but even in this place of lightning elemental about-faces, you know from the cobalt sky and still air that everything will be fine. As Coleridge might say, you're calm and fearless and confident.

That's one way it could go. But there's another. You know you're approaching the plateau because the pitch of the ground is lessening beneath your feet, yet you can't see it. You can't see anything: your world is white. A momentary loss of concentration and suddenly you're aware that you've lost your bearings. You spin round wildly, then forget which way you were originally facing. You can't even see your footprints, just a deepening ditch of snow in which you stand. You know that somewhere on this plateau gullies race in, gullies that overhang with cornices bent at grotesquely delicate angles. You could be standing over a drop and never know it until you hear that sound of shearing snow beneath you, a sound like thick cardboard being torn, followed by your own thin yelp, then oblivion. You try to concentrate on your map, but the wind is battering both it and you so hard you can't think with any kind of clarity. You pull out your GPS device and try to make sense of the screen, but in the building cold – and with panic bubbling up inside you – you forget the skills you were taught. You try to stop, to think, to slow down. You try to have a drink but your water has frozen solid inside the bottle and is now a useless deadweight. The snow beneath you is deep. The sky is grey and darkening. You're on the plateau of storms somewhere near the top of Ben Nevis, it's approaching nightfall and you don't know how to get down. This is what kills people on Ben Nevis, you think. You should have turned back when you could see where you were going. Turned back before you got into this mess. Avoided this mess altogether by listening to the forecast. But you don't want to think any of that. You just want to close your eyes and pretend you're not here.

Ahead of us through a break in the cloud I could see the curve of the mountain. We were nearly on the plateau. We were nearly up. But things were no longer in control.

In the last hour of increasingly difficult upward sloughing, the snow had become desperate. In an attempt to counterbalance the gusts I was leaning into the wind at a pitch that almost brought my right elbow down to the snow – which would be a remarkable feat were the snow not already level with my upper thigh. The path had become a slope of powder snow, and in places where it met rocks or the now almost imperceptible turn of the path it was now chest-deep. Our clothes were frozen heavy to our bodies. Every step was difficult, our progress the tortured crawl of a wounded bug. And whilst we both still felt warm and fairly strong, I knew that neither of these would last – and nor would the light. Through a hole in the cloud we could see that the eastern distance was beginning to lose its definition. Slowly but unmistakably it was getting dark.

Earlier, as we'd begun to climb the zigzags, I'd said to Jim that we had a cut-off point of 3 p.m. Cut-off points were things Himalayan mountaineers used in order to avoid becoming benighted on some hideous 8,000-metre giant, and the wise stuck to them. Summit fever was the result of ignoring them. Death was the outcome for some.

But we weren't caught up in the delicate timescale of a Himalayan mountain. There wasn't less oxygen available to breathe in the rarefied air of extreme height. We were on Ben Nevis. Yet there was little difference. People died in far less extreme conditions than these. And mortality doesn't care about the height of a summit: it's a grimly efficient leveller. Whether you're on Ben Nevis or Everest; being dead on one is precisely the same physical condition as being dead on the other.

When I saw the gradient begin to lessen ahead at 3.30 p.m. I felt a glimmer of hope. It was then that I felt a gloved hand on my shoulder, and a voice, muffled by fabric.

'Mate, we're going to struggle.'

I looked ahead through the racing cloud and again caught a glimpse of the flattening skyline. We were almost up.

'We're almost up.'

'But we're not almost *back*.'

With that, the fragile resolve I'd been clinging on to collapsed. He was, of course, right. What's more, I knew he was right, but I'd been too stubborn to call it sooner. From the lip of the plateau it was a brisk twenty minutes to the summit in good conditions, then twenty minutes back. Add in thick snow like this and you could triple each, at least. Add in the gale – which would be unimpeded on the summit – and impending darkness, and the fact that the snow on the zigzags might deepen to dangerous levels on the descent and it was obvious. We simply wouldn't make it. With what we had in our packs we'd probably *survive* it – and for a second I thought about pushing on, giving in and gambling. Then my thoughts turned to home, and my wife, 400 miles away and pregnant with our first baby, to comfort, to easy safety, and I felt a sudden and overwhelming urge not to be here anymore, to unplug from this situation before it got silly. There will be some who'd have pushed on, who'd have thrown all of this to the wind, and who by fair odds would have emerged heroes having taken on the mountain and won, and come home with a tale of hell to tell.

But I'm rather proud to say I'm not one of those – and so Jim and I did what any reasonable person would have done. Without so much as a backward glance towards the top, we turned around.

And that was that. The descent was slow and careful back to the halfway lochan, where we left the snow and found our way back into the shelter of the lower path. Goggles were removed in the twilight, zips were loosened and after a while the wild, weird wilderness of the mountain's higher reaches we'd been struggling through was a surreal memory. This renewed security caused doubt to creep in, of course. Had we quit too soon? Should we have pressed on for another half hour? Maybe Ben Nevis would have performed one of its famed about-faces and with the moonrise would come a cloud inversion, filling the valleys and at least part-realising the dream we'd had of being on top of Britain beneath starry heavens and valleys filled with stunning fluff. Silly thoughts. Glancing back and up towards the top suggested the weather had not improved one bit up there, and in all likelihood we'd still be floundering in waist-deep snow on the plateau.

We arrived back at the Clachaig Inn tired and with our skin burning from the cold. This is always a thing to look forward to: a re-appreciation of simple things. Shelter. Food. Warmth. Safety. You went, now you're back.

We ate. We drank, a lot. Talked about returning and having a rematch with Ben Nevis one day, maybe not soon, but one day. And occasionally we revisited the day and reassured each other – or ourselves – that we'd made the right decision. That sometimes it's OK to let the mountain win. They're mountains, after all. They'll always be there.

A little after 9 p.m. I wandered alone outside into the dark, beer in hand, to see if the skies had cleared. With nightfall a hard frost had descended and away from the lit wood of the inn, filling the sky where the steep sides of Glen Coe's mountains made a 'V', the stars were peeping through thinning scarves of cloud. The year was supposed to be a good one for the aurora borealis – the famed northern lights, which can often be seen in the winter skies of Scotland. I'd hoped we'd be lucky to catch a glimpse of them during this trip, perhaps from a position of repose on the calm summit of Ben Nevis. It had been an ambitious but not an unreasonable hope. Walk the mountains and you're allowed to expect the sight of wondrous things. You see them all the time.

Dizzyingly far above, where the flat, black outline of the mountain met the depthless sky, something caught my eye. A twinkle, then another. Little bobbing stars, following the line of the ridge. Head torches.

There were climbers up there, descending from the Aonach Eagach towards the inn. What a day they must have had. They'd be looking down at the lights of the Clachaig, thinking of the fire, of beds, of warmth and comfort. Of everything that the mountain couldn't give them, where they could recover from what it had.

The following morning dawned clear, crisp and white beneath a rich sky of blue. If conditions were like this thirteen miles north on Ben Nevis, someone would have a cracking day up there. It was wrenching to see, but nothing we could help. We were going home. Maybe next time we'd be lucky. Tired and aching, we loaded up the car and pulled out of the Clachaig. Soon after, we were travelling back south, back through the ancient nobility of Glen Coe – perhaps the grandest, most famous mountain place of them all.

W. H. Murray's line quoted earlier – 'No man will ever know Ben Nevis' – opens his evocative account of climbing the mountain's huge North-East Buttress. He ends it by repeating his opening statement, but then follows it with a great evocation of man's simple, strange relationship with any mountain, anywhere: 'On the other hand, Nevis will always help him to know himself. There is no end to such knowledge. And there is no end to the joy of getting it.'

It's true. Nobody can ever know these mountains. Because quite simply, there's too much to know. Too much to feel. Far too much to see. But for those of us who seek even to transiently inhabit these wild mountain places – those rough links between earth and sky – that can only be a good thing. They aren't just things. And they aren't just places, either. They are much more than that.

How much more is really up to you. Geoffrey Winthrop Young knew this when he wrote a poem titled, simply, 'A Hill'.

Only a hill: earth set a little higher
Above the face of the earth: a larger view
Of little fields and roads: a little nigher
To clouds and silence: what is that to you?
Only a hill: but all of life to me,
Up there, between the sunset and the sea.

I watched the mirror for a last view, for now, of the frozen mountains of Glen Coe. As the road bent and the outline of Buachaille Etive Mòr slid into sight I did what I always did, and always would. I felt for that flutter of awe and that indefinable, unmistakable quickening of the pulse.

ACKNOWLEDGEMENTS

Too many people have helped in too many ways to summarise so briefly here, both on a personal and a professional level. Works by people far more stately than I are listed in Selected Reading, and I urge anyone who has found interest in this book to investigate these, as they're all worthwhile.

Warmest thanks to Lyle Brotherton, for acres of encouragement and for being a friend; Myles Archibald at HarperCollins, for his faith and ability to 'see' this idea; editor Mark Bolland for his splendid and sharp-eyed work on the draft; and Julia Koppitz for seeing the idea through to completion. Also Guy Procter, who taught me most of what I've ever remembered about writing; Andrew Kennedy, for dragging me up my first mountain; Tom Bailey, with whom I've shared the most since; and my friend James Provost, for walking the toughest bits of this project with me and being a brilliant mountain mate.

Also thanks to Emma Kendell, Nigel Boothman and Kingsley Singleton for feedback, which was more valuable than you could know; Jackie and Ian Robertson for making us welcome in their home; Thomas Newbolt, for kind permission to reproduce his grandfather's beautiful words here, and also Peter Burns, Mal Creasey, Julian Cooper, Deborah Hughes, Robert Macfarlane, Sandy Maxwell, Jean Napier, Audrey Salkeld, Simon Wellings, Maxine Willet, Walter Tafelmaier, Kate and Darren Colombo, Jillian and Daren Cumberbatch, Keith Moody and Ben Barry.

The most important by far: to my wife Rachel Andrews-Ingram, for her support in putting up with me, and with all of this; my beautiful baby daughter Evelyn Grace, for not arriving into our lives early whilst I was somewhere far away; and to my parents and family – to whom I've no doubt given many sleepless nights since I discovered the world outside the door.

And finally, to the readers and makers of *Trail* magazine, who helped me along this path and whose unconditional love of exploring the country's most uncomfortable, unforgettable mountain places continues to be a daily inspiration.

SELECTED READING

Books

Allen, John, *Cairngorm John* (2010)

Baker, E. A., *The Highlands with Rope and Rucksack* (1923)

Brotherton, Lyle, *The Ultimate Navigation Manual* (2011)

Brown, John, *A Description of the Lake at Keswick ... in Cumberland* (1767)

Bryson, Bill, *A Short History of Nearly Everything* (2004)

Burke, Edmund, *Philosophical Enquiry into ... the Sublime and the Beautiful* (1756)

Burton, John Hill, *The Cairngorm Mountains* (1864)

Butterfield, Irvine, *The High Mountains of Britain and Ireland, Vol. 1* (1986)

Butterfield, Irvine, *Dibidil: A Hebridean Adventure* (2010)

Coleridge, Samuel Taylor, *Letters of S. T. Coleridge, Vol. 1* (1895)

Covell, Geoffrey & Timings, Leslie, *An Teallach: The Forge*

Crocket, Ken & Richardson, Simon, *Ben Nevis: Britain's Highest Mountain* (2009)

Crowley, Aleister, *Confessions* (1969)

Crumley, Jim, *The Great Wood* (2011)

Danson, Edwin, *Weighing the World* (2006)

Dawson, Alan, *The Relative Hills of Britain* (1992)

Defoe, Daniel, *A Tour Through ... Great Britain* (1724–27) (1978 reissue)

Drummond, Peter, *Scottish Hill Names* (2007)

Earl, David W., *Hell on High Ground* (1995)

Fiennes, Celia, *Through England on a Side Saddle in the Time of William and Mary* (1888)

Gannon, Paul, *Rock Trails: The Scottish Highlands* (2012)

Gilpin, William, *Observations ... Cumbria and Westmoreland* (1786)

Gray, Affleck, *The Big Grey Man of Ben MacDhui* (1994)

Gray, Thomas, *Thomas Gray's Journal ... Lake District* (2012)

Griggs, E. L., *Wordsworth and Coleridge* (1967)

Hemans, Felicia, *The Poetical Works of Felicia Dorothea Hemans* (1914)

Hendry, George, *Midges in Scotland* (2011)

Hewitt, Rachel, *Map of a Nation: A Biography of the Ordnance Survey* (2011)

Jackman, Brian & Miles, Hugh, *The Great Wood of Caledon* (1991)

Keats, John, *Keats: The Complete Poems* (1977)

King, Dean H., *Patrick O'Brian: A Life Revealed* (2012)

Kington, John, *Climate and Weather* (2010)

Lauder, Thomas, *The Wolf of Badenoch* (1827)

Lewis-Jones, Huw, *Mountain Faces: Portraits of Adventure* (2011)

Lopez, Barry, *Arctic Dreams* (1986)

MacCaig, Norman, *The Poems of Norman MacCaig* (2005)

Macfarlane, Robert, *Mountains of the Mind: A History of a Fascination* (2003)

Manley, Gordon, *Climate and the British Scene* (1952)

Murray, Alexander, *Who's Who in Mythology* (1992)

Murray, W.H., *Mountaineering in Scotland* (1947)

Murray, W.H., *Undiscovered Scotland* (1951)

Murray, W.H., *The West Highlands of Scotland* (1985)

Napier, Jean, *Rhosydd: A Personal View* (2004)

Newton, Isaac, *Principia, Vol. II: The System of the World* (1728)

Nicholson, Norman, *Five Rivers* (1944)

O'Brian, Patrick, *Three Bear Witness* (also published as *Testimonies*) (1952)

Pearsall, W.H., *Mountains and Moorlands* (1950)

Perrin, Jim, *Visions of Snowdonia* (1997)

Prebble, John, *The Highland Clearances* (1992)

Rhys, Siôn Dafydd, *The Giants of Wales and Their Dwellings* (c. 1600)

Rixson, Dennis, *Knoydart: A History* (1999)

Roberts, Andy, *Strangely Strange but Oddly Normal* (2010)

Roy, Marjory, *The Weathermen of Ben Nevis 1883–1904* (2004)

Shepherd, Nan, *The Living Mountain* (1977)

Simons, Paul, *Since Records Began: The Highs and Lows of British Weather* (2008)

Smith, Roly, *National Parks of Britain* (2008)

Styles, Showell, *The Mountains of North Wales* (1973)

Swire, Otta, *Skye: The Island and Its Legends* (2006)

Thomas, Keith, *Man and the Natural World: Changing Attitudes 1500–1800* (2001)

Thompson, Simon, *Unjustifiable Risk?: A History of British Climbing* (2010)

Turnbull, Ronald, *The Riddle of Sphinx Rock* (2005)

Turnbull, Ronald, *The Life and Times of the Black Pig* (2007)

Wainwright, Alfred, *Wainwright in Scotland* (1990)

Wainwright, Alfred, *A Pictorial Guide to the Lakeland Fells, Book 7: The Western Fells* (1992)

Walker, Malcolm, *History of the Meteorological Office* (2011)

Wells, Colin, *A Brief History of British Mountaineering* (2001)

Wood, John D., *Mountain Trail* (1947)

Wordsworth, William, *A Guide Through the District of the Lakes* (1820)

Wordsworth, William, *Complete Poetical Works* (1888)

Young, Geoffrey Winthrop, *Mountain Craft* (1920)

Other sources

I'd also like to acknowledge the following sources of information: *The Scottish Mountaineering Club Journal*, *The Fell and Rock Climbing Club Journal*, the British Library, the National Library of Scotland, Ordnance Survey, *Guardian*, *Daily Mail* and MailOnline, NOAA, Good Words for 1887, Subterranea Britannica, the Tornado and Storm Research Organisation, Mountain Rescue England and Wales, the Mountaineering Council of Scotland, the websites of Richard Sillitto (www.sillittopages.co.uk) and Robert Palmer (www.bearmead.co.uk), *Aberdeen Press and Journal*, *Inverness Courier*, *Inverness Advertiser* and *Trail Magazine* (www.livefortheoutdoors.com).

INDEX